Lin MacDonald
Set Decorator

Public Square Landscapes

DESIGN MEDIA PUBLISHING LIMITED

CONTENTS

Memorial

4 Chicago Riverwalk

8 Šiluva Square

Transportation

12 Square des Frères-Charon

18 Place d'Youville

22 Place Bourget

28 Sydney Olympic Park Jacaranda Square

Educational

32 The Brochstein Pavilion at Rice University

38 Parade Ground, University of the Arts London

42 Angel Field

48 National Center of Indigenous Excellence

52 BGU University Entrance Square & Art Gallery

56 Universitätsplatz Frankfurt (Oder)

Heathcare

60 LAC+USC Medical Center

66 Therapy Garden, Children's Specialized Hospital

70 Extension of the St. Bonifatius Hospital in Lingen

76 Chang Gung Hospital

Commercial

82 Arena Boulevard and Amsterdamse Poort

86 City Square Urban Park

92 Quincy Court

96 Clarke Quay

102 Shanghai Gubei Gold Street

110 Melbourne Convention Exhibition Center

116 Malvern City Square

120 1111 Lincoln Road

126 Plaza Dalí, Madrid

130 Jockey Plaza Boulevard

134 Circle on Cavill

140 Santa Monica Place

146 Southport Central

Corporate

152 Fukuoka Bank

158 EnBW City

164 Enterprise Plaza at 1100 Louisiana

168 Red Soils Plaza

174 Solingen Townhall Square

Distribution

178 Station Square Apeldoorn, The Netherlands

184 ULAP-Square Berlin

188 Ursulines Square

194 Koelnmesse Nord

200 Target Plaza at Target Field

206 Plaza Indautxu

212 Vancouver Convention Center Expansion Project

216 Frederiksberg New Urban Spaces

222 Place des Festivals

Recreational

228 Mathilde Square

232 Town Hall Square

236 Piazza Municipio, Povegliano

242 West Hills Corporate Pointe Cafe and Conference Center

248 Tecnoparque

254 Furtwängler Garden

260 Southeast False Creek Plaza

266 Fahrzeugwerke Falkenried

272 Fontana Square in Quinto de Stampi

278 Coquitlam Spirit Square

286 Index

Chicago Riverwalk

Location: Chicago, USA **Designer:** Ross Barney Architects **Photographer:** Kate Joyce, Hedrich Blessing Photographers **Completion date:** 2009 **Site area:** 5,946 sqm

The new Chicago Riverwalk is a major public amenity at the river level along lower Wacker Drive, extending from Michigan Avenue westward to the Lake Street. Completely built out, the Chicago Riverwalk will offer a mix of concessions and public activities. Following the guidelines established by the City of Chicago for riverside development, the Riverwalk includes reproduction light fixtures, planters, railings and other features that provide symbolic links to the City's past.

The Wabash Memorial Plaza is a new focal point along the Chicago Riverfront. It provides a green refuge in the center of the City while creating a vital link between upper Wacker Drive and the future riverwalk development. Reclaimed by the rebuilding and relocation of Wacker Drive, the plaza creates an urban park, with terraces and bench-lined ramps that gently transition from busy city streets to more quiet spaces near the river.

The Chicago Vietnam Veterans Memorial Fountain is both educational and symbolic. A wall of water, cuts into the limestone wall along Wacker Drive, spills into a pool that harmonizes with the upper plaza's fountain. A timeline, of significant events during the war, line the sides of the pool. The names of Illinois soldiers who died during the war parallel the timeline, linking each name with a moment in time.

1. State Street Bridge
2. Riverwalk Extension
3. Landscaping
4. Wabash Avenue Bridge
5. Wabash Plaza Vietnam Veterans Memorial

Right: The Chicago Vietnam Veterans Memorial Fountain is both educational and symbolic

CHICAGO REMEMBERS

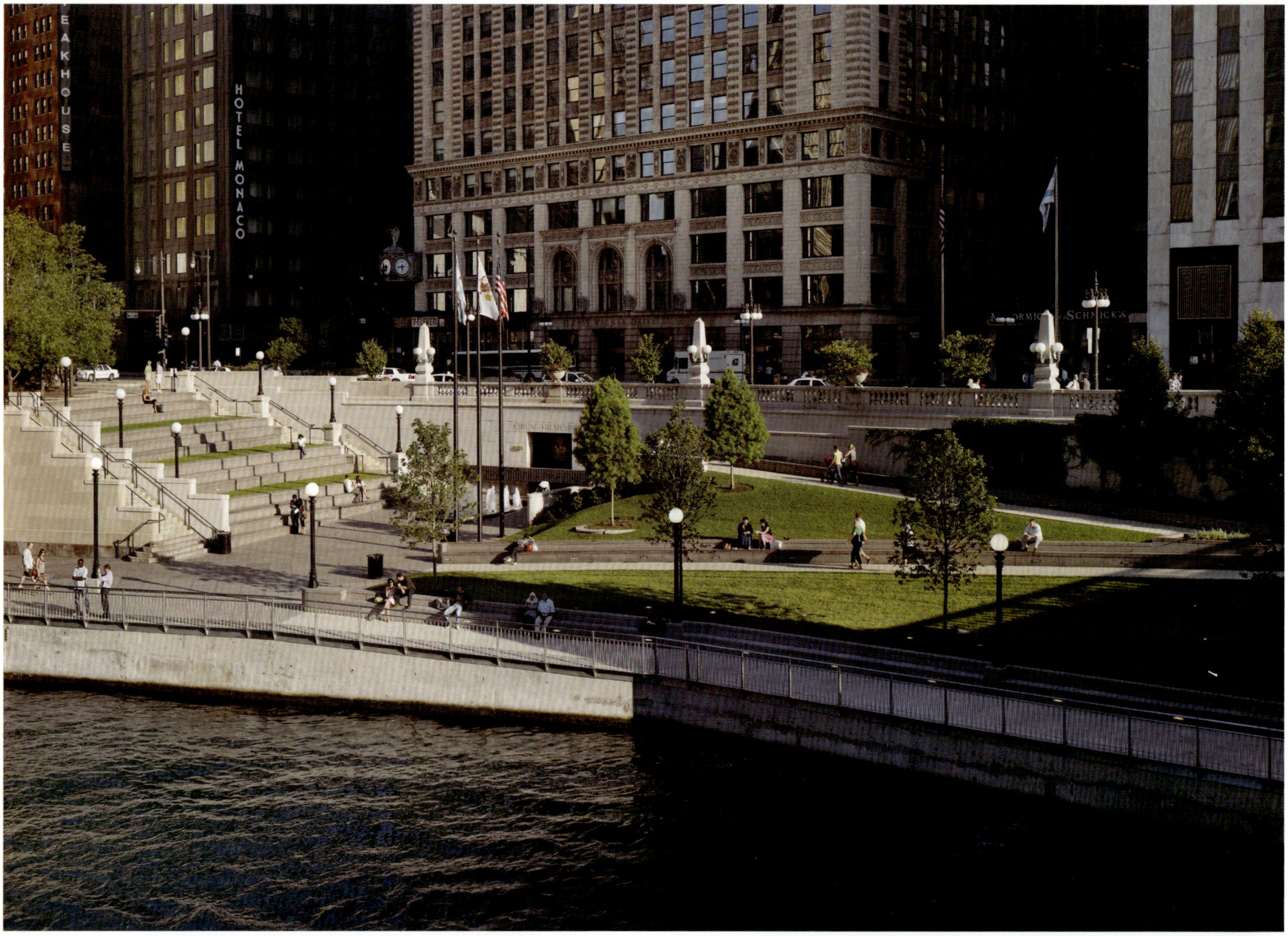
HOTEL MONACO

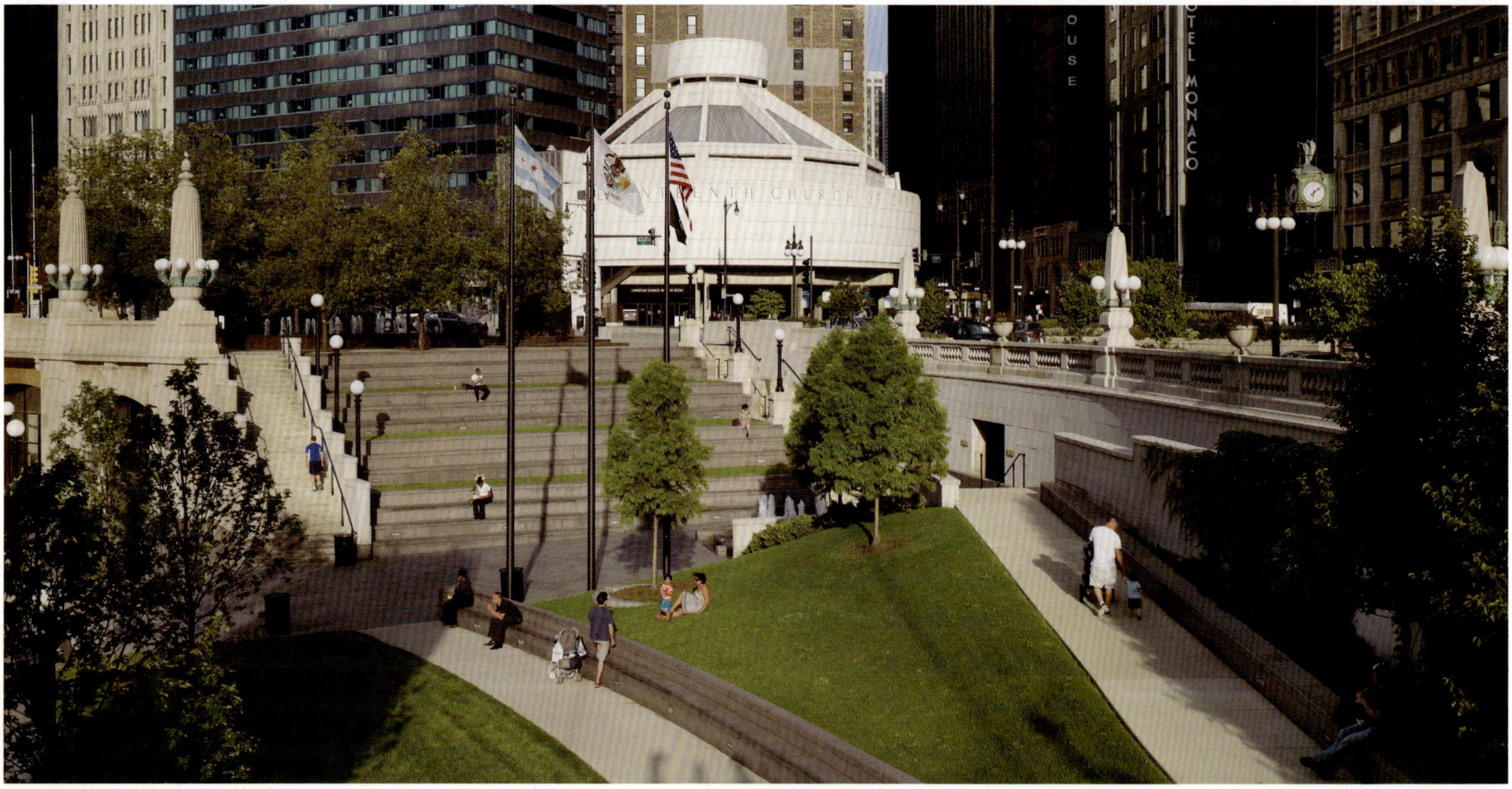

Upper left: The Chicago Riverwalk will offer a mix of concessions and public activities
Lower left: Wabash Plaza Vietnam Veterans Memorial
Upper right: State Street bridge

Šiluva Square

Location: Šiluva, Lithuania **Designer:** G.Natkevičius, J.Skalskytė, T.Kuleša, A.Natkevičiūtė **Photographer:** G.Česonis **Completion date:** 2009 **Site area:** 14,500 sqm

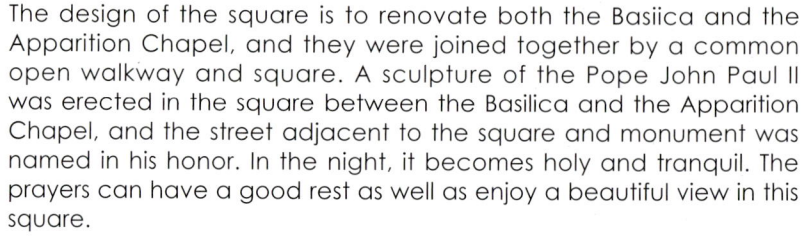

The design of the square is to renovate both the Basiica and the Apparition Chapel, and they were joined together by a common open walkway and square. A sculpture of the Pope John Paul II was erected in the square between the Basilica and the Apparition Chapel, and the street adjacent to the square and monument was named in his honor. In the night, it becomes holy and tranquil. The prayers can have a good rest as well as enjoy a beautiful view in this square.

Part of the central square is dedicated to mass rituals, facing the front of the Basilica and an outdoor altar in front of it. Its main plane is covered in milled cast concrete, like a pattern of Lithuanian fabric cut in rustic metal stripes. The light band of concrete is framed by a dotted line of black basalt blocks and green lawn. In order to preserve the fragile village scale, the designers narrowed the wide square space by framing it with rows of customised rustic metal chandeliers, seated trees, hedgerows, lined 3.5 meters high stone crosses / stations and solid oak benches. Thanks to these elements, the square is comfortable and functional both during mass events as well as on casual days when there are almost no one.

1. Chairs
2. The Square
3. The Statue

Right: Lined oak benches

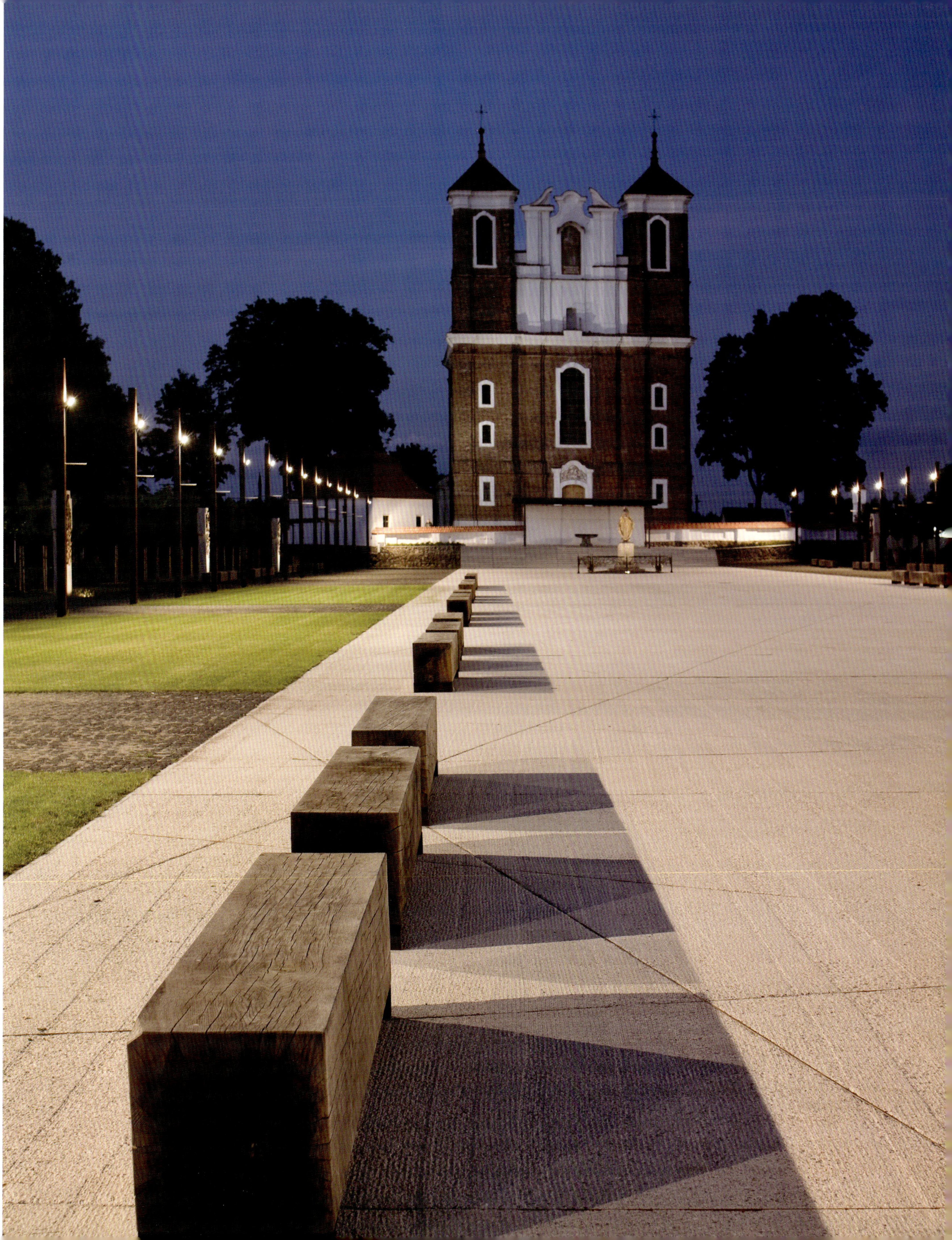

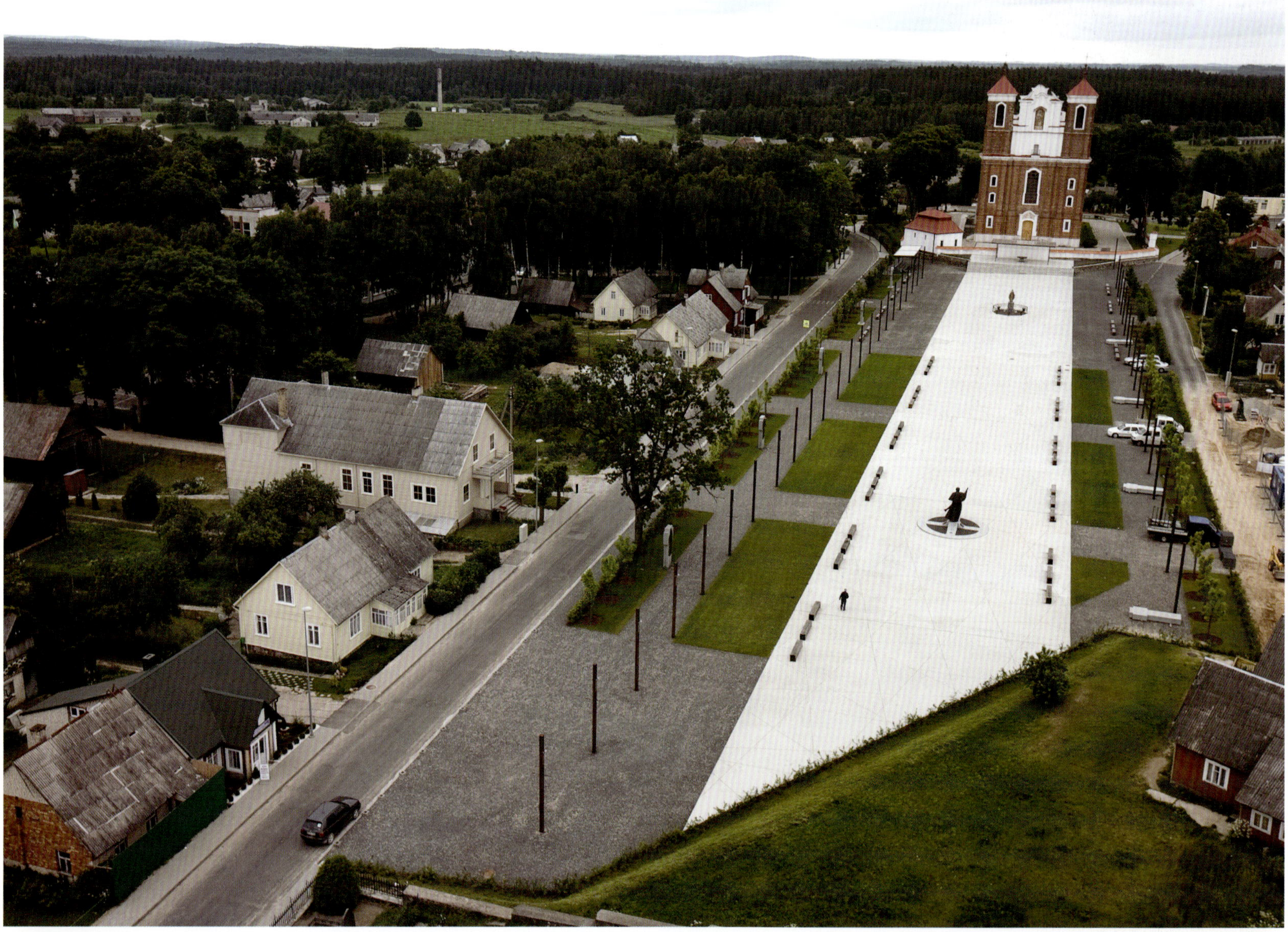
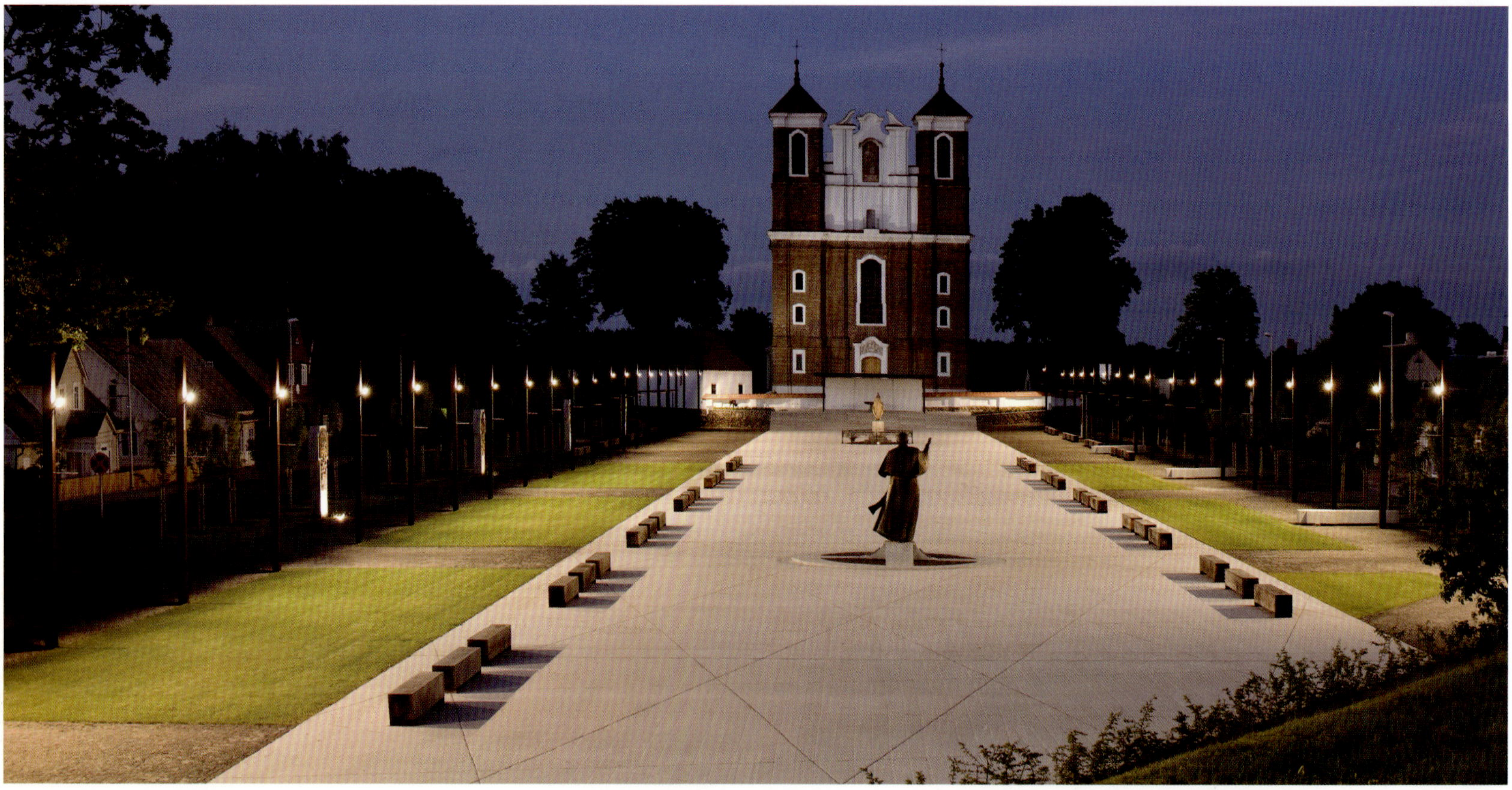

Upper left: The Square in the day
Lower left: The Square in the night
Upper right: People resting in the square
Lower right: Details of the benches

Square des Frères-Charon

Location: Montreal, Canada **Designer:** Affleck + de la Riva Architects
Photographer: Marc Cramer **Completion date:** 2008 **Site area:** 1,800 sqm

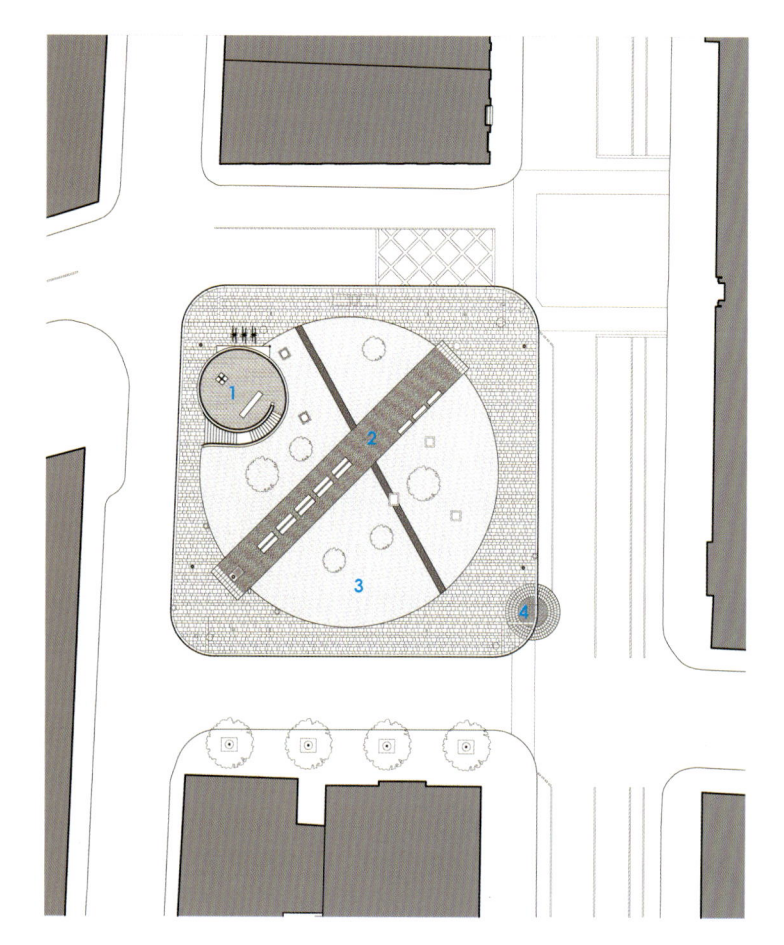

Square des Frères-Charon is part of a network of public spaces organized along the axis of the McGill Street, a historic thoroughfare that links the Old Port to the contemporary city center. The square offers the experience of a contemporary urban landscape inspired by the original vocation of the site, a prairie wetland where the Charon brothers built a windmill in the seventeenth century. The square is an experience in contrast and connection where the prairie wetland, surrounded by the city, takes on new dimensions and raises public awareness of the history and geography of the site.

The project uses a simple, refined, and minimalist architectural language to create a dialogue between circular and cylindrical forms including a garden of wild grasses, the vestiges of the windmill and a park pavilion in the form of a belvedere-folly. Complementing these gestures, the lighting scheme proposes a chromatic garden that alludes to the changing seasons.

Built as a response to the urban revitalization of a disaffected industrial sector, Square des Frères-Charon is an entirely new public amenity in a space that is more than 150 years old. The new square provides identity, civic pride and generous outdoor areas for all-season public use.

Award description:
2009 Design Exchange Award
2009 Prix Aménagement Les Arts et la Ville
2009 The Canadian Society of Landscape Architects Award of Excellence

1. Belvedere-Folly
2. Rest Area
3. The Prairie
4. Marking the Vestiges of the Windmill

Right: The square takes on new dimensions and raises public awareness of the history and geography of the site

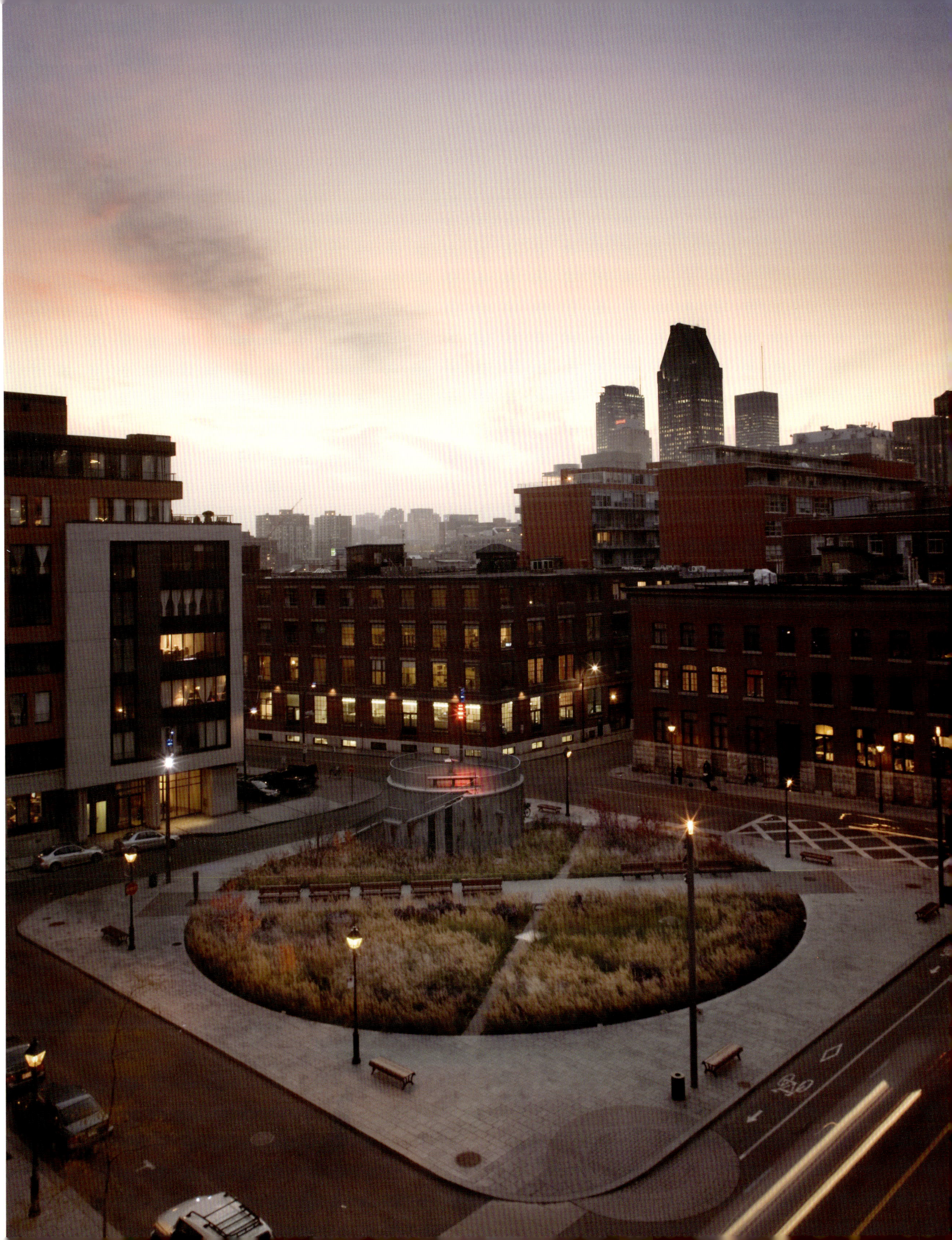

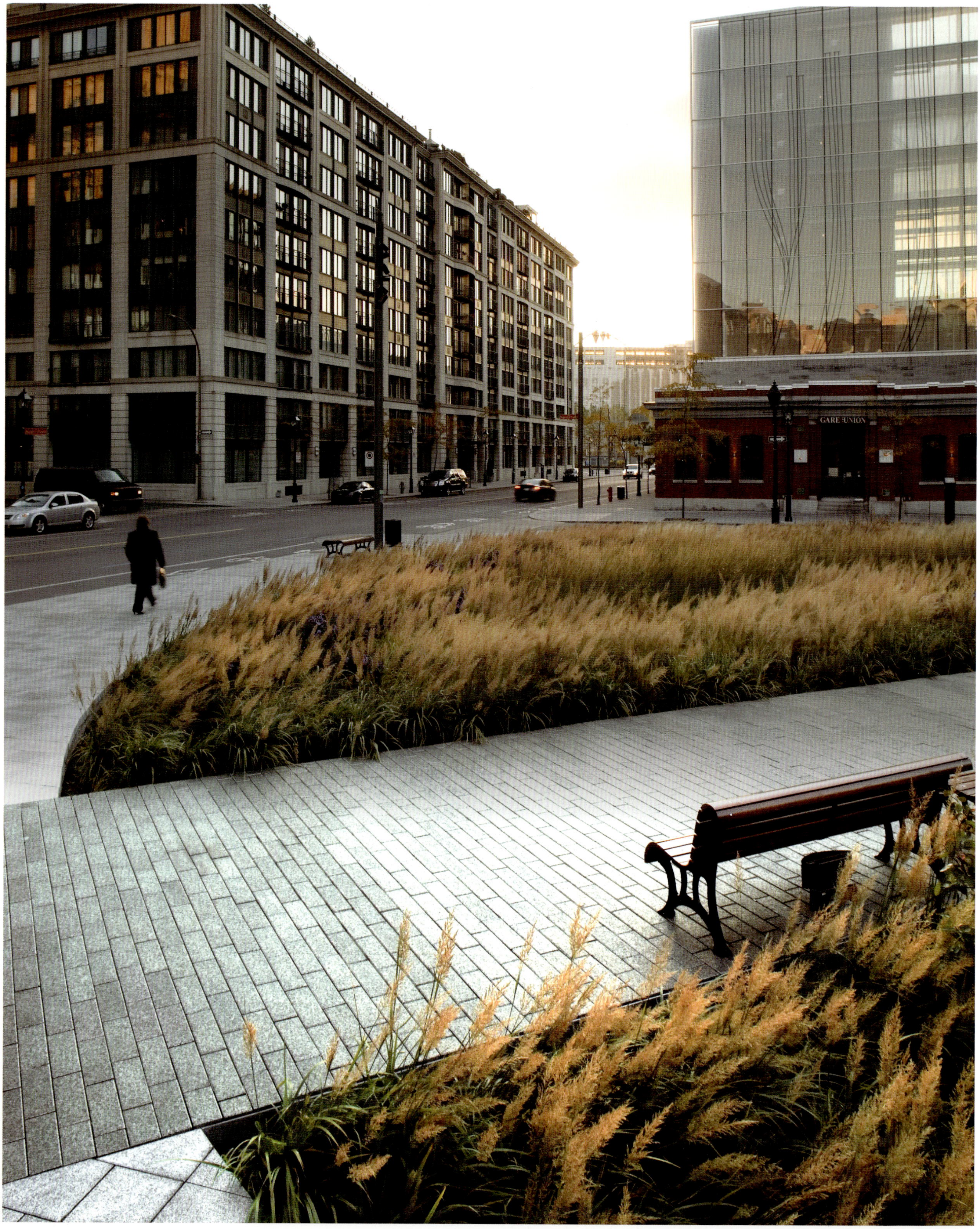
GARE UNION

Left: Sustainable initiatives include the planting of local species of wild grasses which take a significant load off the municipal irrigation system
Upper right: The square uses a simple, refined and minimalist architectural language to create a dialogue between circular and cylindrical forms

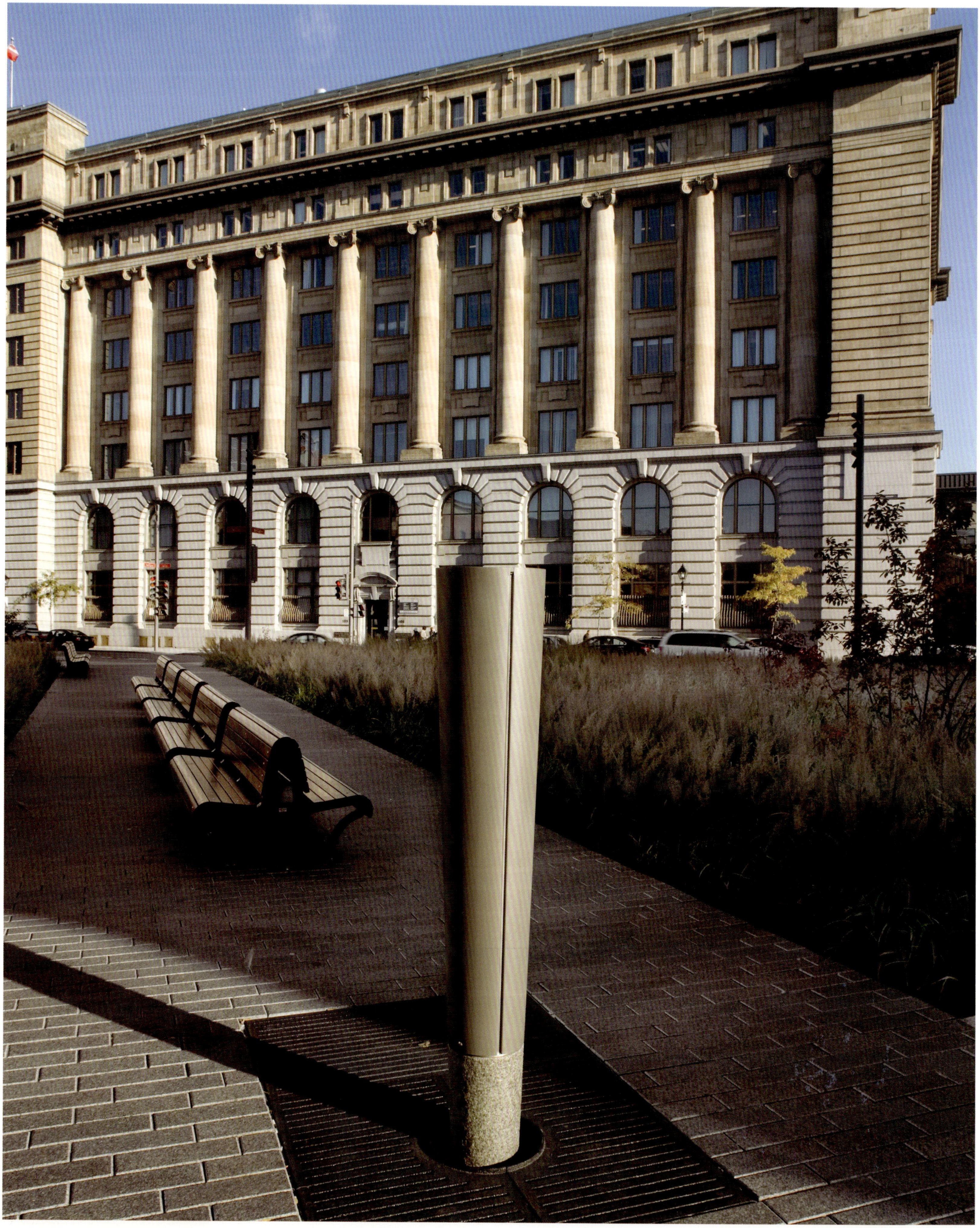

Left: The use of durable Quebec granite for hard landscaping
Upper right: The lighting scheme proposes a chromatic garden that alludes to the changing seasons

Place d'Youville

Location: Old-Montreal, Canada **Designer:** Claude Cormier Architects Paysagistes Inc. and Groupe Cardinal Hardy **Photographer:** Jean-François Vézina & Denis Farley **Completion date:** 2008 **Site area:** 15,000 sqm

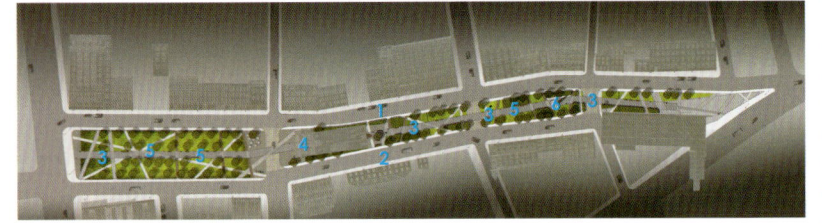

This project transformed an empty space into a truly public place that reflects contemporary lifestyles and attitudes characteristic of Montreal. Respect for the historical character of the space was a prime objective.

A quilt of sidewalks was created and laid over the ground, like a protective blanket, a criss-cross of pathways constructed through techniques and materials taken from the city's history of sidewalks. Cobblestone streets, sidewalks made out of wood, limestone, granite and concrete reflect this history, from Montreal's early days as a settlement to the present day metropolis. The site's history became neither an obsession nor an obstacle: room was made to allow for the unpredictable nature of archaeology at the center of the design strategy, with the archaeological site research serving as a contemporaneous addition to the design process.

The design lays down a blanket of sidewalks over the space, each comprised of wood, concrete, or different patterns of granite, that weave links between the museums, offices, restaurants and homes standing on both sides of the space. They all feed into a central alley situated over the ancient river bed. Benches are installed in a lowkey light, bushes and greenery springing through every gap left in the fabric. The pattern is complex, but not complicated; the textures are evocative, but not overbearing.

1. Place d'Youville North
2. Place d'Youville South
3. The Promenade
4. The Building
5. Bench
6. The Tower

Right: Long view

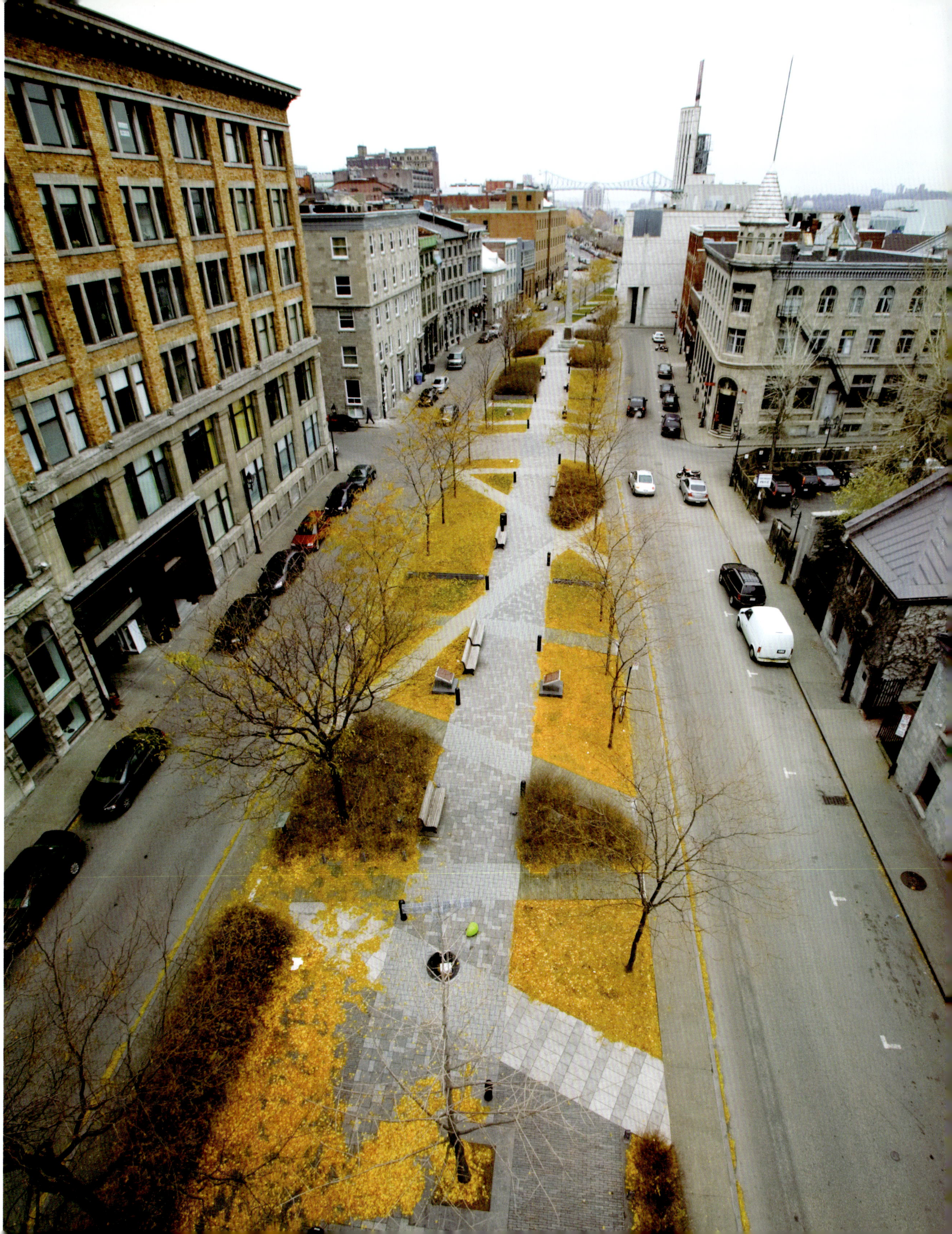

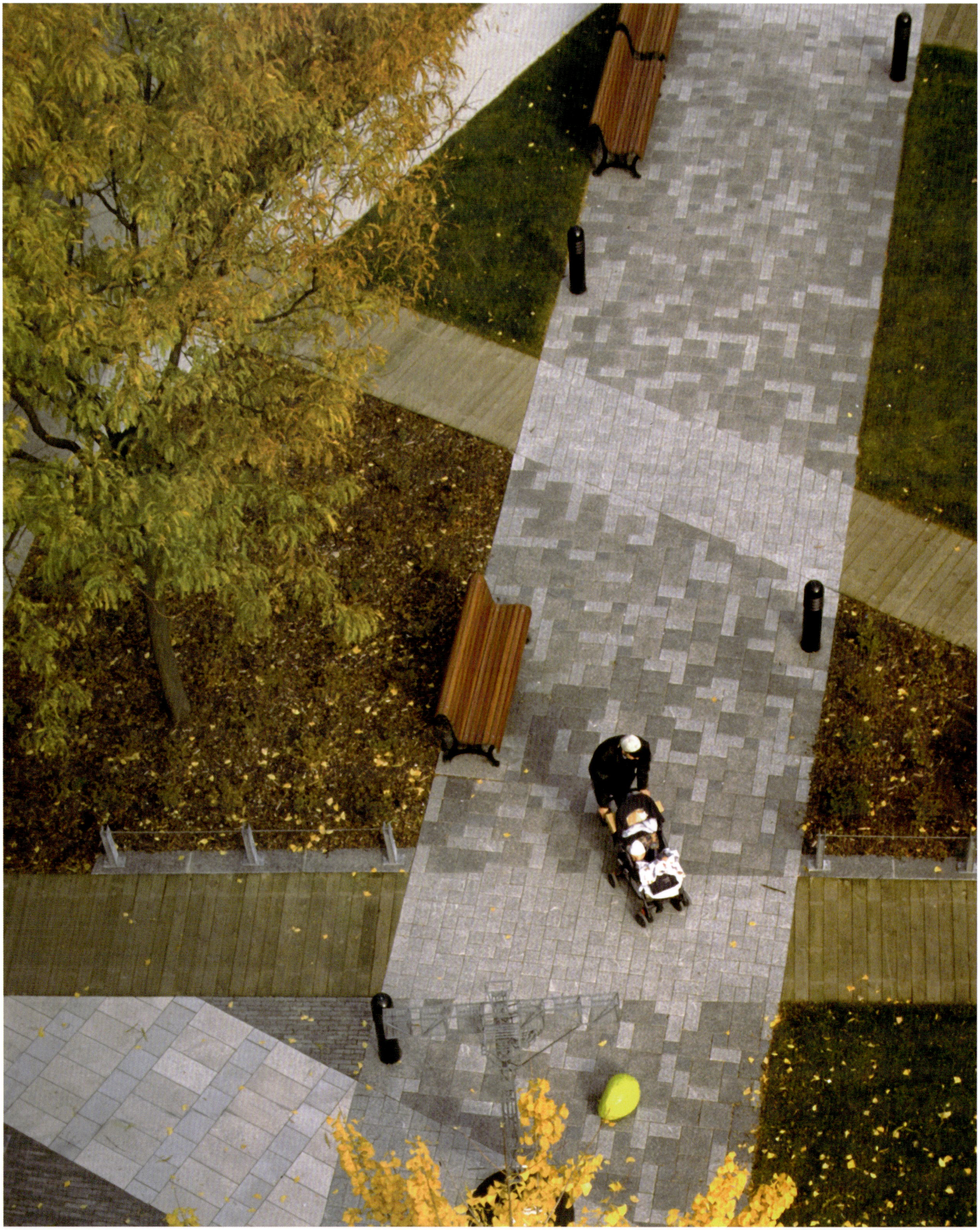

Left: Pavement
Right: Summer and fall views at Youville

Place Bourget

Location: Joliette, Canada **Designer:** DAOUST LESTAGE Inc. Architecture Design Urbain **Photographer:** Marc Cramer **Completion date:** 2009 **Site area:** 14,000 sqm

The repositioning of the downtown area as a friendly, attractive space for drivers, pedestrians, and cyclists involved a complete review of the layout of streets and sidewalks in order to recover as much space as possible for the new Place Bourget and peripheral sidewalks. The project expanded the space from the current configuration with a width of about 16 meters, to that of a true public square of almost 30 meters wide, with streets and sidewalks recalibrated to create terraces and install trees and street furniture.

Cut through the paved surface, the gardens offer planted sub-spaces. The structure, with its orthogonal and transversal circulation axes, is echoed in a geometric composition.

Traces of history and planting structure are subtle reminder of the traces of the old market and city hall. More than 40 trees are planted in the square in discontinuous alignments framing various perspectives. Slightly accentuated tones in the paving and the arrangement of trees of a different color (red) recall the presence of buildings.

Finally, the water power of Rivière l'Assomption, the original reason for founding the city around the establishment of mills and other industries, has inspired a series of monolithic fountains made of Cambrian granite situated on either side of Boulevard Manseau in the new, large square.

1. Place Bourget South
2. Place Bourget North
3. Courthouse
4. Marketplace

Right: View toward the south

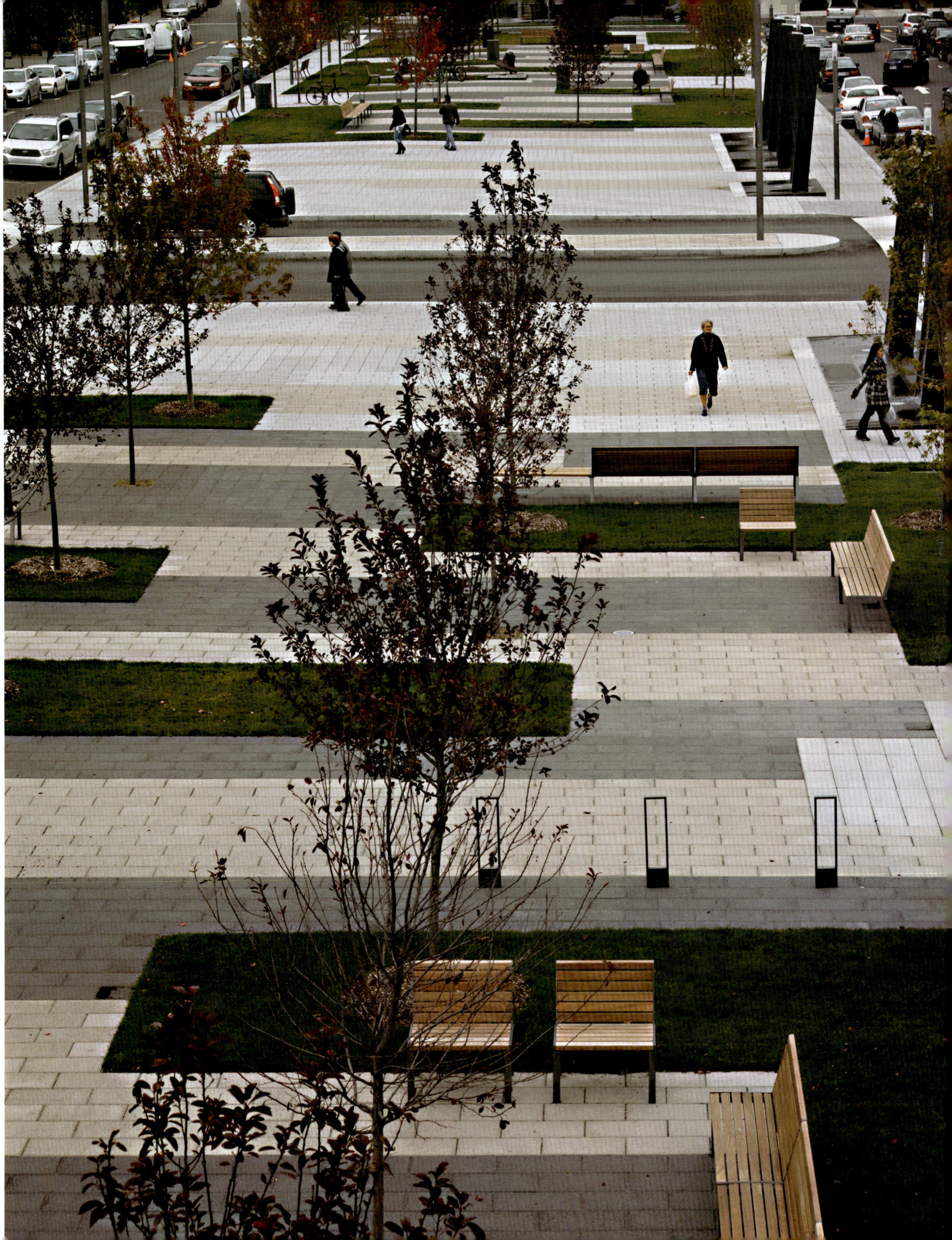

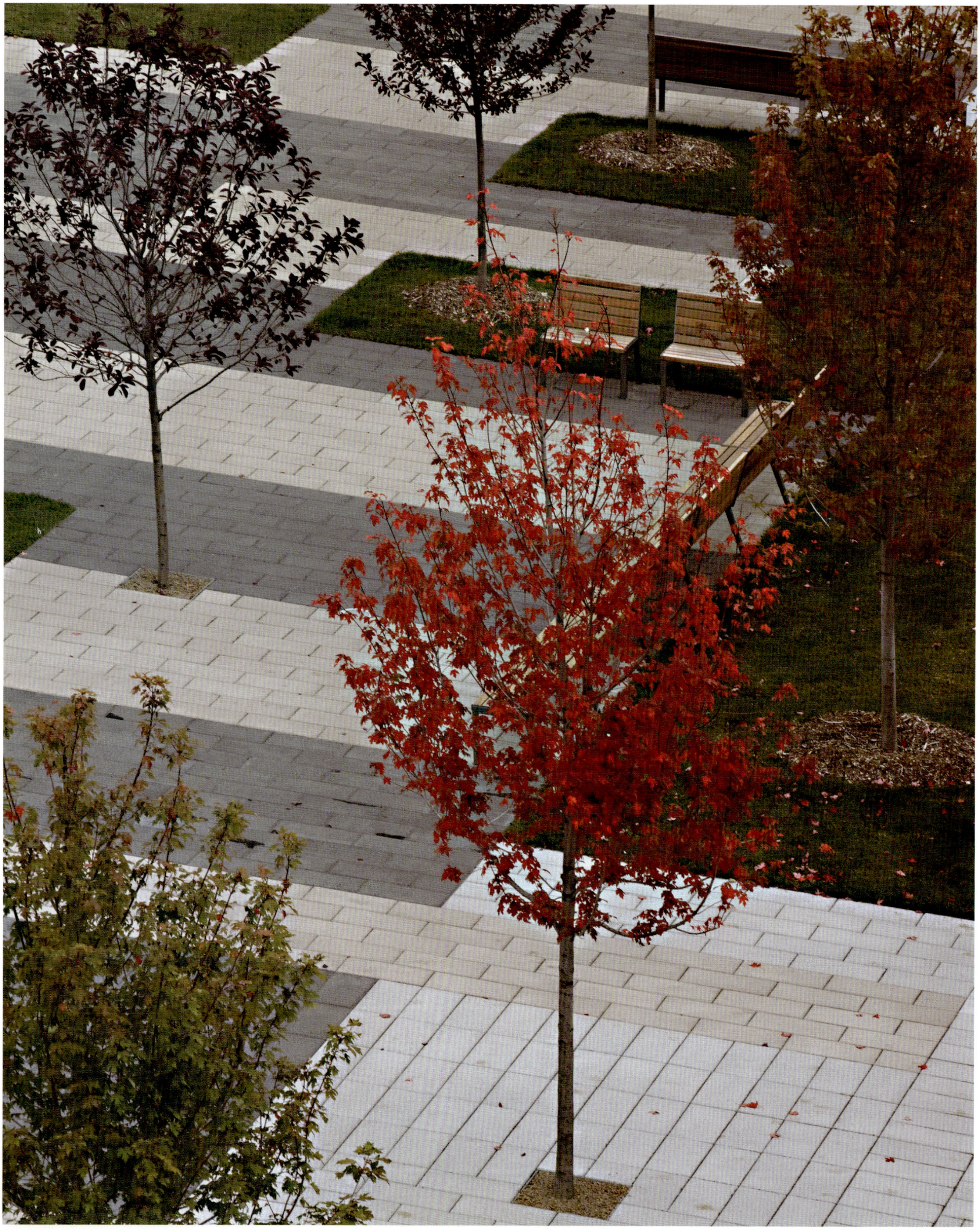

Left: Geometric composition
Upper right: Trees alignments
Lower right: Urban furniture

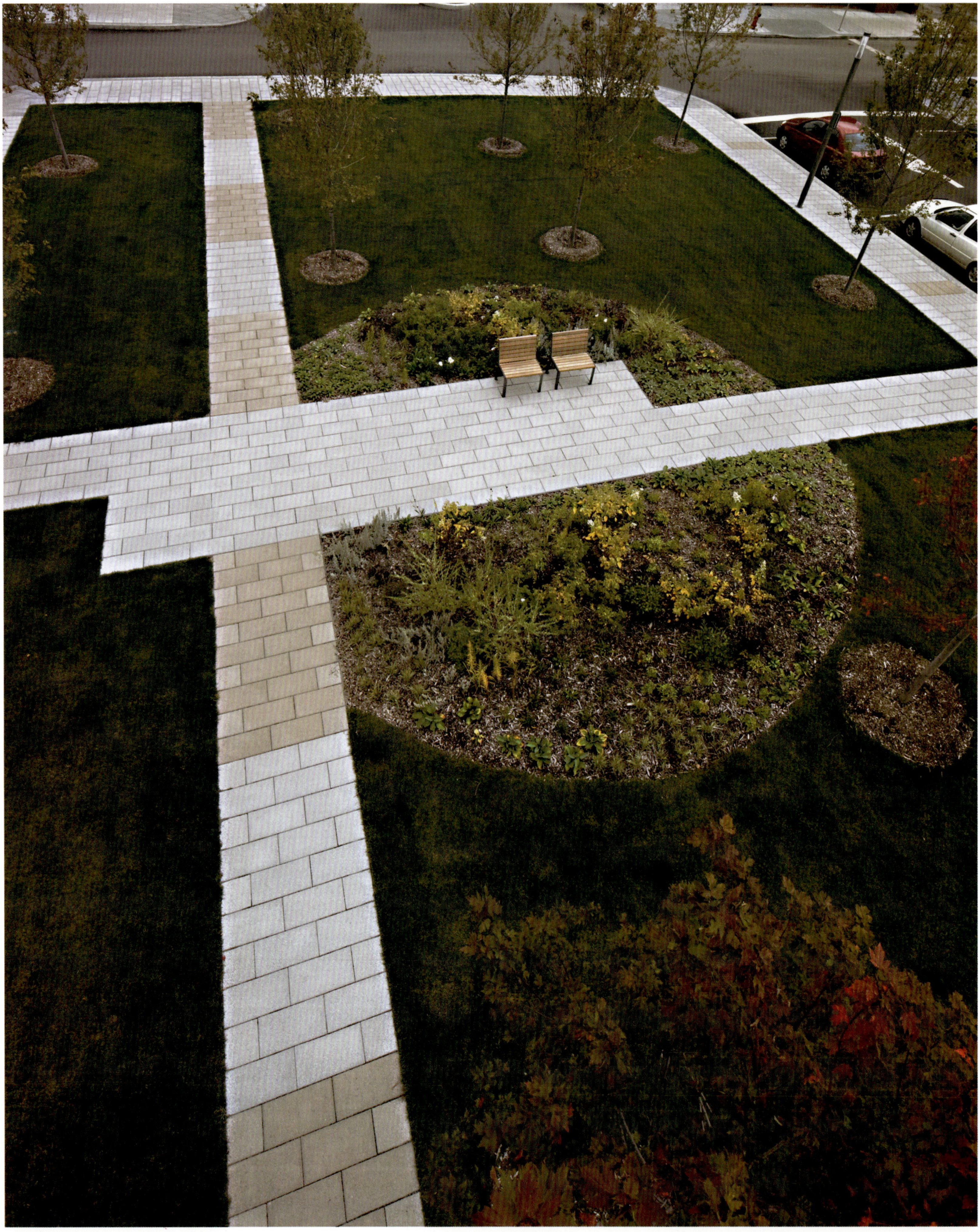

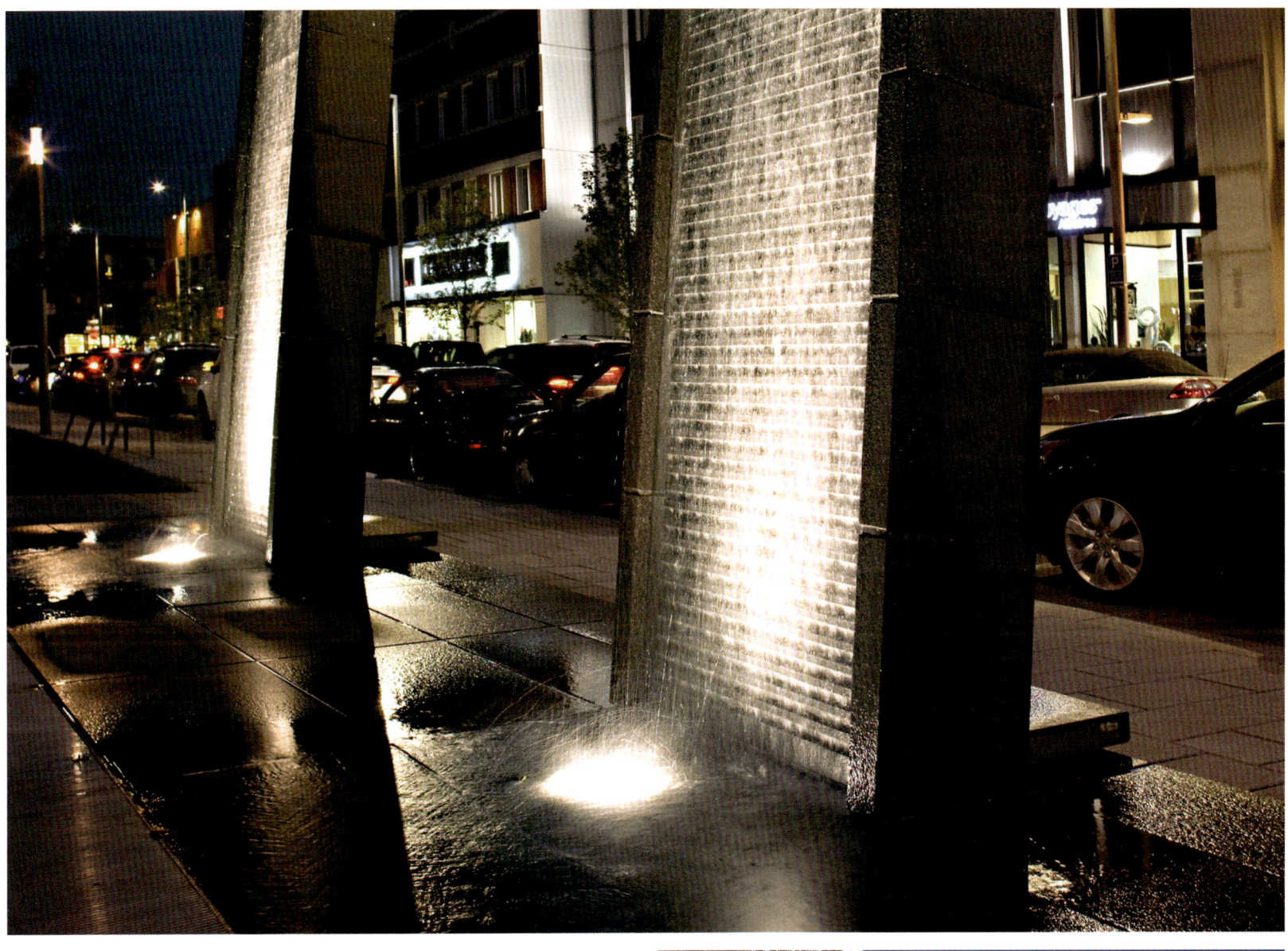

Left: St-Marie garden
Upper right: Water walls made of Cambrian granite
Lower right: Detail of the water wall

Location: Sydney, Australia **Designer:** ASPECT Studios Pty Ltd, McGregor Westlake Architecture, Deuce Design **Photographer:** Simon Wood, Sacha Coles
Completion date: 2008 **Site area:** 4,000 sqm

Sydney Olympic Park Jacaranda Square

The resulting award-winning scheme is a new urban park for passive recreation and community gathering. The term 'The Everyday Stadium', is both a gentle, ironic nod to the Olympic legacy and a description of the design concept, which is made up of three elements: a large central open space, an edge of walls and seats and large perimeters of shade – one built and the other through trees.

Brick was used extensively in the project, in part due to the site proximity to the former Homebush brick pit and to give the park a dynamic, textural and colorful character.

Glazed bricks were used as a cladding on the perimeter walls, interspersed with Austral Gertrudis to give a striking visual pattern.

Recycled bricks were used on edge in a concrete stretcher pattern for the paved area adjacent to the cafe. The recycled bricks harmonize their rustic quality with the sharply crafted adjacent precast concrete elements.

The final result is colorful, clean and green. The design features a series of modular precast-concrete lounge suites; a canopy of polychrome greens; walls of glazed pixilated bricks set amongst a landscape of native trees.

Green in theory and design, the park features include: a recycled brick pavement, recycled materials and recycled water for irrigation combined to achieve a meaningful environmental and socially sustainable place.

This is a 'complete project', which successfully fuses Landscape Architecture, Industrial and Graphic design with Architecture to create an intelligent and memorable open space.

Award description:
2009 Think Brick Horbury Hunt Award
Winner in Landscape category
2009 Australian Institute of Architects Award (NSW)
Commendation in Urban Design
2008 Master Builders Association Award
Civil Engineering category

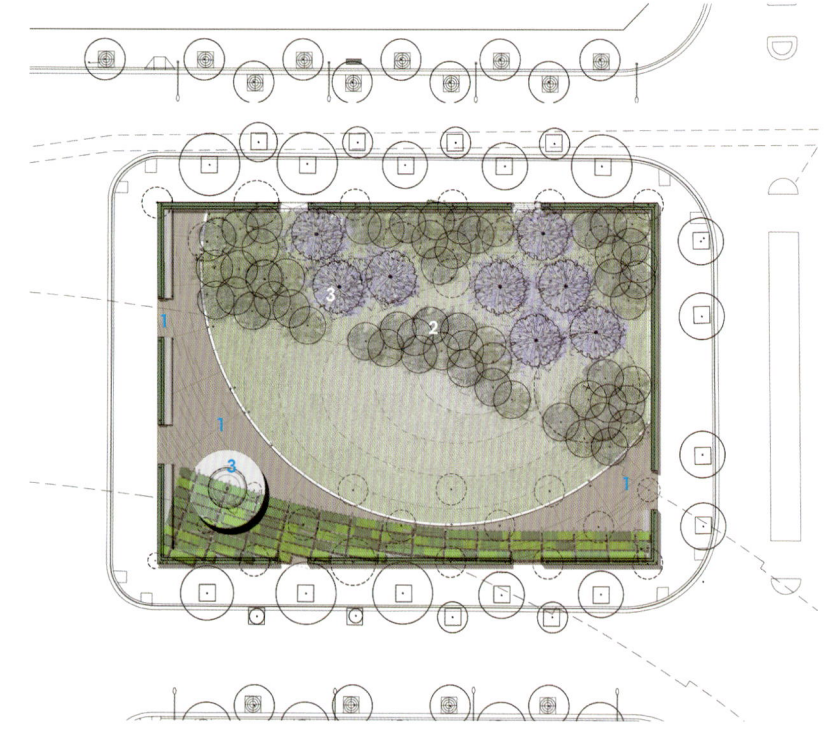

1. Entrance
2. Green Grass
3. Cafe

Right: Aerial view

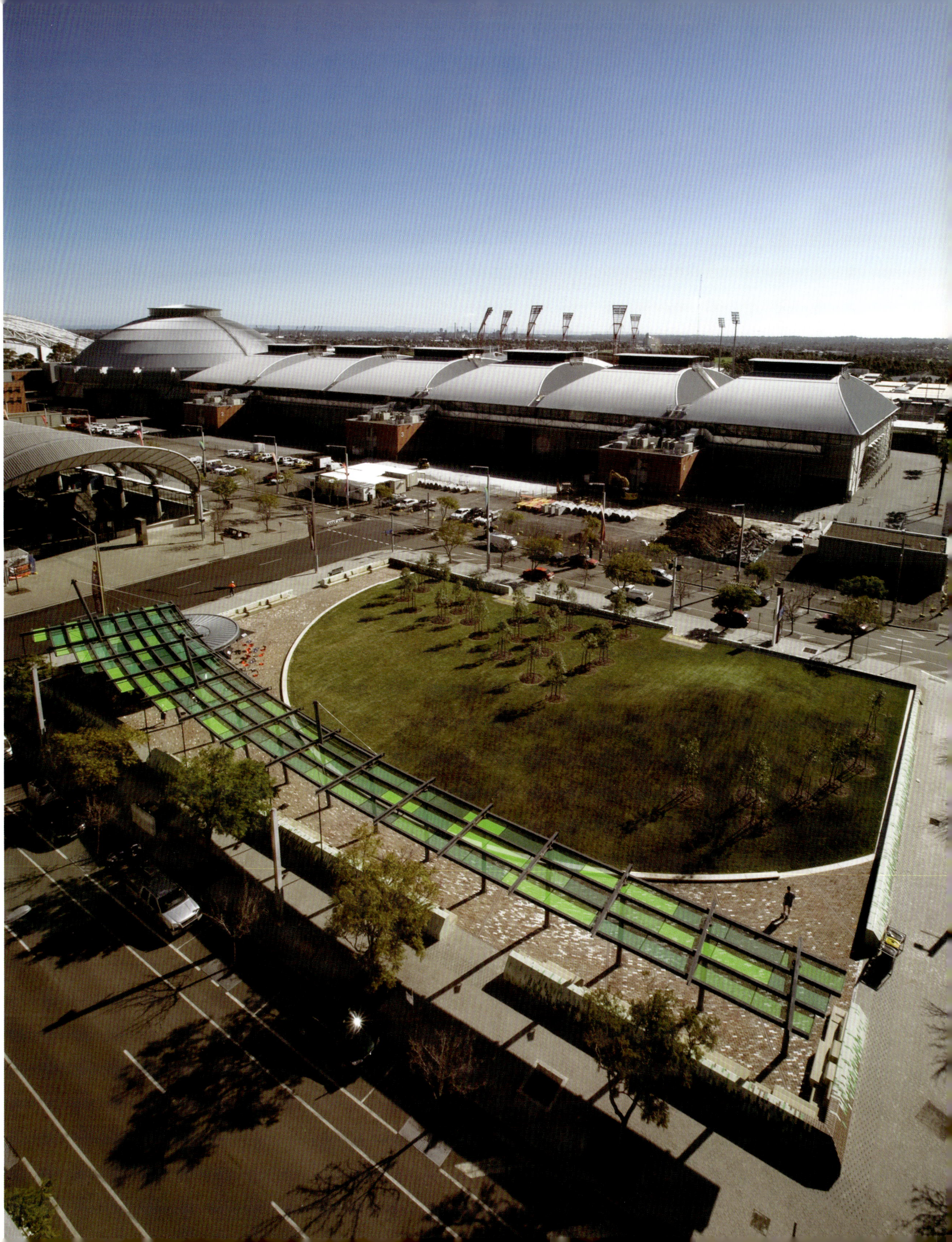

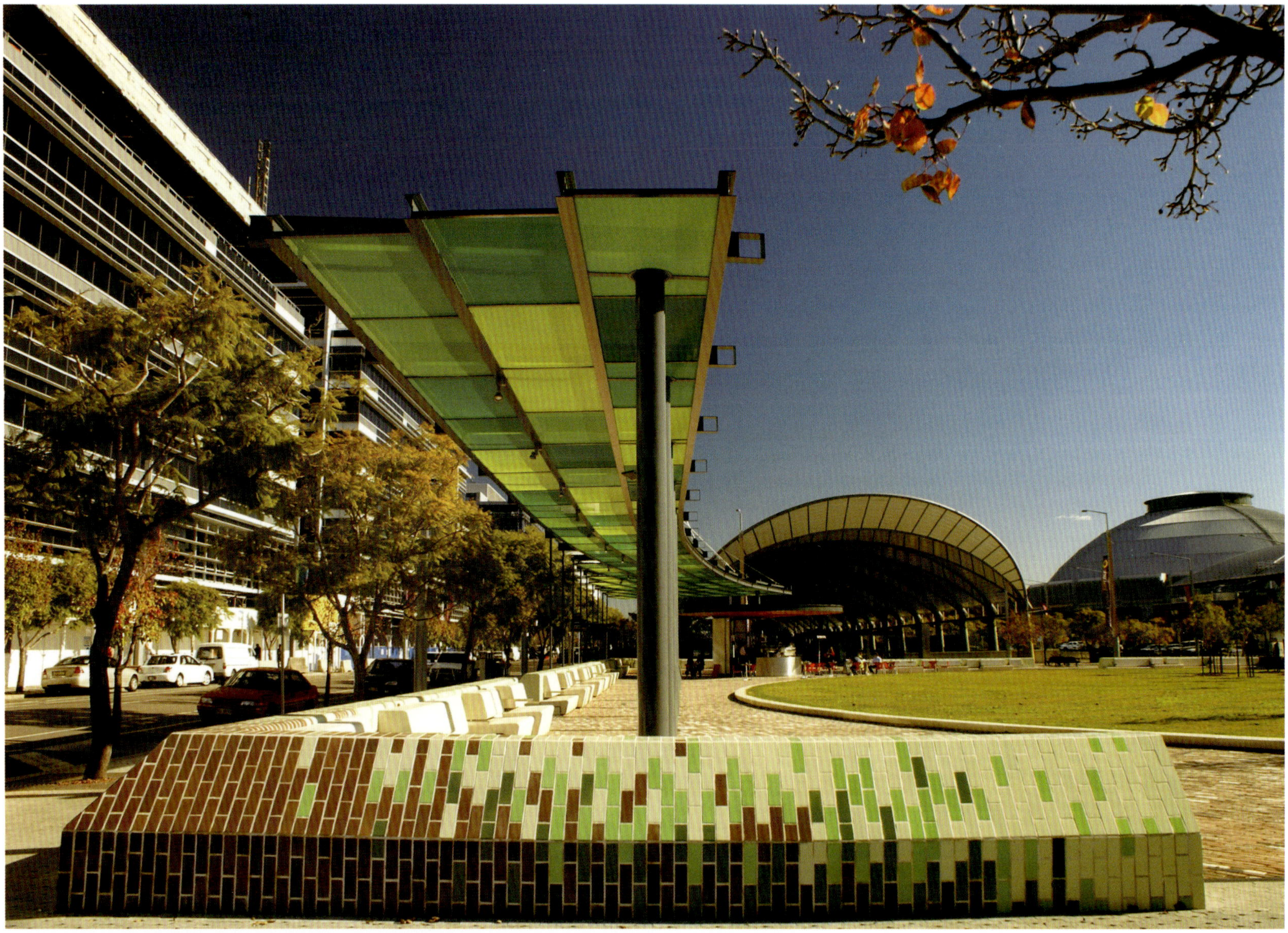

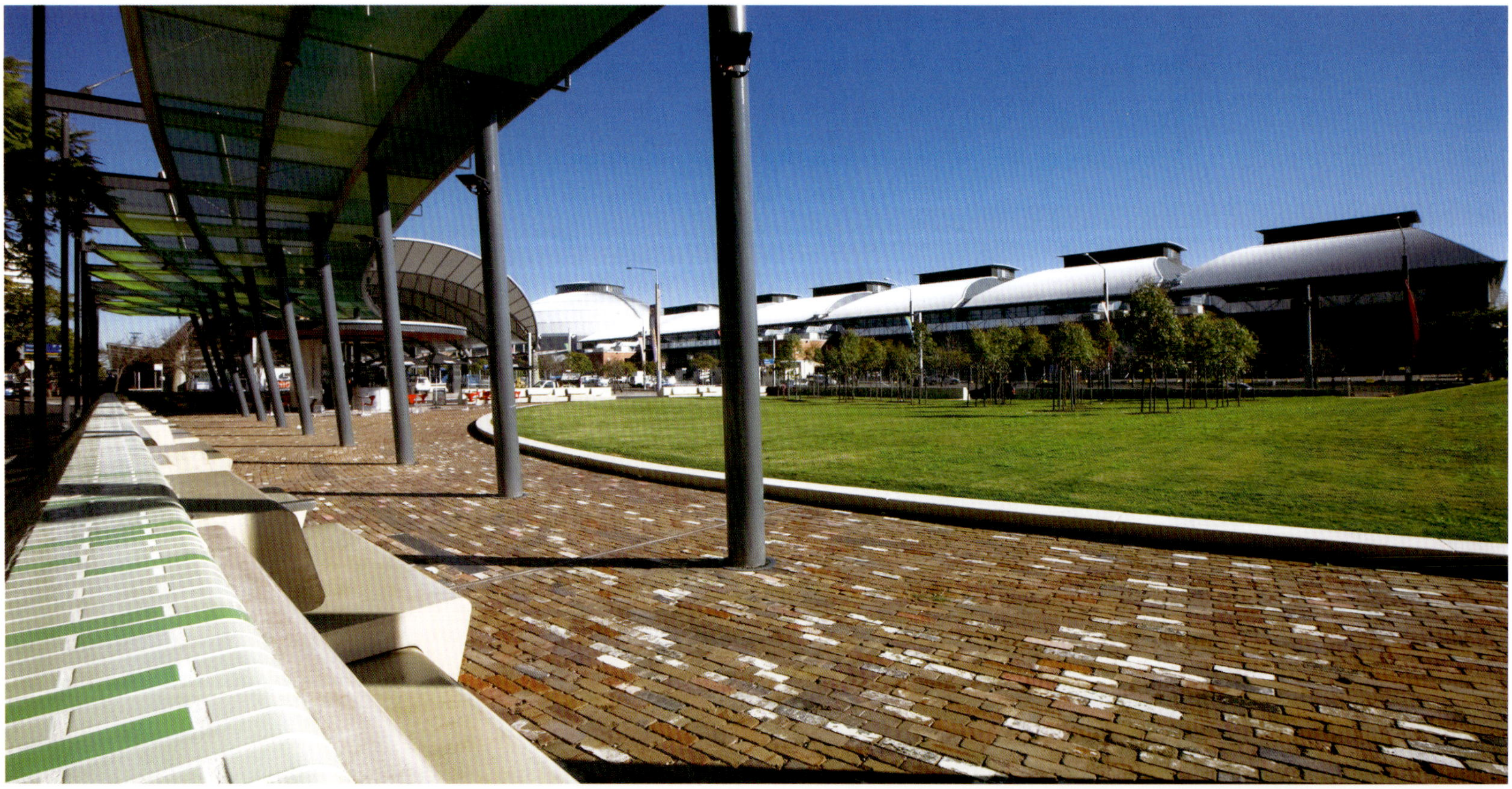

Upper left: Decorative colored brick walls and colorful canopies
Lower left: The Brick Pavement as a reflection of history
Lower right: Details of the brick wall

The Brochstein Pavilion at Rice University

Location: Houston, USA **Designer:** The Office of James Burnett **Photographer:** Hester + Hardaway **Completion date:** 2009 **Site area:** 1,486 sqm

Meticulously detailed and unpretentious, the transparency of the 1,486-square-meter glass, steel and aluminum pavilion offers a sublime contrast to the adjacent buildings. To complement the modesty of the building, the landscape architect surrounded the structure with a 10,000-squar-foot concrete plaza scored and sandblasted in a simple geometric pattern that references the plan of the building. Linear bands of horsetail reed define the edge of the outdoor dining and separate the adjacent pedestrian paths.

Interventions to the area of the Central Quadrangle to the west were limited to those that reinforced the existing framework of the space but the newly created interstitial space between the library and the pavilion required a more complex approach. Responding to the grid of the building, a bosque of 48 specimen Allee Lacebark Elms rise from a plane of decomposed granite and provide an organizational framework that humanizes the scale of the space. A generous concrete walk connecting the library and the pavilion bisects the grove into garden rooms defined by plantings of African Iris. Long black concrete fountains filled with beach stone occupy the center of each space, filling the garden with the murmur of running water and reflecting the filtered light through the canopy. Movable furniture and subtle site lighting allow impromptu gatherings of visitors to enjoy the oasis created by the dense shade and running water.

Respecting the lightness of the building, the landscape architect made minimal interventions elsewhere. New concrete walks and a row of specimen Live Oaks reinforce the existing spatial framework of the quadrangle. Although the floodplain requirements necessitated a finish floor elevation considerably higher than existing grade, the architects favored a solution that would not isolate the building on a dramatic plinth. Carefully considering the existing trees, the landscape architect subtly manipulated the grading of the approach walks so that building feathers into the landscape and overcomes the flatness of the campus.

Award description:
2010 ASLA National Honor Award
2009 ASLA Texas Chapter Merit Award
2010 AIA National Award

1. Live Oak Groves
2. Decomposed Granite Grave Court
3. Elm Bosque
4. Water Fountain
5. Library Entrance
6. Brochstein Pavilion
7. Plaza Around Building
8. Limit of Overhead Canopy
9. Lawn

Right: Protected from the intense Houston sun by a continuous canopy of Allee Elms, visitors rearrange the bistro chairs and tables to suit their changing needs

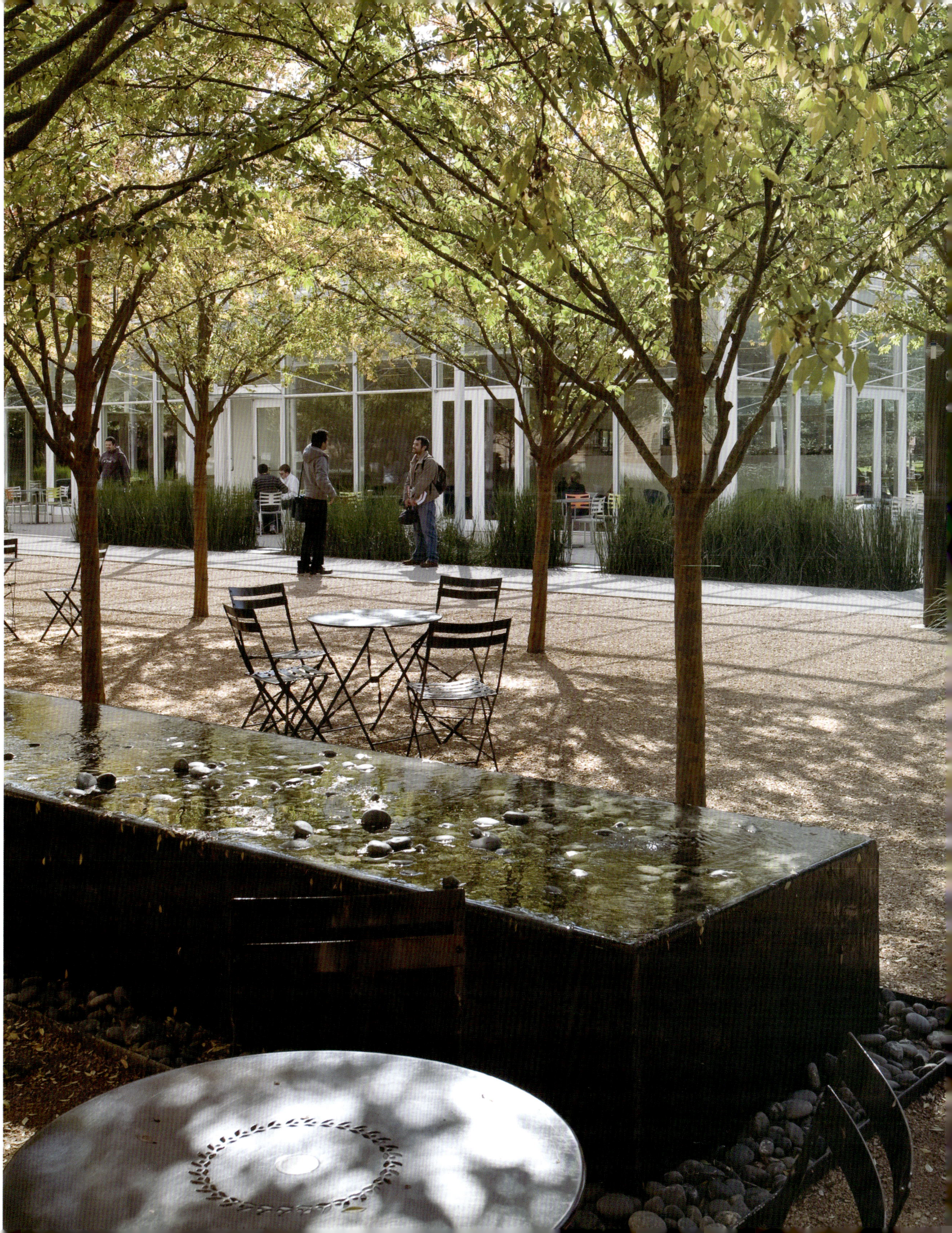

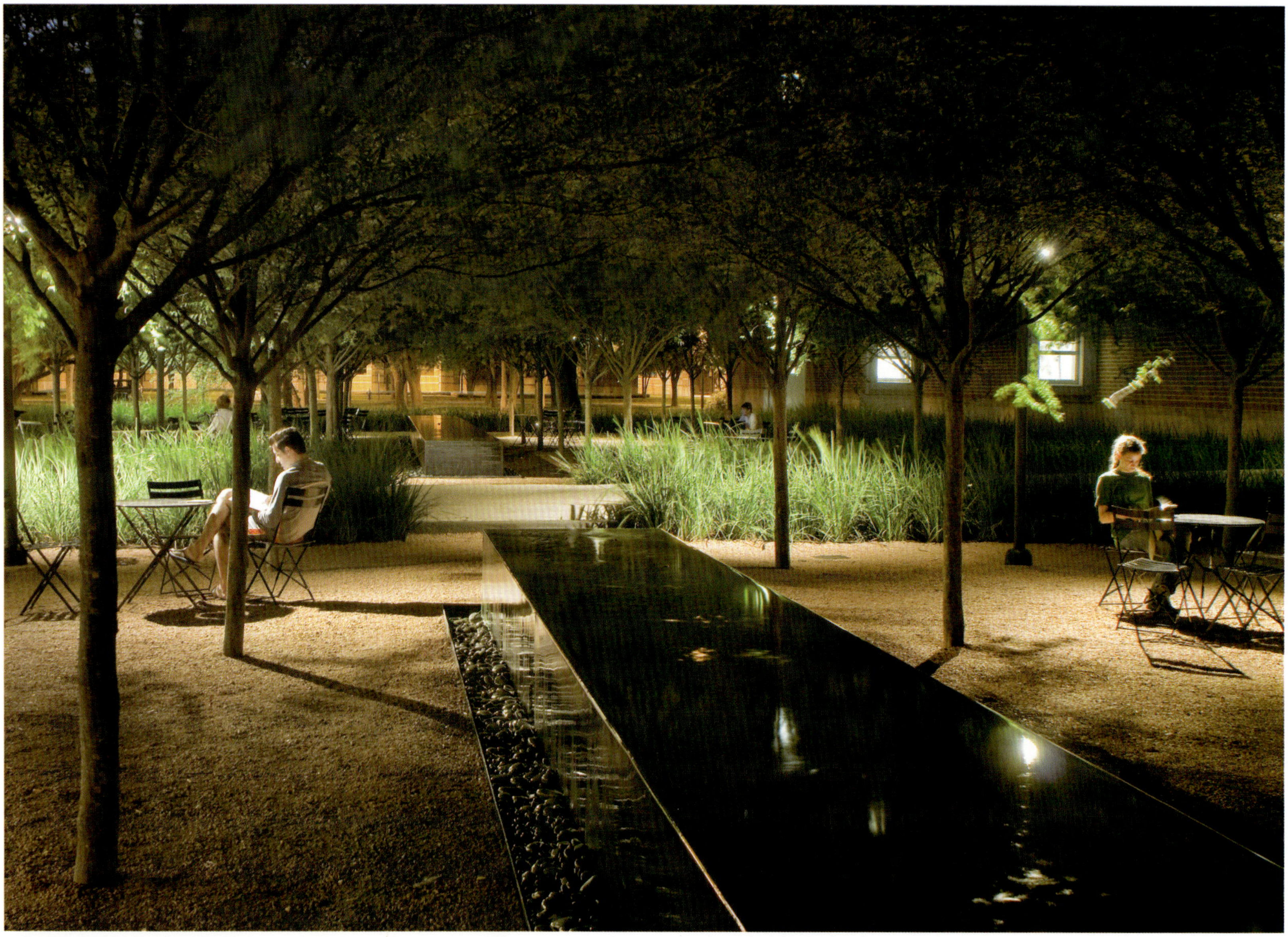

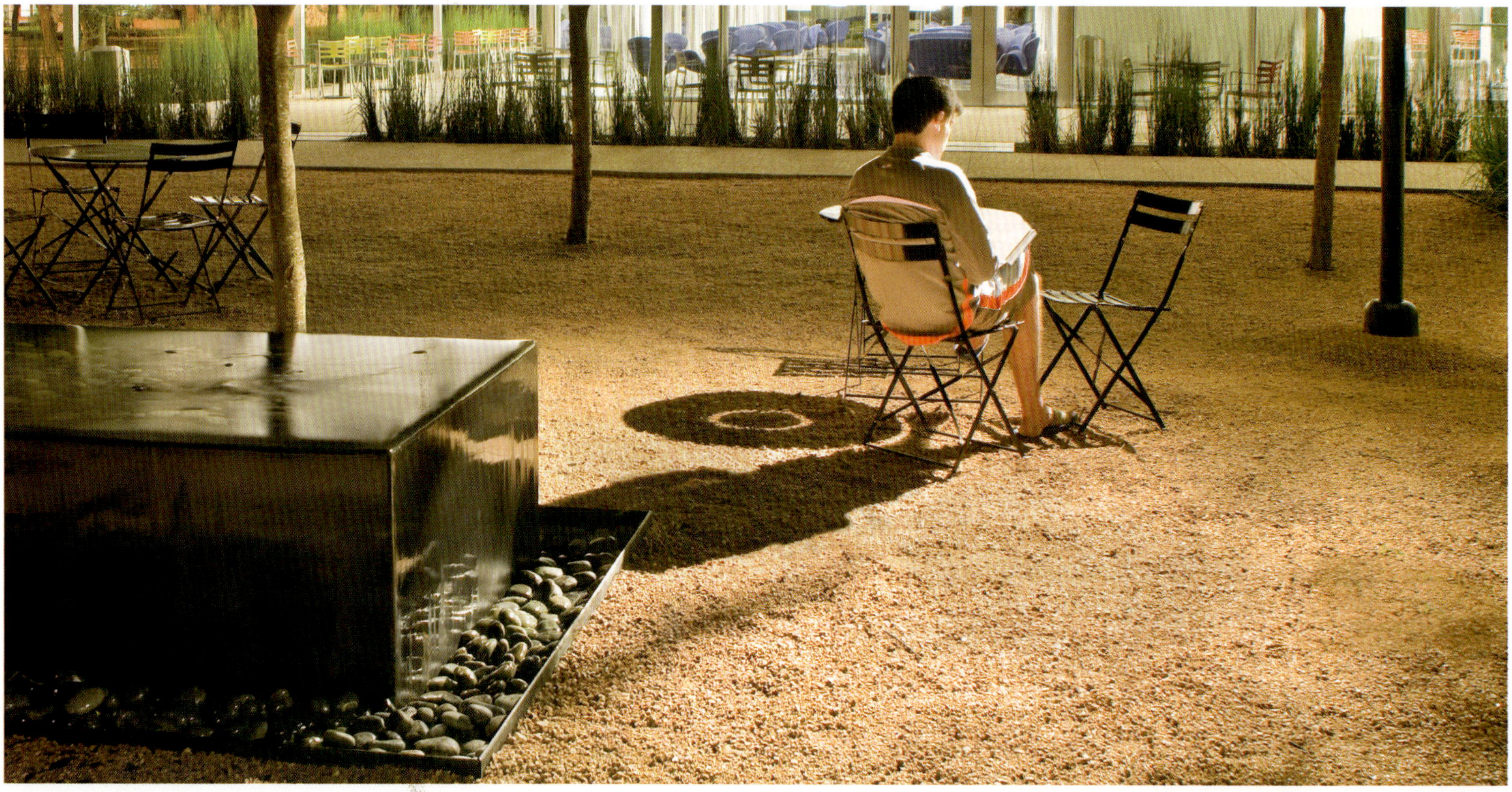

Upper left: Site lighting provides a sense of security that encourages students to study and socialize at all hours. The water trays provide drama and depth to the garden at night
Lower left: Students can experience the garden at all hours of the night
Upper right: The water trays provide a calming and continuous sound in the garden. They are more interactive than we had envisioned as people enjoy moving the stones within the basin to expose the clusters
Lower right: The fall color of the Elms provides a wonderful contrast with the lustrous green of the Iris and Horsetail. The Horsetail provides a buffer between the 'porch' and the adjacent campus walks

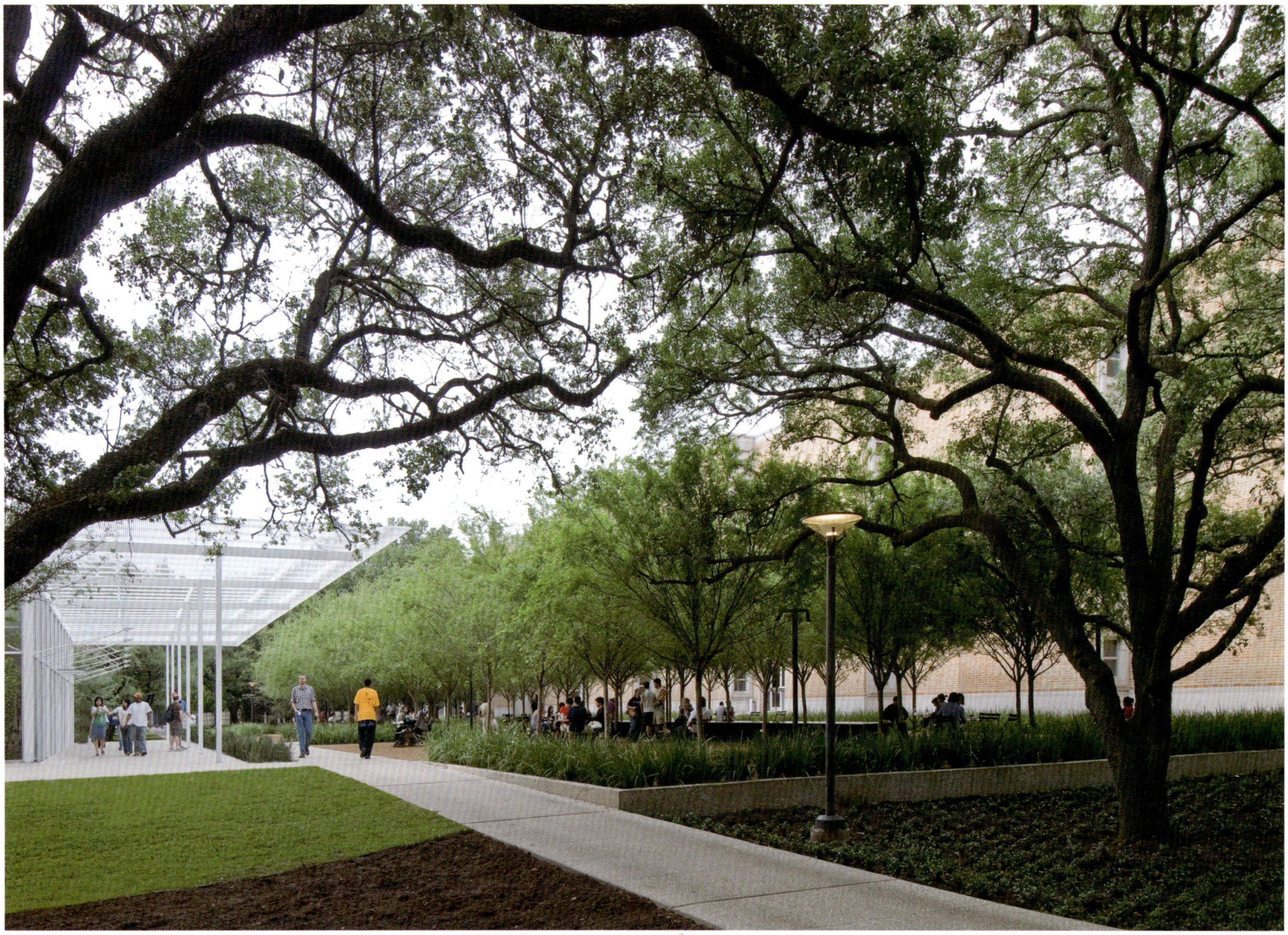

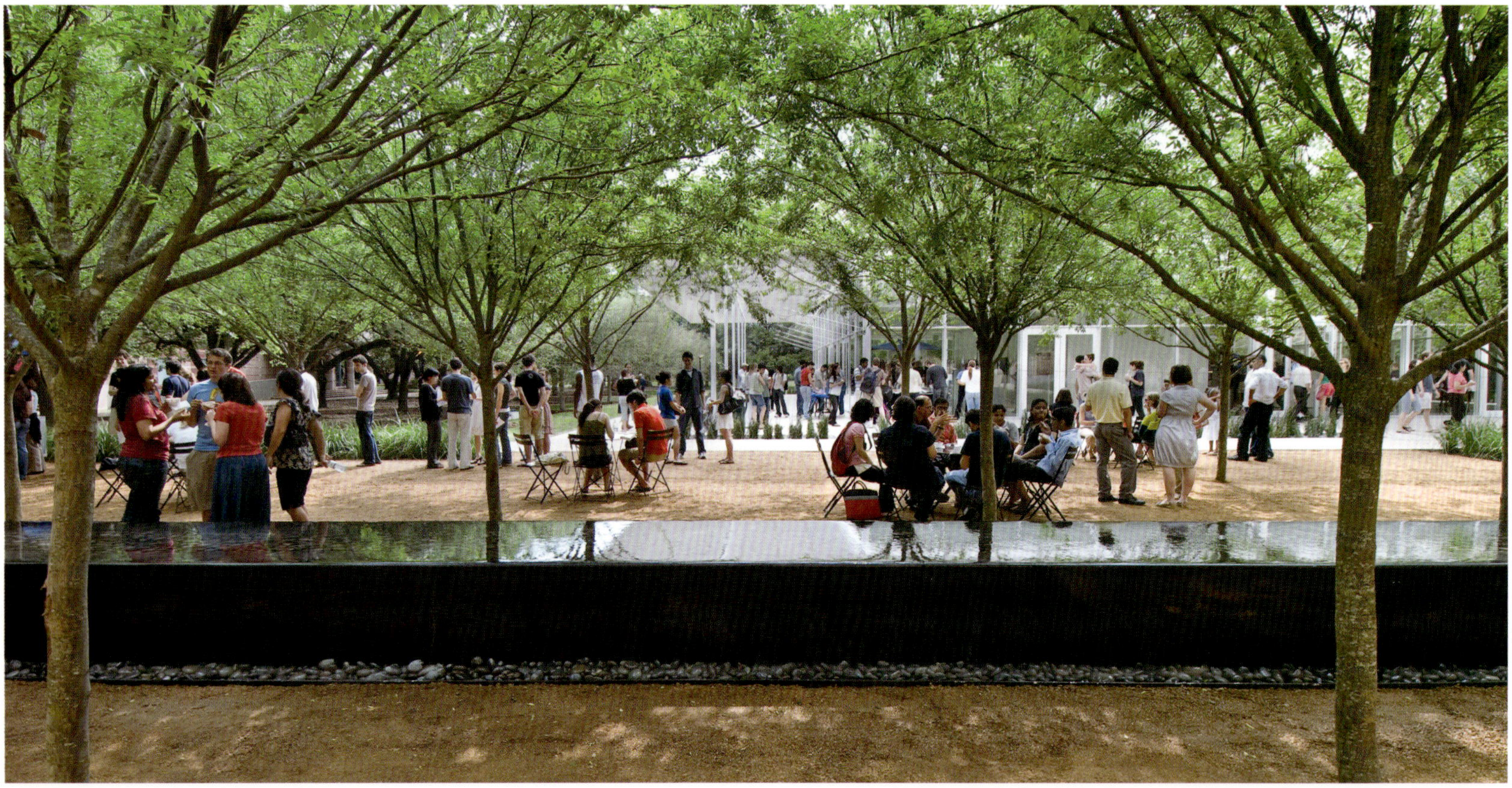

Upper left: A bosque of Allee Lacebark Elms organizes the space between the Pavilion and creates a new entry to the Fondren Library. This garden and pavilion has become the new 'Heart of the Campus' at Rice
Lower left: The new 'Heart of the Campus' has become a popular location for receptions, parties and celebrations at the campus
Upper right: The height and proportion of the basins invite children and adults to interact with the water, moving stones and touching the water as it sheets across the basins
Lower right: The surface of the basin spectacularly mirrors the sky and the canopies of the Elms

Parade Ground, University of the Arts London

Location: London, UK **Designer:** Planet Earth Ltd **Photographer:** Nathan Willock
Completion date: 2008 **Site area:** 3,500 sqm

The design divides the space into a geometric grid according to 'golden section' measurements which reveal proportions and harmonies discovered in the design of the surrounding buildings. The grid is defined by subtle straight and curved polished stainless steel lines and linear and curved LEDs embedded into new granite paving. The grid can be illuminated in a variety of sections and sequences to create stunning evening effects and to assist artist in aligning and exhibiting their work.

The elegant design enhances the surrounding college buildings whilst offering maximum flexibility, as a working/leisure space featuring seating and a central turfed area, with ninety-nine anchoring points inset within the grid that are used for marquees and other temporary structures.

Planet Earth studied the energy generation capacity of the Parade Ground to offer the University of the Arts sustainable energy solutions for their buildings' heating and cooling, now and in the future.

The vast area of constructed surface at the Parade Ground is a good potential solar radiation collector. As the impacts of climate change indicate, a rise in summer temperatures will bring an increasing demand for the cooling of internal environments, as well as the need for heating in cooler winters.

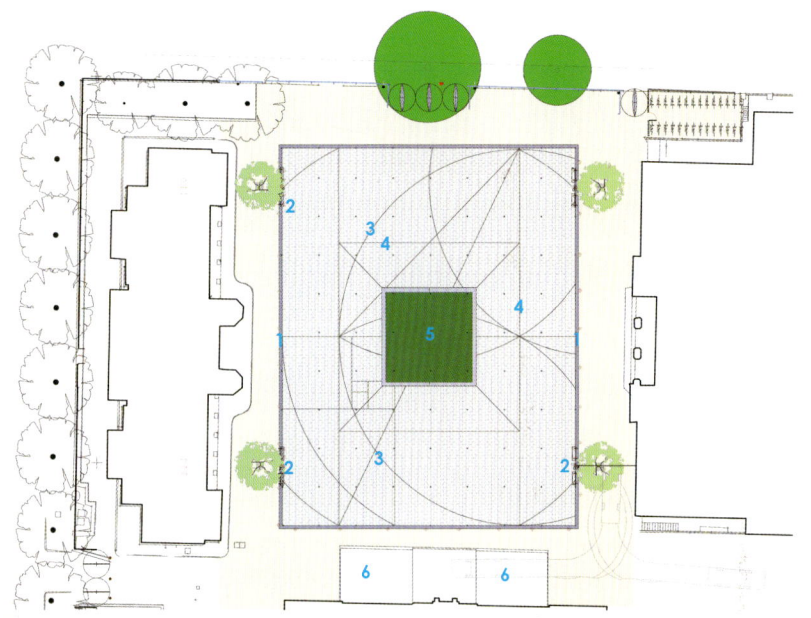

1. Floor Recessed Uplighters to Wash the Facades
2. Floor Recessed LED Uplighters Used Beneath the Benches
3. Curved in-ground Light Channel, 25 millimeters Wide
4. Linear in-ground Light Channel, 12 millimeters Wide
5. Central Turfed Area
6. Ramp

Right: Lightlab and building

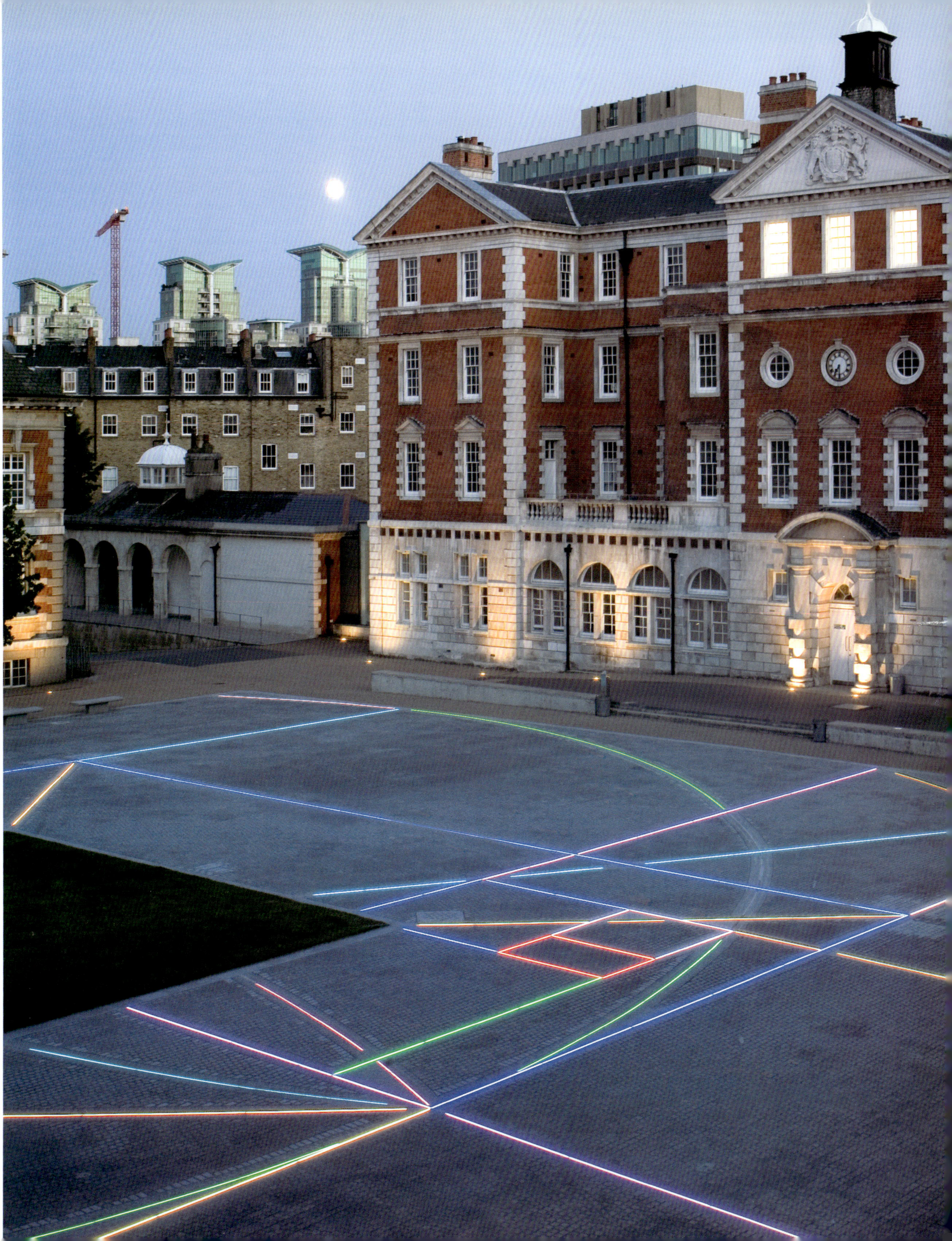

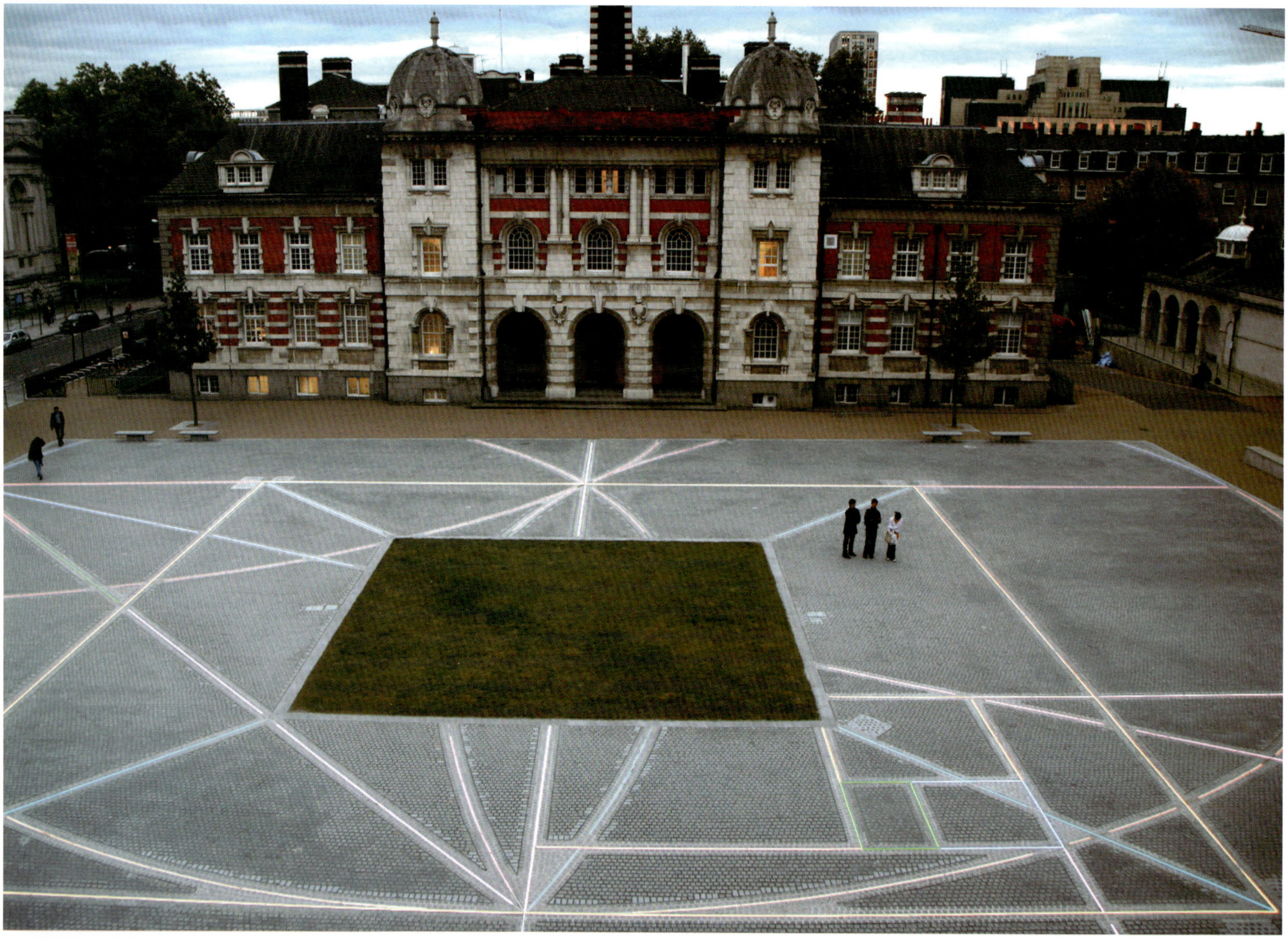

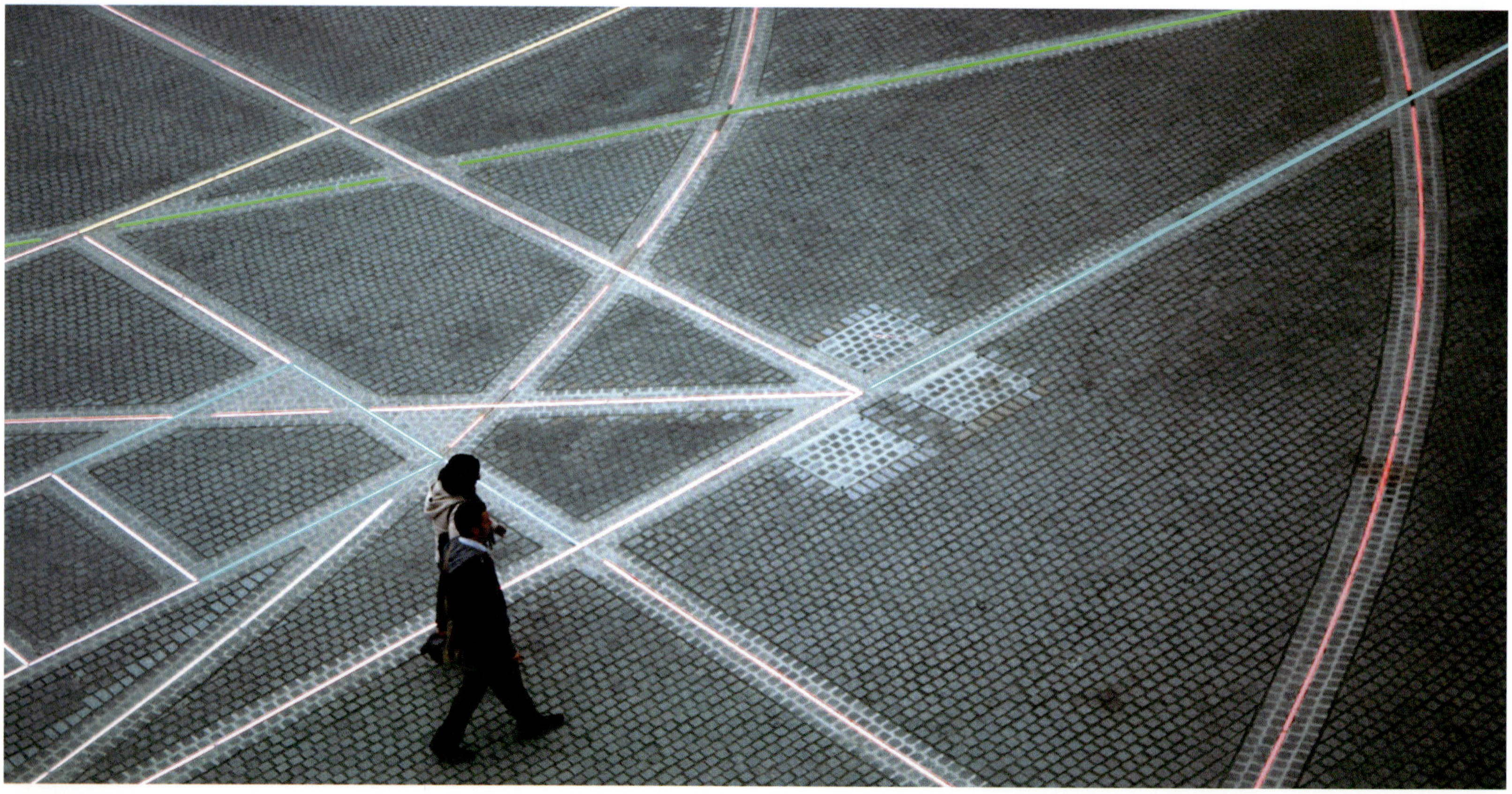

Upper left: Lightlab
Lower left: Lightlab detail
Upper right: View of the lightlab in the daytime
Lower right: Close view of the lightlab

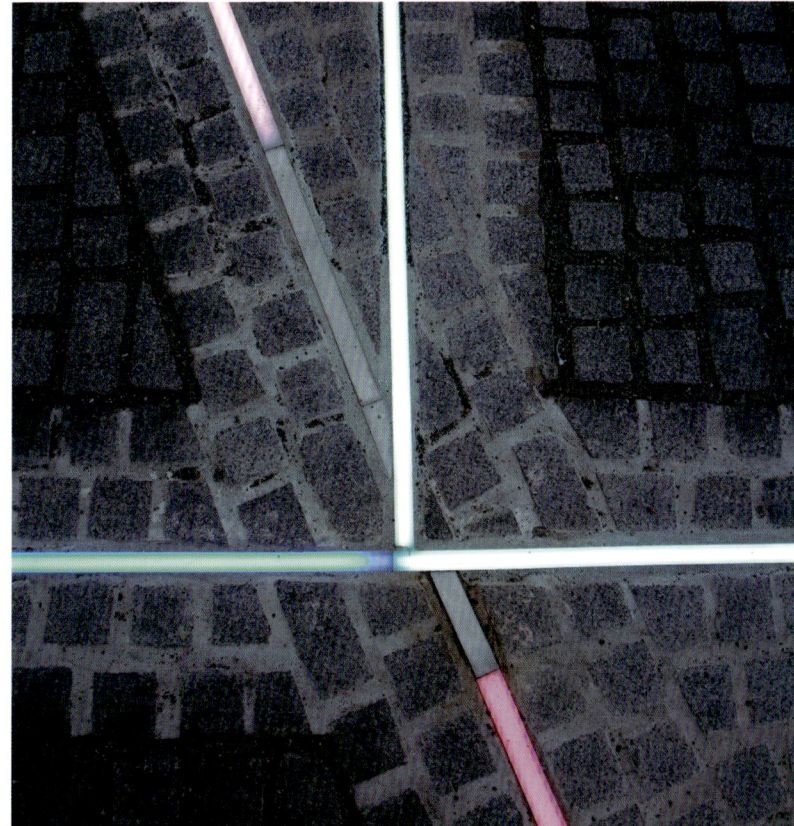

Angel Field

Location: Liverpool, UK **Designer:** BCA Landscape UK **Photographer:** Dan Kenyon, BCA Landscape **Completion date:** 2010 **Site area:** 5,000 sqm

Angel Field links The Cornerstone and The Capstone which houses the new Hope Theater on the Creative Campus in south Everton, Liverpool. It is one of the finest small gardens to have been created in Britain in recent years and has already won wide acclaim for its blend of tranquillity and intellectual stimulation and for its variety of its fountains, hedges, trees, and literary quotations.

Inspired by the gardens of the Renaissance and emblematic of Liverpool Hope University's educational philosophy, it is a place of calm contemplation in the midst of a busy city center. The vision has been realized in beautiful and spectacular fashion. 'Origins' is a belt of native mature woodland with a circular pool (or spring) and the words of St. Thomas Aquinas: "Nothing is in the intellect that was not first in the senses." 'The Body' is an apple orchard set in a native wild flower meadow. On scattered stones are the words of Pied Beauty, by local poet-priest Gerard Manley Hopkins. 'The Mind' features a performance area surrounded by hedges, pom-pom pines, pleached limes and the fibbonacci planting beds – nature controlled and manipulated by human intervention. A pool surrounded by Shakespeare's immortal line: "All the worlds a stage and all the men and women merely players". 'The Soul' is a cloister adjacent to the Cornerstone building. A light translucent cast resin angel stands guard – a re-imaging of the heavy stone greek gods of Villa Lante. With the garden, the University has set a public place of beauty into one of the poorest wards in the country.

1. Tilia Cordata (Greenspire)
2. Ilex Aquifolium Hedge
3. Native Tree Planting
4. Native Forb Underplanting
5. Amelanchier Lamarkii (Umbrella Form)
6. Pool of Life
7. Saint Thomas Aquinas' Quotation
8. T.S. Eliot Quotation
9. Gerard Manley Hopkins Poem
10. Malus Boskoop Apple Orchard Trees
11. Native Wildflower Meadow Underplanting
12. Perennial Grass Planting Bed
13. Bible Quotation
14. Tilia Platyphyllos Rubra
15. Fibonacci Beds
16. Paving Stones
17. Carpinus Betulus
18. Paving Border
19. Fountain Pool
20. Shakespeare Quotation
21. Malus 'Evereste' Hedge
22. Pinus Austriaca
23. Magnolia Loebnerii 'Merrill' Tree Group
24. Mixed Species Hedge
25. Taxus Baccata
26. Shady Perennial Underplanting
27. Bronze: Bible Quotation
28. Cast Resin Angel Sculpture

Right: Aerial view of the plaza

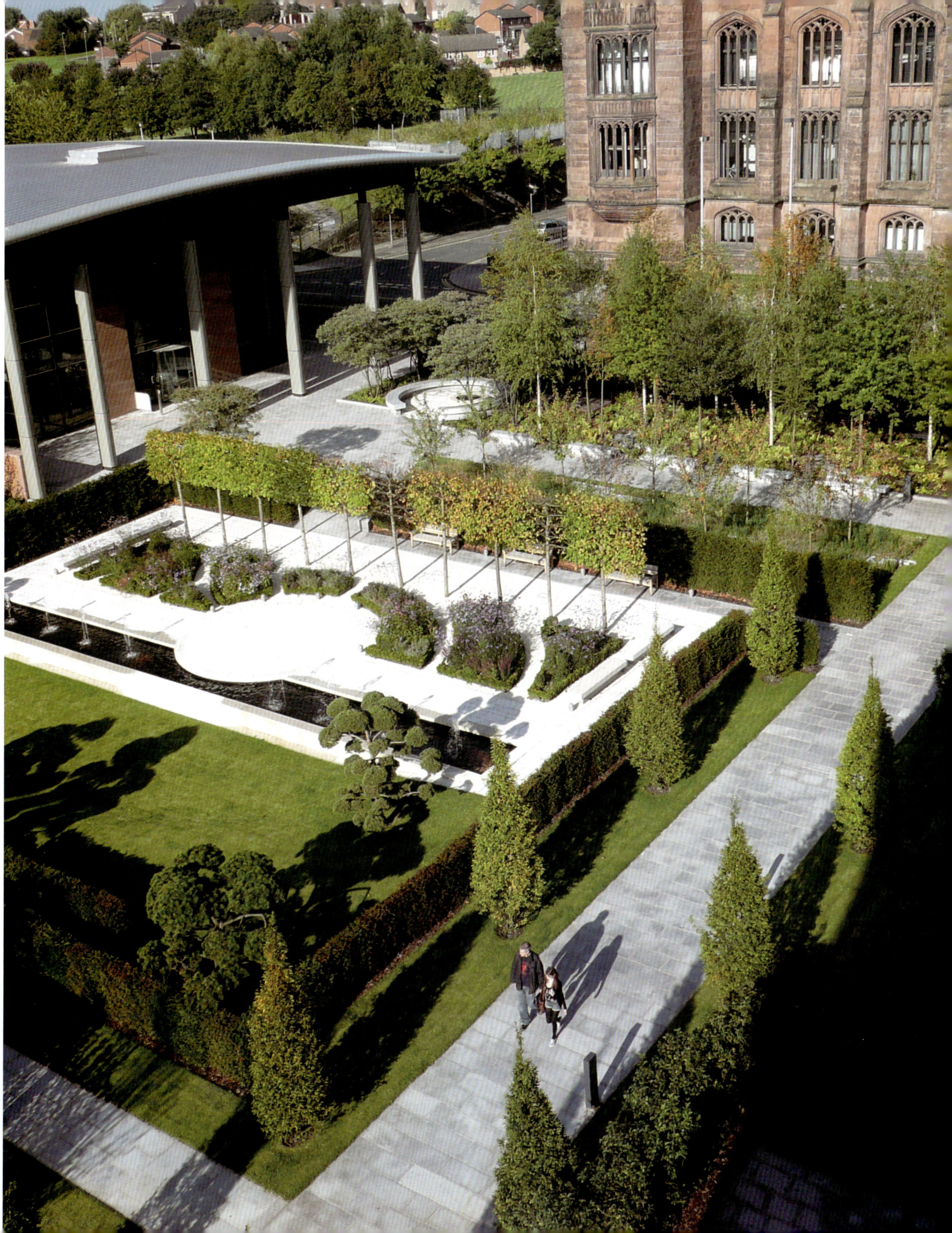

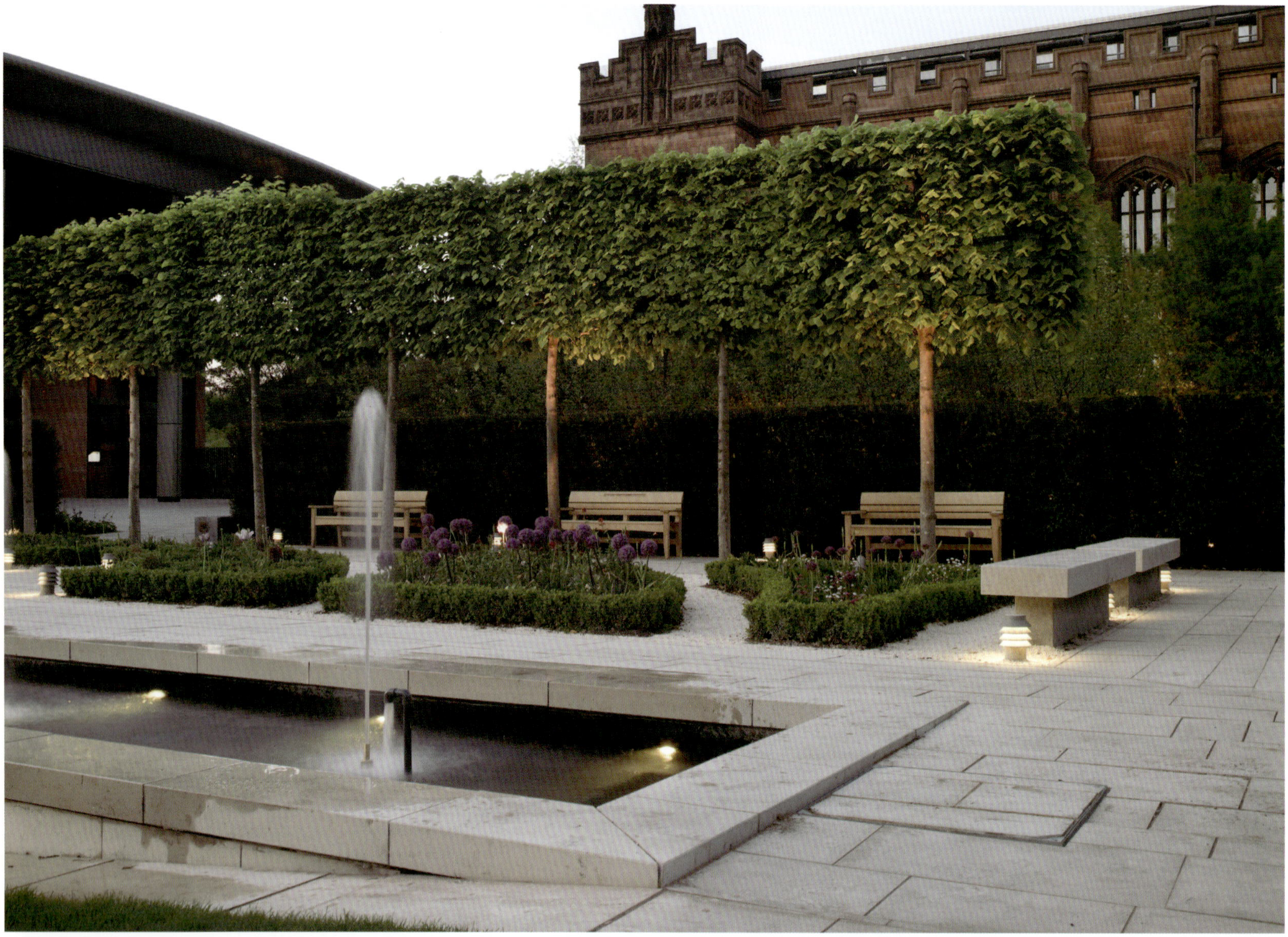

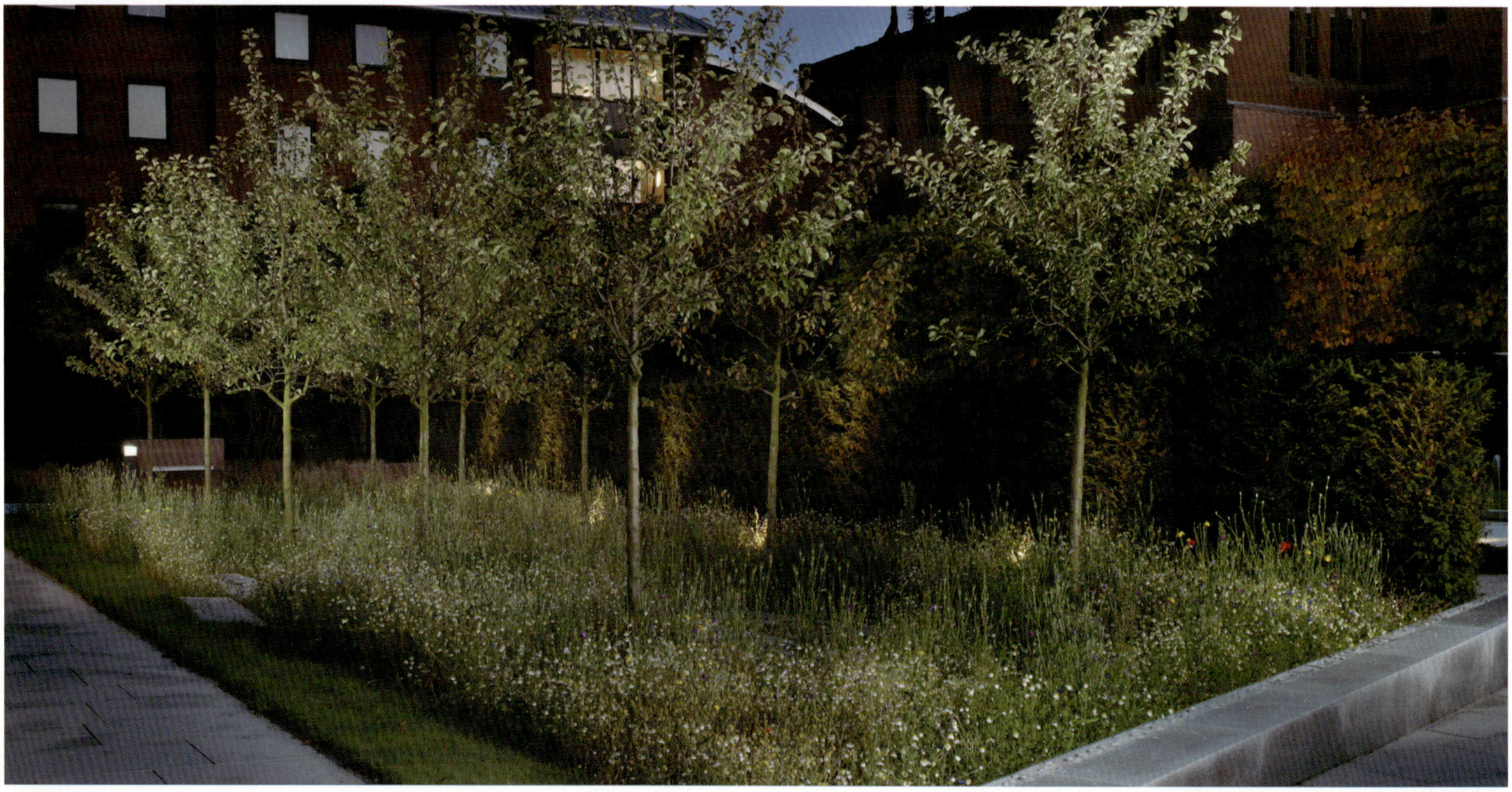

Upper left: Fountain pool
Lower left: Orchard and wildflower
Upper right: Path with hornbeams
Lower right: Wildflowers and poem stones

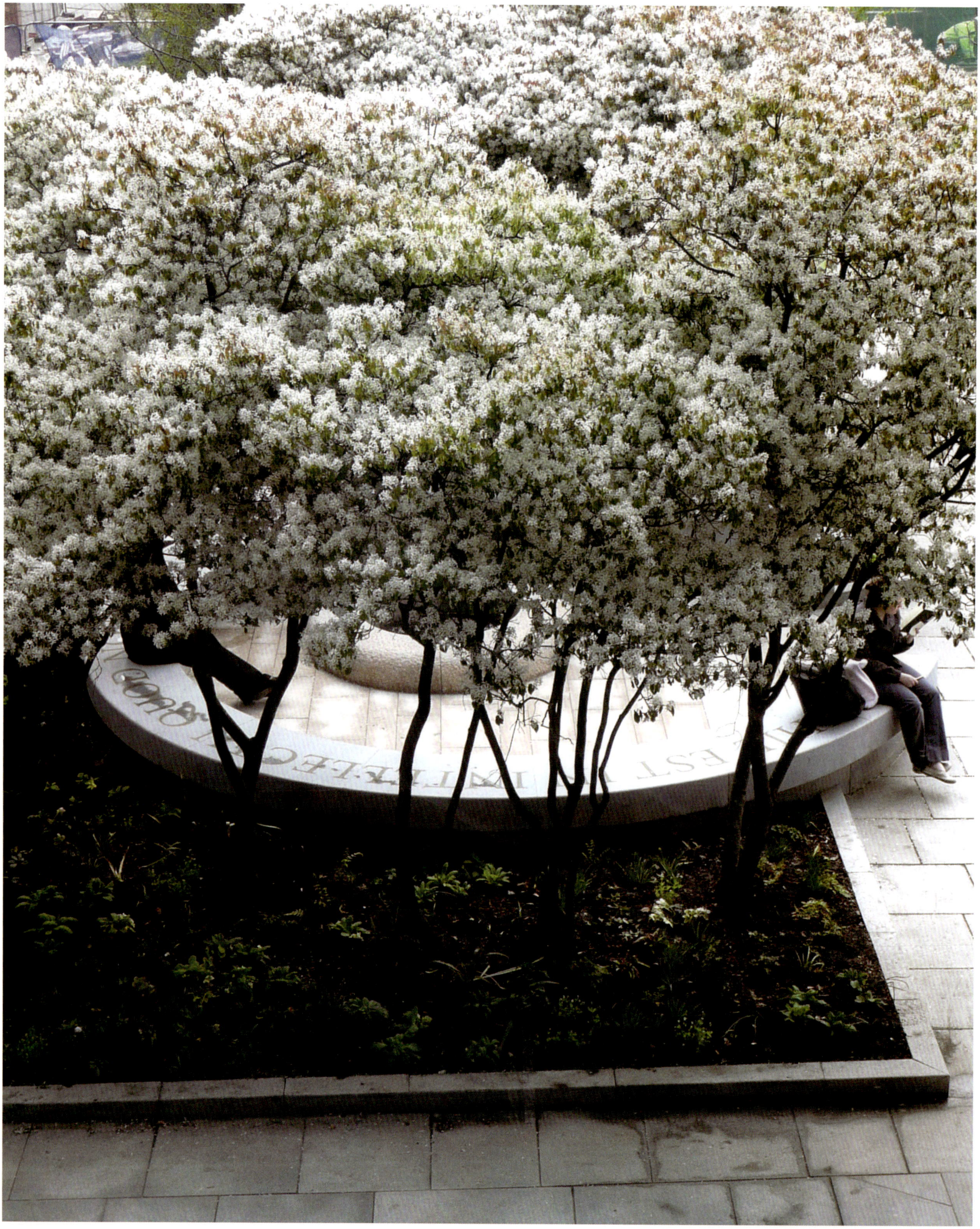

Upper right: The planting pattern forms a semi-enclosed effect
Lower right: Seat detail

National Center of Indigenous Excellence

Location: Sydney, Australia **Designer:** 360°Landscape Architects **Photographer:** Brett Boardman **Completion date:** 2010 **Site area:** 16,000 sqm

The landscapes are characterized by a restrained material palette of concrete, timber, softfall, bitumen, sandstone and extensive native 'bushtucker' plantings.

At the main George Street frontage, a central vista welcomes visitors through the entry courtyard to the central terraces and playing fields below. Three Queensland Kauri trees mark the entry courtyard.

The YMCA and Pool is accessed from the main courtyard. A raised turf area runs along the western side of the Pool terrace, and planted with three Screw Pine offers a soft social edge with opportunities to enjoy both sun and shade.

Below the entry courtyard, to the south of main axis is a space between two former school buildings that have been converted to dormitories and dining rooms. An organic geometry of winding walls resolve a complex slope, and creates a series of terraces and planter boxes that provide informal sitting areas and play edges, shaded by a grove of Cabbage Tree Palms. This is a key space for the NCIE and at its heart is a unique firepit.

The main axis terminates at the playing field's concrete and turf spectator terraces. The terraces benefit from the shade of existing Tallowoods and new plantings of Tuckeroo. In the residual landscape space to the south of the field is a screen planting of bushtucker species.

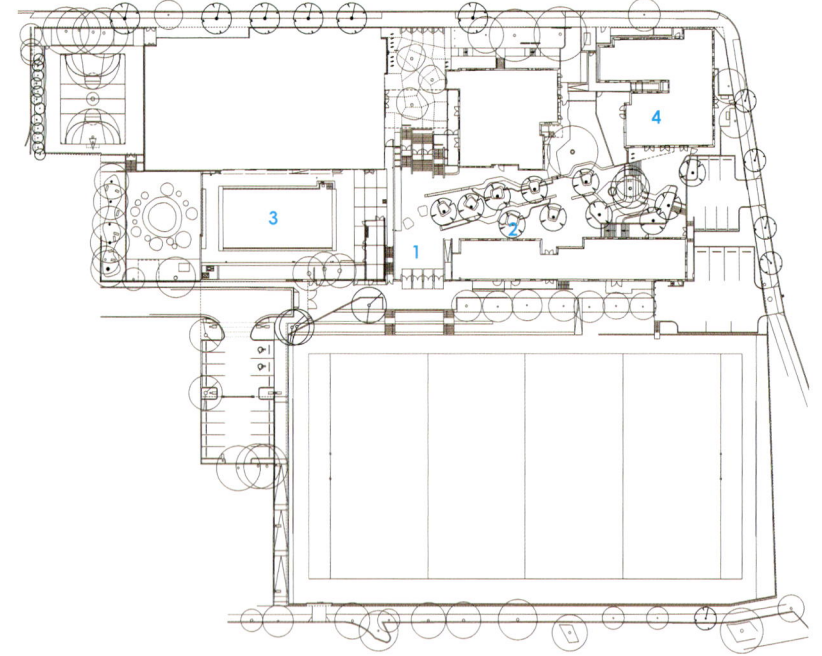

1. Entrance
2. Planter for Sitting
3. Swimming Pool
4. Building A

Right: Grove of Cabbage Tree Palms

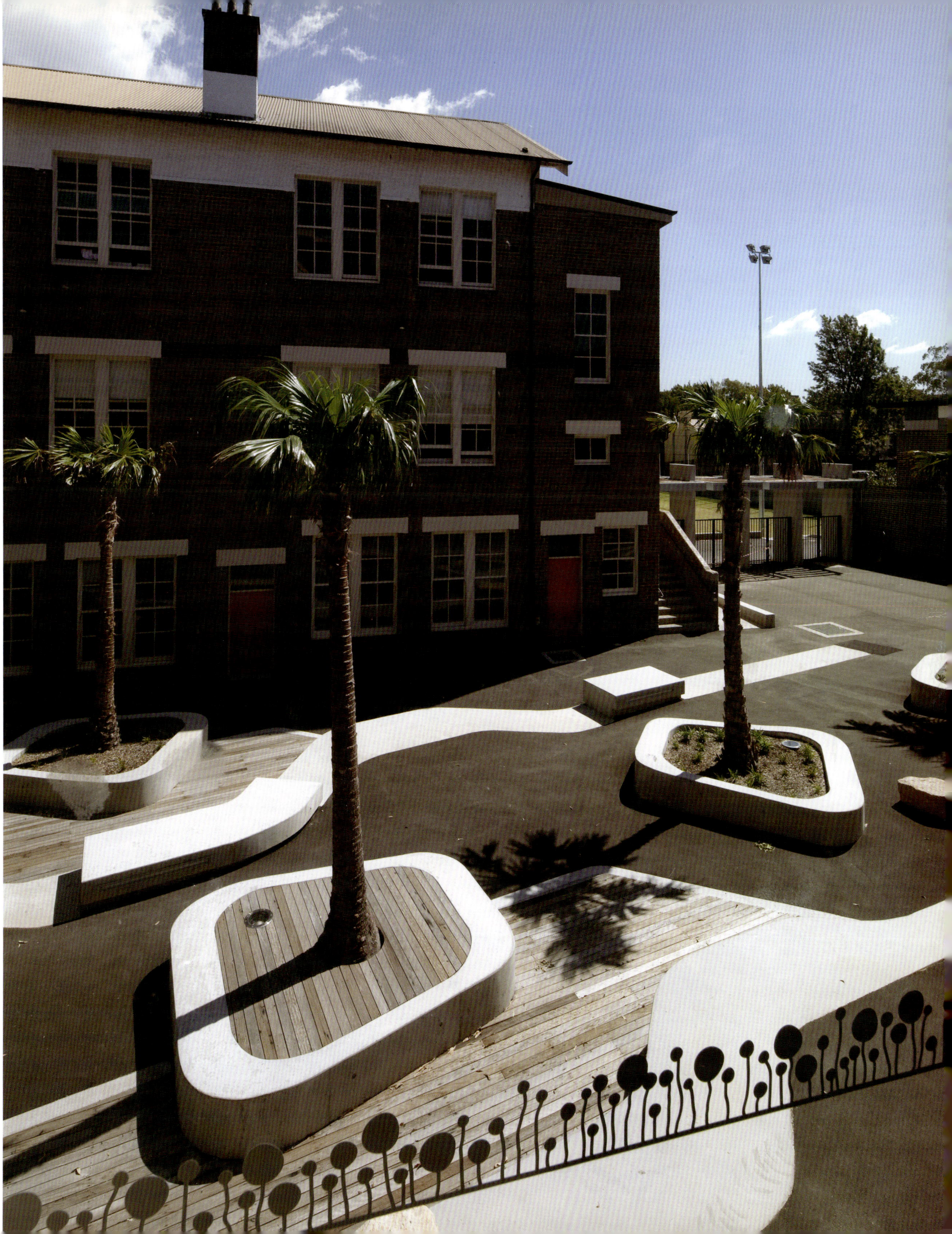

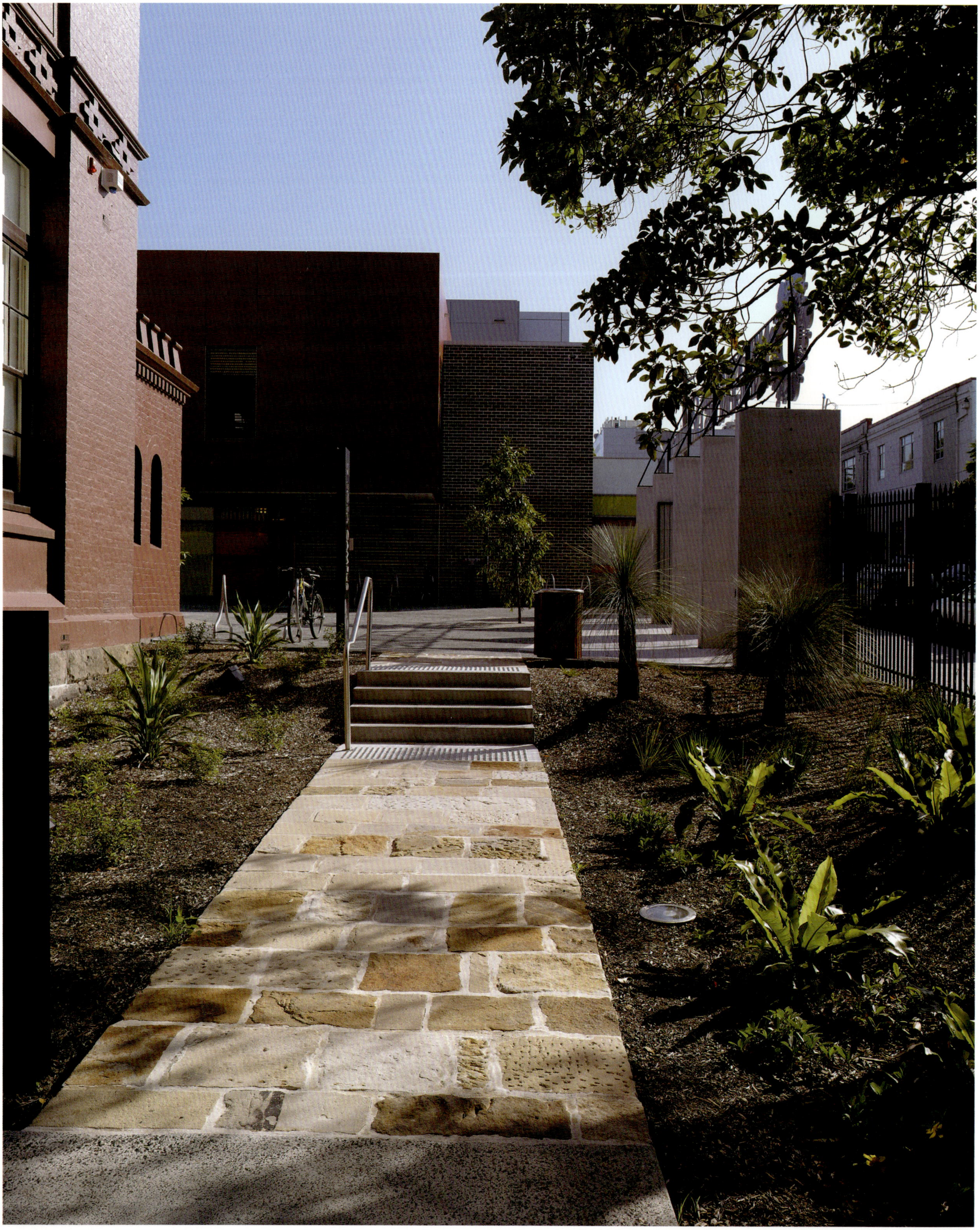

Left: Sandstone and native planting
Upper right: Timber amphitheater sited under shade of existing Eucalyptus microcorys
Lower right: Organic geometry of winding walls

BGU University Entrance Square & Art Gallery

Location: Beer Sheva, Israel **Designer:** Chyutin Architects Ltd **Photographer:** Sharon Yeari **Completion date:** 2009 **Site area:** 4,500 sqm

The Square serves as an entrance gate to the western side of the campus, surrounded by existing buildings and the future Negev Gallery. The Square offers an outdoor space for cultural and social activities for students and for the city population.

The Square is bordered by the elongated structure of the gallery facing both the city and the campus. The gallery's continuous façade (160 meters in length) unifies the heterogeneous appearance of the existing buildings behind the gallery into a cohesive urban unit. The city façade is accompanied by a sculpture garden creating a green edge to the campus. The two-story high monolithic body of exposed concrete emerges from lawny topography of the northern part of the campus and hovers above an entrance courtyard in the southern part, where it appears to be leaping toward the urban space.

Since the Square was designated to accommodate intensive congregation of youth and students, the preferred solution was to allocate limited areas for vegetation. The design of the square with various elements of exposed concrete connects the surrounding buildings both physically and visually, accentuating their common features.

The Square appears as a carpet of integrated strips of concrete paving, vegetation and lighting with concrete benches and trees scattered randomly. The strips of vegetation consist of lawn, Equisetopsida and seasonal plants.

The first phase to be realized includes the Deichmann Square, followed by the Negev Gallery.

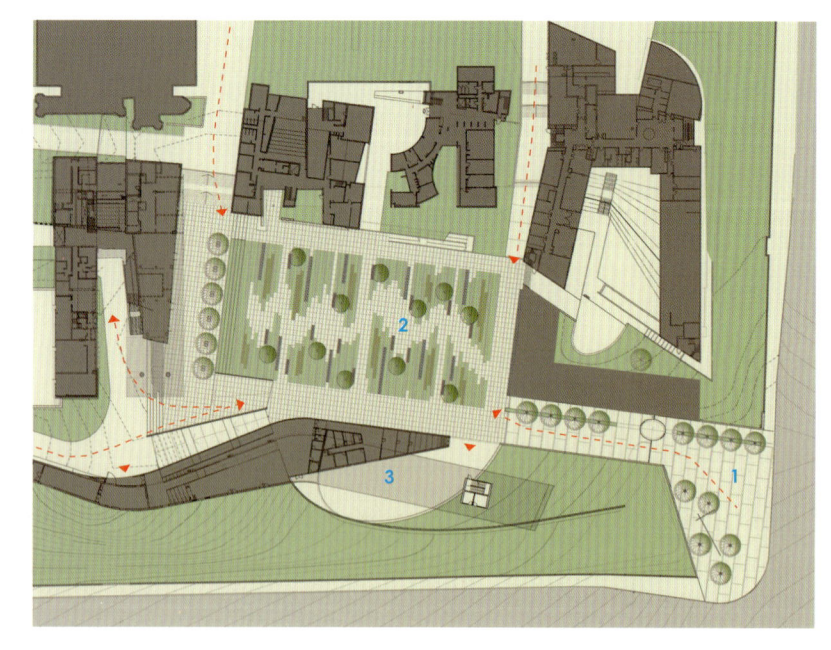

1. Entrance Plaza
2. Deichmann Square
3. University Gallery

Right: Night view with lighting effect

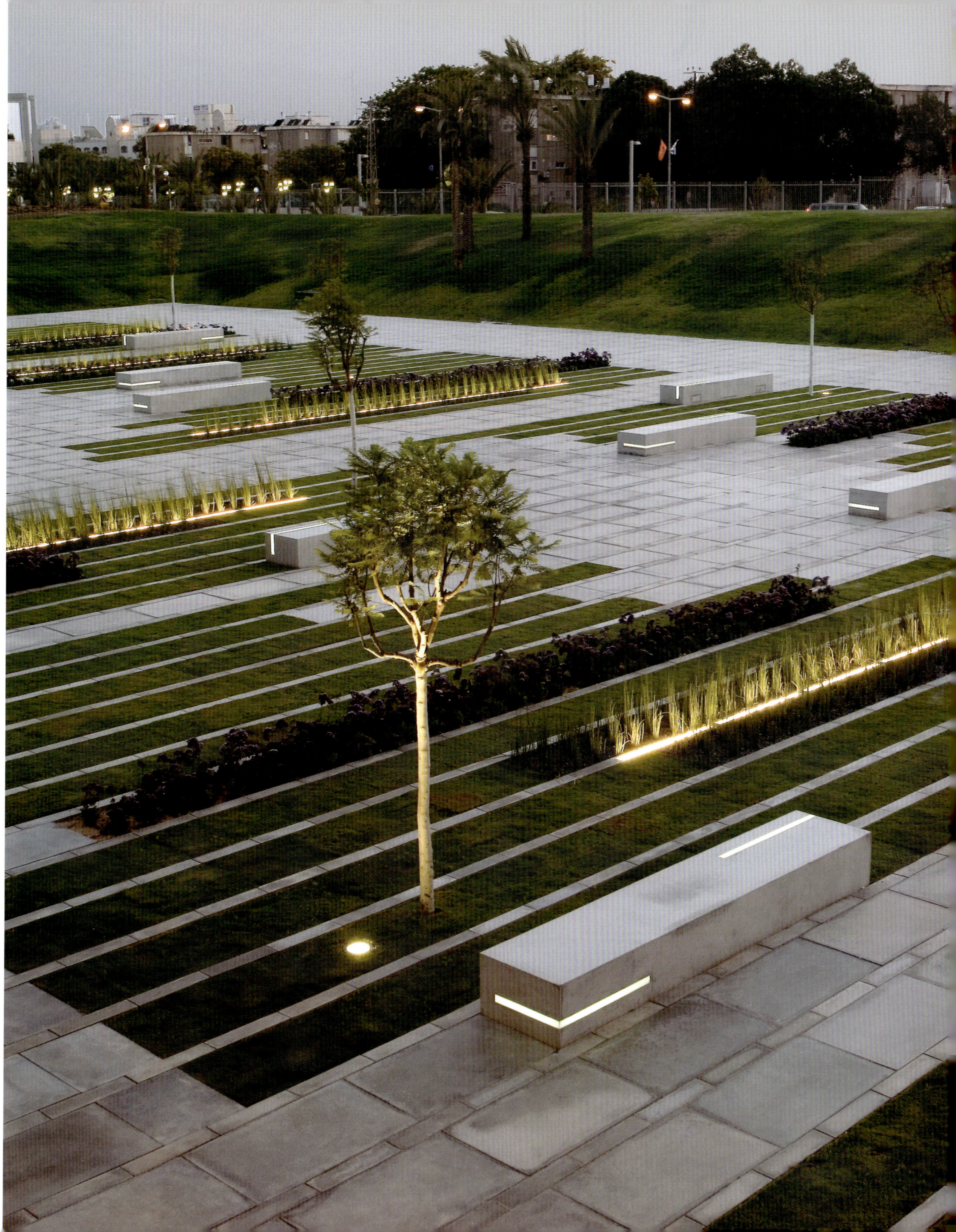

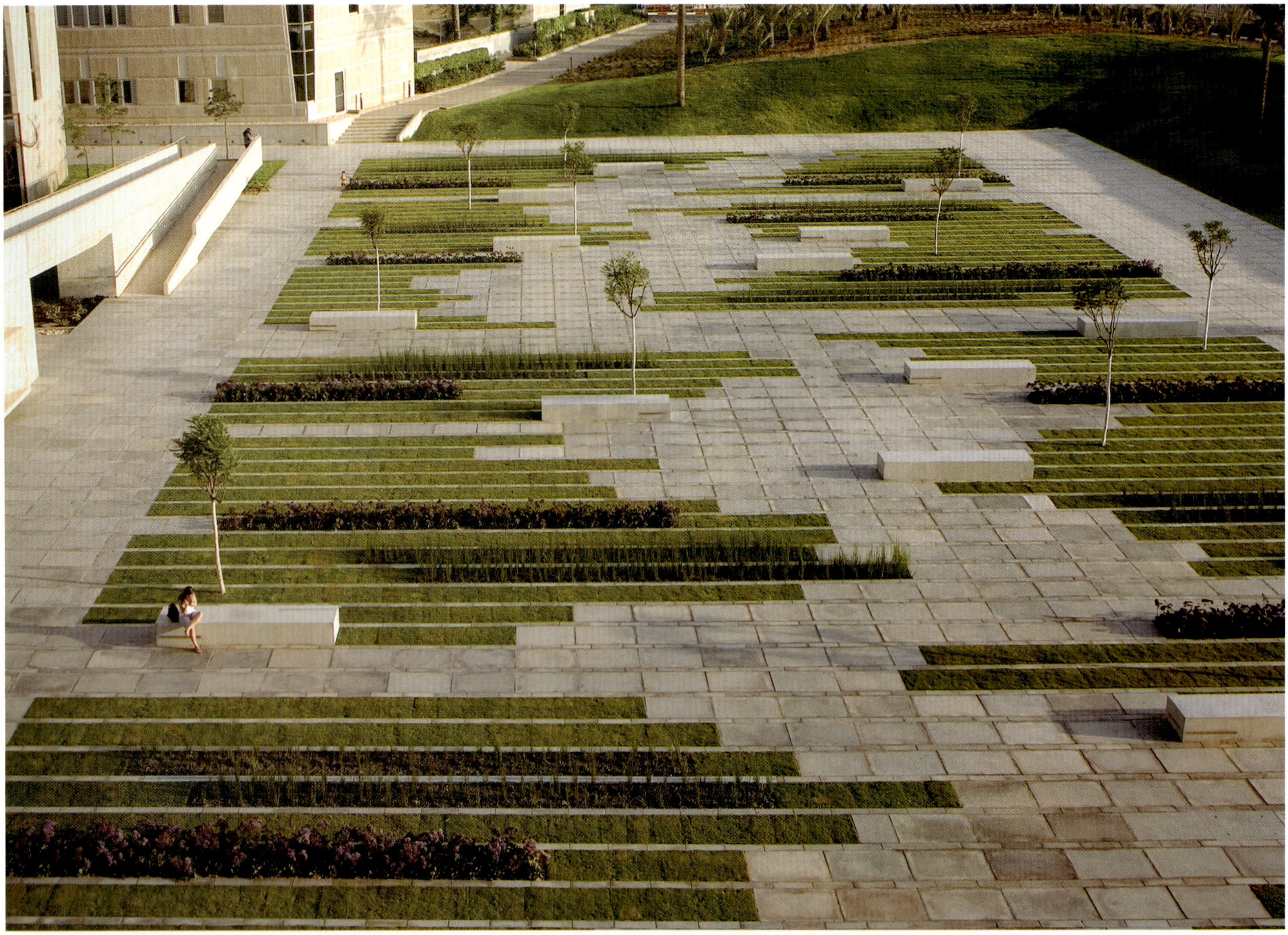

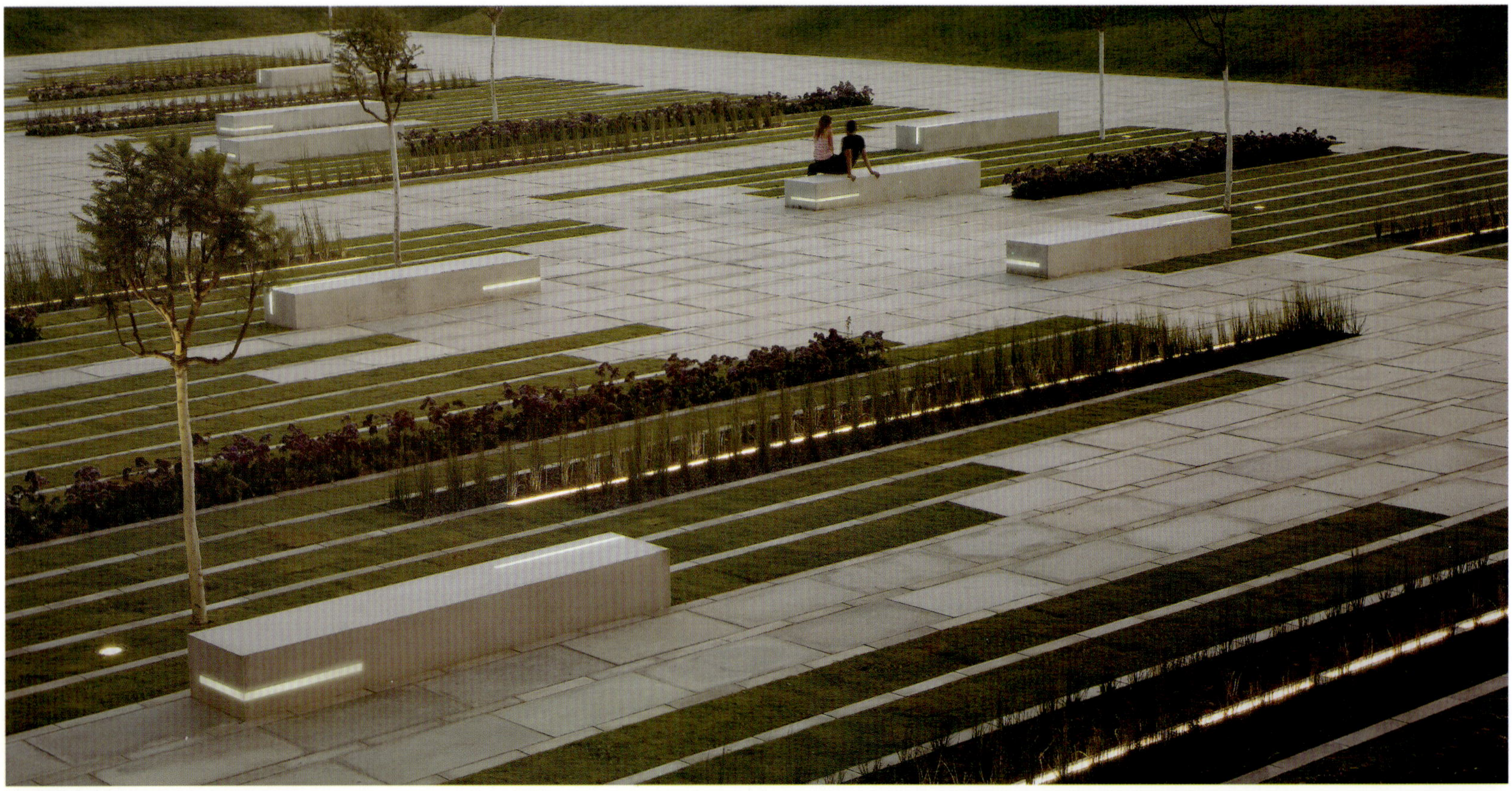

Upper left: The bird's view of the plaza
Lower left: The shape of the benches
Upper right: Building and the square

Universitätsplatz Frankfurt (Oder)

Location: Frankfurt (Oder), Germany **Designer:** Henningsen Landschaftsarchitekten BDLA Berlin **Photographer:** Christo Libuda, Lichtschwärmer **Completion date:** 2010 **Site area:** 10,100 sqm

This public open place in the heart and historic center of the east German town Frankfurt (Oder) is located between modern university buildings and the historic Church of Our Lady.

The square 'Universitätsplatz' creates together with square 'Europaplatz' nearby the central campus of the 'European University Viadrina Frankfurt (Oder)' in the middle of the city. This campus is not only open to students, but also to all residents and other public as well.

Based on the first prize of a competition in year 2006 this urban free space is made of wide paved areas, tree lined lawn terraces and a temporarily used playground. Some single extant trees order together with colorful seatings in the 'Universitätsplatz' and give him special quality and identity.

Most of the big and especially made yellow and blue seat units, the so-called 'campus-pillows', have integrated light-bands underneath the seats, which sets a special course at the whole square together with other light orchestrations in colors of the university.

Beside the paved areas the new built lawn terraces create a retirement and rest area inside the mostly stony setting. Groups of existing lime-trees form here together with in-between planted Amelanchier trees a sheltering roof of leaves. The bright and heavy concrete walls, lying between the lawn fields and building borders between the terraces, invite the students and inhabitans of Frankfurt (Oder) to stay and relax on them.

The temporarily used area was paved with light grey synthetic material and framed by huge bamboo pillars. Inside there is a playground, two chess tables and some concrete seating furniture.

1. Paved Area with Colorful Seatings and Groups of Maple Trees
2. Forecourt Lecture Hall
3. Lawn Terraces Separated by Low Concrete Walls
4. Temporarily Used Playground with Seating Furniture
5. Memorial Lime-tree for the Poet Heinrich von Kleist
6. Square 'Europaplatz'

Right: Chess tables and concrete seating furniture at the temporarily used area, which was fenced by bamboo pillars and marked with light grey synthetic material

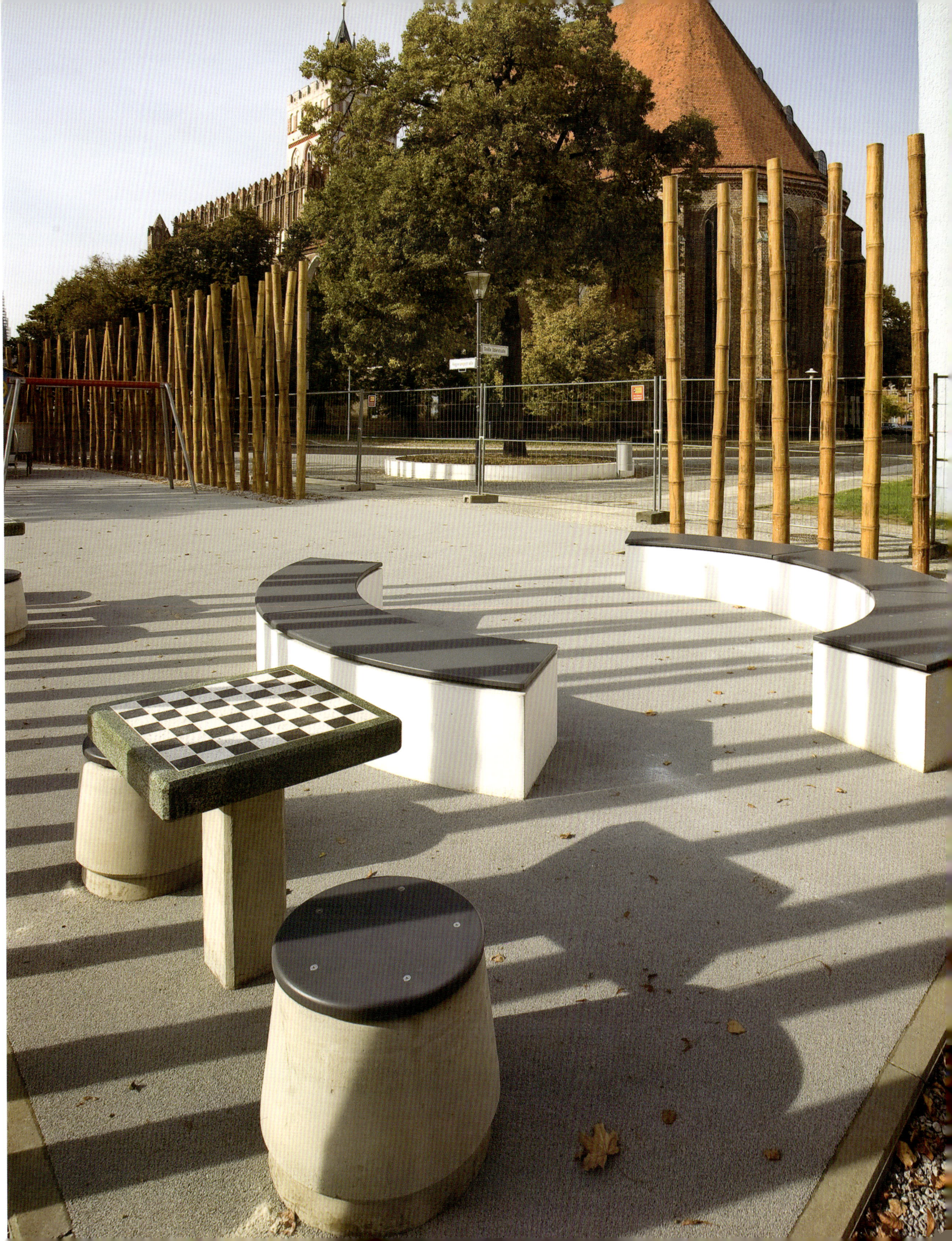

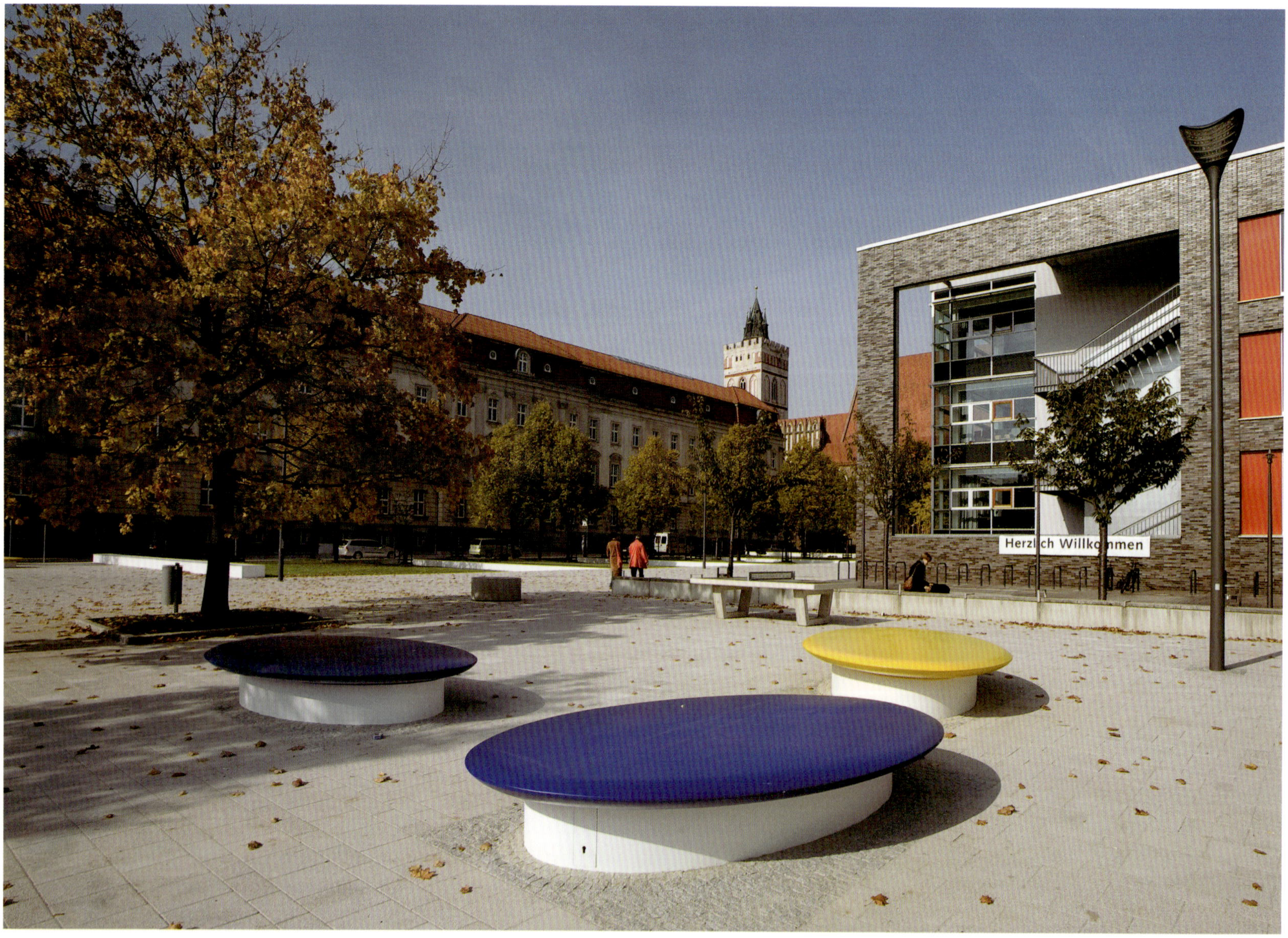

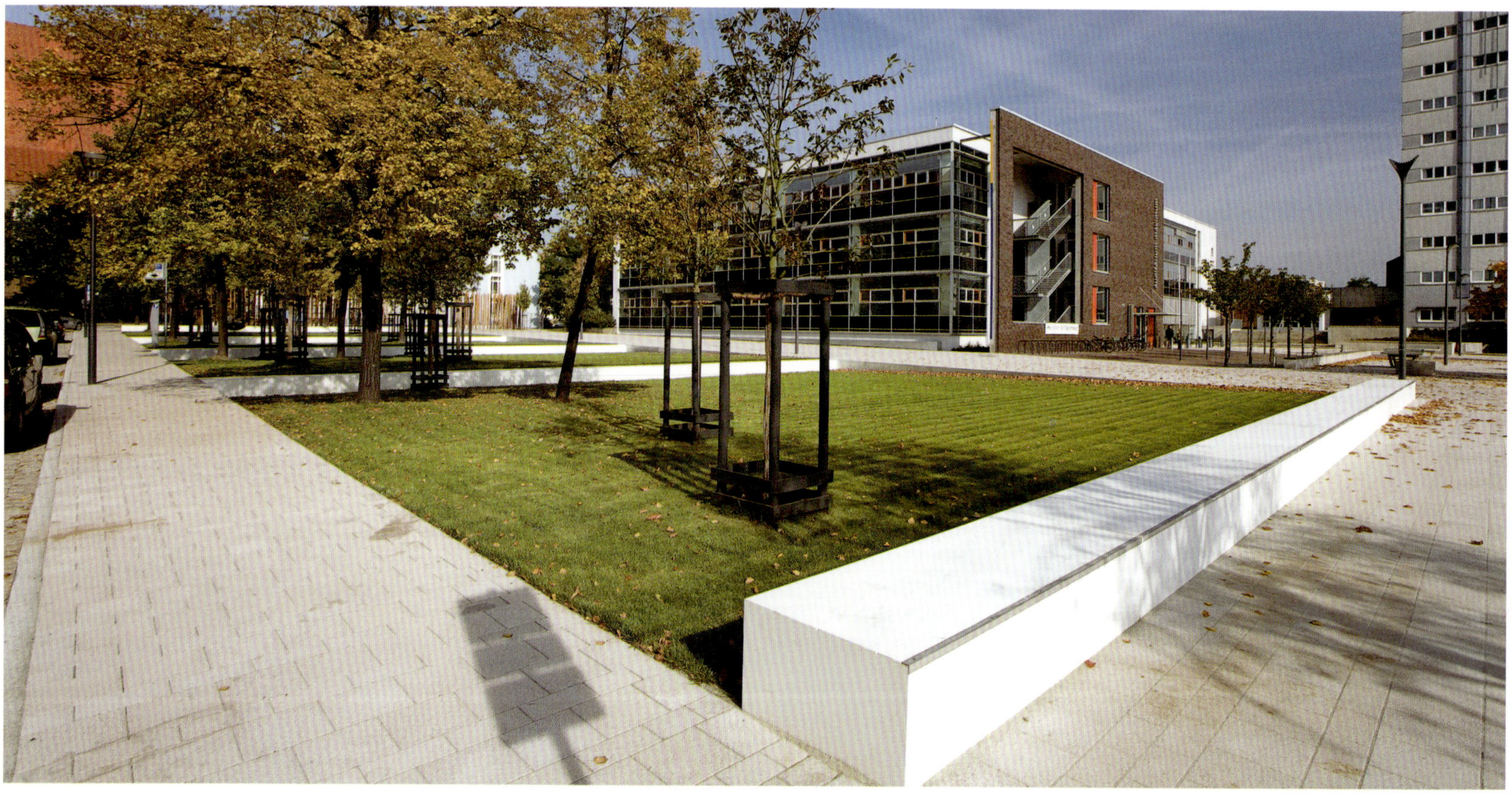

Upper left: Main entrance to the lecture hall with a group of blue and yellow seatings in front
Lower left: A bright and wide concrete wall marks the border between the lawn fields and the paved area
Upper right: View from the square to the Church of Our Lady
Lower right: Seat unit in yellow, one color of the 'European University Viadrina', with lecture hall in the back

LAC+USC Medical Center

Location: Los Angeles, USA **Designer:** Rios Clementi Hale Studios **Photographer:** Tom Bonner **Completion date:** 2008 **Site area:** 80,937 sqm **Plants:** Koelreuteria Bipinnata, Washingtonia Robusta, Canna, Equisetum hyemale, Euphorbia milii, Tulbaghia violacea, Agave attenuate

In conceiving the landscape architecture for the new Los Angeles County and University of Southern California Medical Center (LAC + USC) site, Rios Clementi Hale Studios used large, bold, geometric patterns abstracted from regional history and geology. The design re-interprets and integrates elements and patterns from the new building and existing site throughout the campus.

An animated juxtaposition of circular and rectilinear shapes blankets the tiered ground plane like a Mexican tapestry, giving way to a mosaic of paving patterns and site features. Elements include a long grove of oak trees set diagonal to a curved lawn amphitheater – a ribbon-like ramp leads to a pedestrian walkway above. Refreshing tree bosques, colored concrete, sand-colored decomposed granite hardscape, drought-tolerant underplantings and shrubs, and seating areas and gardens of various sizes play into the overall pattern.

The landscape architecture further addresses 30 meters of elevation change across the 80,937 square meters. At the site's lowest level, abstract wave-like patterns run through the concrete paving surface. At the high point, columnar Canary Island pine trees evoke the mountain peaks and vistas surrounding Los Angeles. Throughout, graceful lines, ramps, stairs, plazas, and walkways traverse the pedestrian-friendly topography.

Rios Clementi Hale Studios also designed a line of concrete and metal site furnishings expressly for LAC + USC's outdoor environs. Examples include the curved concrete benches that ring a series of circular meditation gardens, each planted in a distinct fashion. Nearby, a round, plant-free seating plaza is embedded with a ground design suggesting a meditative labyrinth. Other areas feature rows of rectangular concrete benches detailed with a slatted-wood treatment on the seating surfaces.

1. Outpatient Building
2. Diagnostic and Treatment Building
3. Inpatient Building
4. Central Plant

Right: Circular meditation garden with Chorisia speciosa

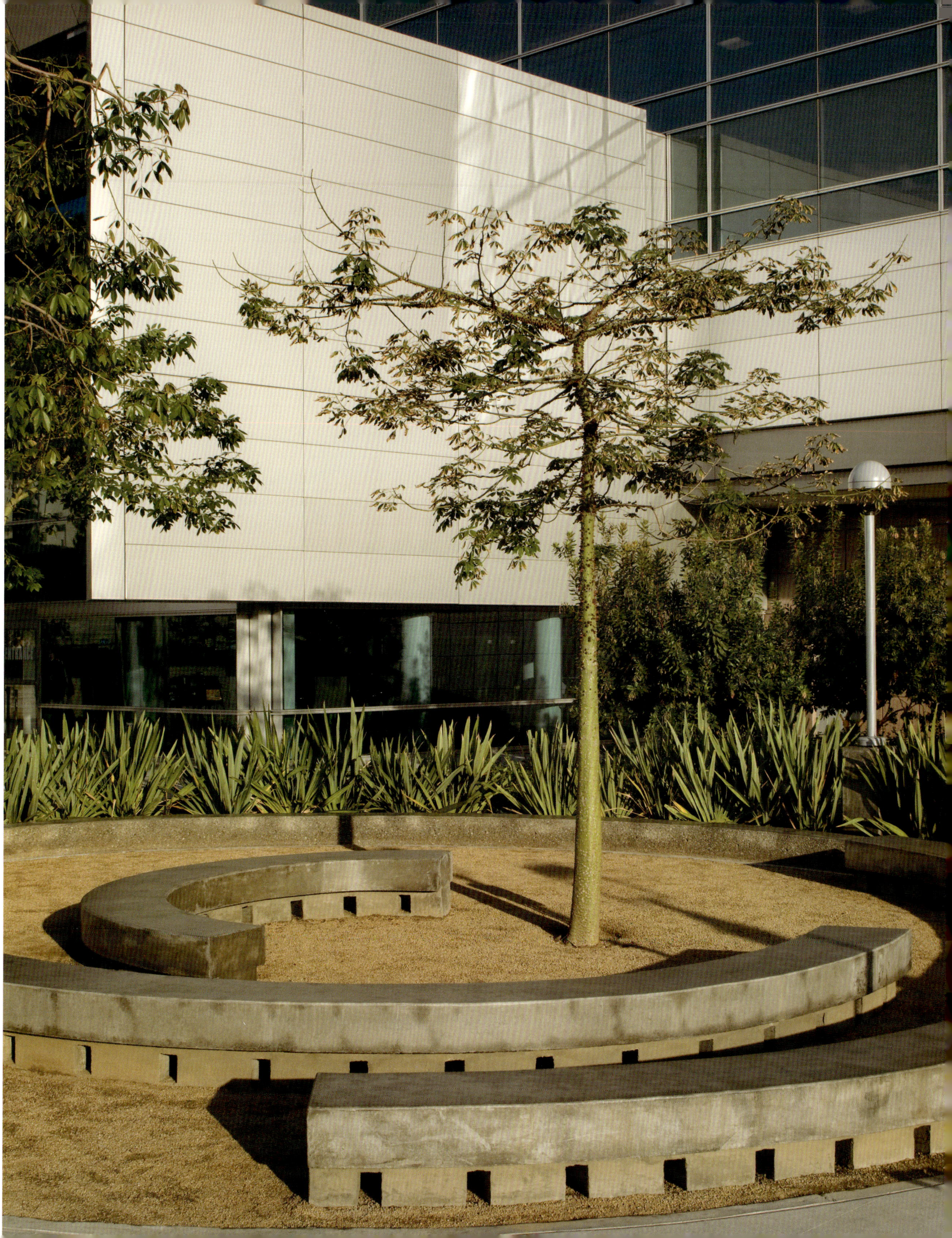

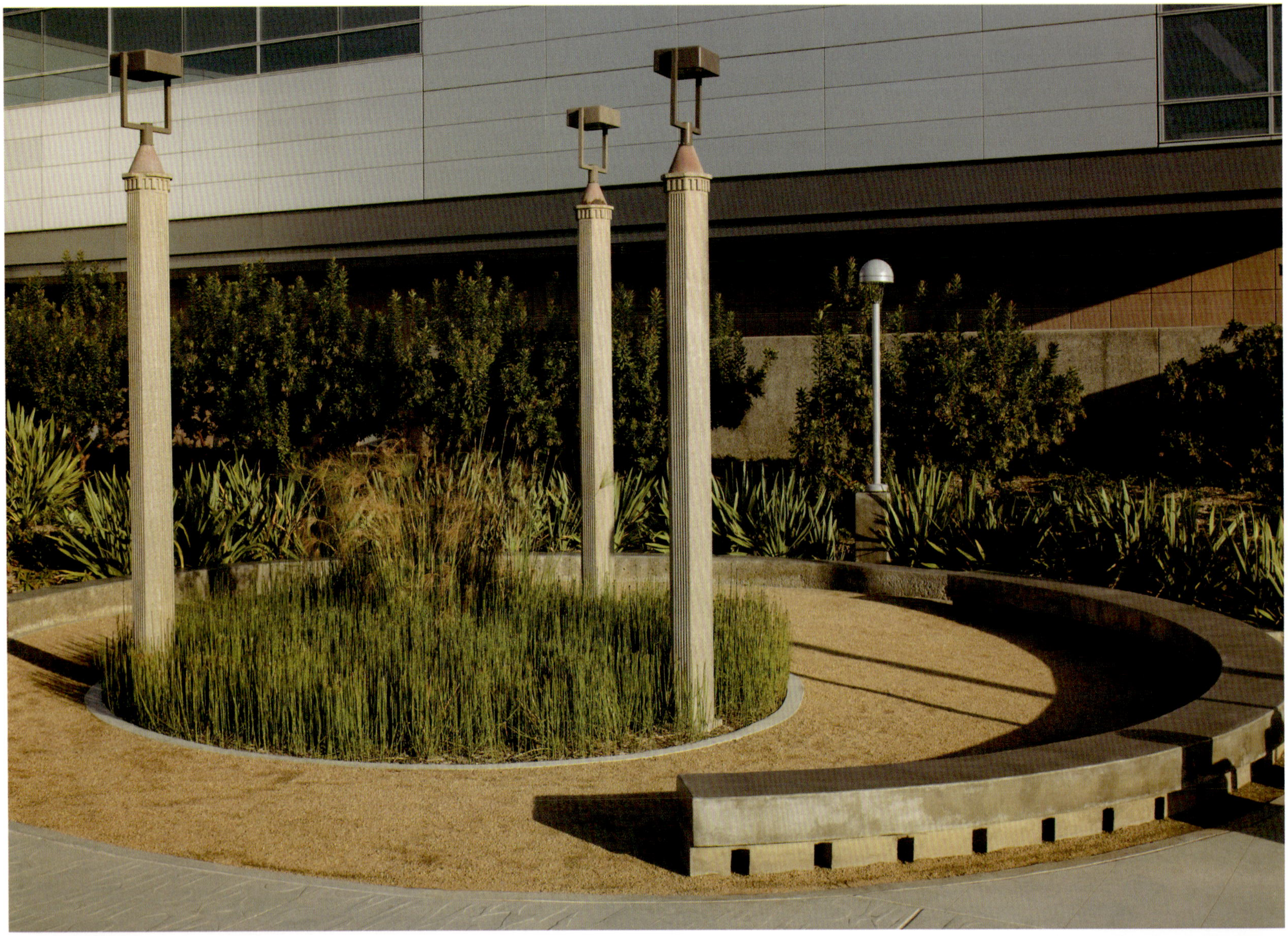

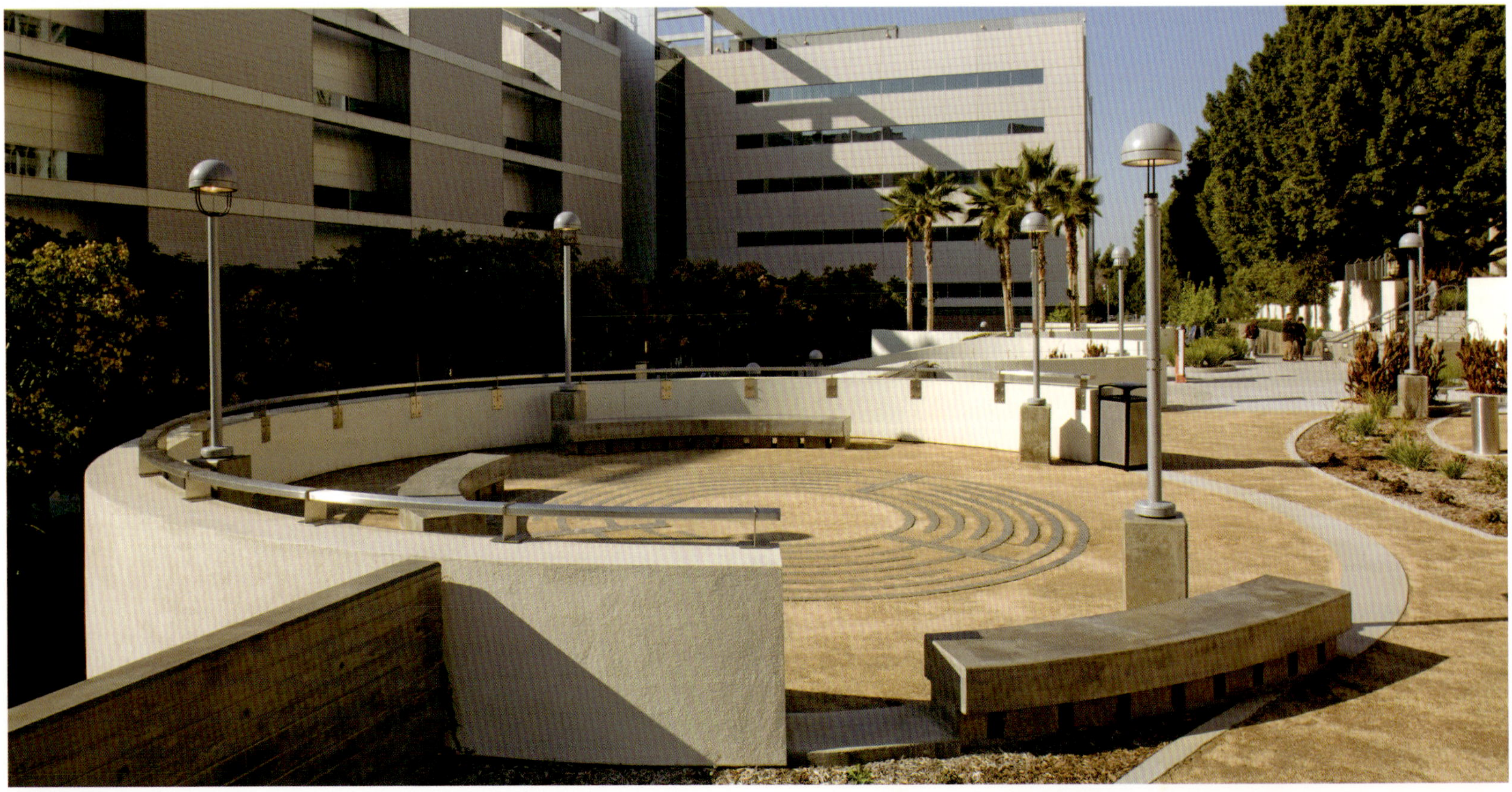

Upper left: Circular gardens provide seating along the entry walk
Lower left: Circular garden with seating and meditative labyrinth
Upper right: Small circular planters showcase diverse flora along the courtyard walk
Lower right: Undulating seat wall forms edge to native garden

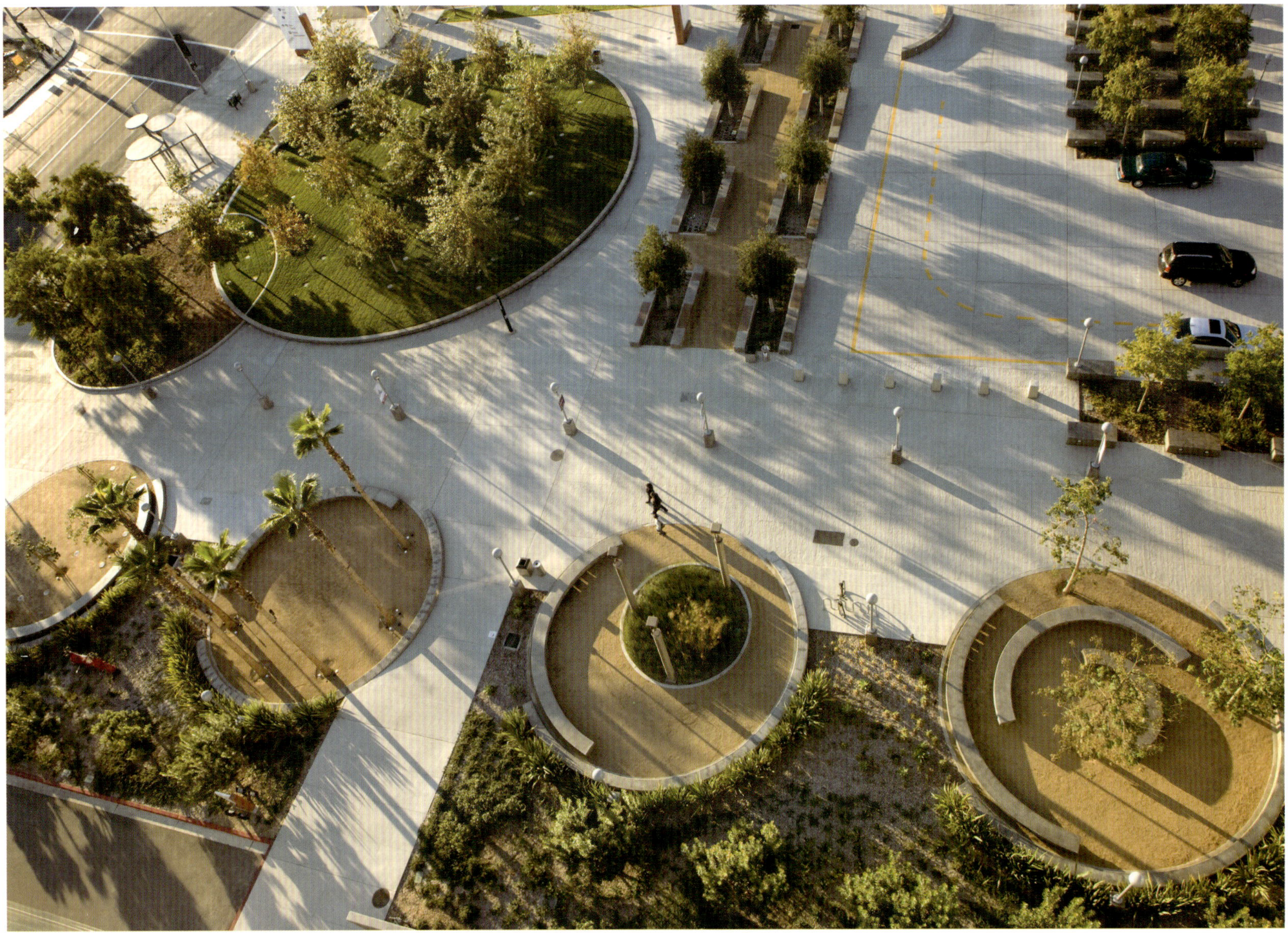

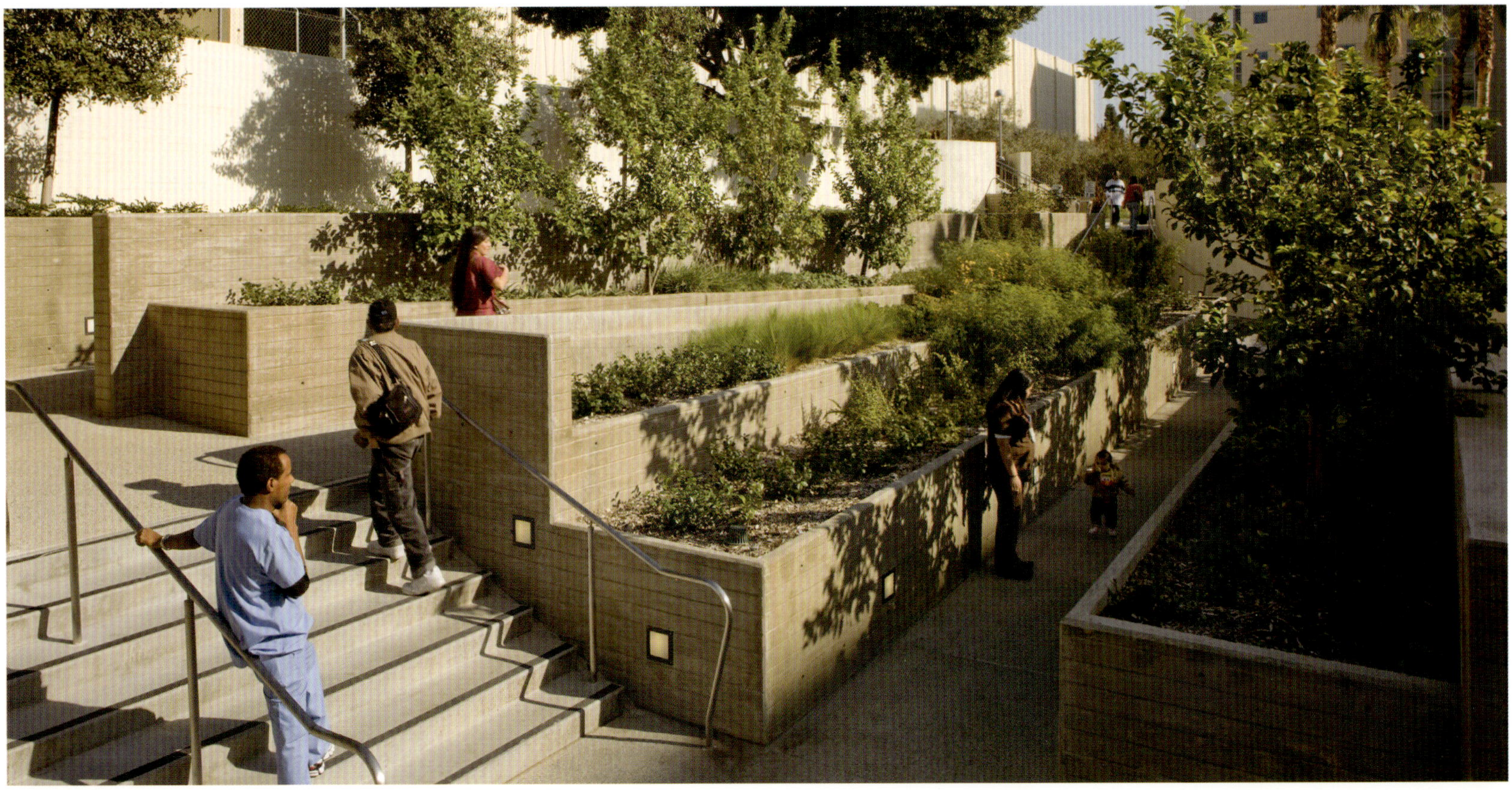

Upper left: Circular gardens of various sizes provide a range of outdoor experiences from meditation to children's play at the main plaza
Lower left: The Garden of the Senses includes fragrant flowers and foliage, textures for the touch and leaves that rustle in the wind
Upper right: The inner garden courtyard with circular gardens provides a quiet landscape setting for the busy hospital complex
Lower right: The Garden of the Senses incorporates tiered planters to allow touching and smelling the plants

Therapy Garden, Children's Specialized Hospital

Location: New Jersey, USA **Designer:** Thomas Biro Associates **Photographer:** Olivia Holmes **Completion date:** 2009 **Site area:** 406 sqm **Plants:** Deciduous shrub

Thomas Biro Associates was asked to design a therapy garden for their new facility being built in New Brunswick. It became obvious that the challenge of this design would be how to fit this ambitious program onto a 9 meters by 38 meters rooftop.

A major concern for any roof project is waterproofing. The roof was first covered with a bituminous moisture barrier, then a 12.7 centimeters layer of insulation which also accommodated the drainage and utilities. Another layer of moisture barrier was applied and finally a 7.6 centimeters colored concrete wearing course. Various surfaces such as cobbles, aggregate concrete, and synthetic lawn were used to create areas for wheelchair practice and walker therapy. Curved and circular elements were used to create interest, softness and a sense of whimsy. Poured-in-place concrete planters were raised for seating and to allow handicap access to plantings. Three copper trellises create a living canopy of colored vines over a ramp leading to an upper patio. The focal point of the garden, the Kugel Fountain is a 91 centimeters granite globe etched with a map of the world floating on a thin sheet of water. The globe is interactive and can easily be spun by a child. The water then flows along a curved runnel and falls into a circular fish pond below. Deciduous shrubs, evergreens and perennials provide year-round interest.

Award description:
2010 ASLA New Jersey Honor Award

1. Ramp
2. Arbors
3. Raised Planters
4. Kugel Fountain
5. Seatwalls
6. Runnel
7. Steps
8. Fish Pond
9. Donor Patio
10. Synthetic Lawn

Right: Overview

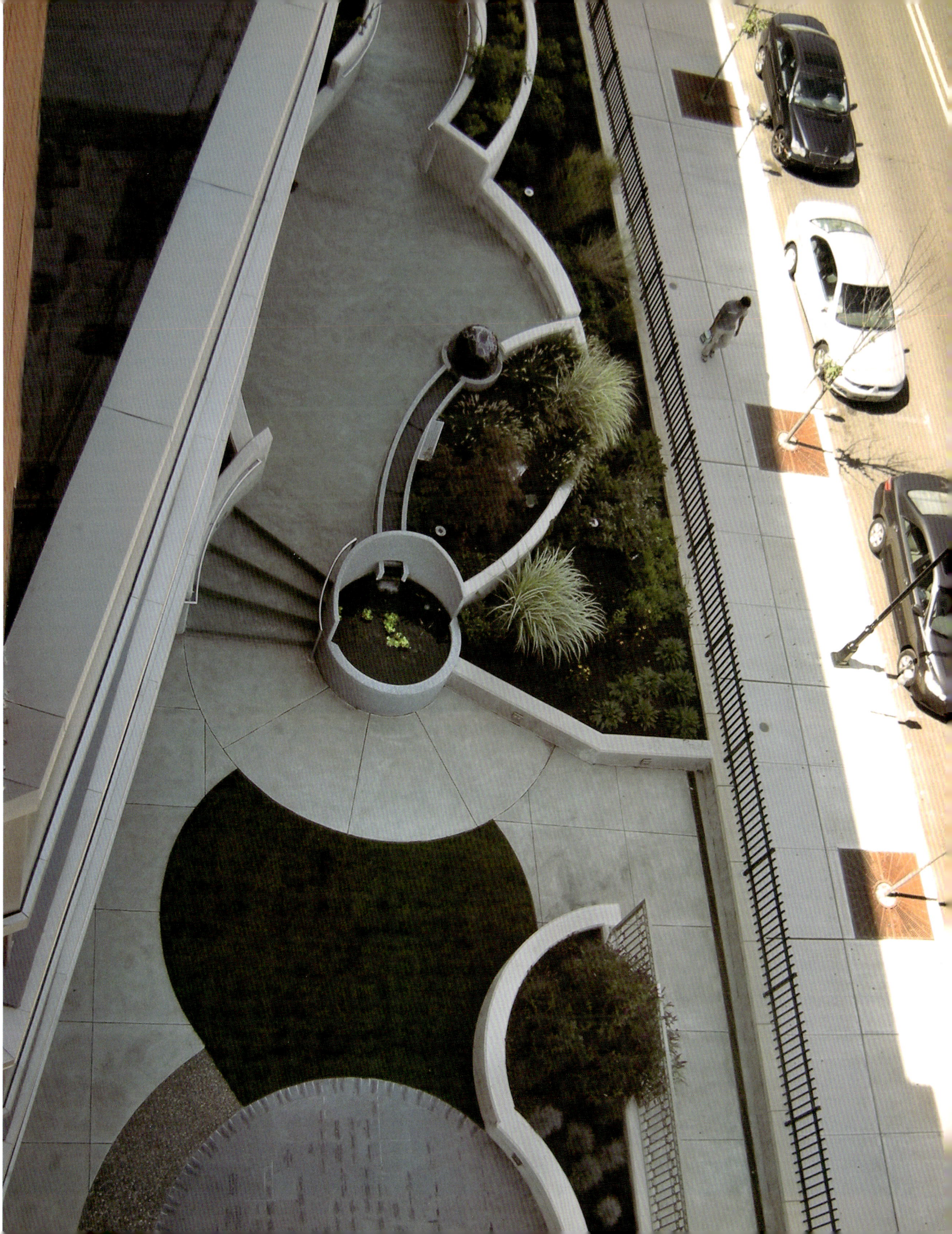

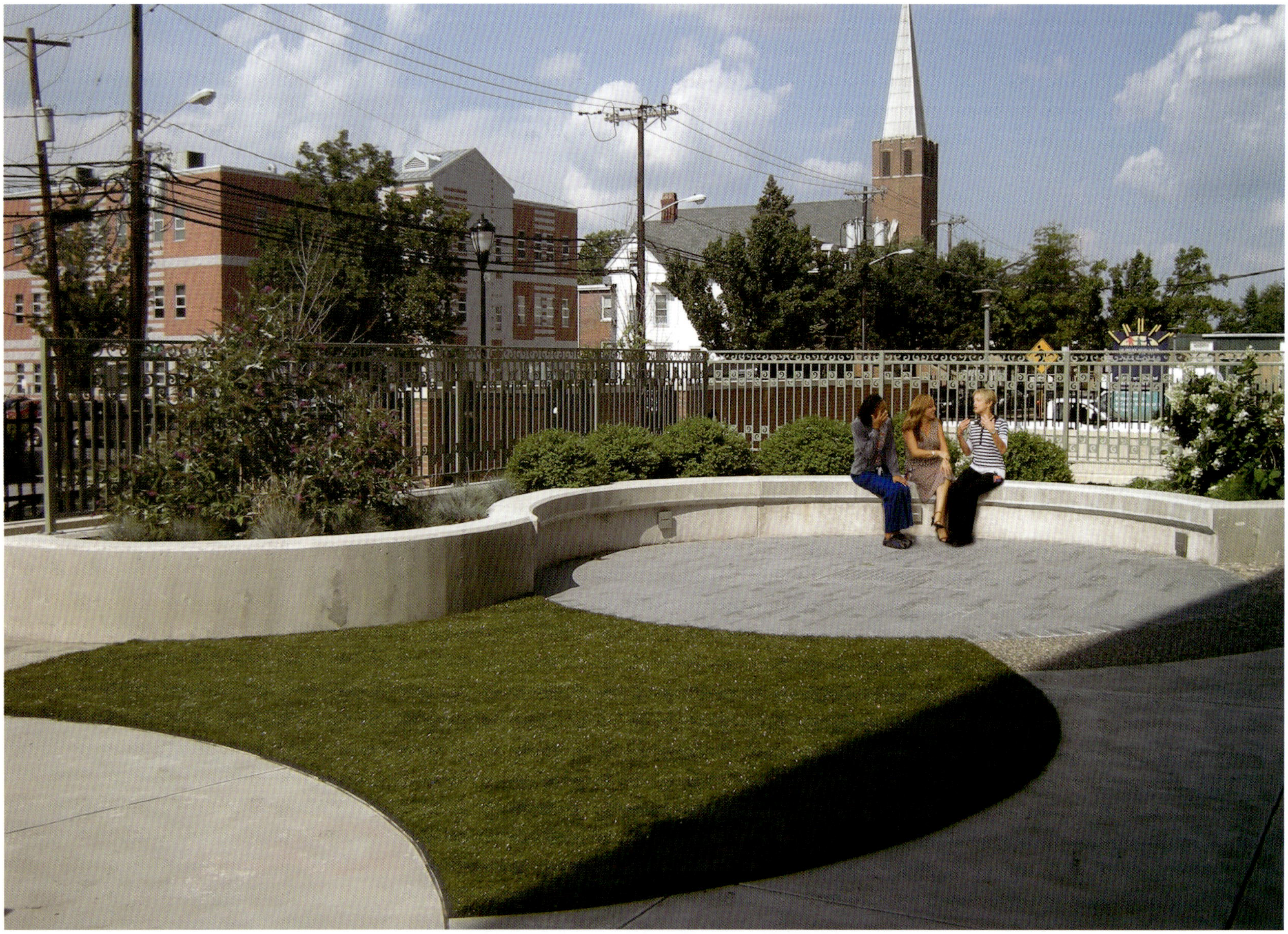

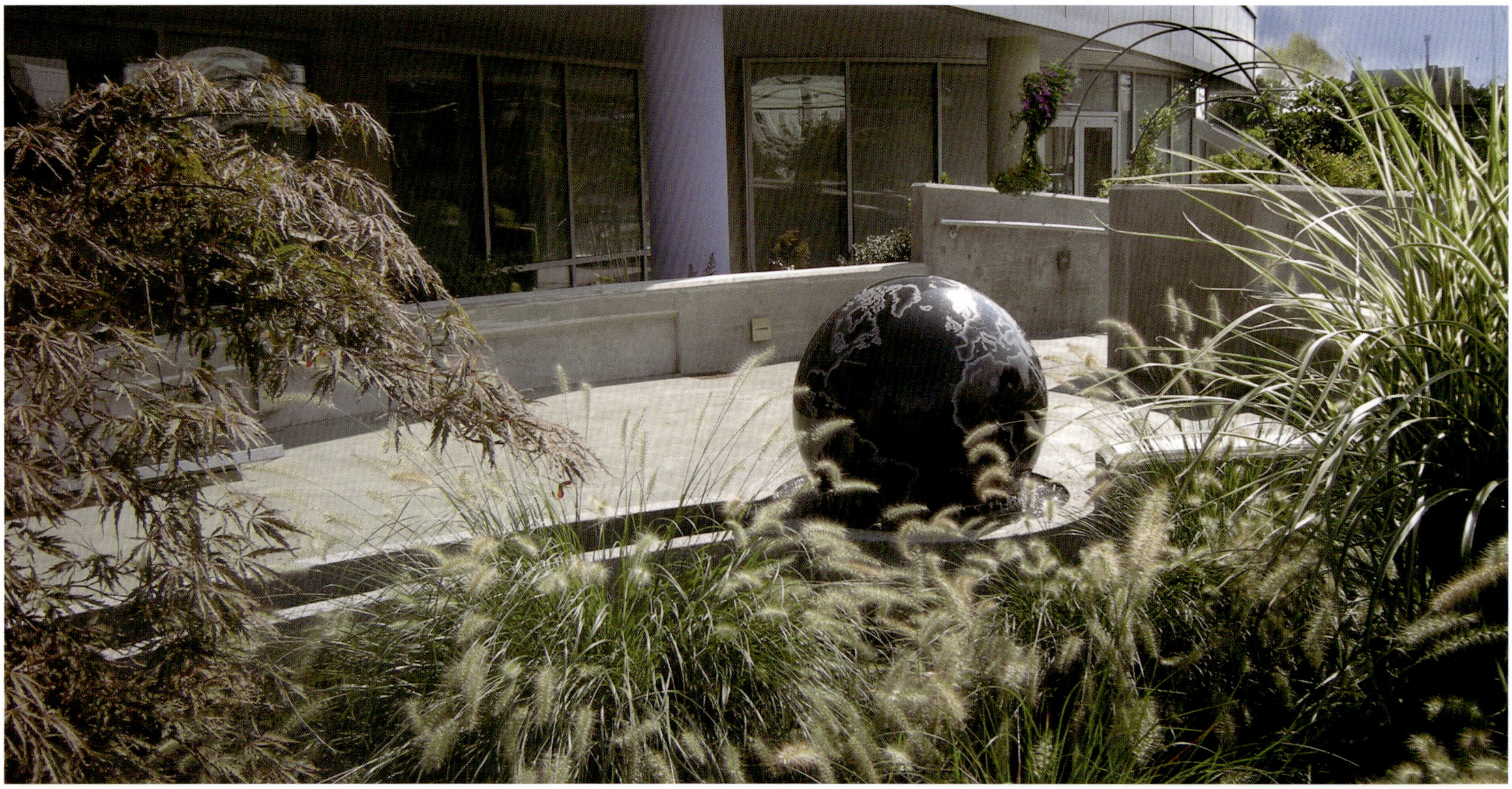

Upper left: Donor patio
Lower left: Kugel fountain
Upper right: Steps close view

Location: Braunschweig, Germany **Designer:** Gnuechtel Triebswetter Landscape Architects **Photographer:** Tim Corvin Kraus **Completion date:** 2008
Site area: 10,000 sqm

Extension of the St. Bonifatius Hospital in Lingen

The new outdoor area design in the scope of the extension of the St. Bonifatius Hospital offers a great opportunity of not only designing the entrance situation and the reception area for patients and visitors of the hospital in a suitable way, but also of integrating these areas into the overall context of outdoor areas of the city of Lingen.

The access to the underground car park, which has been newly defined in the meantime, creates a continuous outdoor area, which leaves the city with a sufficient space for achieving the set-up targets of interweaving the hospital outdoor area with the basis of the city and of defining a 'beautiful usefulness'.

1. Recreational Landscape
2. Leisure Area
3. Plaza
4. Pathway
5. Flower Bed
6. Pedestrian Path

Right: Waterscape

AUEN UND

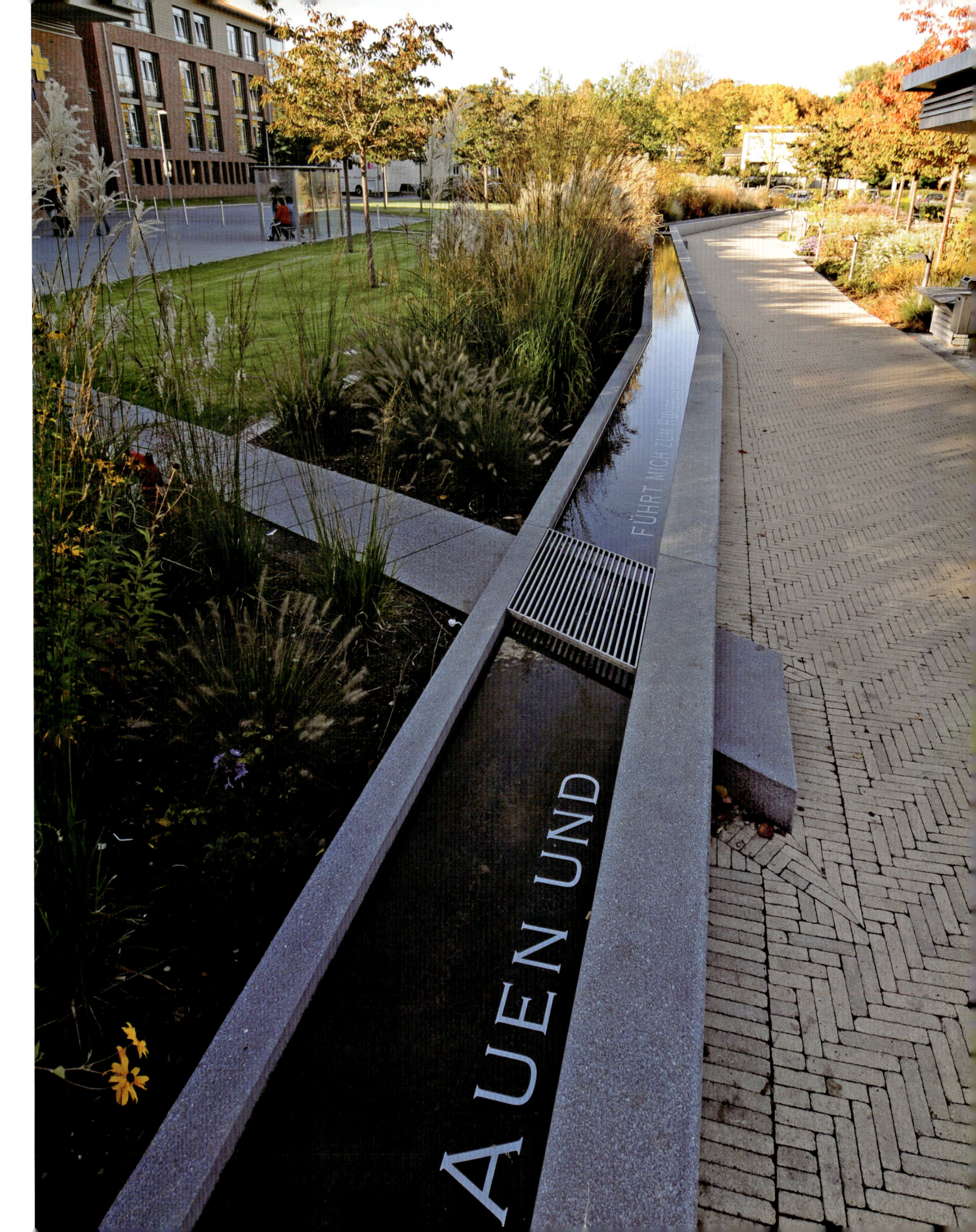

FÜHRT MICH ZUR

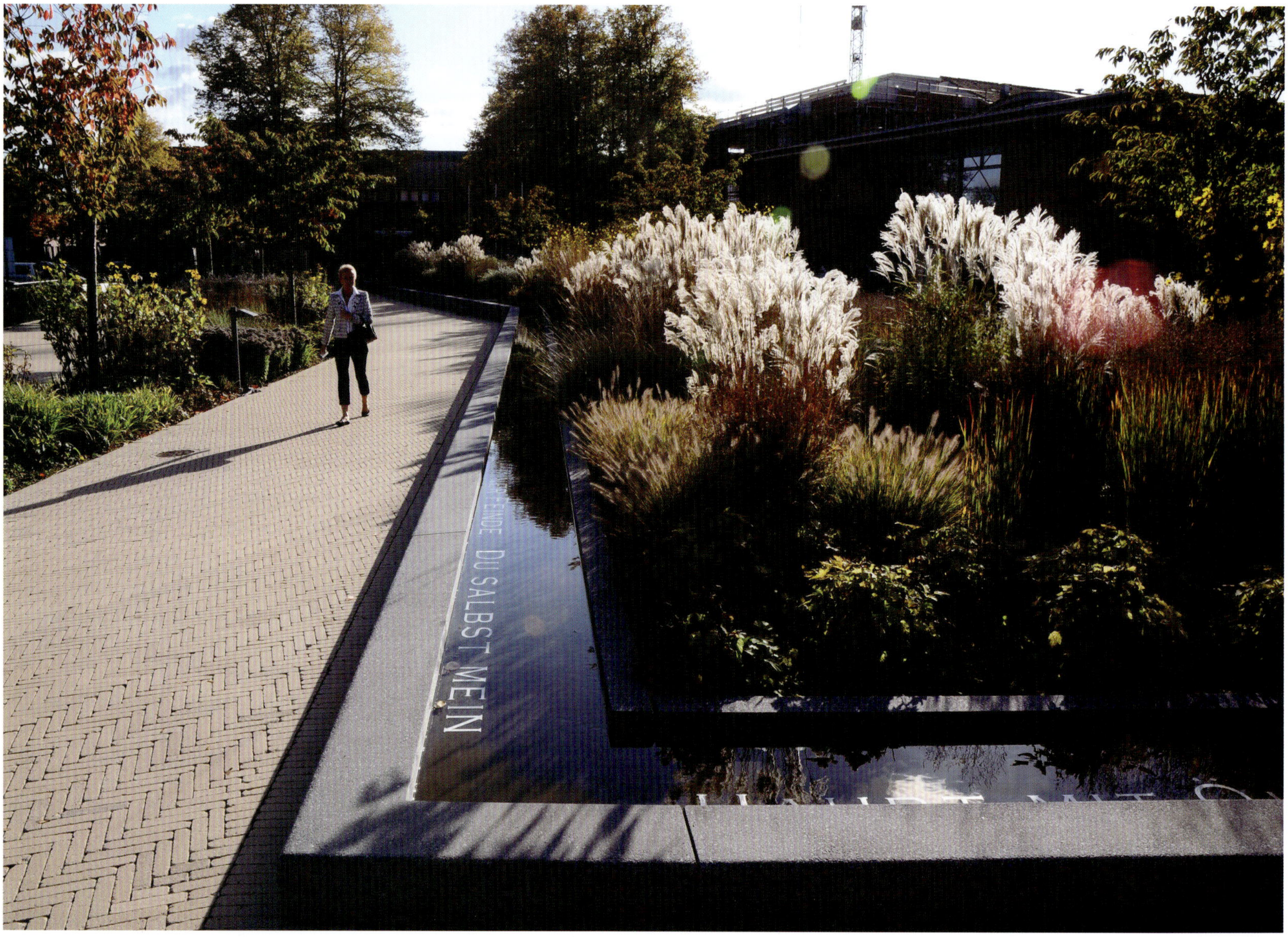
DU SALBST MEIN

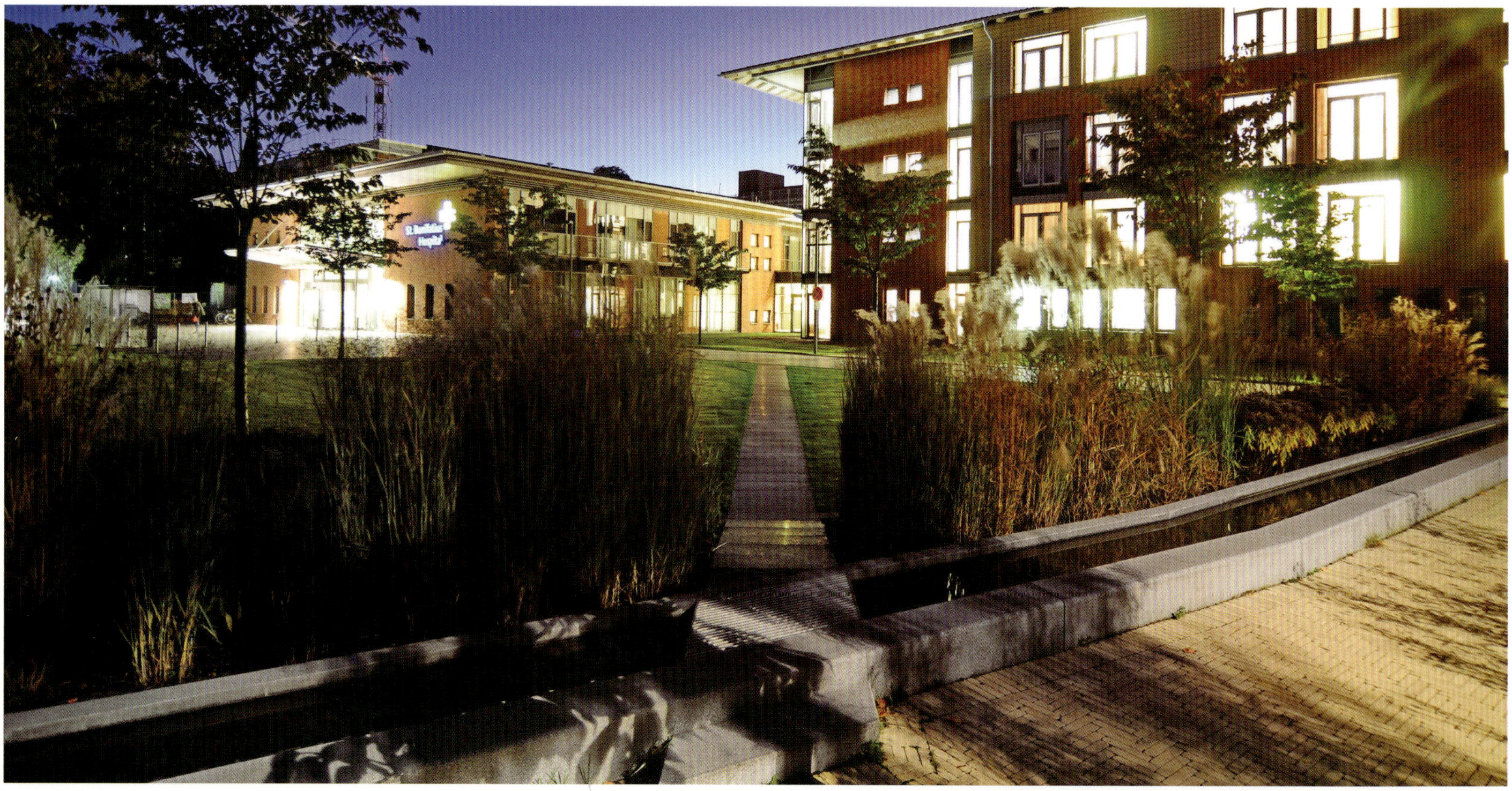

Upper left: The corner of the flower bed
Lower left: The night view of the pathway
Upper right: Leisure area

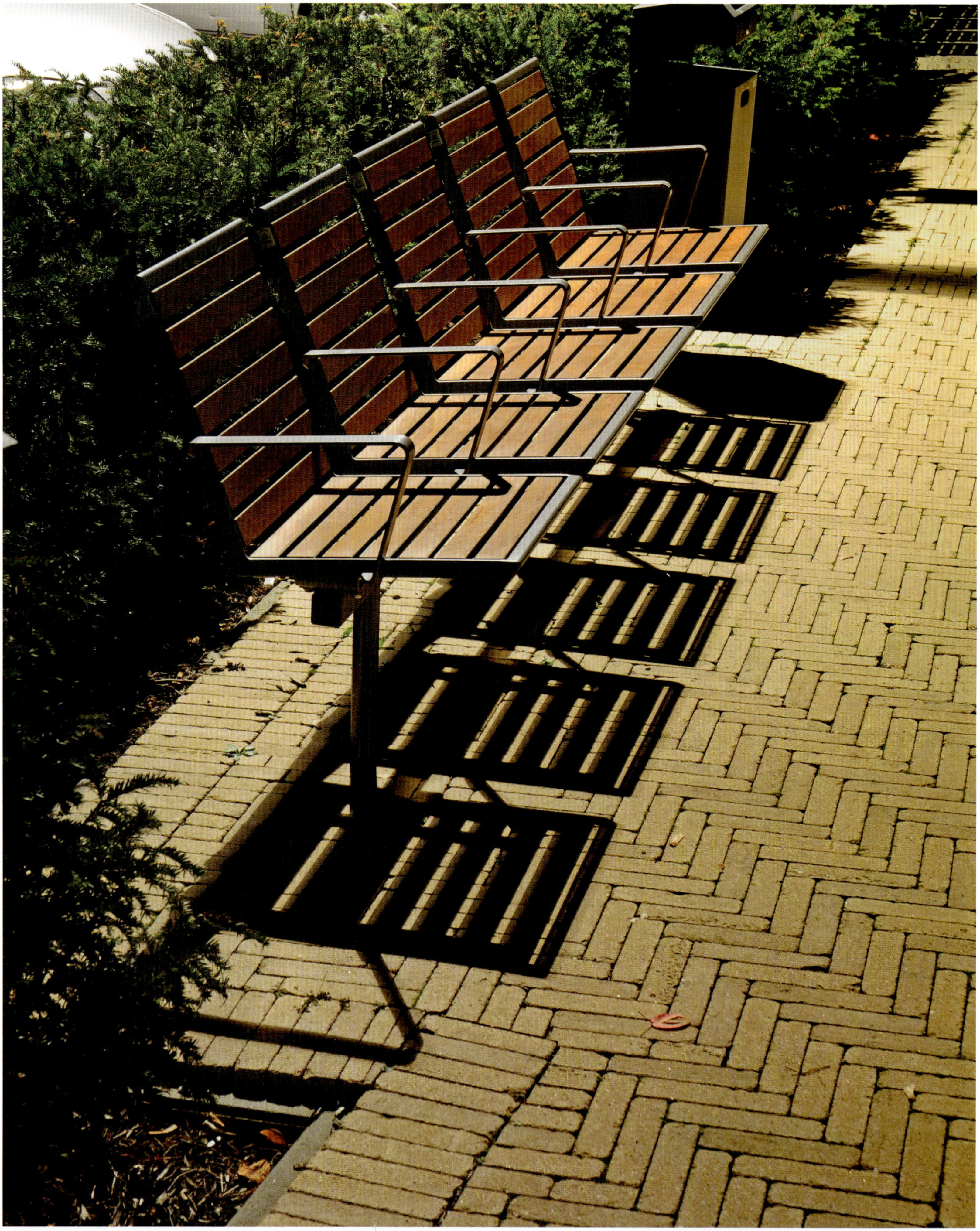

Left: Seating area
Upper right: Recreational landscape

Chang Gung Hospital

Location: Taiwan, China **Designer:** McGregor Coxall **Photographer:** Cheng Chin Ming **Completion date:** 2007 **Site area:** 175,000 sqm **Plants:** Ixora Chinensis, Juniperus conferta, Hymenocallis Littoralis, Nephrolepis Cordifolia, Delonix Regia, Canna Indica

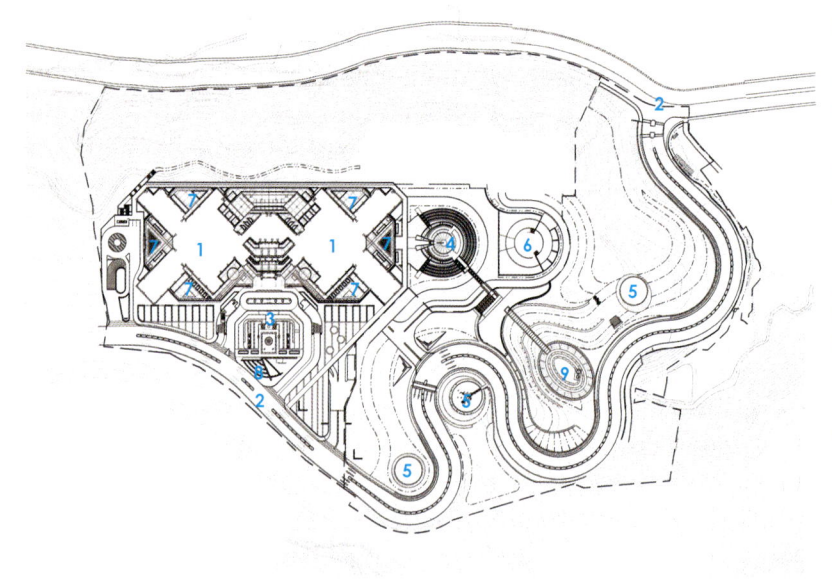

The Taoyuan Branch of Chang Gung Hospital at the time of the proposed completion was to be the largest hospital in Asia. It was developed on a 175,000-square-meter site by Formosa Plastics, owners of a number of private hospitals in Taiwan. The gross ground floor area of the building is 280,000 square meters. The facility has approximately 3,000 beds servicing both day surgery and a large percentage of patients who generally stay for periods longer than three months. The designers were commissioned for site planning, design, documentation and site review of the entire external works including green roofs.

The site program was conceived from the thinking that physical and psychological experience of a landscape environment is important in the healing process for patients. Design components include extensive roof gardens, an outdoor cafe, interactive water features, walking trails, sun dial, tea gardens and outdoor art/craft workshop plazas. Storm water from the building is channeled to a 30-meter-long cascading viaduct into an elliptical wetland detention pond for recycling as irrigation. All non potable water for the project is supplied through a black water treatment plant. The building is designed to accommodate social and medical advancements well into the future.

1. New Hospital Buildings
2. Main Entry Road
3. Entry Plaza
4. Sun Dial and Terrace
5. Planted Markers
6. Lower Garden
7. Courtyard Garden
8. Sunken Garden
9. Rain Pond

Right: Aerial view

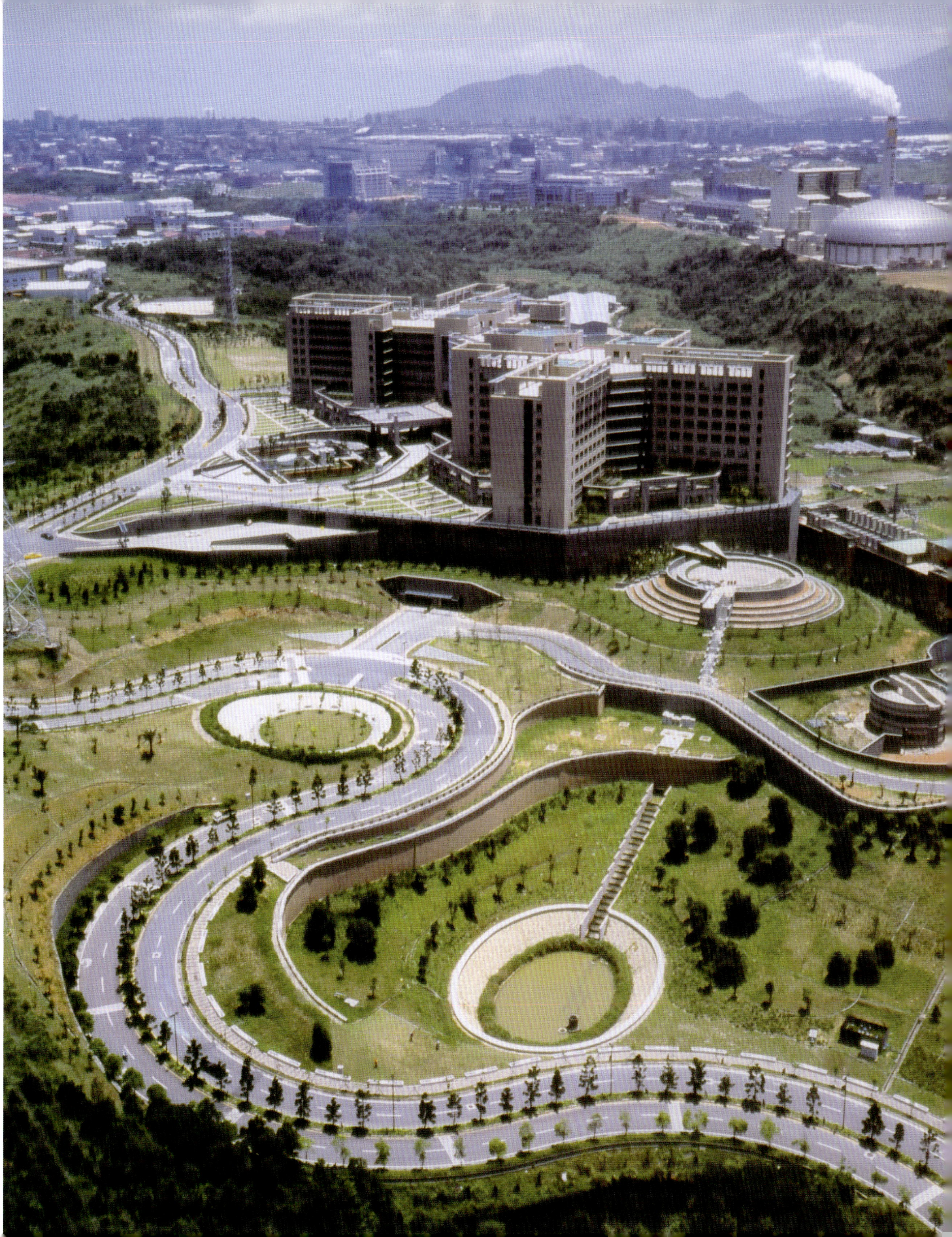

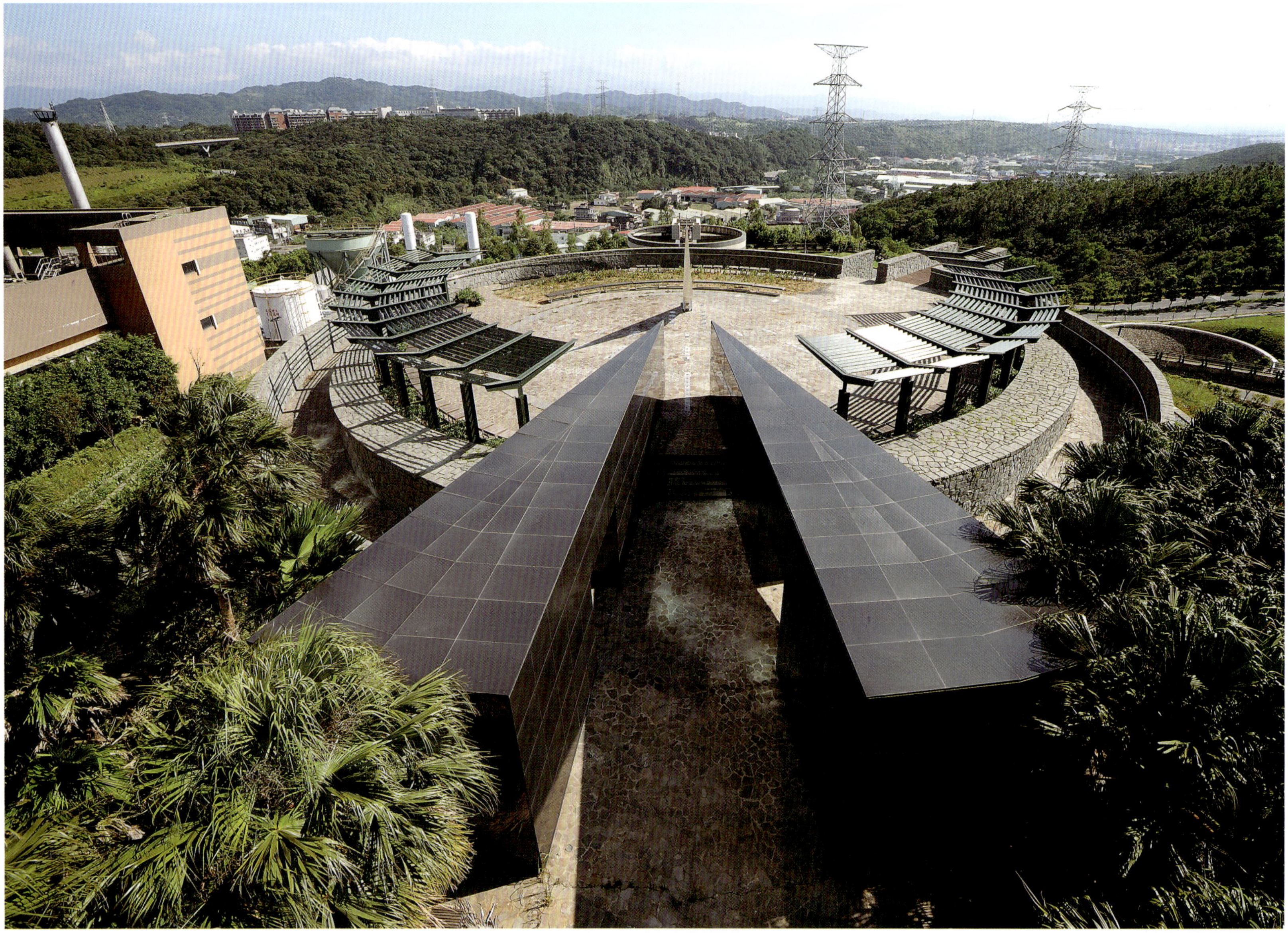

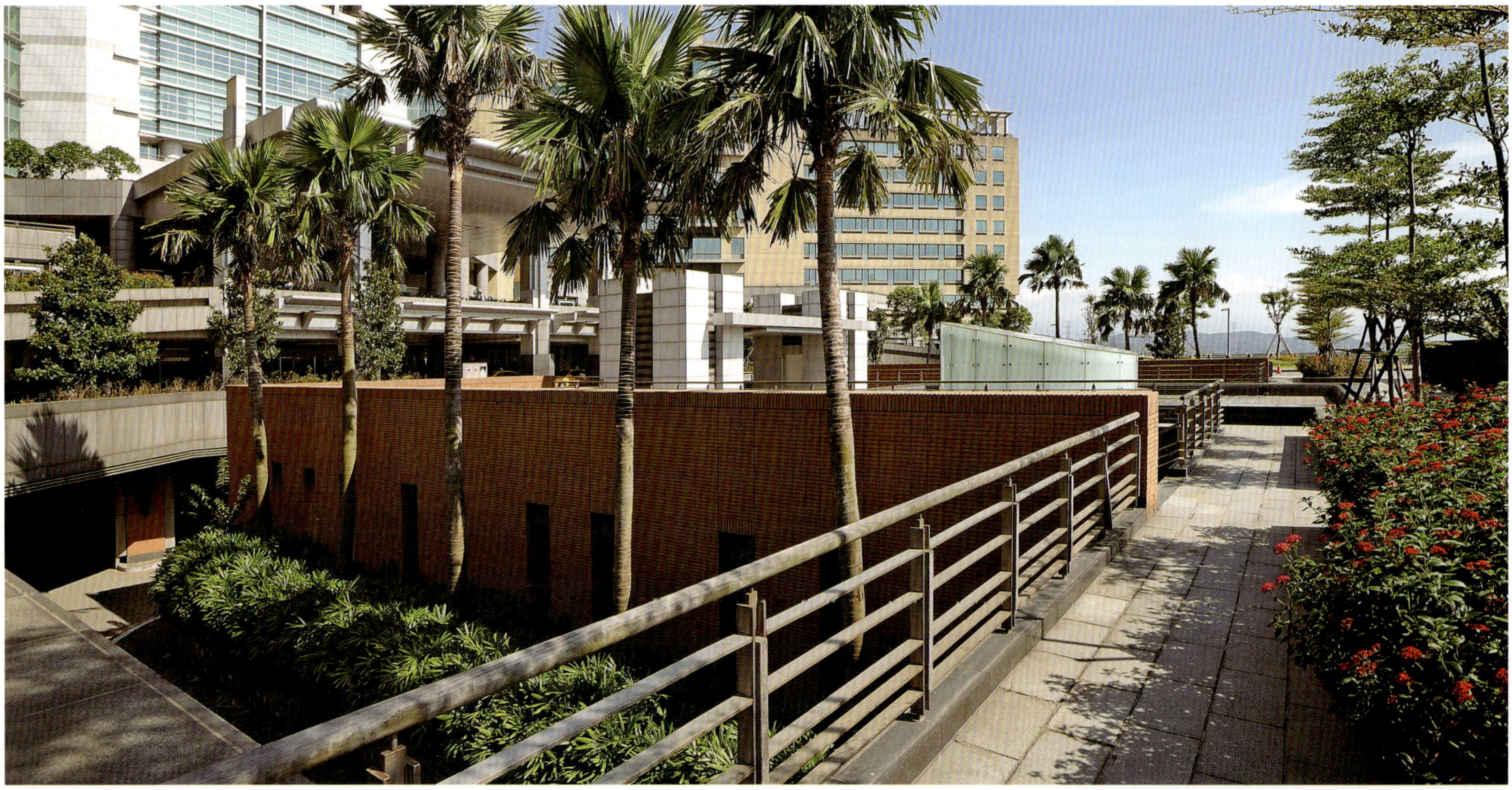

Upper left: Sundial plaza
Lower left: Entry plaza
Upper Right: Tea terraces
Lower right: Sunken cafe court

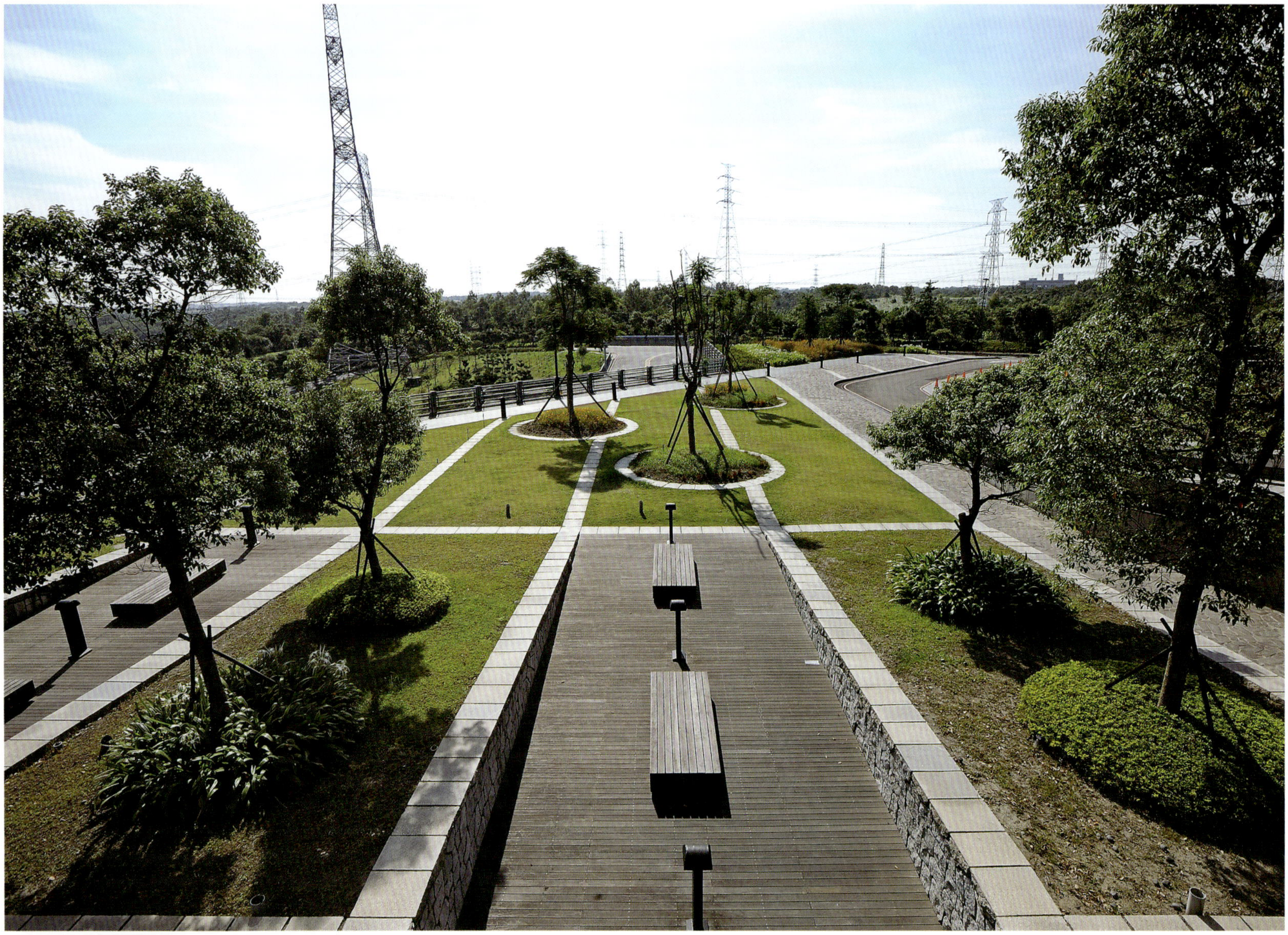

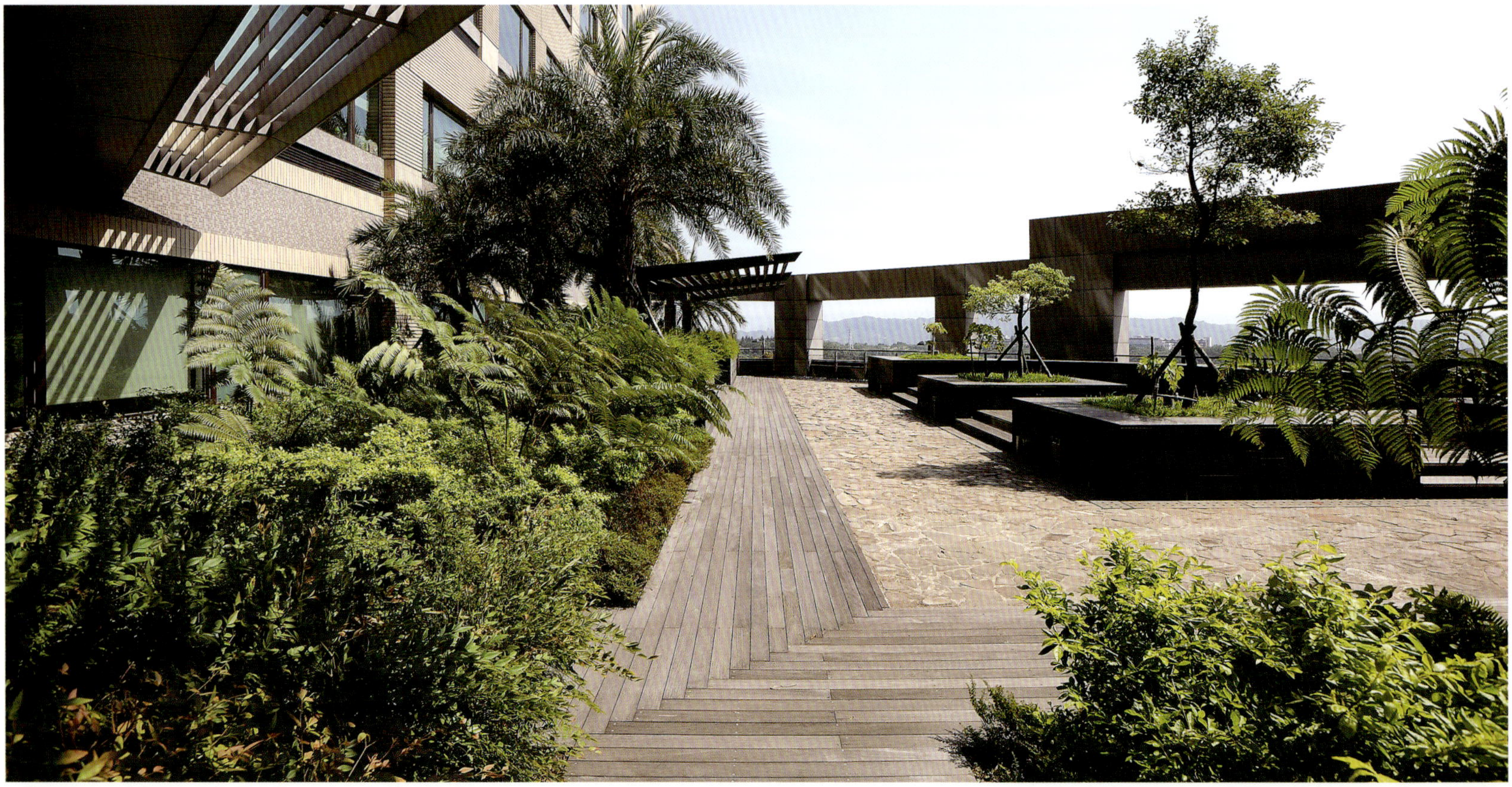

Upper left: Roof top garden
Lower left: A corner of roof top garden
Upper right: Main entry plaza and roof top garden
Lower right: Detail of roof top garden

Location: Amsterdam, The Netherlands **Designer:** Karres en Brands Landschaps Architecten bv **Photographer:** Karres en Brands Landschaps Architecten bv **Completion date:** 2008 **Site area:** 42,000 sqm

Arena Boulevard and Amsterdamse Poort

The cue for redesigning Arena Boulevard and the Amsterdamse Poort shopping area was provided by a doubling in the number of visitors to both areas, and by the new spatial connection between them. Two key objectives were to provide these areas with greater coherence, and to provide people with reasons to repose there.

Currently, Arena Boulevard and Amsterdamse Poort have two different faces: the lively, small-scale shopping center of Amsterdamse Poort, and the spacious but often deserted Arena Boulevard. The design for Arena Boulevard will therefore break the linearity and scale of this environment, creating a space that is as pleasant for ten people as it is for 50,000.

Crosslinks between the northern and southern sides are reinforced by the creation of space between the buildings on the boulevard; the design helps the public space to arrange itself naturally. The transitions between areas for movement and those for stationary activities are marked by long benches in wood and stone, along which the ground-level rises and falls, creating gentle undulations in the paving. Certain areas will be reserved for sport. Others will be raised and have trees and grass for people to lie on. By creating a public space that invites people to linger, the design provides scope for a wide range of uses.

In the evening, a three-dimensional web of lighting created by wires and spotlights will provide a fabulous 'starry' sky over Arena Boulevard. In particular areas, the network will become denser and the lights brighter, the dynamic lighting responding to events and pedestrian flows.

1. Paving
2. Cycling Lane
3. Water Feature with 2,500 Lights
4. Underground Container

Right: People sitting on the resting seats
Lower right: The road between buildings

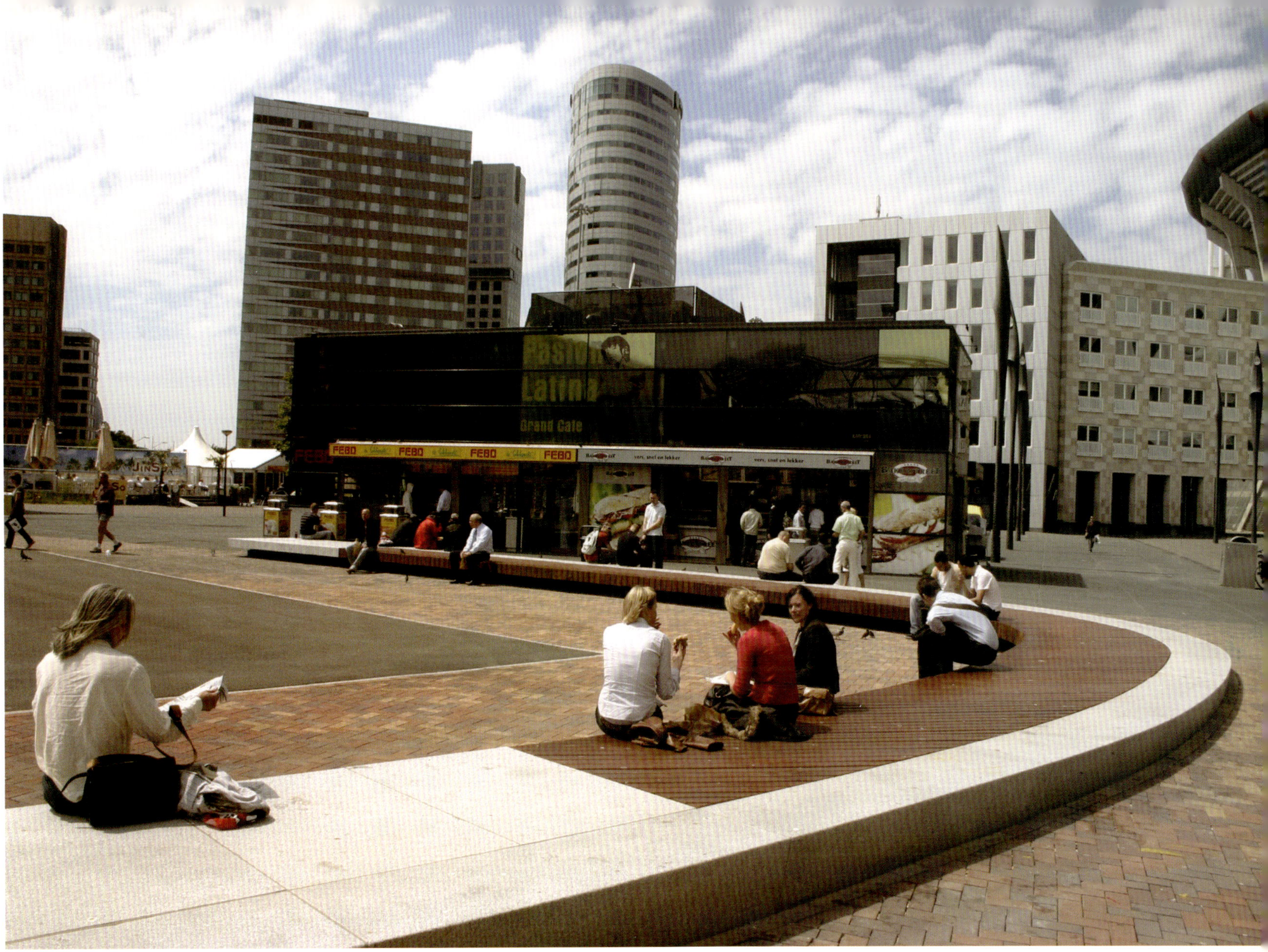
FEBO

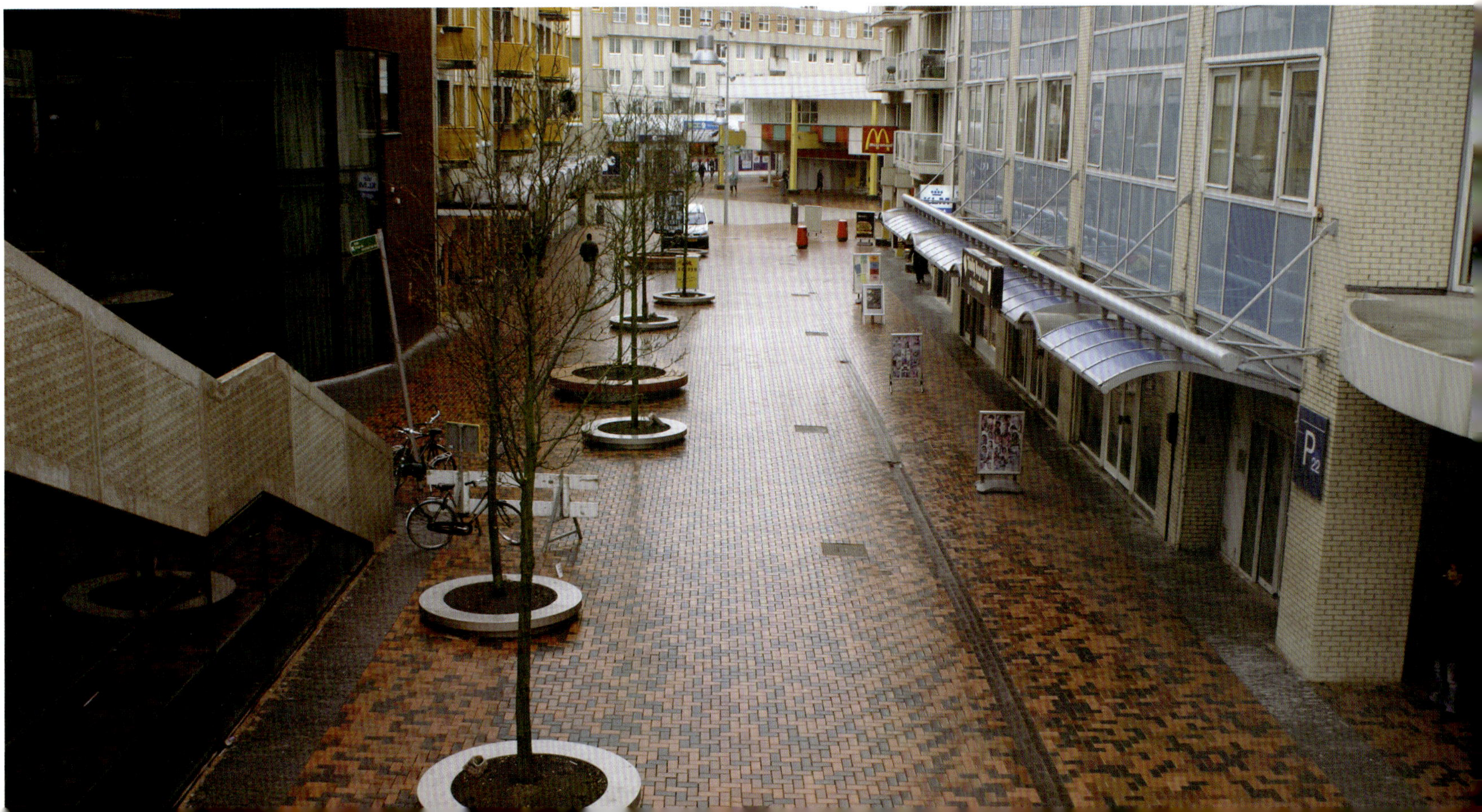

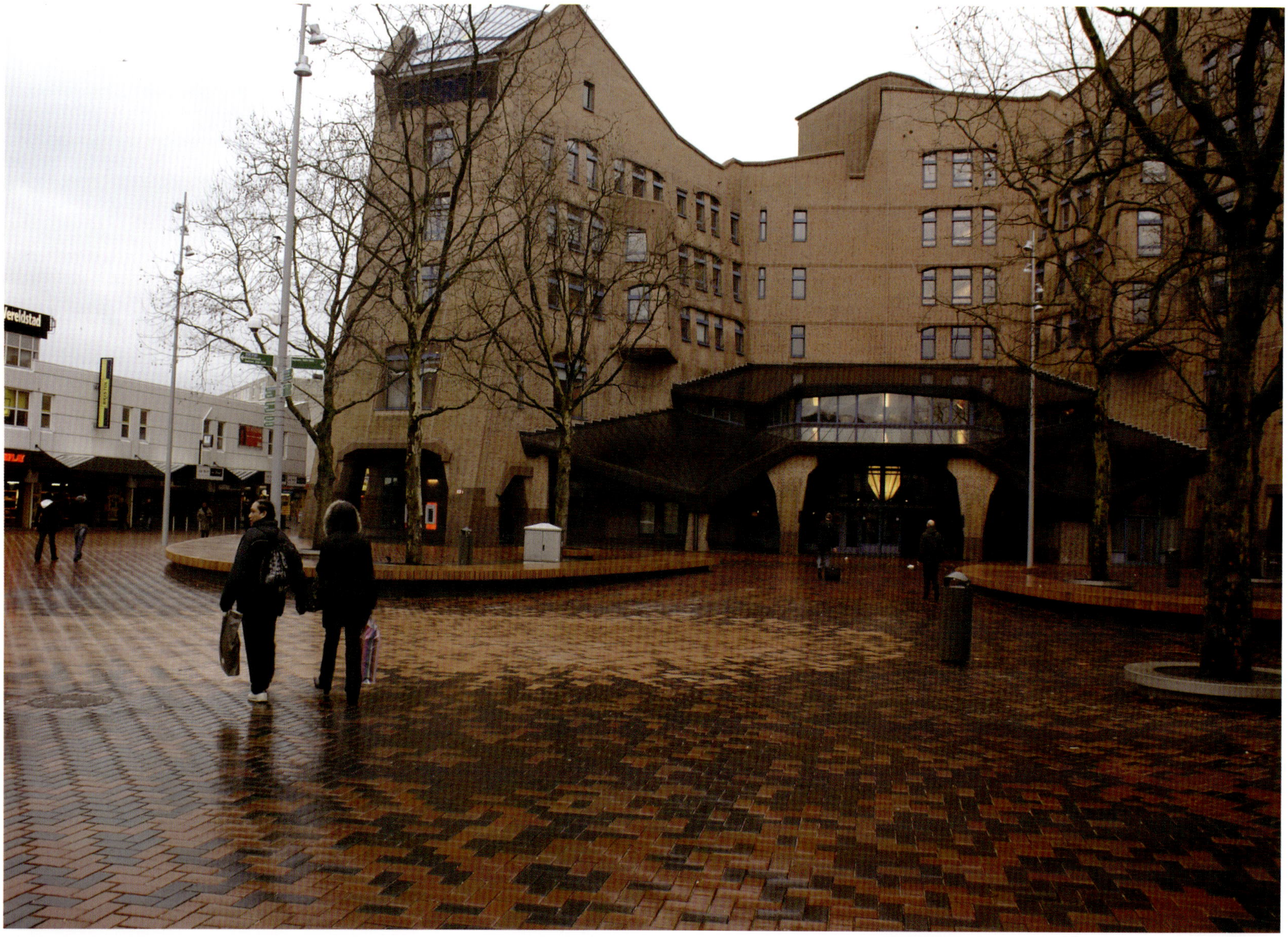

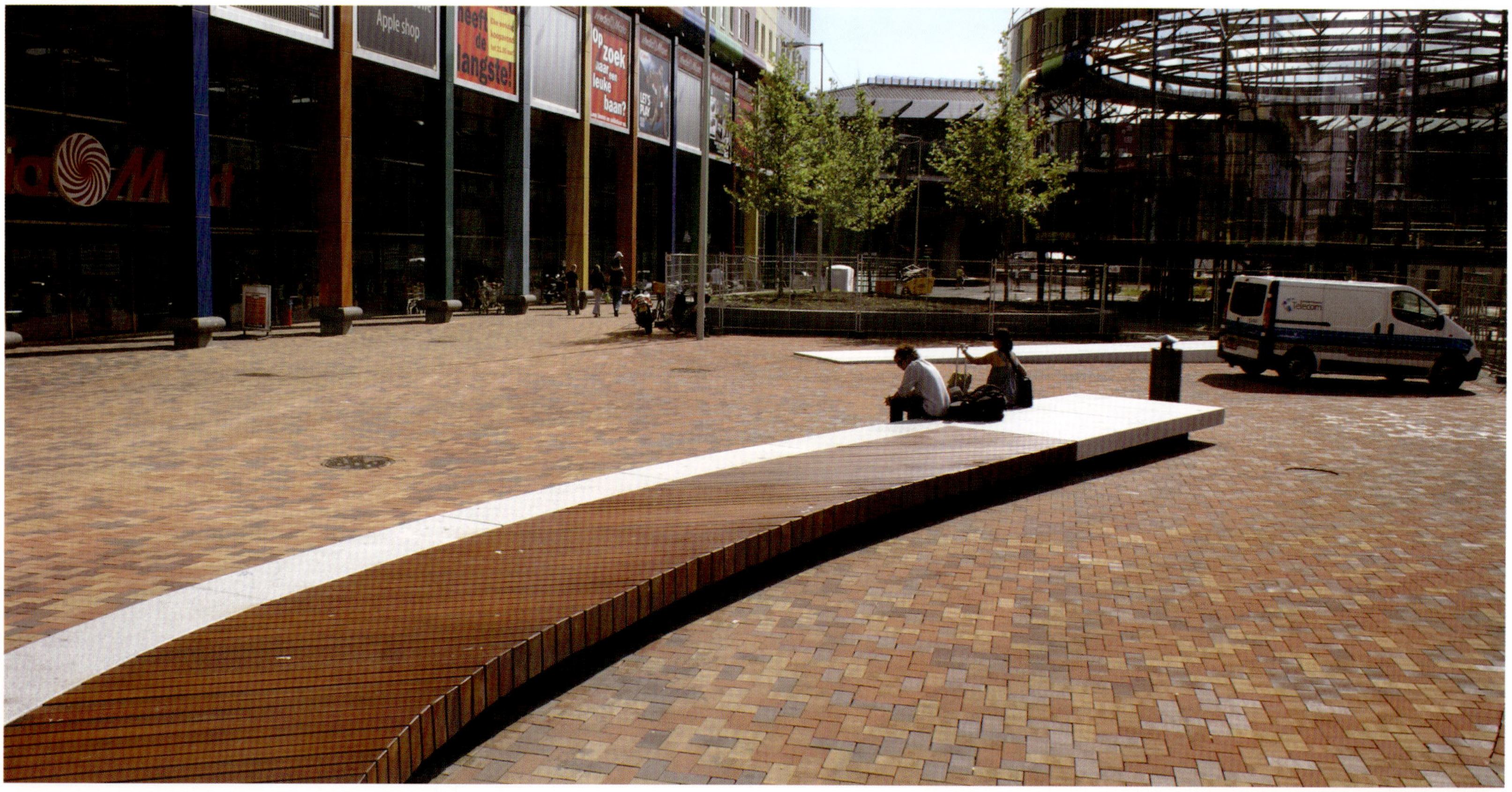
Apple shop

Upper left: Pavement
Lower Left: Resting seats

City Square Urban Park

Location: Singapore City, Singapore **Designer:** ONG&ONG Pte Ltd
Photographer: ONG&ONG Pte Ltd **Completion date:** 2009 **Site area:** 3,500 sqm

City Square Urban Park fronts the City Square Mall's entrance and provides a recreational environment for nearby residents and visitors alike. In addition, the natural space serves as a constant reminder of the importance of environmental conservation.

The sunken plaza is the focal point of the park, serving as a multi-purpose space while also acting as a passageway linking the MRT station to the mall. An eco-roof, comprising of solar panels, low-e glass panels and a green roof, traps naturally produced energy that in turn powers the lightings, regulates temperature and controls wind circulation. This project further maintains its environmentally-friendly status by introducing the application of 'Eco-tiles' – a composite recyclable product that is manufactured with sustainable resources.

The project is designed as a 'green lung' for the neighborhood, and includes a butterfly garden where people can engage with and learn about wildlife, and a 'living maze'; a green garden where children can roam and learn about plants. A fountain park also provides interactive water-play and acts as a distinctive communal meeting point.

Other features include a 'vertical green', an eco-roof showcase and an 'eco-wall', where kids can learn hands-on about recycling, reducing and reusing. In line with the 'City in a Garden' movement, preservation and integration of two huge existing trees is allowed for within the new design.

Award description:
2010 BCA Universal Design Award for Built Environment – Gold

1. Living Maze
2. Green Wall
3. Fountain Park
4. Butterfly Garden
5. Eco Maze
6. Sculpture
7. Stage

Right: Overview of the Square

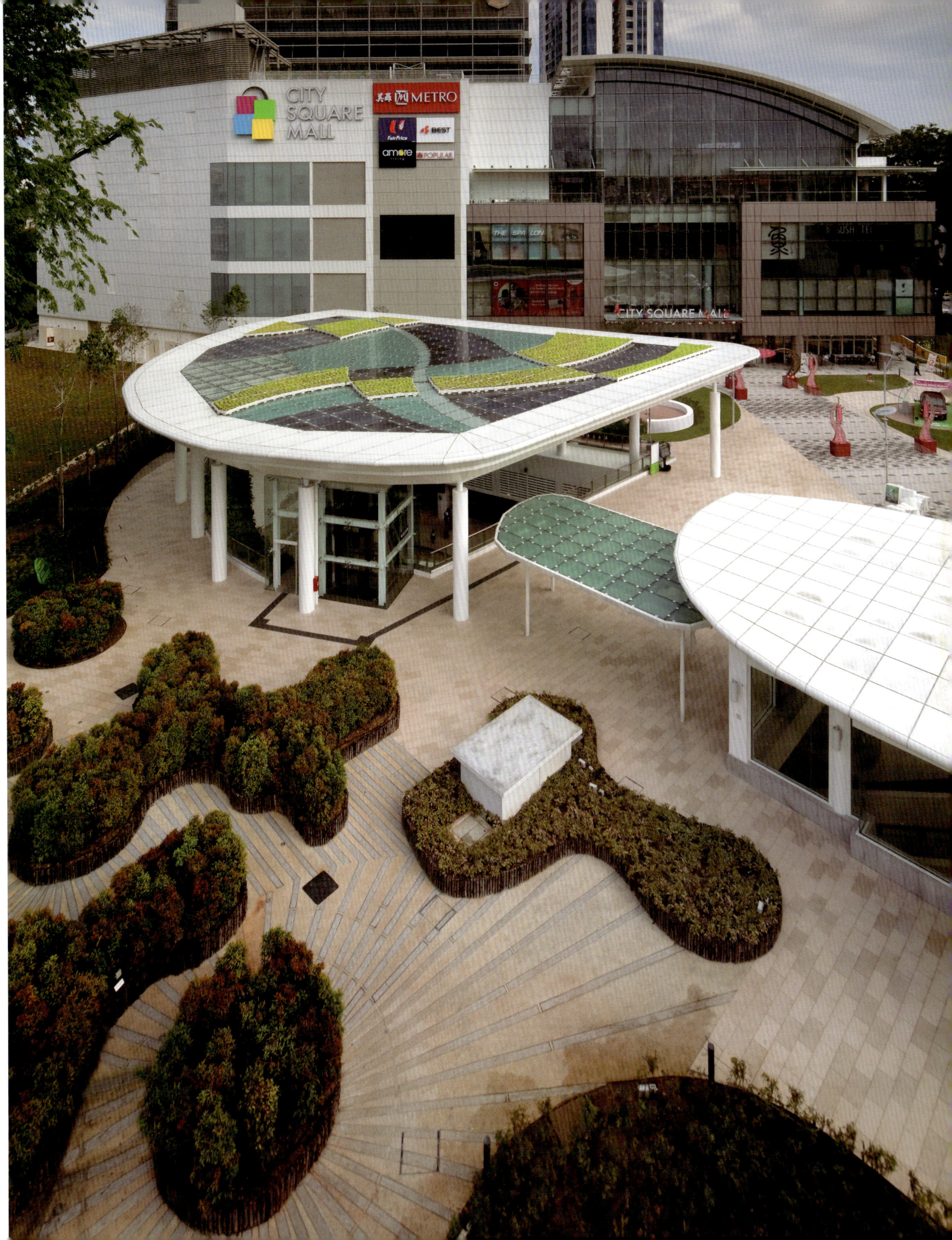
CITY
SQUARE
MALL
METRO
BEST
amore
CITY SQUARE MALL

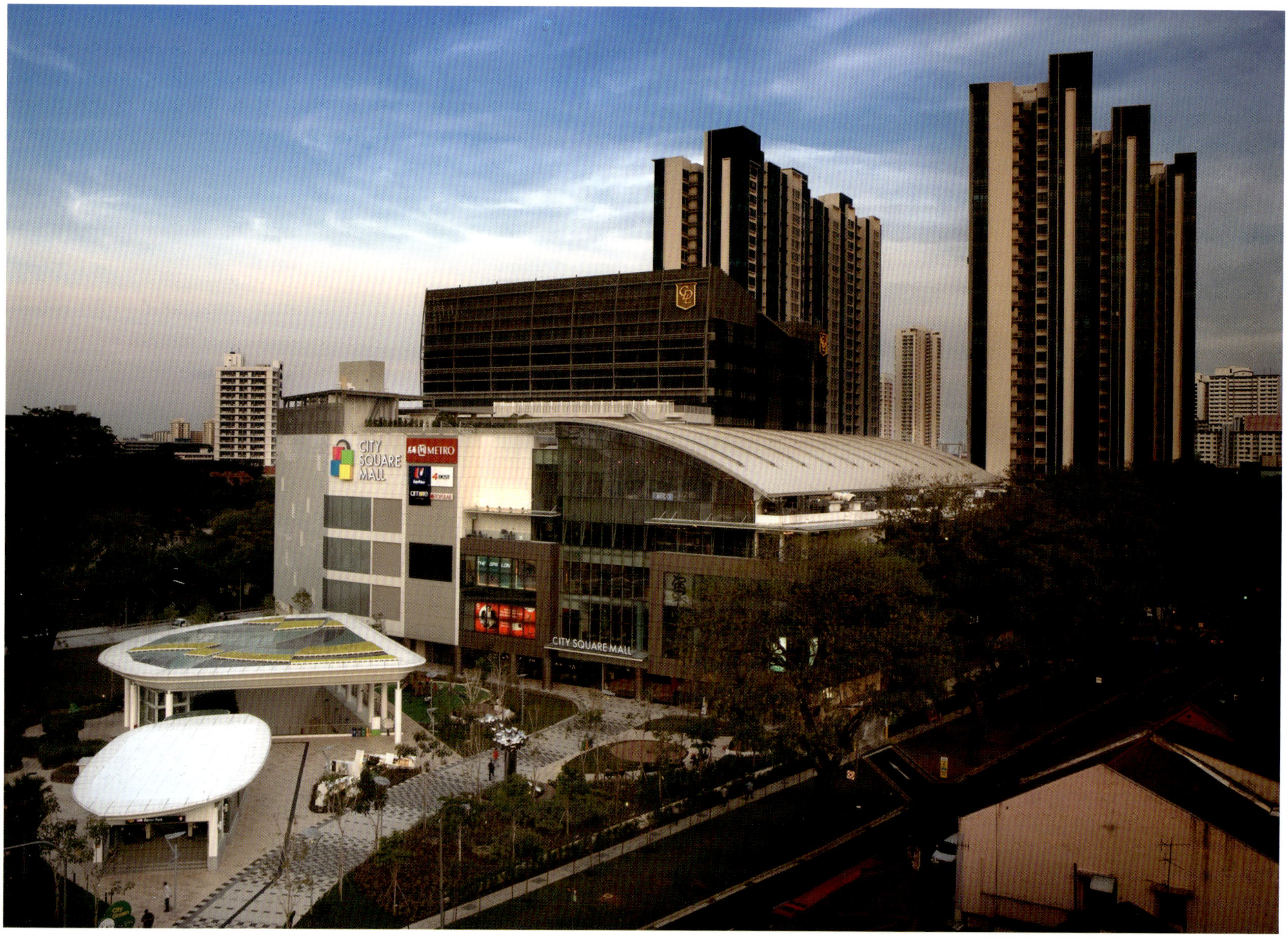
CITY SQUARE MALL
METRO
CITY SQUARE MALL

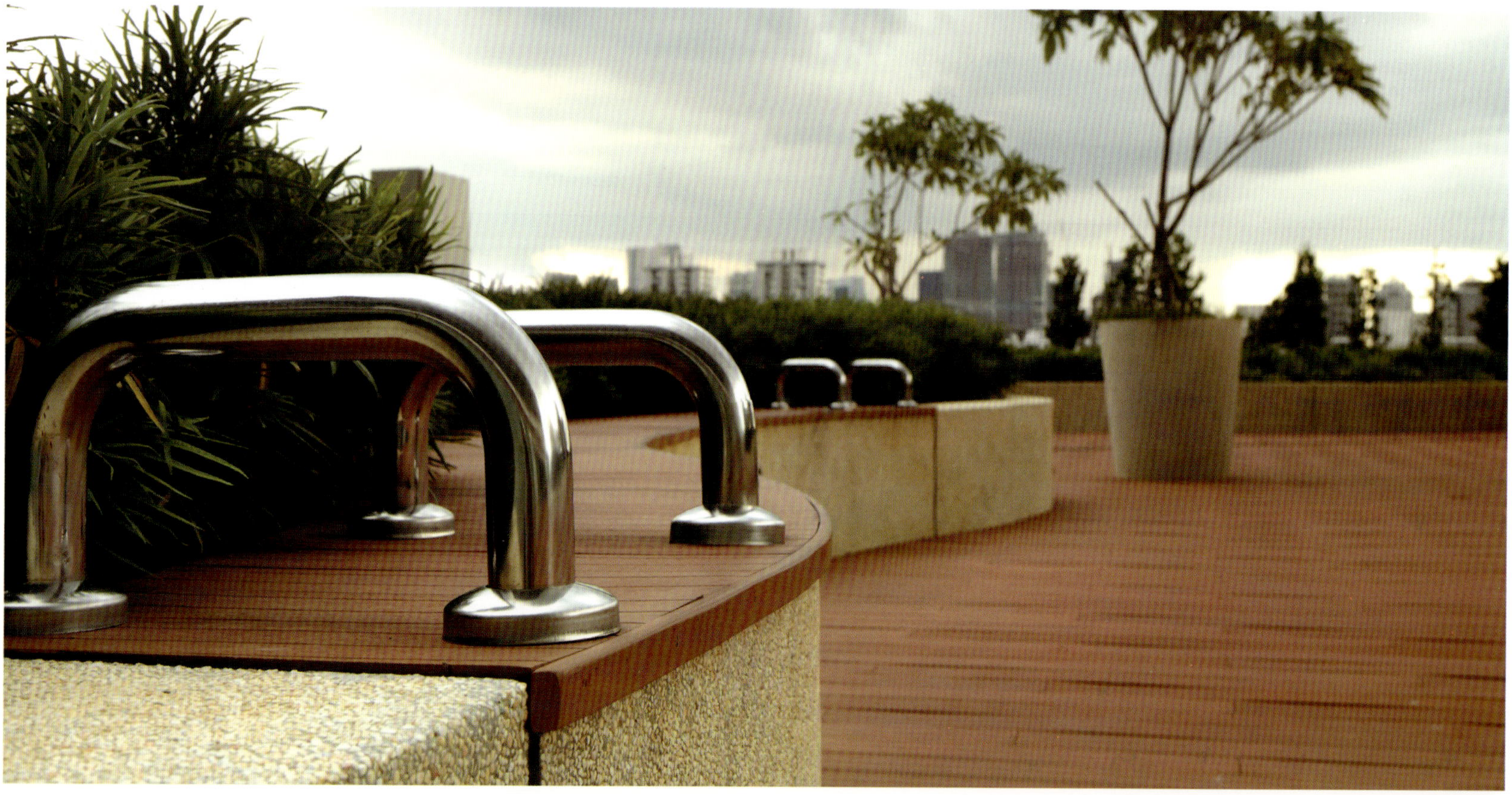

Upper left: Wide view of the facade
Lower left: Detail of the relaxing seats
Upper right: Green roof

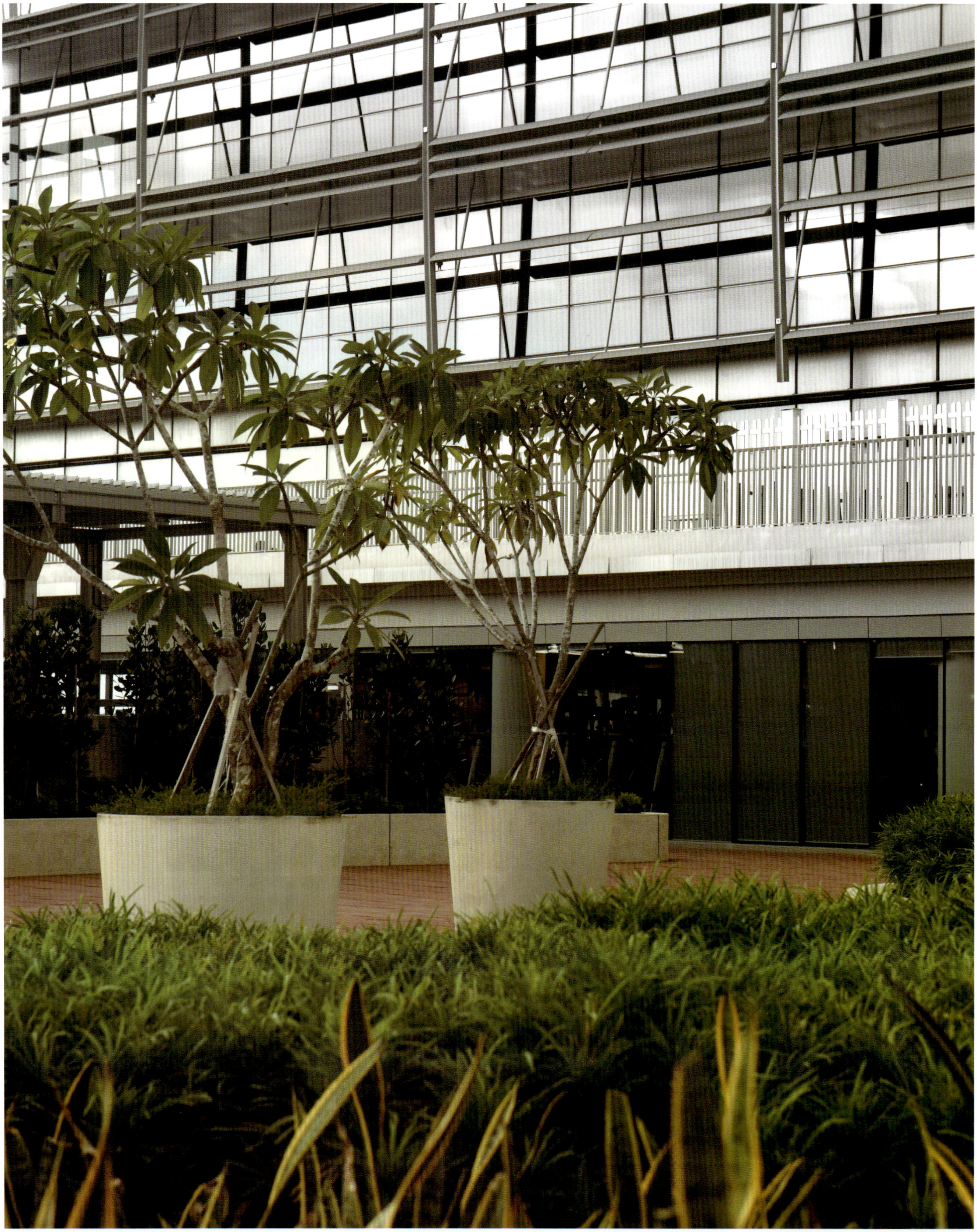

Upper right: Bird's-eye view of the Square
Lower right: Night view of the Square

Quincy Court

Location: Chicago, USA **Designer:** Rios Clementi Hale Studios **Photographer:** Scott Shigley **Completion date:** 2009 **Site area:** 1,115 sqm

The multi-disciplinary design firm transformed the Quincy Court, a remnant of an old downtown street, into an engaging gathering place for Chicagoans and visitors.

Using bold graphic forms, the designers provide canopy elements, a variety of seating configurations, and hardscape improvements to the half-block space. The design elements – abstracted tree forms, translucent tables with integrated lighting, white granite accent pavers – provide transitional scale between the monumental modern architecture of the Federal Plaza and the pedestrian scale of historic State Street.

Mark Rios notes: "The design is inspired by the honey locust trees used throughout the federal campus and prevalent in the City, the white terra-cotta detailing of historic Chicago buildings, the Miesian grid of the modernist plaza, and the reflected light patterns of the Dirksen Federal Building facade."

The new plaza features a series of seven tree-like canopy elements made of steel and three tones of translucent acrylic panels that are lit from above after dark. The 'trees' are rooted by sandblasted concrete in an abstracted leaf pattern. New granite benches and pavers join existing seating and hardscape materials, while a new site furniture language is introduced using concrete benches and translucent resin tables glowing with inner LED lighting. Four large leaves are situated on the ground, seemingly scattered on the pavement.

Award description:
2010 ASLA Southern California Chapter Honor Award for Design

1. Canopy
2. 'Fallen' Leaf
3. Granite Bench
4. Resin Table with Concrete Bench
5. Custom-Patterned Sandblasted Concrete

Right: The designer playfully places a leaf that the 'Windy City' has blown from the branches above

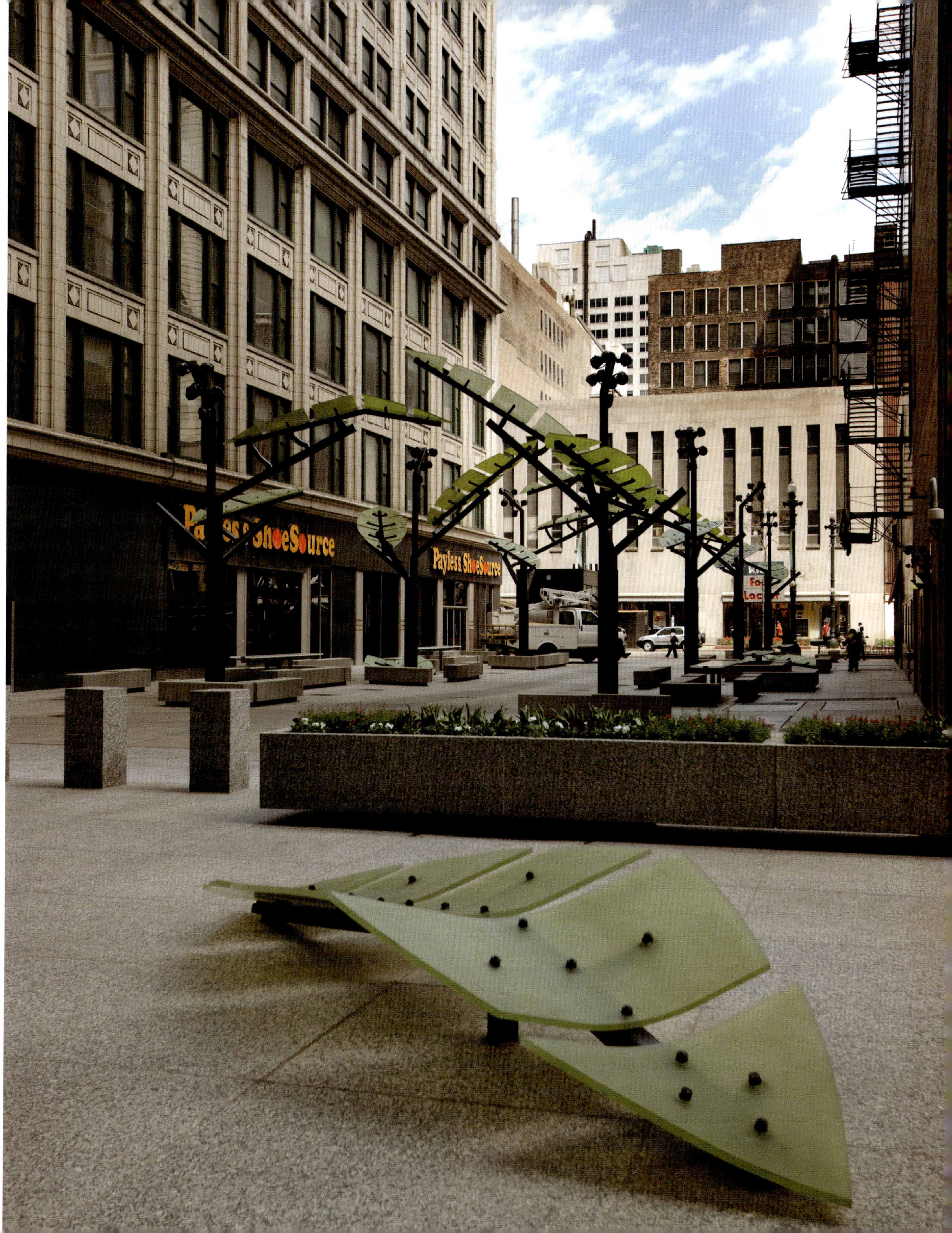
Payless ShoeSource
Payless ShoeSource

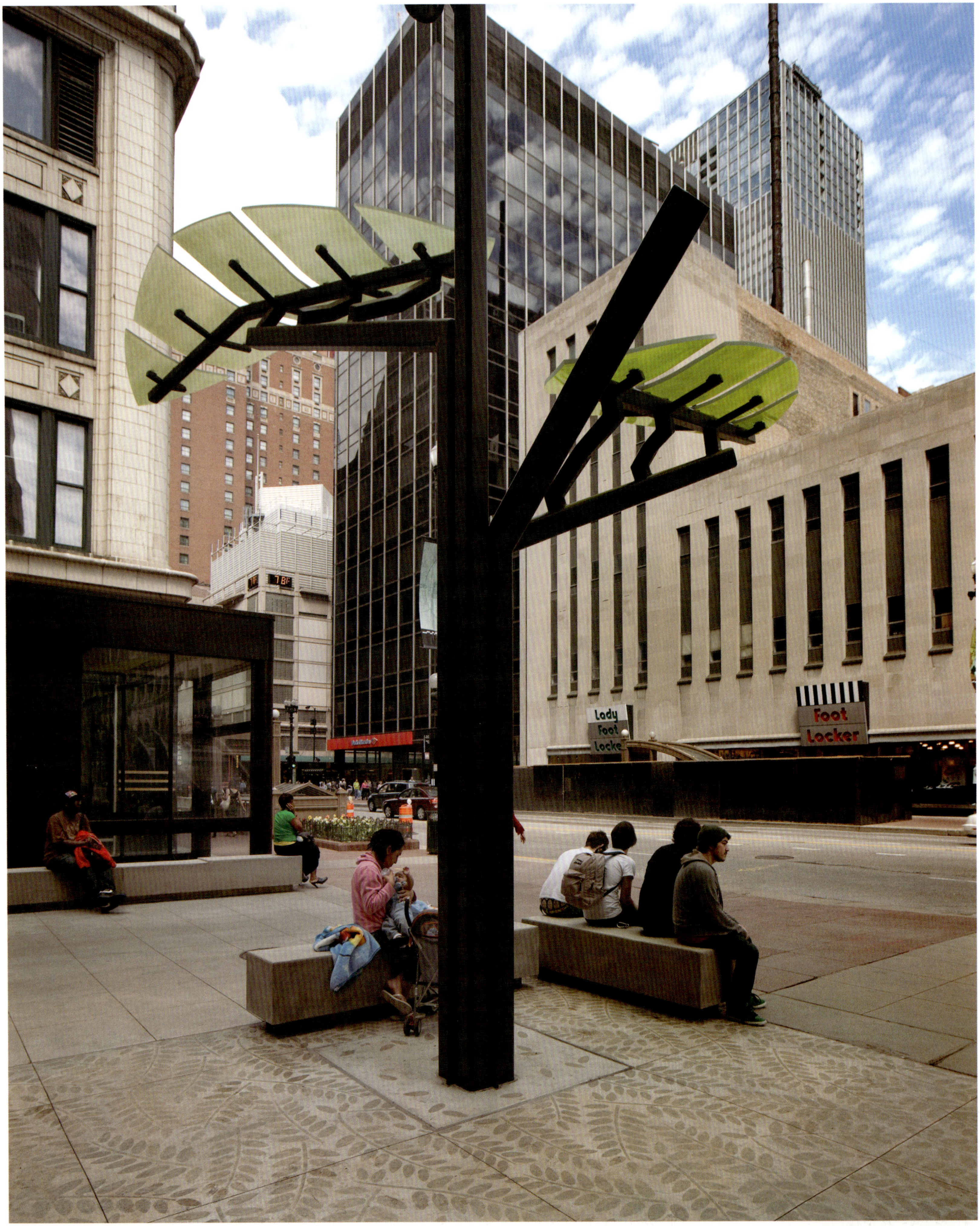
Lady
Foot
Locker
Foot
Locker

Left: New benches provide pedestrians with much needed seating near the State Street entrance
Upper right: The newly designed courtyard complements the Dirksen Federal Building and red Flamingo sculpture
Lower right: Concrete sandblasted with a leaf pattern repeats the theme throughout

Clarke Quay

Location: Singapore **Designer:** Alsop Architects **Photographer:** Jeremy San of Stzern Studio **Completion date:** 2006

Alsop Architects' first major project in Asia, a dramatic redevelopment of the river front district of Clarke Quay in Singapore, is succeeding in drawing tourists and locals back to the historic waterfront. Developed by Capitaland, the SGD 88 million (approx. £30.6 million) mixed-use scheme, designed to increase commercial and leisure activities, gives the riverfront area a new identity and re-positions Clarke Quay as a vibrant and attractive destination.

Crucial to the success of the project has been the architect/engineers ingenious manipulation of the site's micro climate through the design of a distinctive and sophisticated shading/cooling system that provides the Quayside with tremendous visual interest and environmental benefit.

For Alsop Architects the challenge was to provide a new lease of life not just by developing an attractive re-design of the streetscape and waterfront but also to address the perennial climate problem- and to find ways to mitigate against the Singapore ambient temperature and heavy rainfall – without resorting to the traditional scenario of creating an internal air-conditioned mall. The first phase of the waterfront revival, which was completed in March 2006, has effected a total transformation of the area's ambience, activity and appearance through the redevelopment of three main areas; the riverfront, the streets and River Valley Road.

1. Read Street
2. Clarke Street
3. Tan Tye Place
4. River Valley Road
5. Canning Street
6. North Boat Quay
7. Clarke Quay
8. Read Bridge

Right: The space between the shop houses and the waterfront has been turned into a clear zone dedicated to pleasant strolling and observation

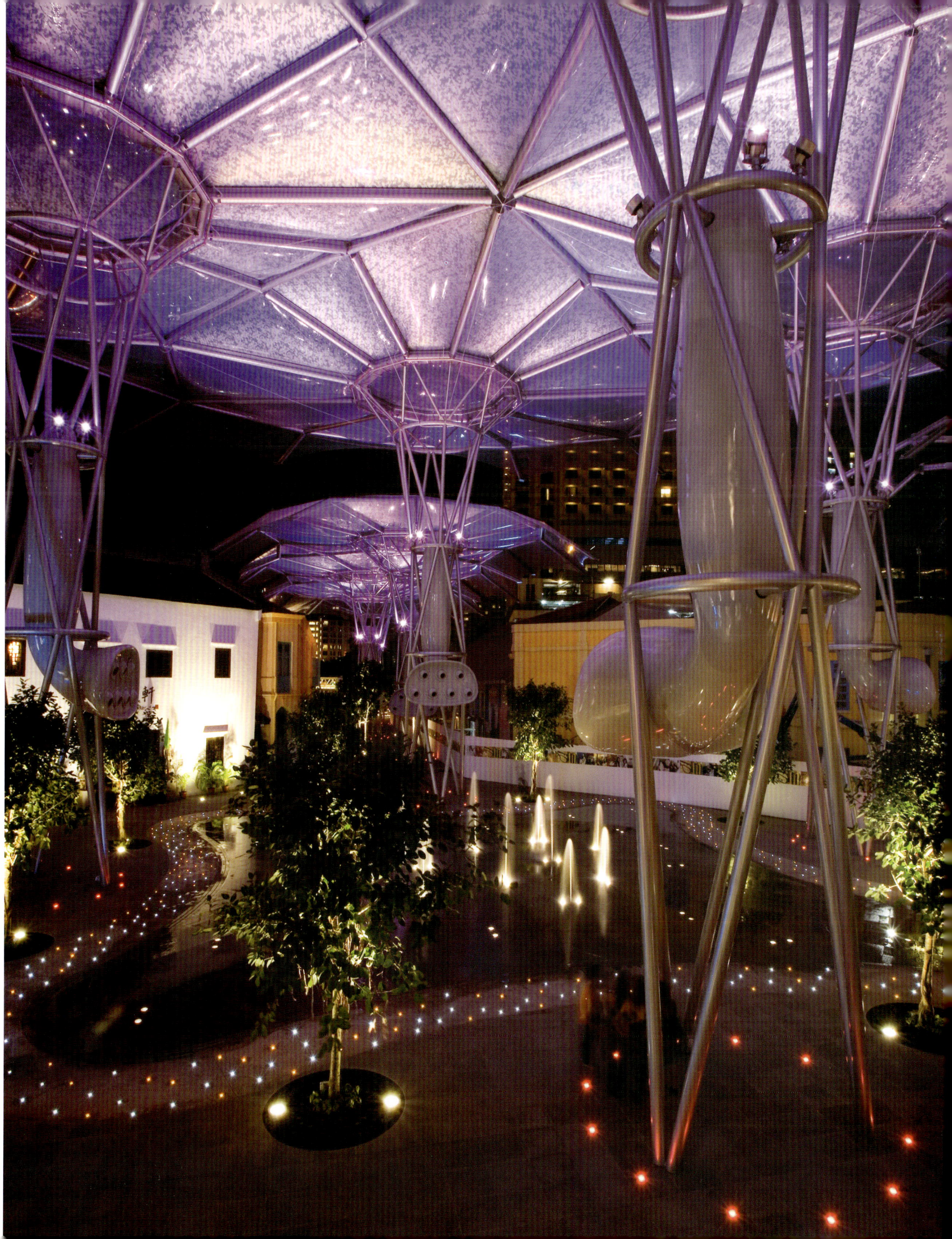

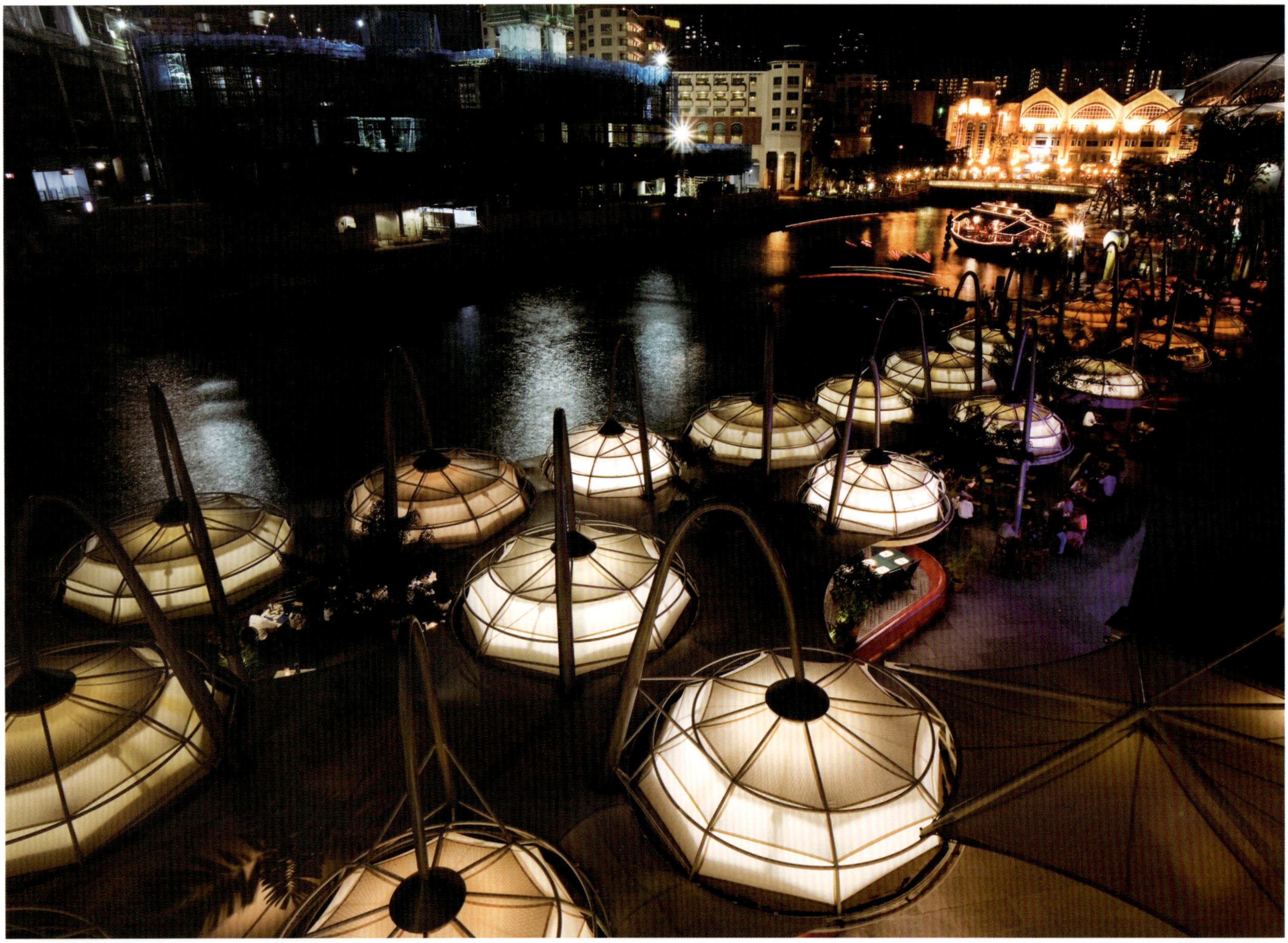

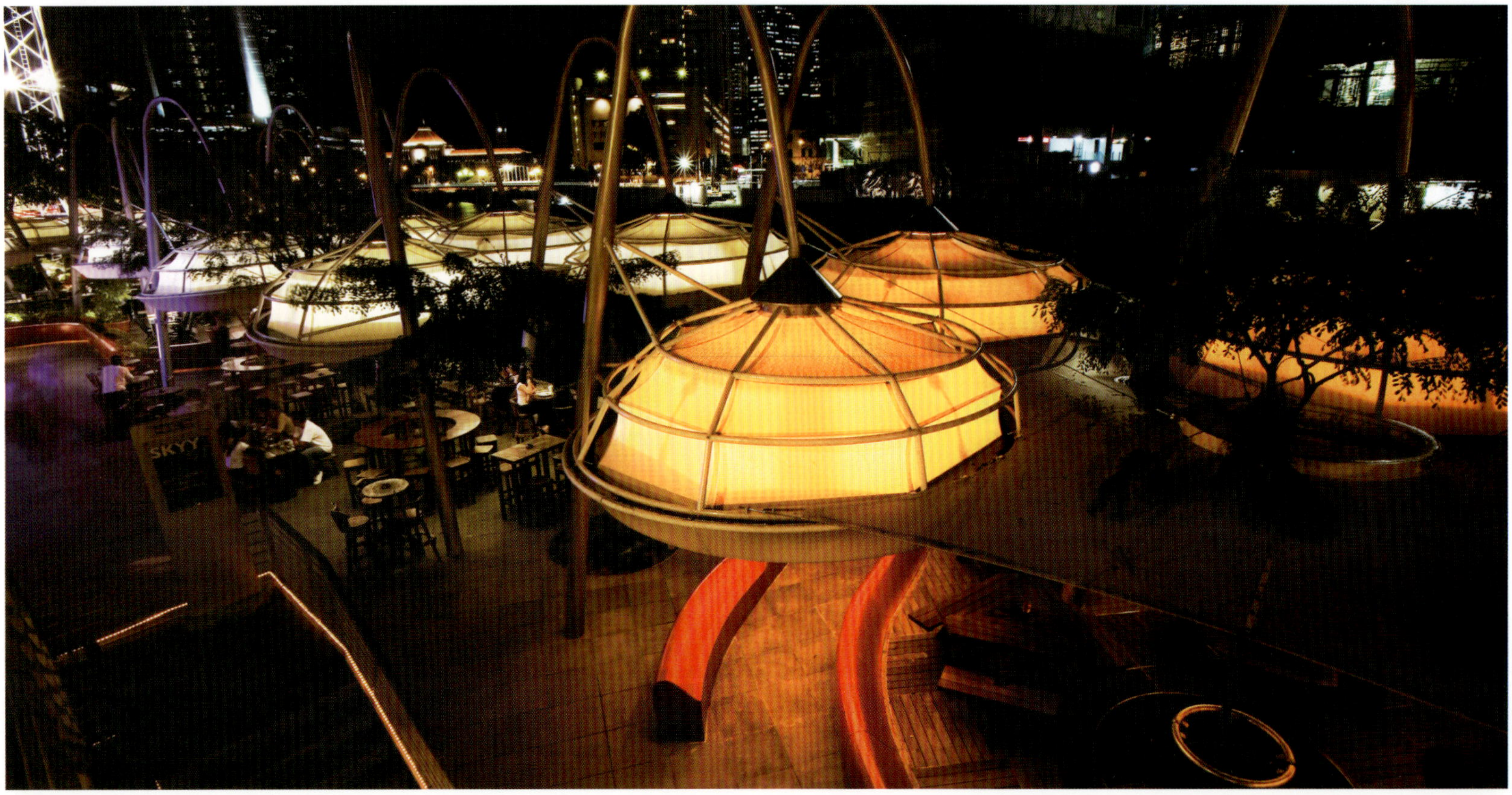
SKYY

Left: Illuminated at night in a variety of colors, the Bluebell umbrellas and their reflection in the Singapore River are delightfully reminiscent of an array of traditional Chinese lanterns

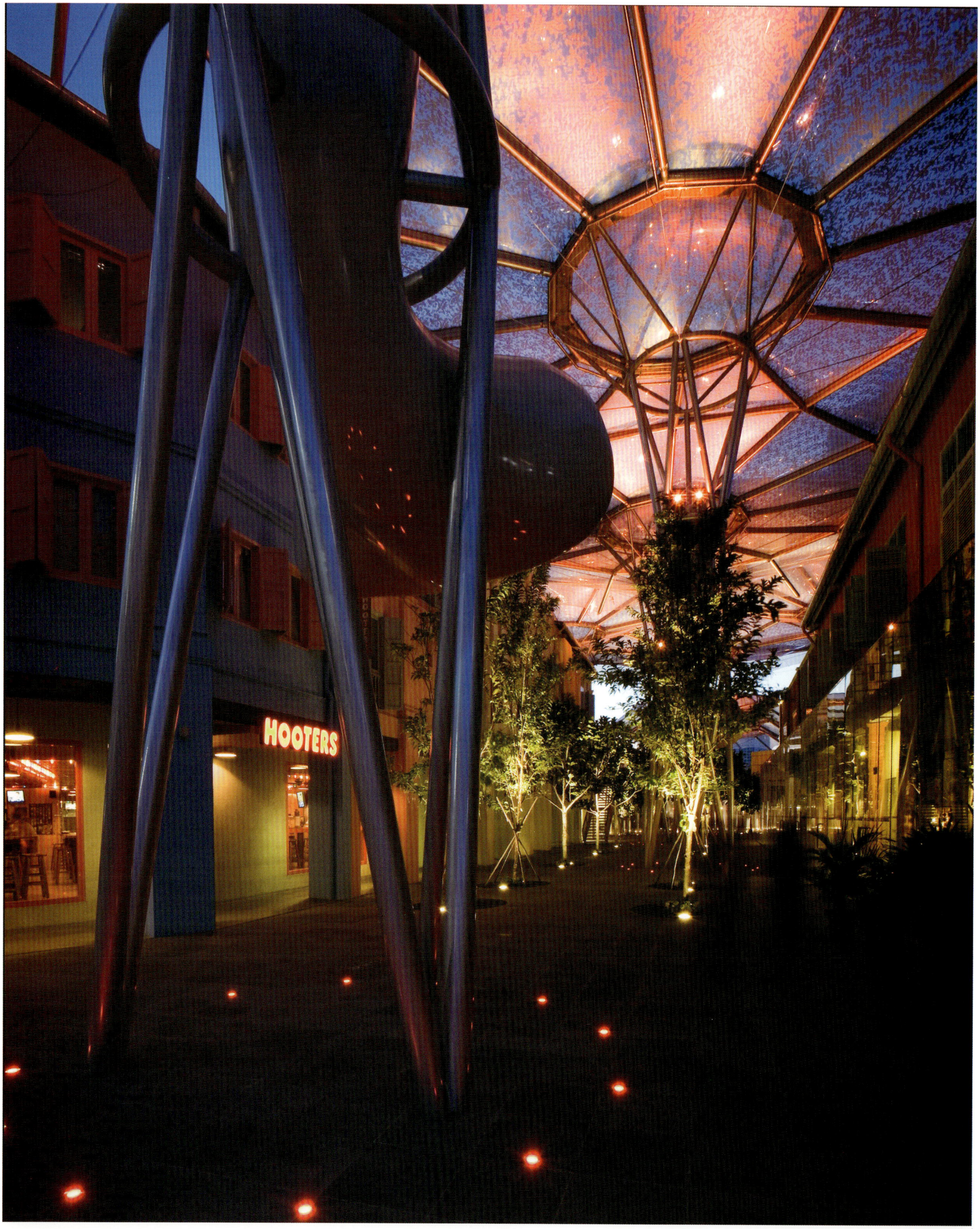
HOOTERS

Left: Elegant canopies provide environmentally friendly shading and cooling, which protect visitors against the extremes of the Singaporean climate and maintain the temperature at 28 centigrade

Shanghai Gubei Gold Street

Location: Shanghai, China **Designer:** SWA Group **Photographer:** Tom Fox
Completion date: 2008 **Site area:** 46,000 sqm

The densely populated Gubei District in Shanghai is a bustling urban district with a growing international community of families and young professionals. SWA was selected to design a new pedestrian promenade to provide the public with an iconic open space and a sanctuary from the hectic city. The new promenade occupies three city blocks, and flanked by 30-story high-rise residential towers. The retail shops at street level form a contiguous edge of the promenade and merge seamlessly with programmed plazas, parks, water features, outdoor dining, an amphitheater, and a monumental tree-lined raised terrace now attract focus and activity. Graphic paving and custom site furniture contribute to this fluid connection from building to open space.

The landscape architecture consists of a hybrid integration of both bold gestures and small garden spaces. Tall Ginkgos line the retail promenade, creating a visual transition from the surrounding towers to the promenade's intimate gardens. Contrasting the city's hard-edged environment, evergreen camphor trees ensure a welcoming canopy year-round, while deciduous cherry trees provide seasonal interest.

The intention of the Gubei Pedestrian Promenade is simple – to provide highly desired and flexible open space in a very dense urban environment. The success of the project has brought new energy to this part of the city of Shanghai. The pedestrian promenade offers a peaceful sanctuary from the hectic street life as well as potential for urban ecology and natural cooling in a dense urban setting.

1. East Entry Park
2. Pedestrian Crossing
3. Clipped Ginkgo Bosque
4. Second Architectural Folly
5. Tree Bosque on Viewing Platform with Seating
6. Park/Garden for Seniors
7. Raised Seating Terrace
8. Interactive Fountain
9. Community Sculpture
10. Architectural Folly
11. Continuous Street Tree Planting
12. Outdoor Dinning at Restaurants
13. Pedestrian Connection to Neighborhood
14. Outdoor Dinning Island
15. Water Feature
16. Open Space Park

Right: Long view at night

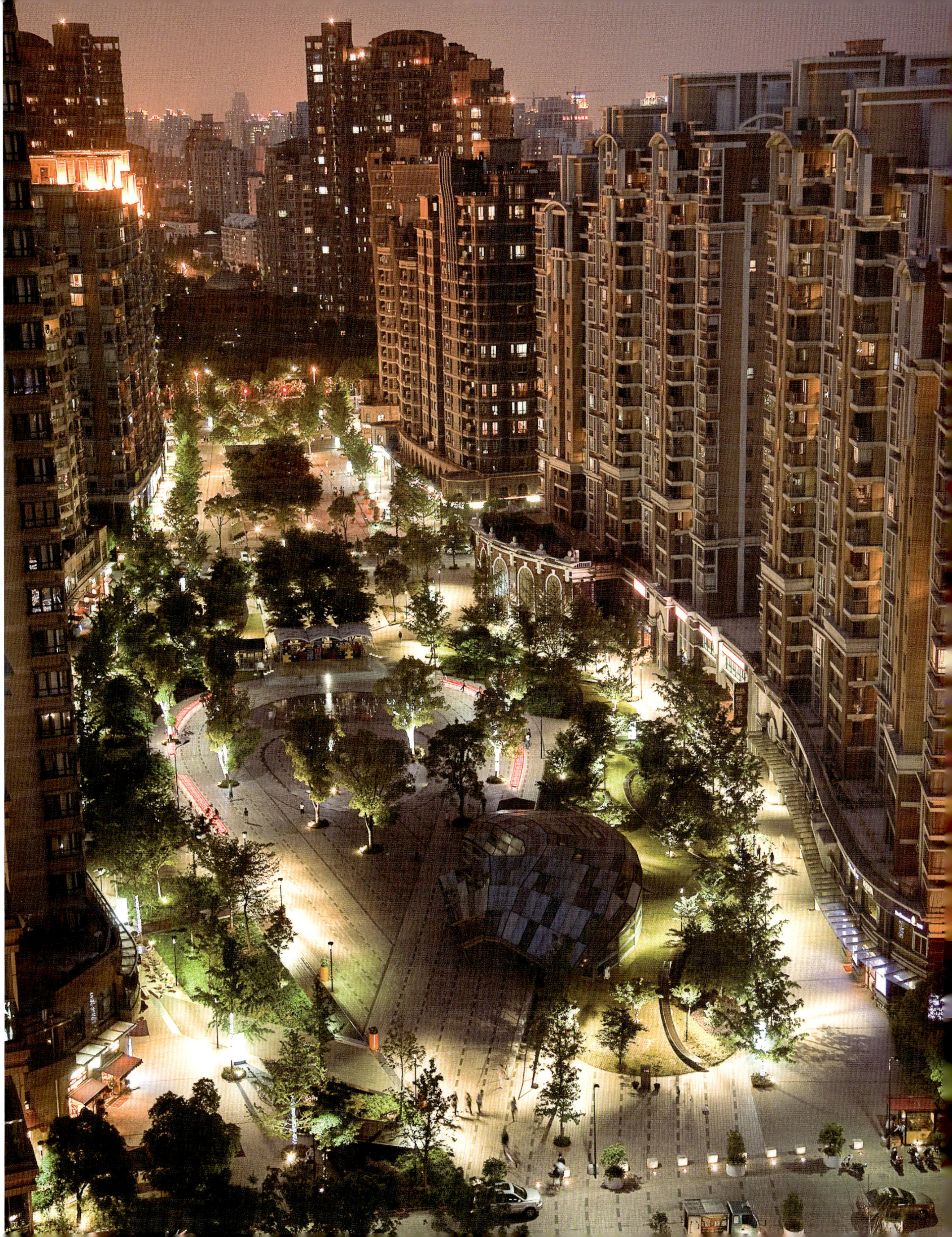

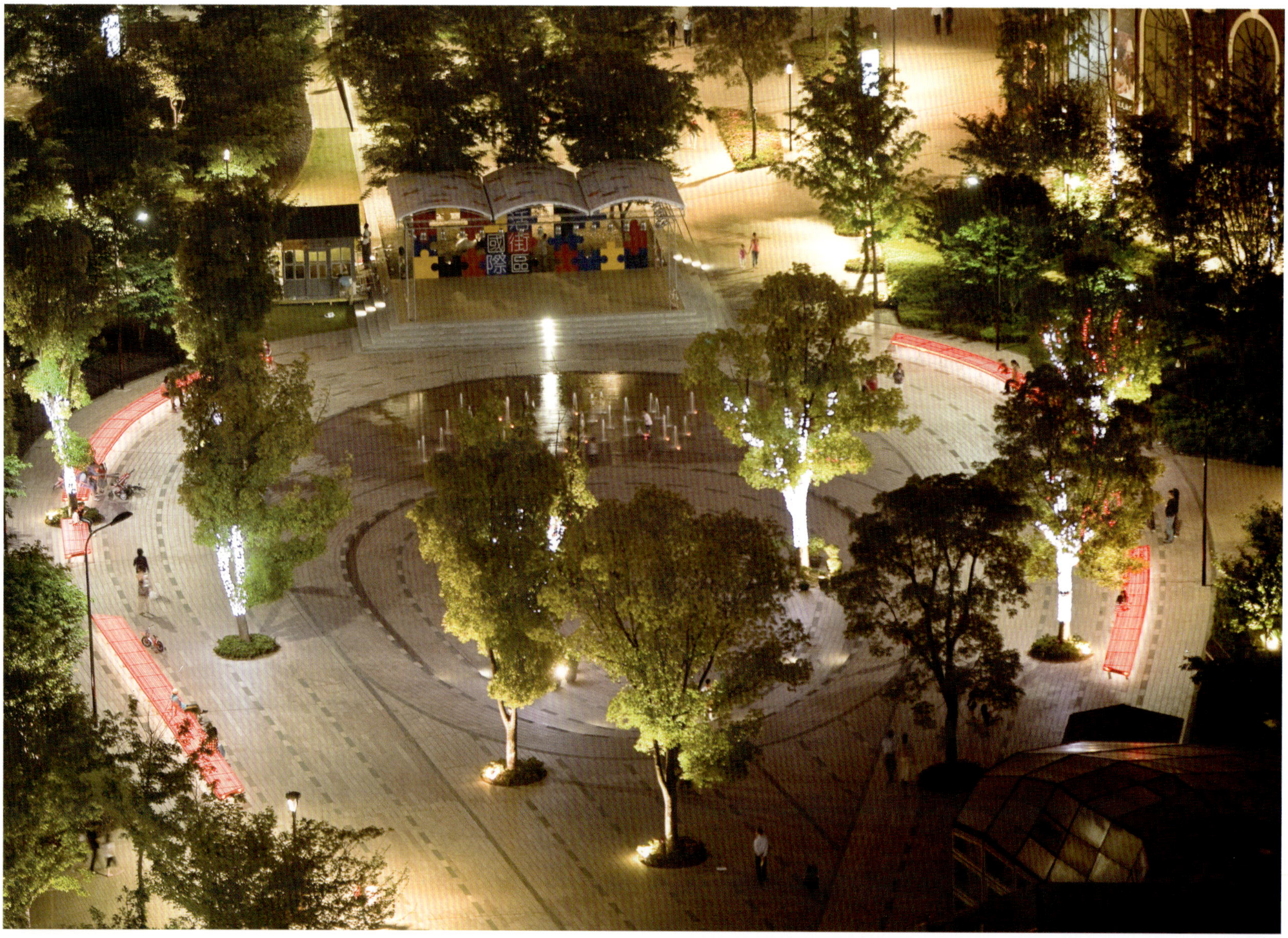
國 街
際 區

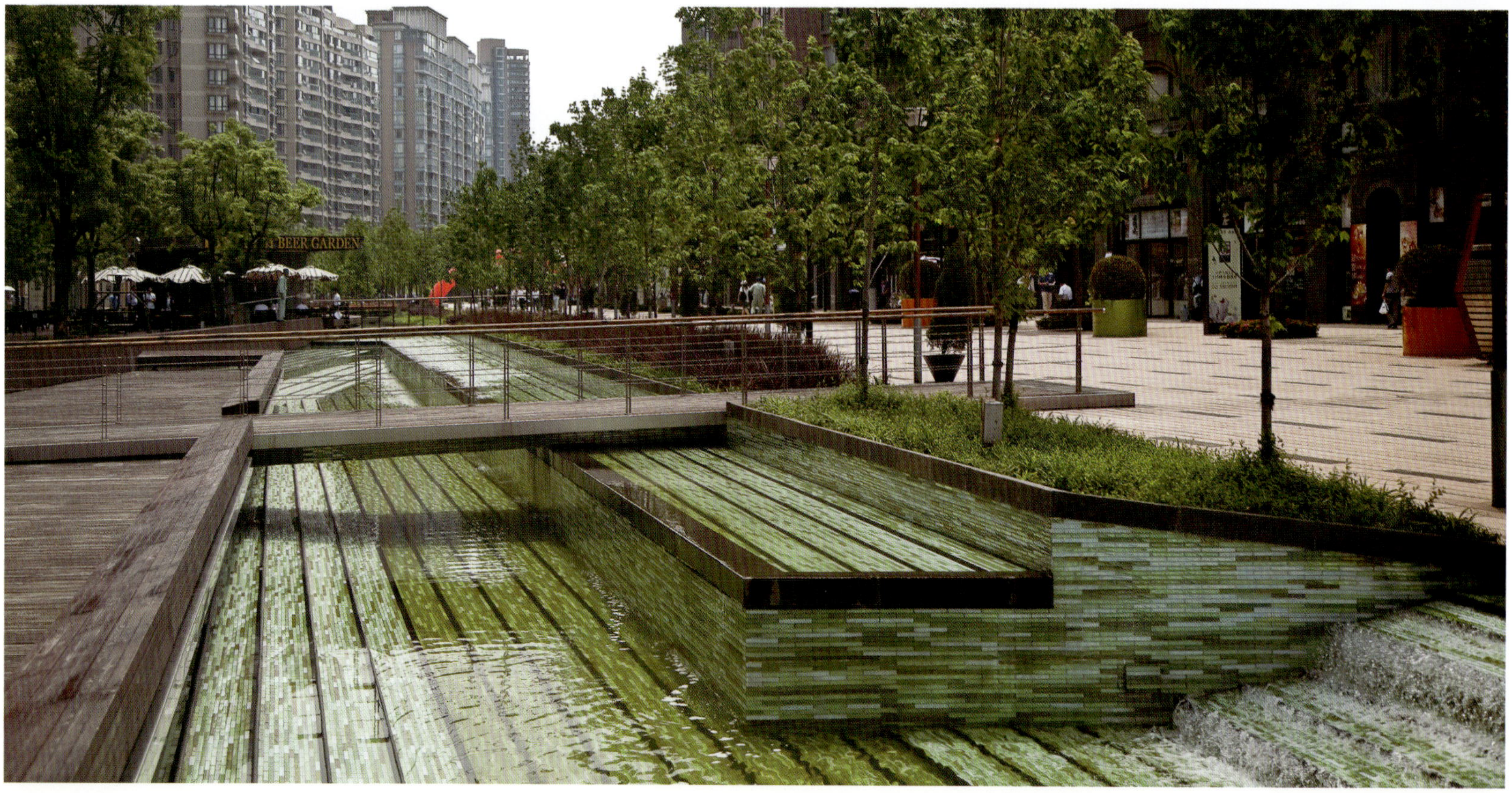
BEER GARDEN

Upper left: Interactive fountain
Lower left: Water feature
Upper right: Open space park
Lower right: Curved seats with inner lights

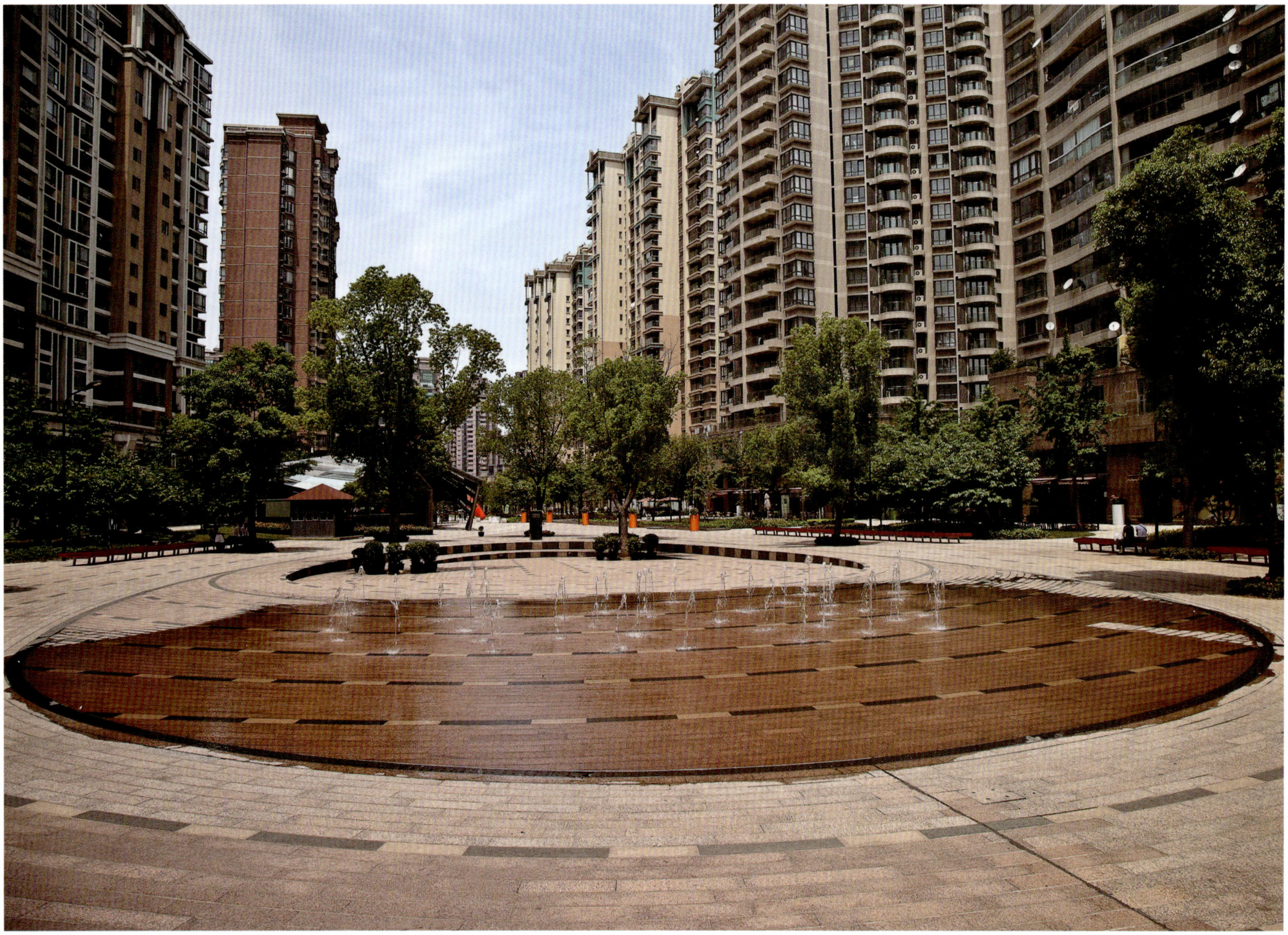

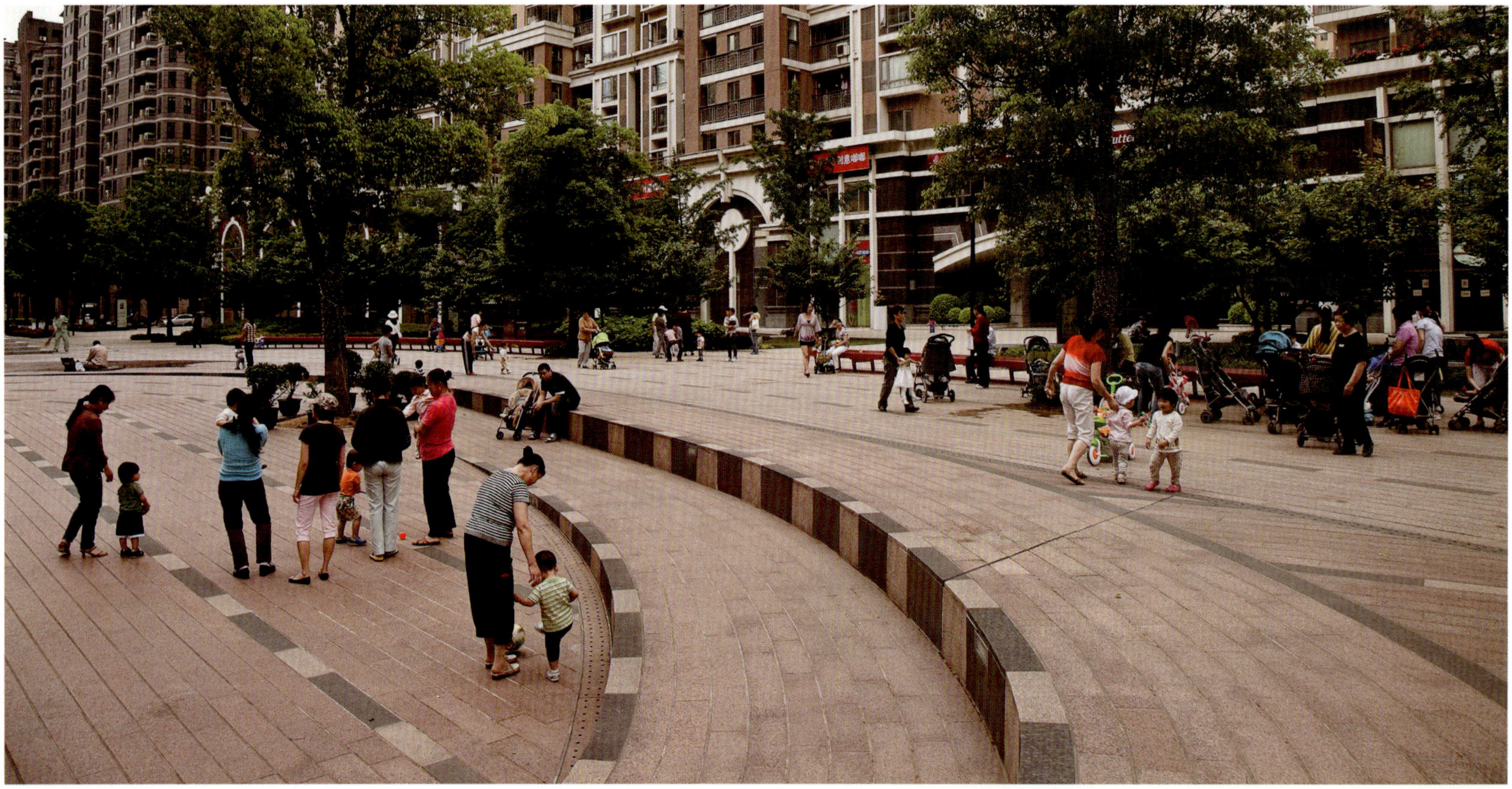

Upper left: Interactive fountain
Upper right: Plantings
Lower right: Raised seating

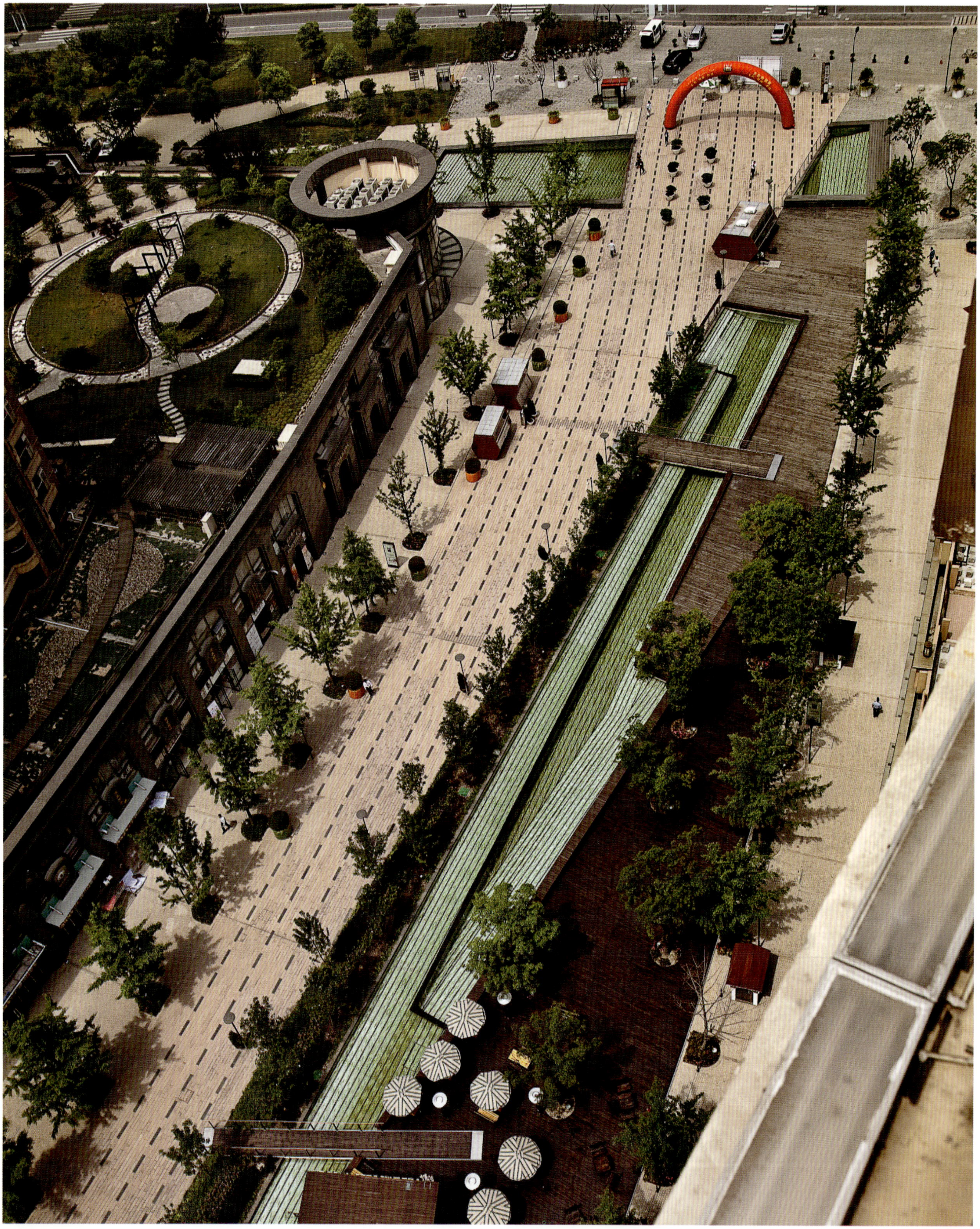

Left: Long view
Upper right: Tree bosque

Melbourne Convention Exhibition Center

Location: Melbourne, Australia **Designer:** ASPECT Studios Pty Ltd **Photographer:** Ian Roony, Andrew Lloyd **Completion date:** 2009

Aspect Studios was commissioned by the Plenary Group, Multiplex and Contexx to undertake the design and documentation of the new public realm for the Melbourne Convention Center and South Wharf Precinct. The Melbourne Convention Center is the first convention center in the world to achieve a 6 Star Green Star environmental rating.

The landscape design for public realm places include:
- Convention Center
- Hotel
- Retail
- Residential
- Public forecourts, promenades and laneways
- Refurbishment of the existing Exhibition Center Park
- Heritage Landscapes

Key principles of the Public Realm:
- 24 hour public access throughout the precinct
- Clear and direct pedestrian and cyclist routes
- An attractive Yarra River Promenade
- Interesting spaces with the precinct for residents, pedestrians, visitors, shoppers and delegates
- Connection of the precincts areas to the Yarra River
- Incorporate of all heritage elements

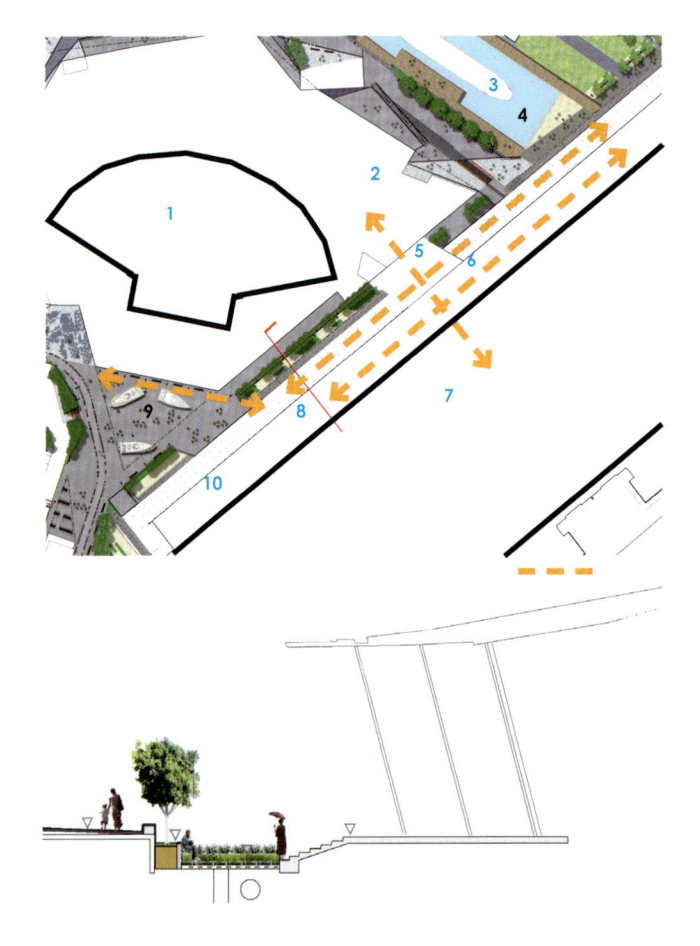

1. Plenary Hall
2. Entrance Doors
3. Polly Woodside
4. Dukes Dock
5. Main Link
6. Entrance Doors
7. Melburne Exhibition Center
8. Entrance Doors
9. South Plaza
10. Entrance Doors

Right: Landscape integrated with architecture

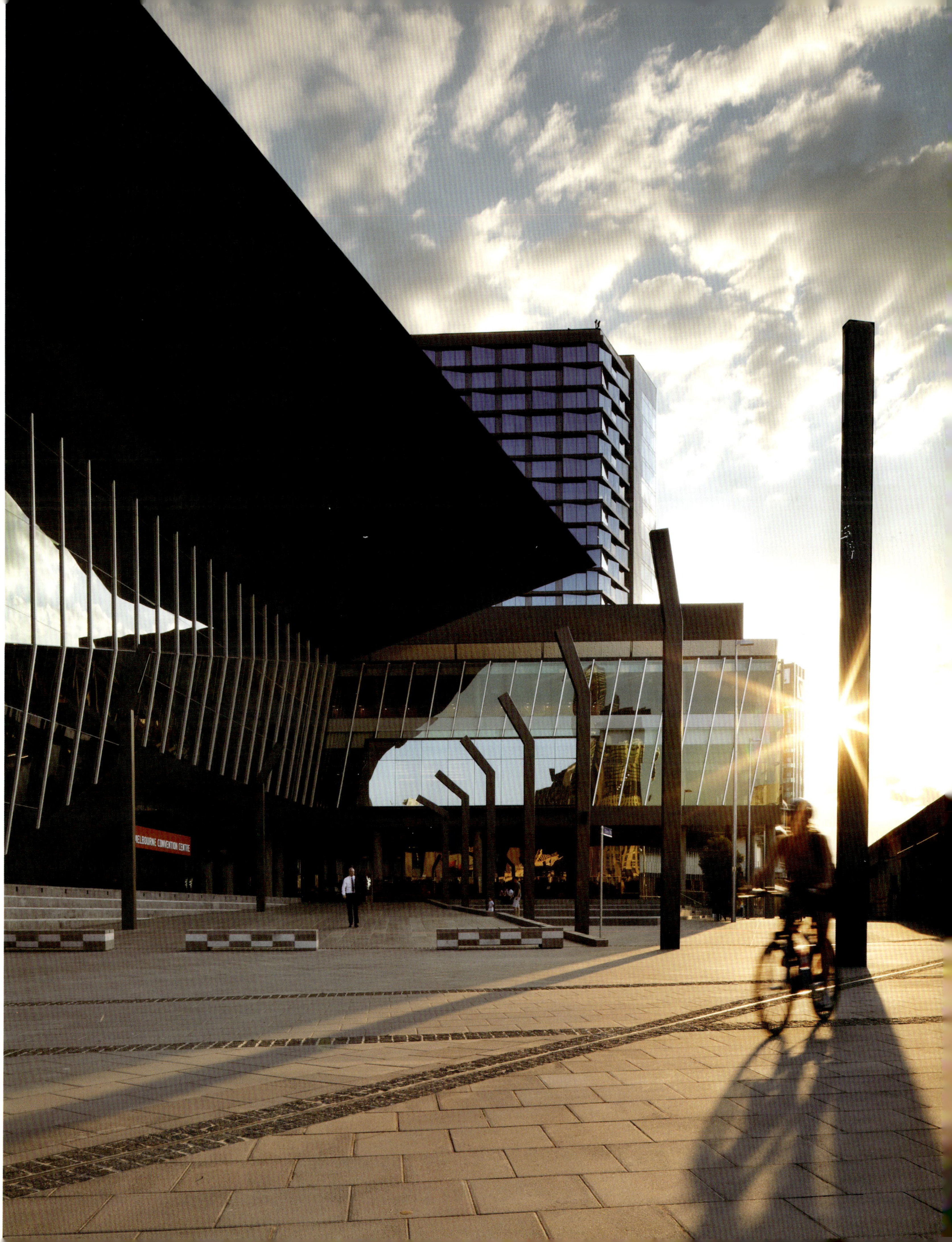
ELBOURNE CONVENTION CENTRE

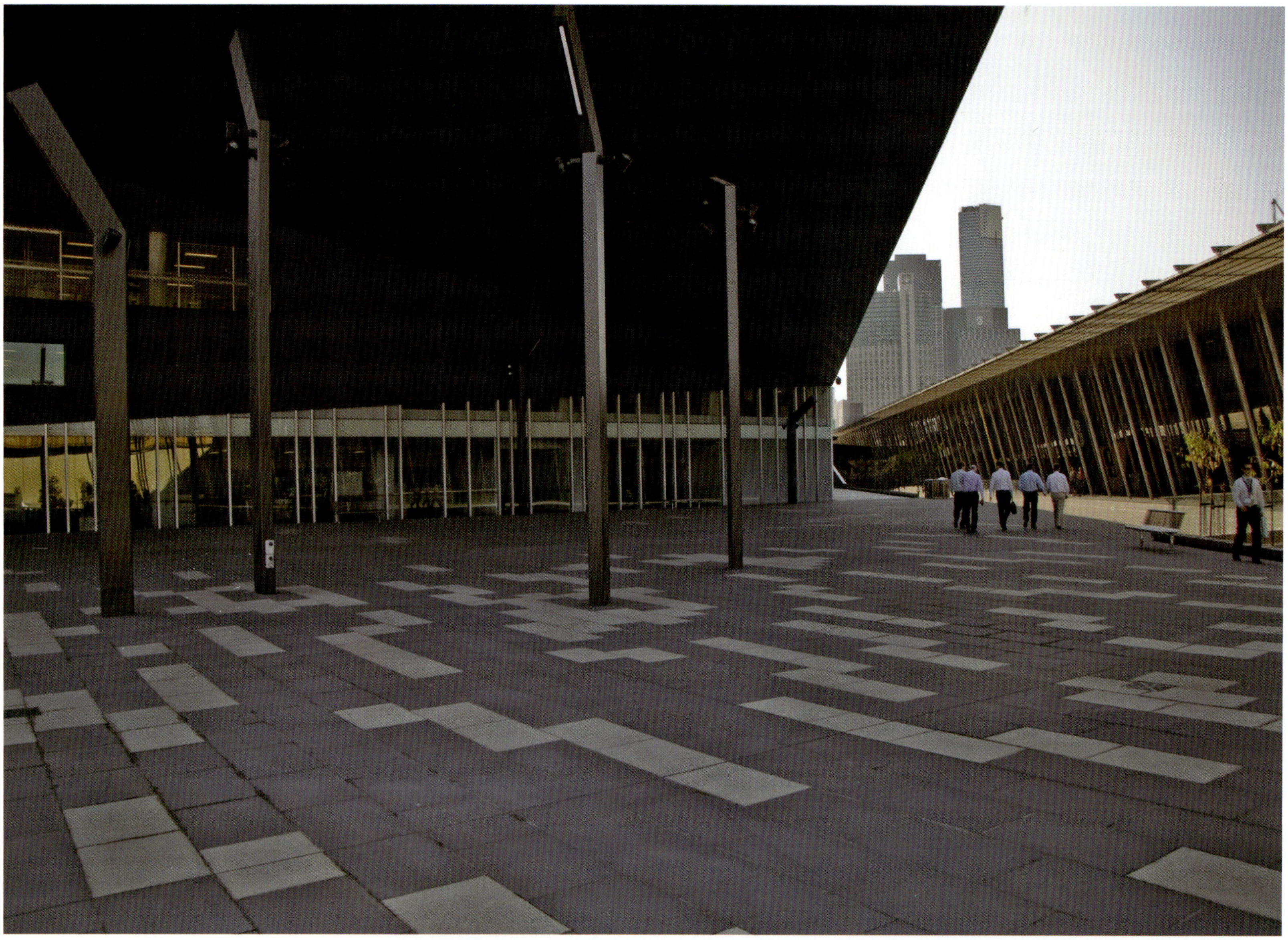

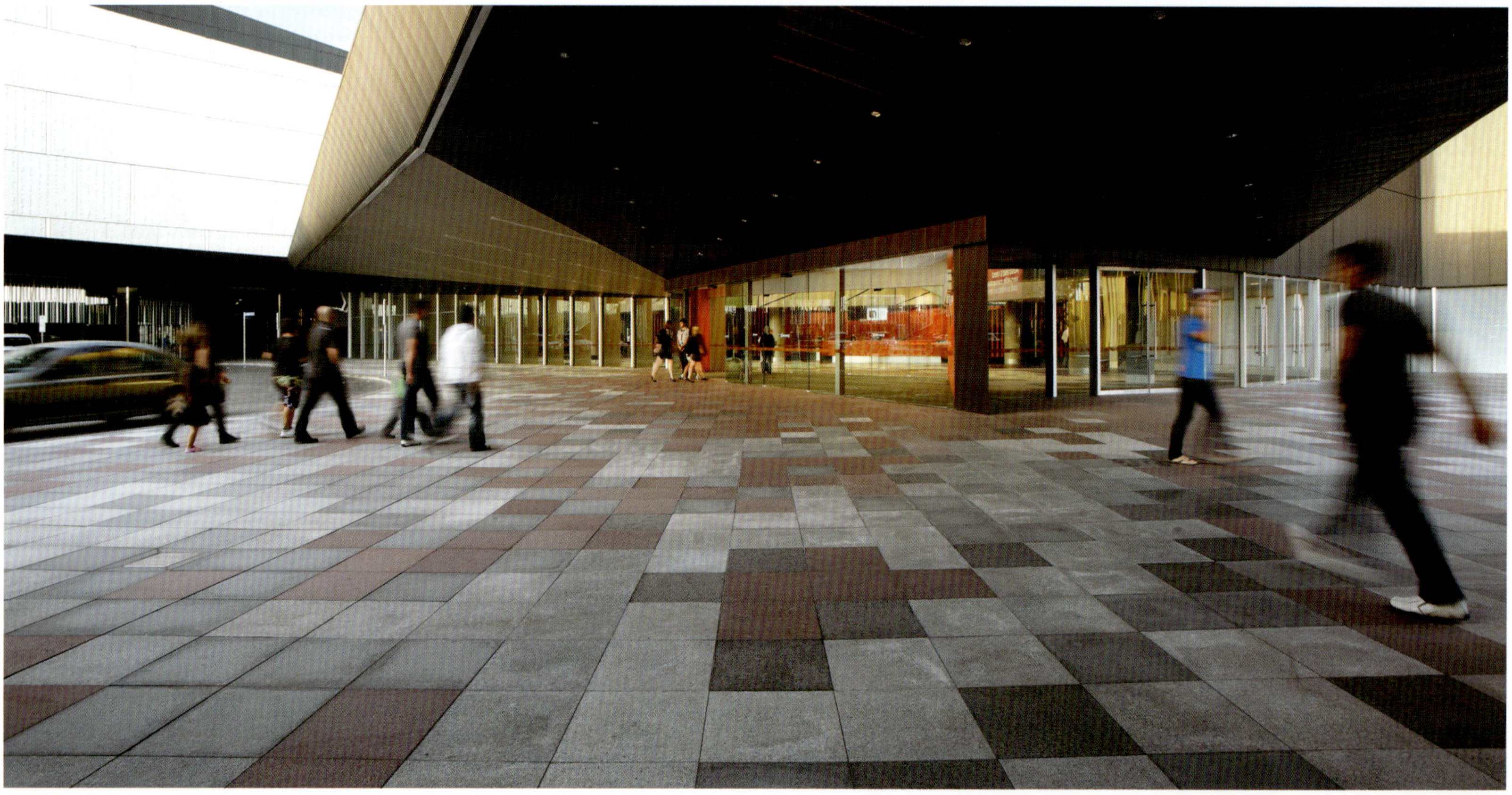

Upper left: Lamps on the square
Lower left: Details of the stone pavement
Upper right: Wooden deck for relaxing
Lower right: Details of the planting bed

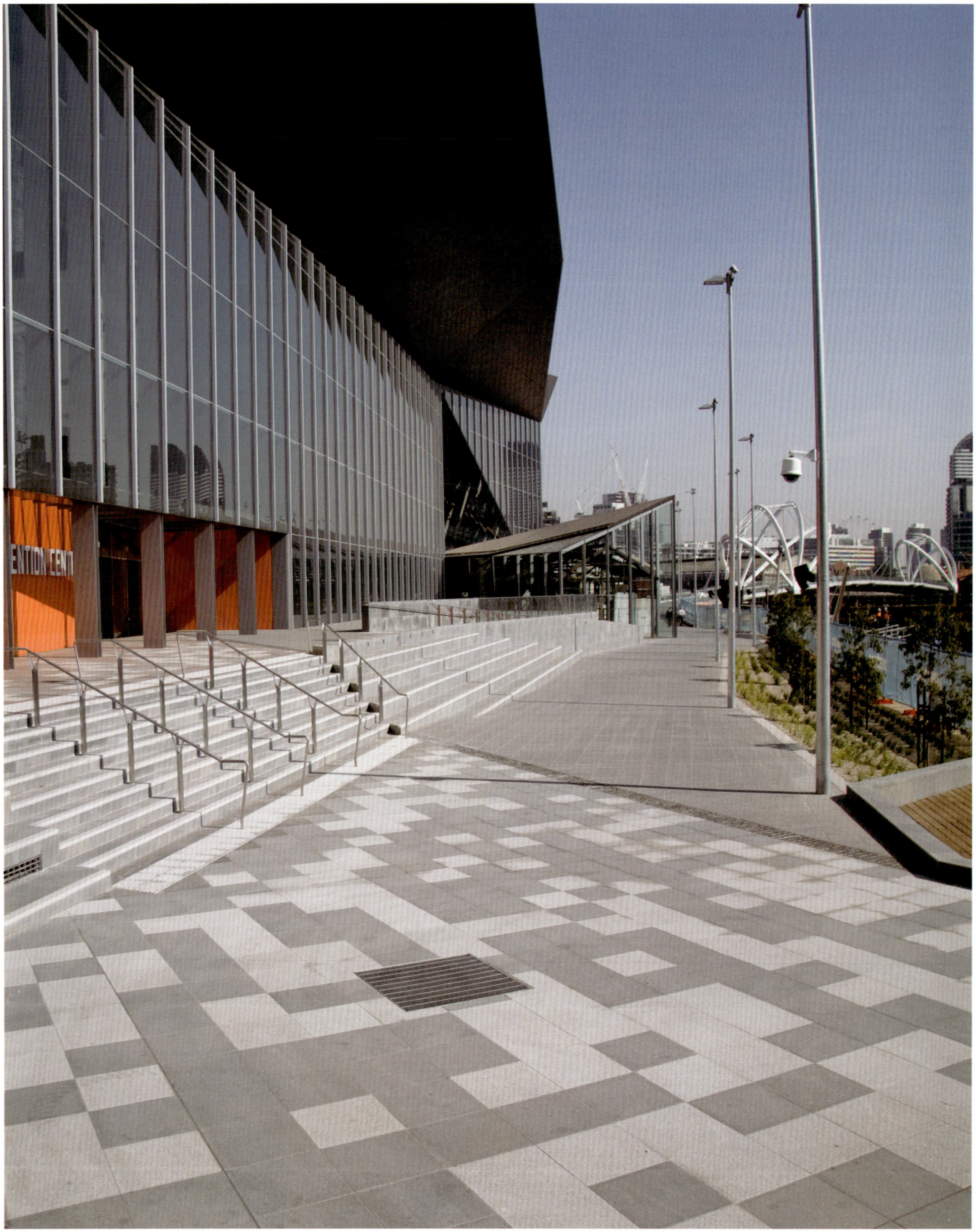
ENTION CENT

Left: Steps and footpath
Upper right: Low water use plants
Lower right: Details of the bench

Malvern City Square

Location: Victoria, Australia **Designer:** Rush\Wright Associates **Photographer:** Michael Wright, David Simmonds **Completion date:** 2006 **Site area:** 1,800 sqm **Plants:** Star Jasmine, Boston Ivy, Boxleaf Azara, Hill's Weeping Fig

The Malvern City Square is located in a dense urban shopping precinct and required a high percentage of paved areas to allow for large volumes of people and the ability to hold functions. Material selection was based on the need for a slip resistant and safe surface whilst adding a dynamic and unique feel to the site. The granite is complimented by stainless steel handrails and mesh forms which surround the existing planters.

The design agenda for the new square was to open up the upper level which previously only had one entrance point from Glenferrie Road. This was achieved by extending the upper level into the site, providing two new entrance points from High Street and a ramped entrance from Glenferrie Road each with wide steps which also provide casual seating. The upper level is still used as an outdoor dining space by Giorgios Restaurant, which is now perceived as an integral part of the square and contributes to the overall amenity of the space as they are open until later every night.

Lighting thus played an important role in providing a safe environment where all areas of the site were visible at night. Light poles form view lines into the site and wash the area with a soft yellow light while feature lighting to the statues and existing Plane trees highlight the site at night and the colors within the site.

1. Colonnade
2. Grass Under Tree
3. Footpath
4. Garden Bed
5. Planter
6. New Vent
7. Terrace Extension

Right: View over the new stainless steel mesh planters

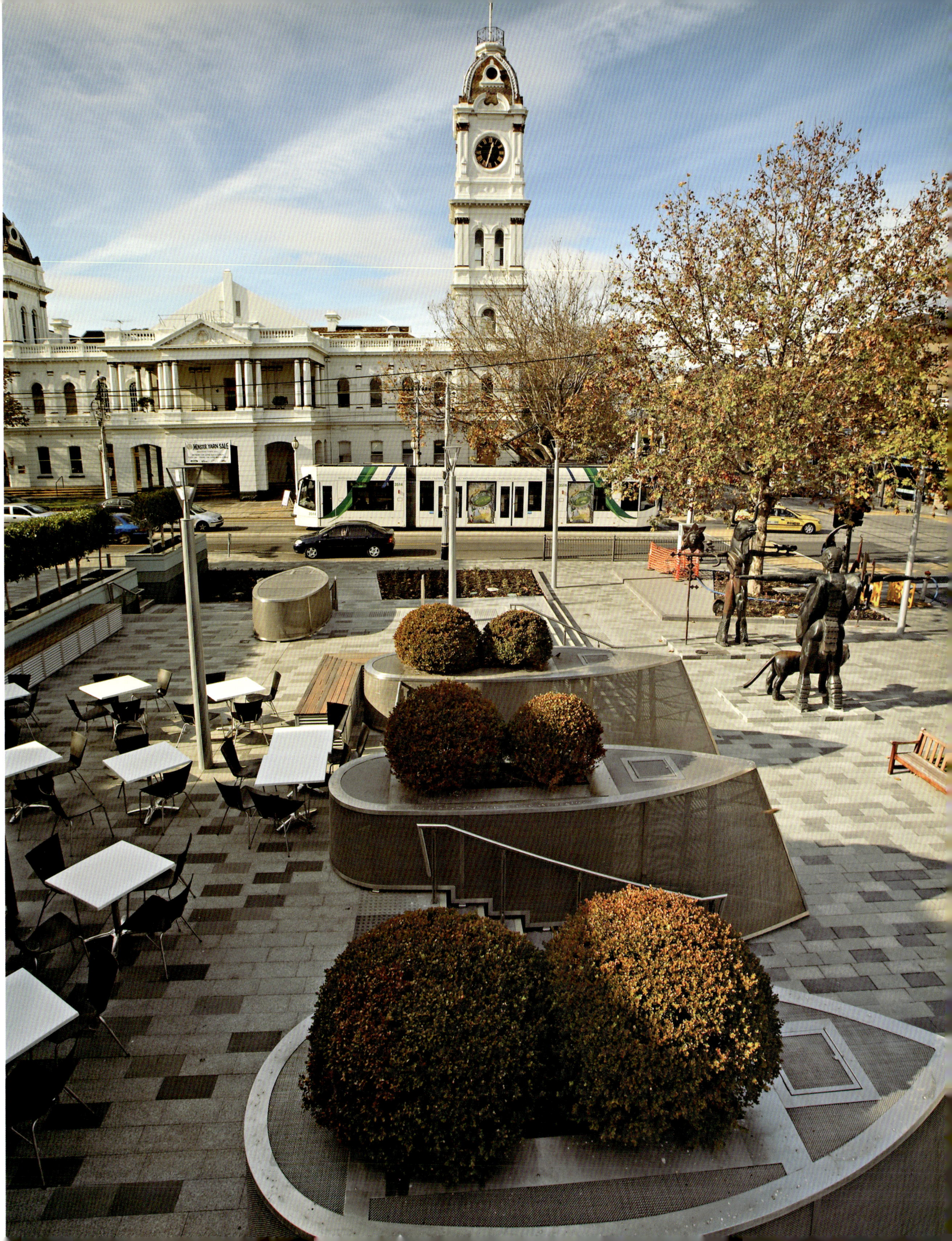
MONSTER YARN SALE

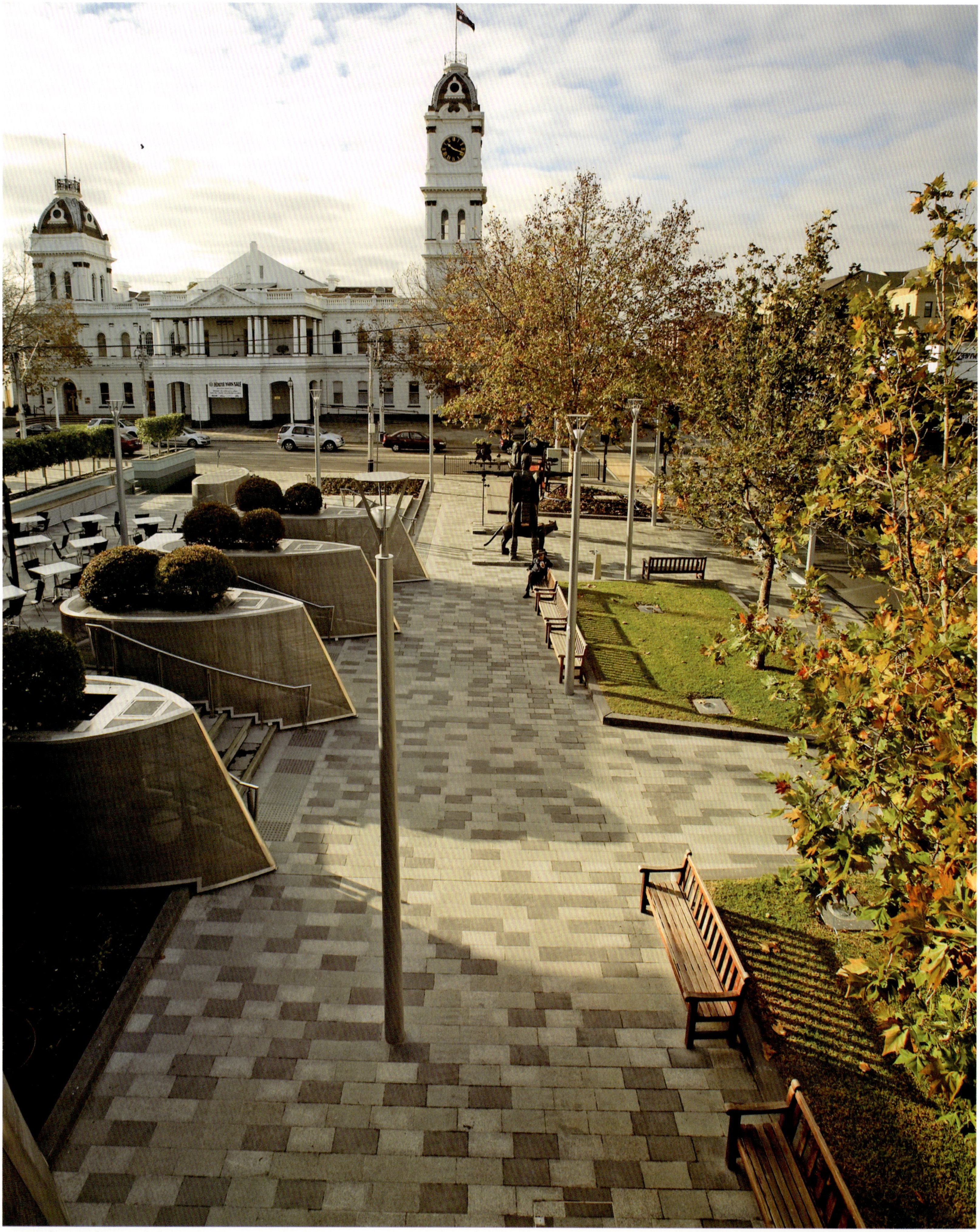

Left: View across the square toward Glenferrie Road and Malvern Town Hall
Upper right: The existing 'Sun God' and 'Moon God' sculptures were an integral part of the design and help to define the main entrance on High Street
Lower right: New stainless steel mesh planter and handrail

1111 Lincoln Road

Location: Miami Beach, Florida, USA **Designer:** Raymond Jungles, Inc.
Photographer: Steven Brooke **Completion date:** 2009 **Site area:** 4,047 sqm
Plants: Guiana Chestnut, Pond Apple, Character Sabal Palms, Mexican Horncone

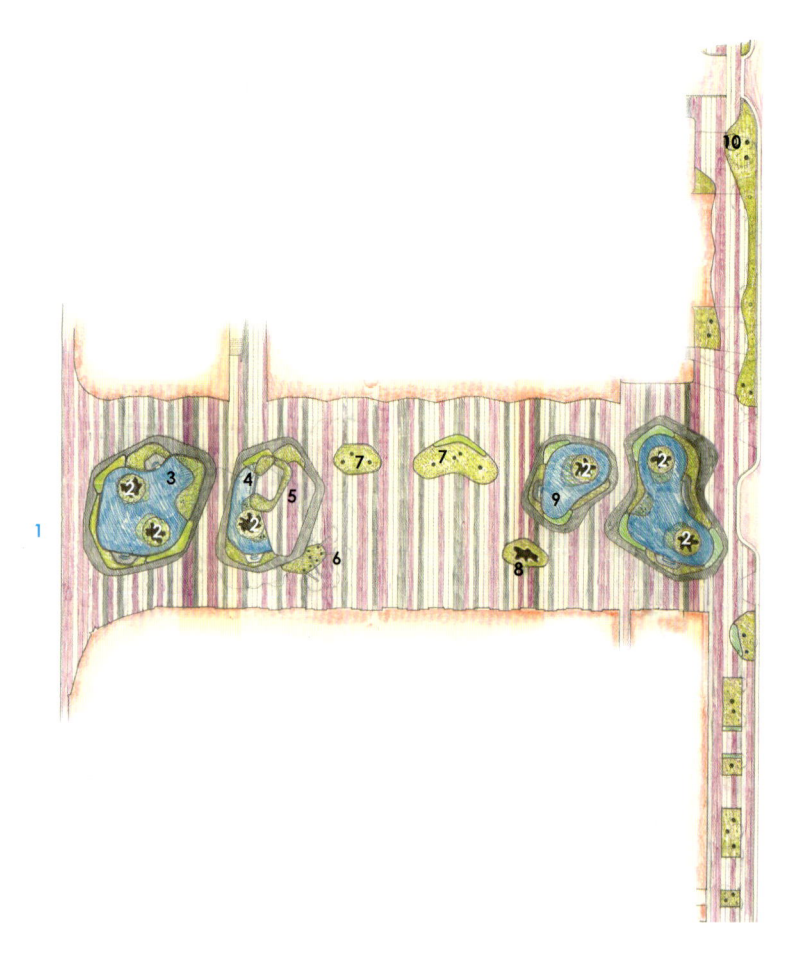

The design of 1111 Lincoln Road aspires to be bold, simple and timeless. The project was a collaboration between Herzog & de Meuron and Raymond Jungles, Inc. The main inspiration was a combination of admiration of the architect's previous work, and the natural Everglades ecosystem. It maintains compatibility with Morris Lapidus' original vision of an outdoor 'tropical' setting for shopping, dining and public gathering. There were, of course, challenges in the design. The scale of the structures cuts off most light for most of the day in the winter. That was one issue, but the grade change from north to south was also an issue. The designers want to maintain maximum visibility into, and through the space, yet had to create a vault for equipment.

The plaza is structured by water gardens, planting areas and varying width stripes of 'Pedra Portuguesa' that act as an interface by extending and defining pedestrian movement and visibility for the proposed and existing retail businesses, restaurants and entertainment venues.

A central open space defined by a slightly raised multi-functional platform was created for public gatherings, presentations and events. A variety of Florida native trees, palms and grasses recreate a sense of nature while providing a smooth transition between the building and human scale. By bringing nature into a built, urban environment, Raymond Jungles has created an 'Urban Glade', as coined by the City of Miami Beach Planning Department members.

1. Alton Road
2. Specimen Cypress Trees and Pond Apple
3. Water Garden 1
4. Water Garden 2
5. Raised Multi-Functional Platform
6. Character Sabal Palms
7. Specimen Live Oak Trees and Wild Peanut
8. Guiana Chestnut Tree
9. Water Garden 3
10. Planting Along Lenox Avenue

Right: The various plants recreate a sense of nature while providing a smooth transition between the building and human scale

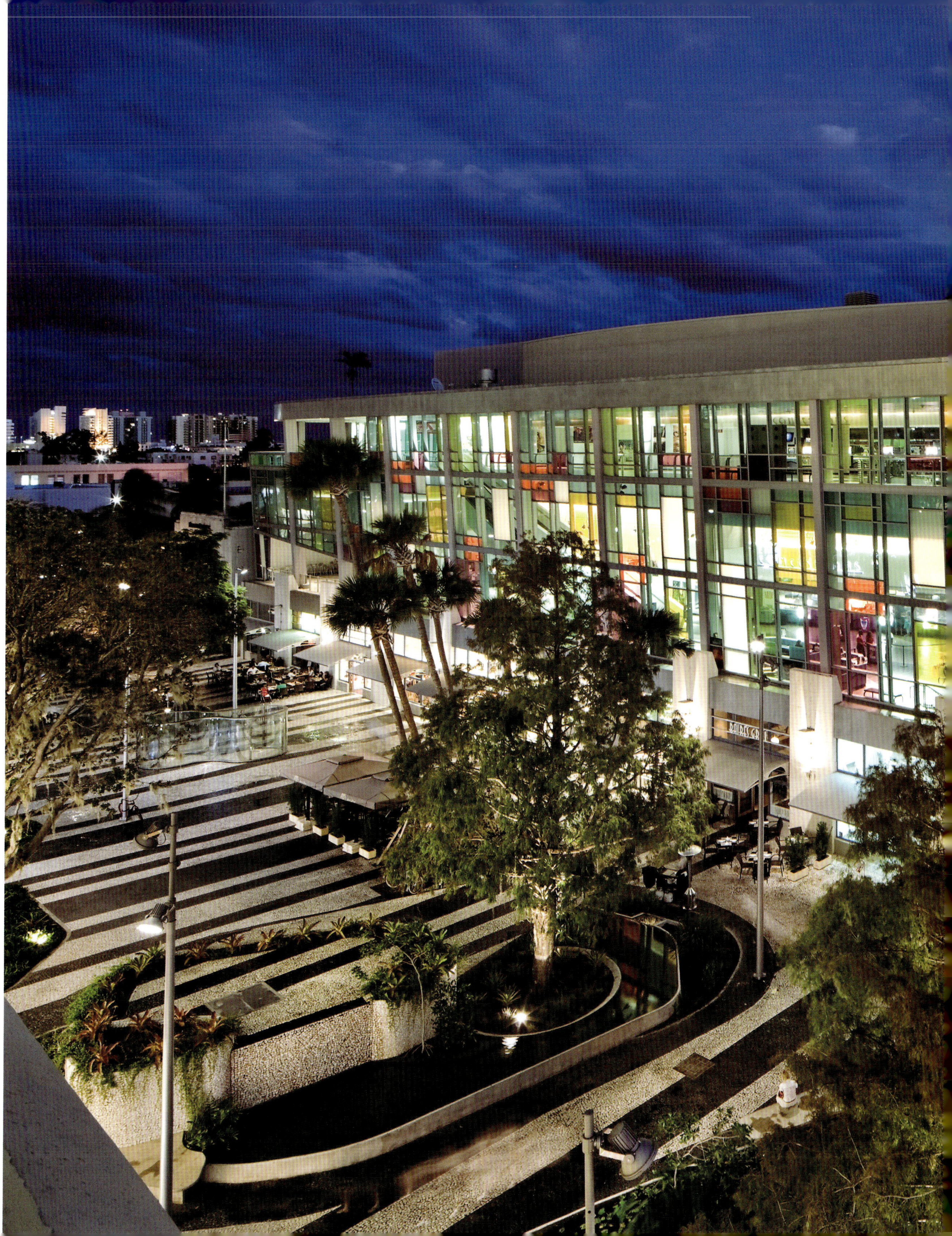

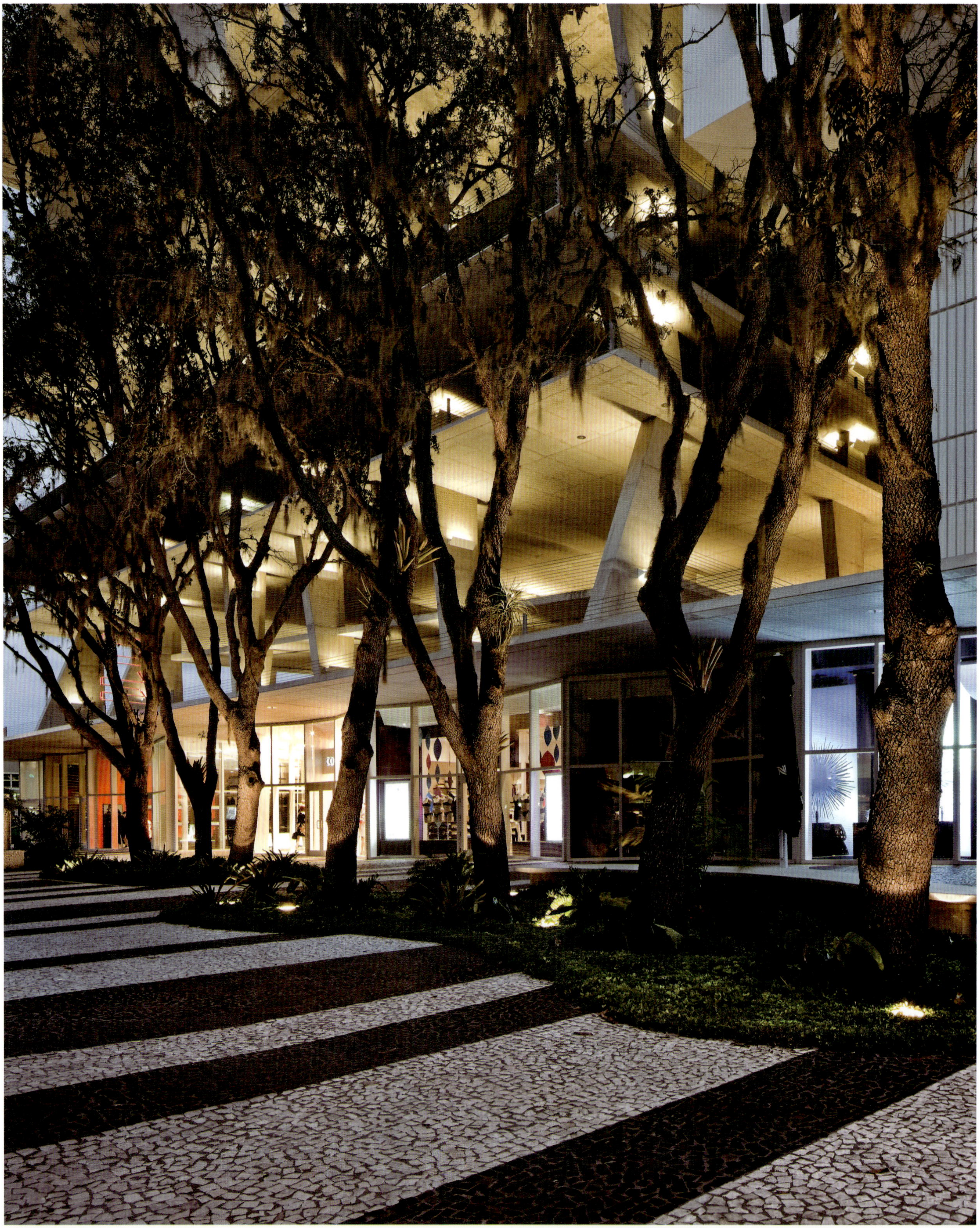

Upper right: The urban glade

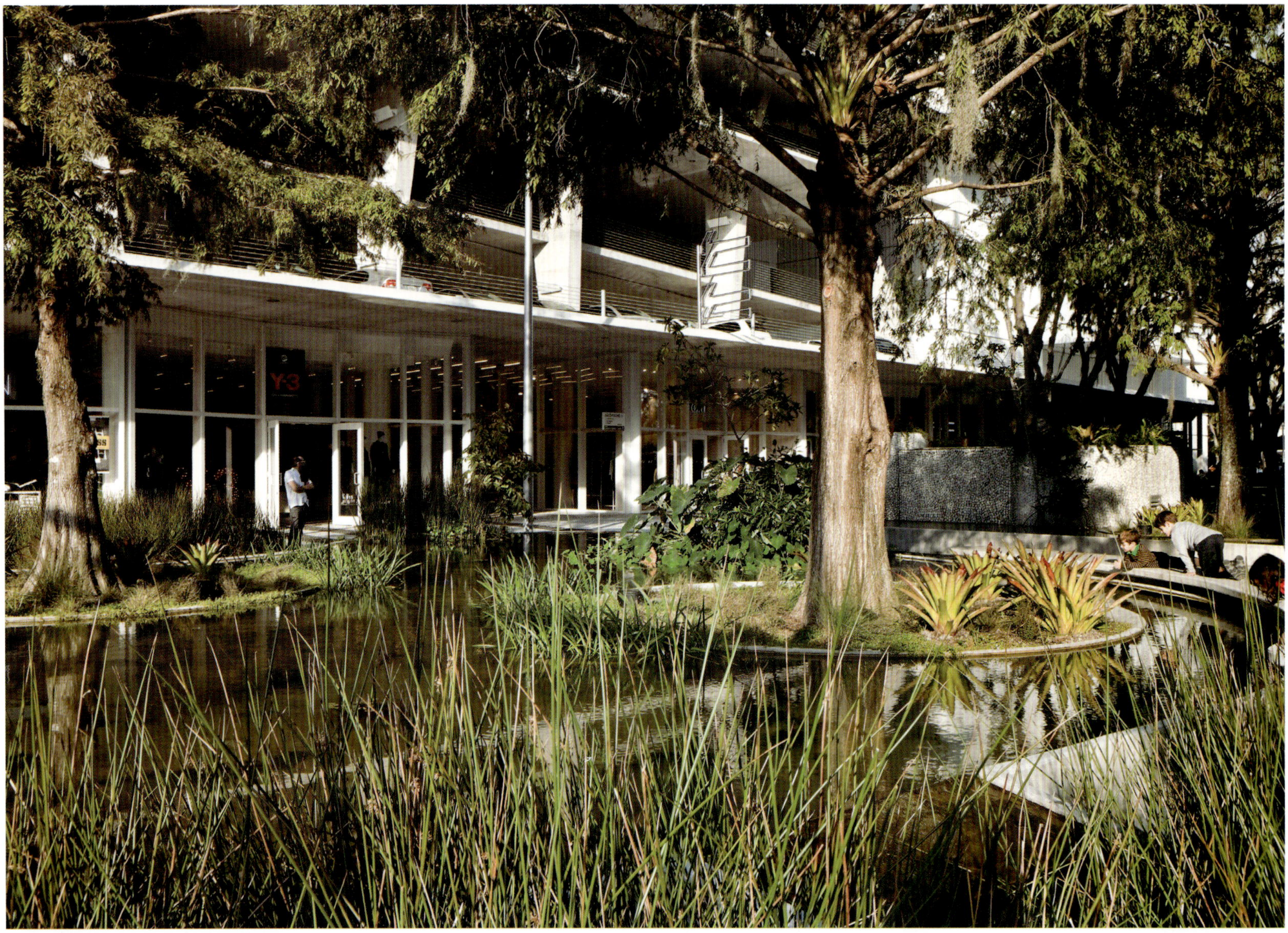
Y-3

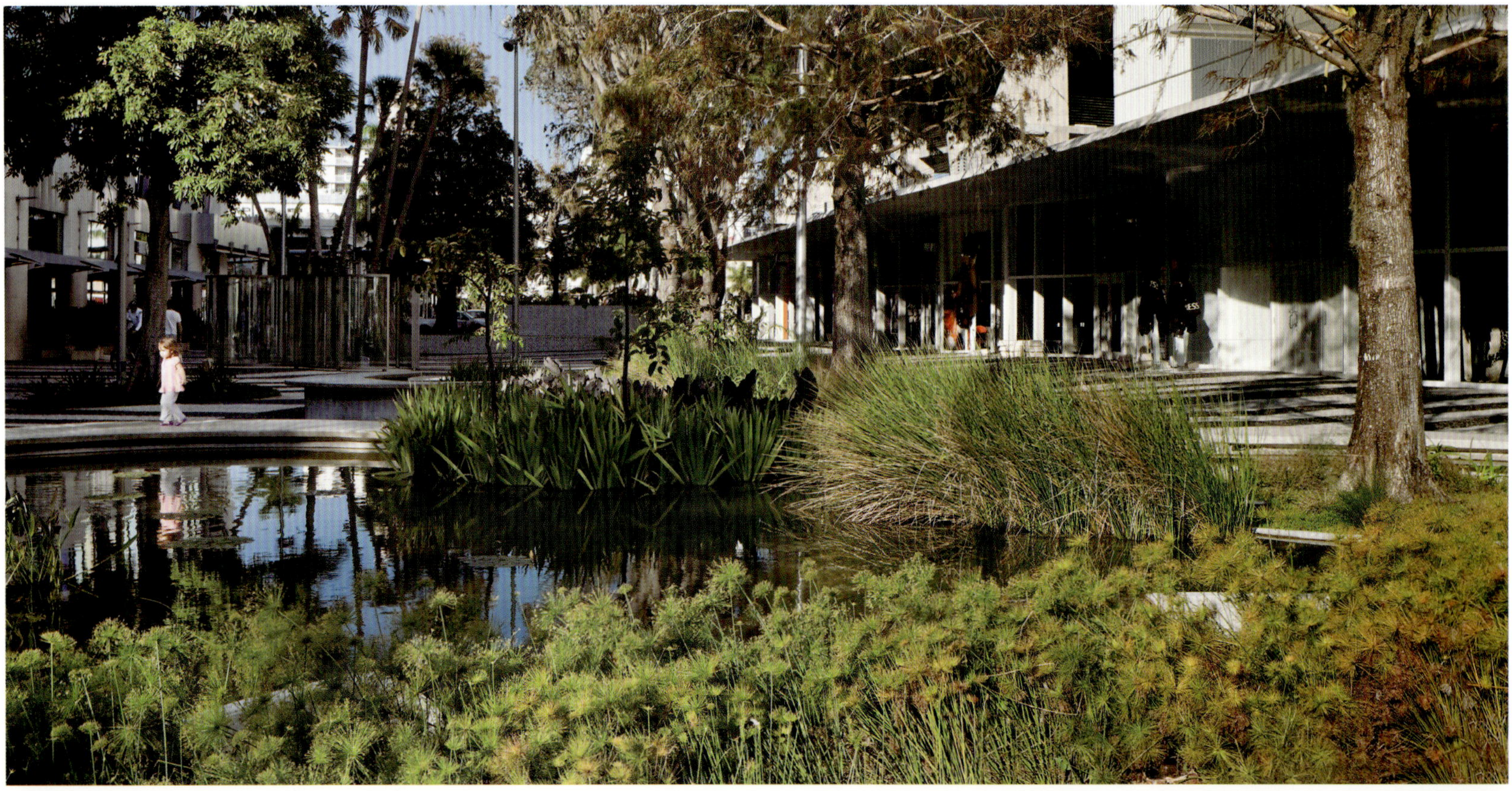

Upper right: The outdoor tropical setting for shopping, dining and public gathering

Plaza Dalí, Madrid

Location: Madrid, Spain **Designer:** Francisco Mangado **Photographer:** Miguel de Guzman, Roland Halbe (127) **Completion date:** 2005 **Site area:** 20,000 sqm

The new project follows two objectives: through the improvement, repaving and restructuring of the complex, to endow it with a formal significance in tune with its importance as a central public space of the city, but also to attain a certain degree of comfort to allow neighbors, who up to now contemplated this area with some distance, to make it their own.

The new paving represents the unit as a whole. A 'dense' paving, built in granite and bronze, highlighted by the sculptures of Francesc Torres, as well as the LED strips that give the square a new geometric order and visual appeal.

The aforementioned framed spaces, with a more pleasant and cozy scale, are materialized here with landscaped surfaces that rise from the paving and slope in the form of wedges filled with soil and deep enough to contain vegetation and trees, as well as urban furniture pieces and benches that turn this space into a welcoming living area.

The consideration of light as a primary 'material' that helps to give shape to the new configuration is another priority. Aside from its use as a physical part of the pavement, light also acts as an element that helps to transform the underground parking accesses (for both pedestrians and cars), whose location could not be changed. So though these accesses initially seemed to be encumbering elements, in the end they have become illuminated pieces that earn a special significance, thanks to their size and location, within the new square.

1. Pavements
2. Rest Zone with Chairs
3. Children's Playing Area

Right: View by night

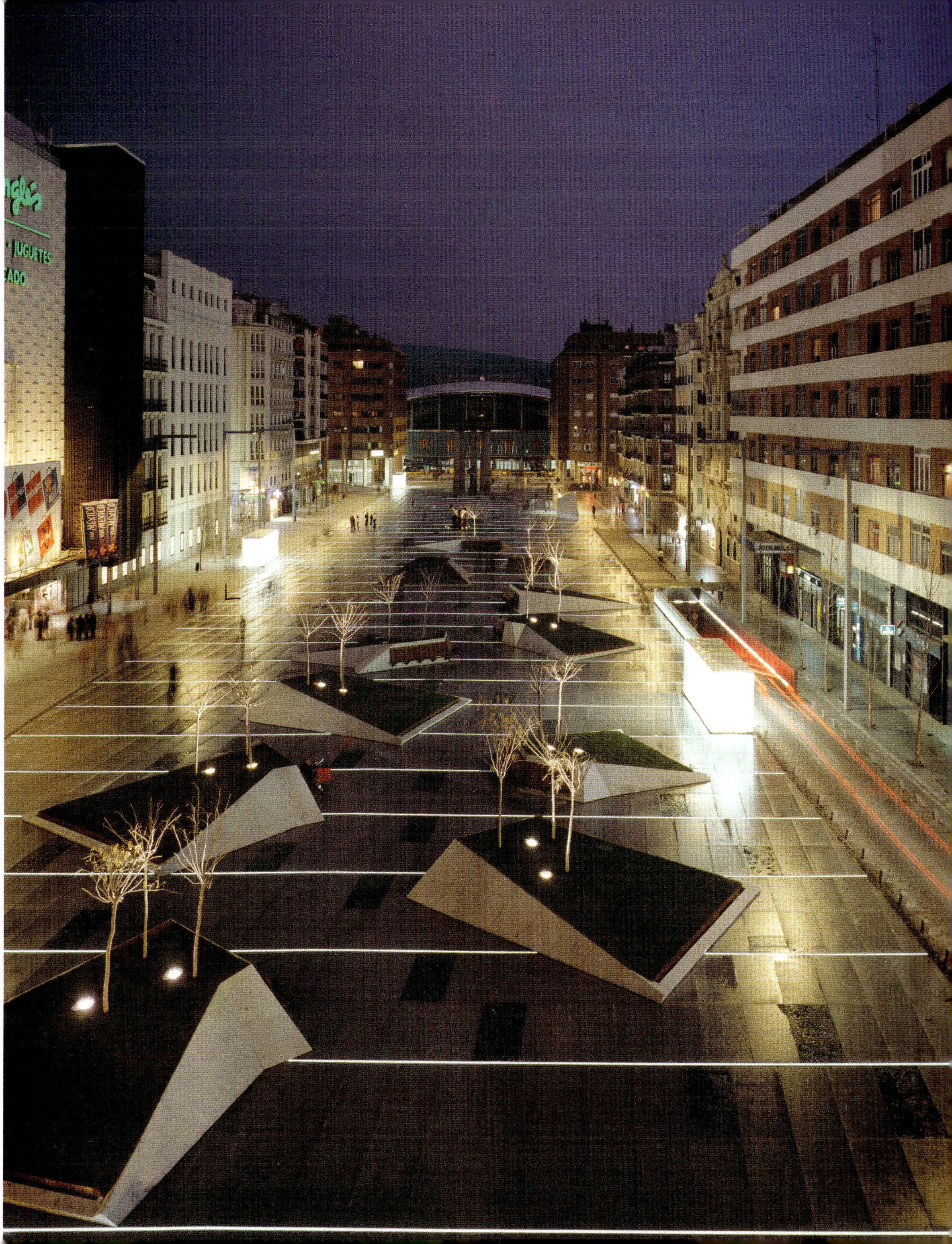
JUGUETES

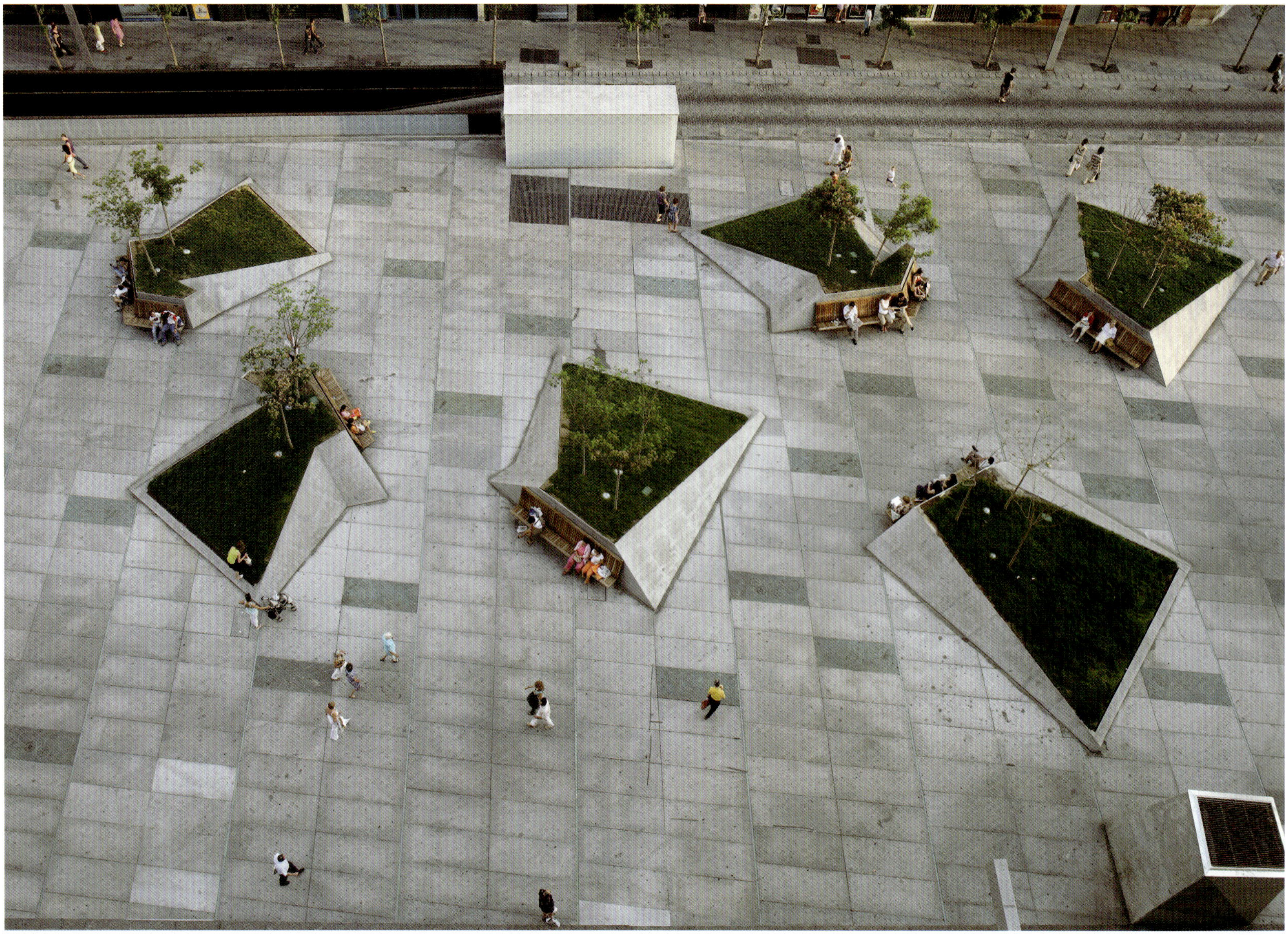

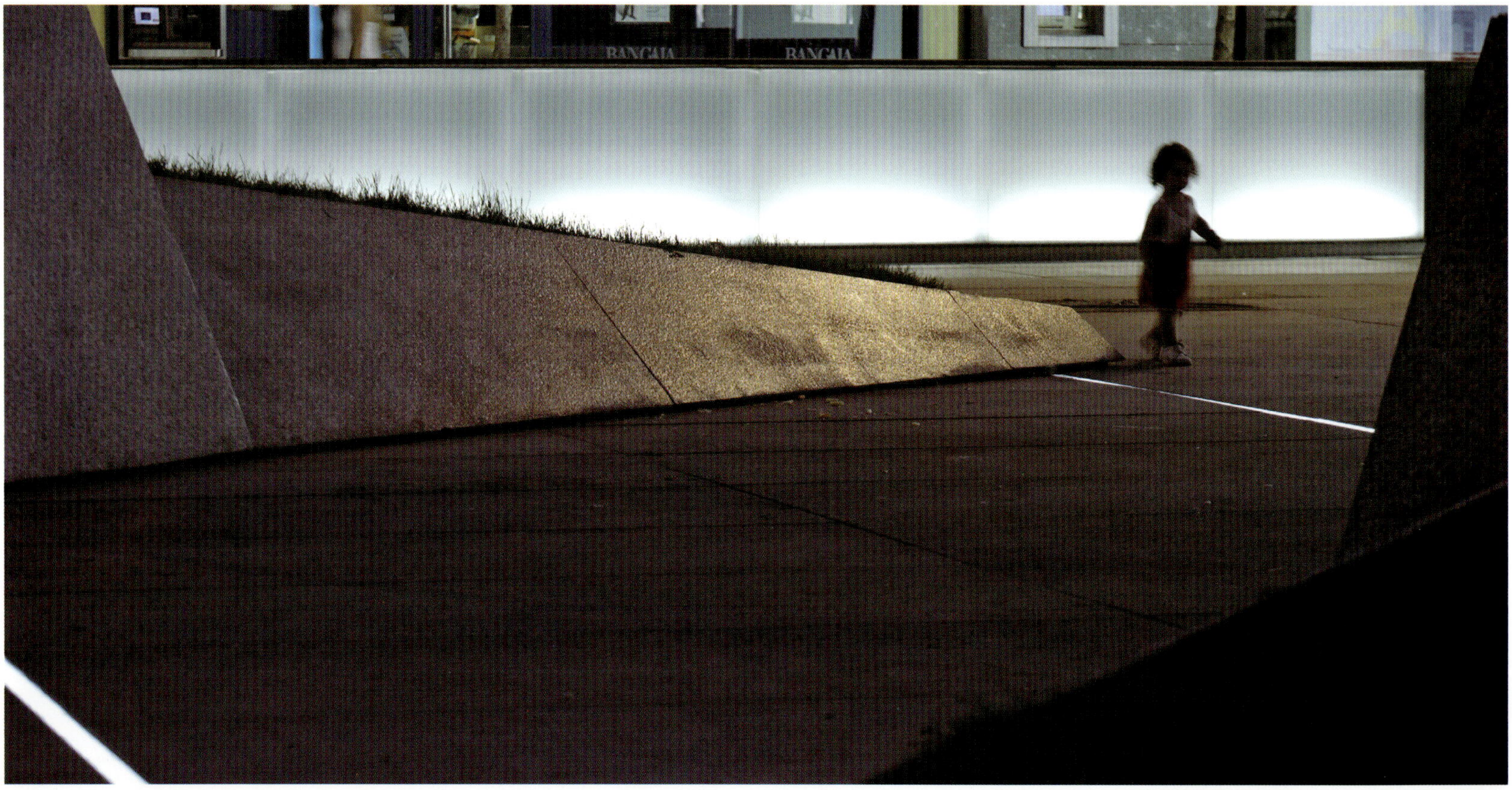
BANCAJA
BANCAJA

Upper left: General view
Lower left: The LED strips running through the granite slabs give the paving surface scale, geometry and rhythm
Upper right: Wedged containers with benches
Lower right: The granite paving is dotted by pieces cast in bronze designed by Francesc Torres

Jockey Plaza Boulevard

Location: Lima, Peru **Designer:** José Orrego (Metropolis Peru) **Photographer:** Metropolis Peru **Completion date:** 2010 **Site area:** 5,610 sqm

This project has been developed in two levels, recreating a villa with small buildings and creating a controlled urban experience. The idea of this proposal is to create a special and fully equipped meeting point as well as a place to interact in a small scale.

That´s how the scheme is based on three articulating elements:

1. The main circular square, which is the most important space and thought as a big attraction. It is playful and its use is associated with entertainment.
2. The central axis, symbolic element that will become the icon of the mall.
3. The new technology applied to create a day-night experience by the use of LEDs, landscaping and facade treatments.

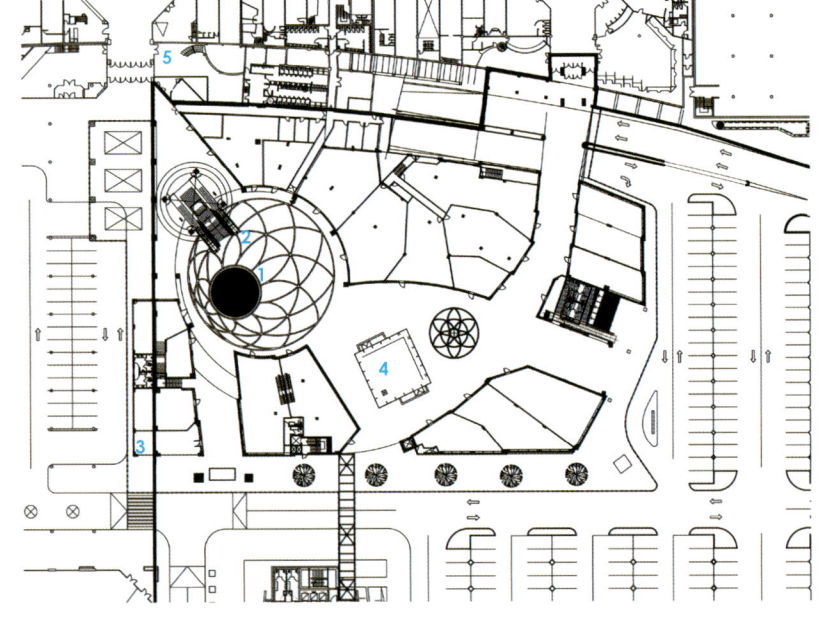

1. Plaza Center
2. Stairs
3. Block 1
4. Block 3
5. Shopping Mall

Right: Plaza center

BILLABONG.
crocs
feel the love
MONT BLANC
BOSS
HUGO BOSS
Coming Soon
Cartier

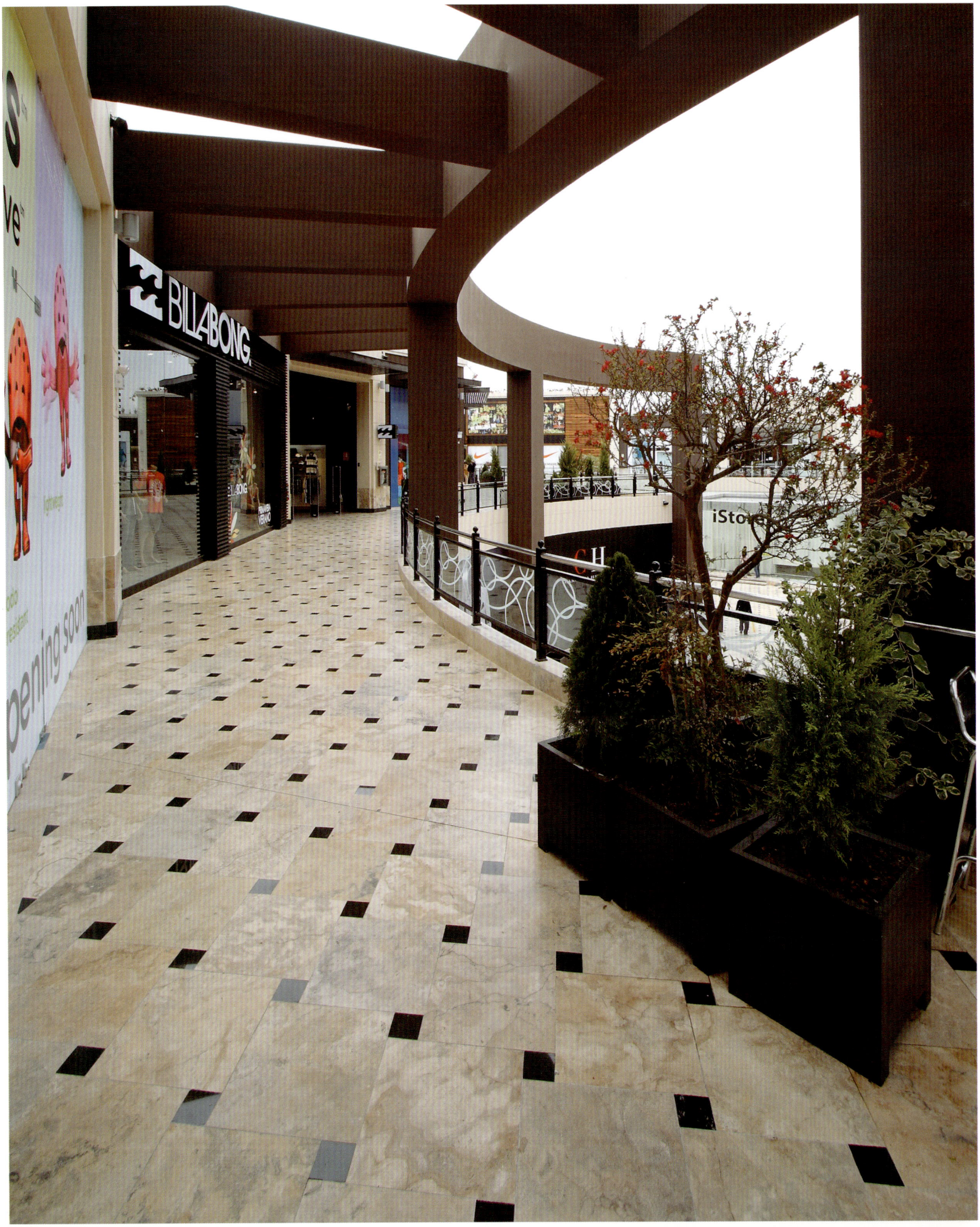
BILLABONG.

Left: Shopping area
Upper right: Fountain in plaza center
Lower right: Plaza center with green lights

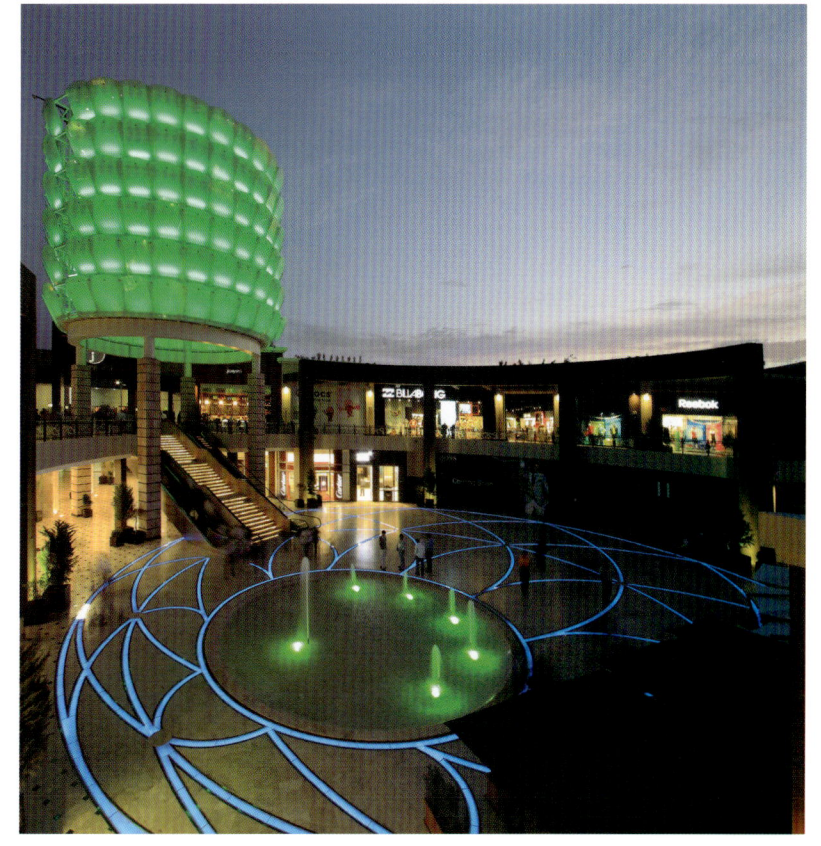

Circle on Cavill

Location: Queensland, Australia **Designer:** PLACE Design Group **Photographer:** Gollings Photography, Denise Yates **Completion date:** 2007 **Site area:** 15,400 sqm

A landmark project in a landmark location, Circle on Cavill in Surfers Paradise combines residential apartment living with a vibrant and contemporary commercial precinct. An award-winning project, this development has set new benchmarks in Surfers Paradise, and reaffirms the special position Cavill Avenue occupies in the public consciousness.

The active, self-policing and dynamic environment offered to the residents integrates elements/materials that guarantee a first class finish to a potentially harsh environment being only 100 meters to the ocean. Water feature placement and plant selection have been made with careful consideration of winds, view lines and amenity of adjacent residences.

Offering heated, lap and lagoon style pools overlooking the retail precinct, Circle on Cavill recognizes the residents need for relaxation away from the 'buzz' of Surfers Paradise. The landscape scale has been sensitive to the building resident's requirements, integrating social zones; children's play areas, with BBQ facilities to allow for different levels of interaction and personal privacy.

The iconic architecture of Circle on Cavill stands out against the Surfers Paradise skyline and serves as a readily identifiable place marker from afar. Up close the strong connection at ground level combined with a fully integrated urban design creates a strong sense of place.

The success of Circle on Cavill exhibits an understanding of the critical synergies, that combined are the three triple bottom line elements of sustainability: social, economic and environmental.

1. Gold Coast Highway South Bound
2. Cavill West
3. Ferny Ave
4. Arcade
5. Feature Pavement Band
6. Tall Canopy Trees
7. Feature Radial Bands
8. Linear Water Feature
9. Lawn
10. Pavement Cross Links
11. Jumbo Screen
12. Ramp from Cavill
13. Cavill Water Feature
14. Stairs and Escalators
15. Water Feature
16. Tower Entry
17. Porte Cochere

Right: Central plaza water feature with view to mixed-use tower

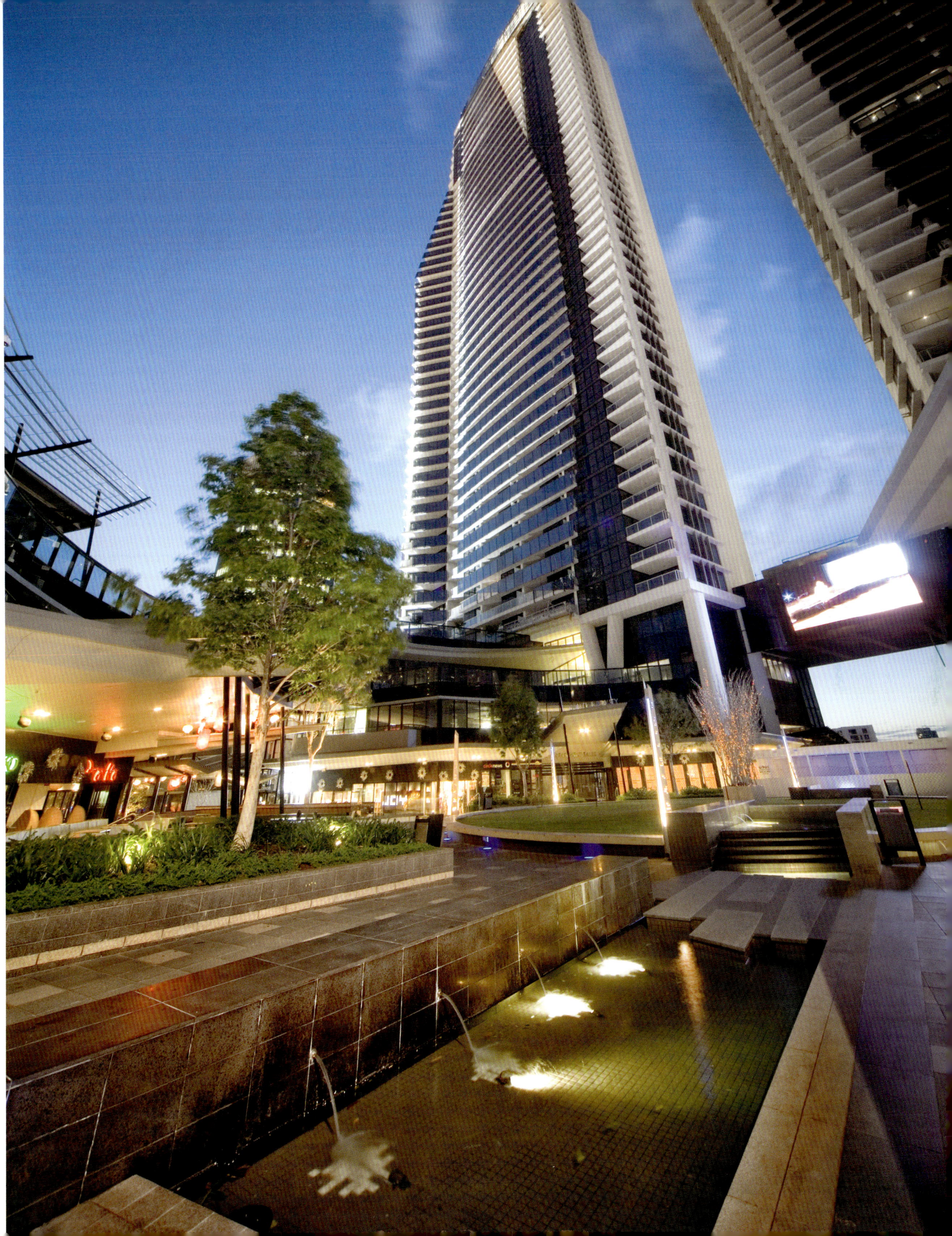

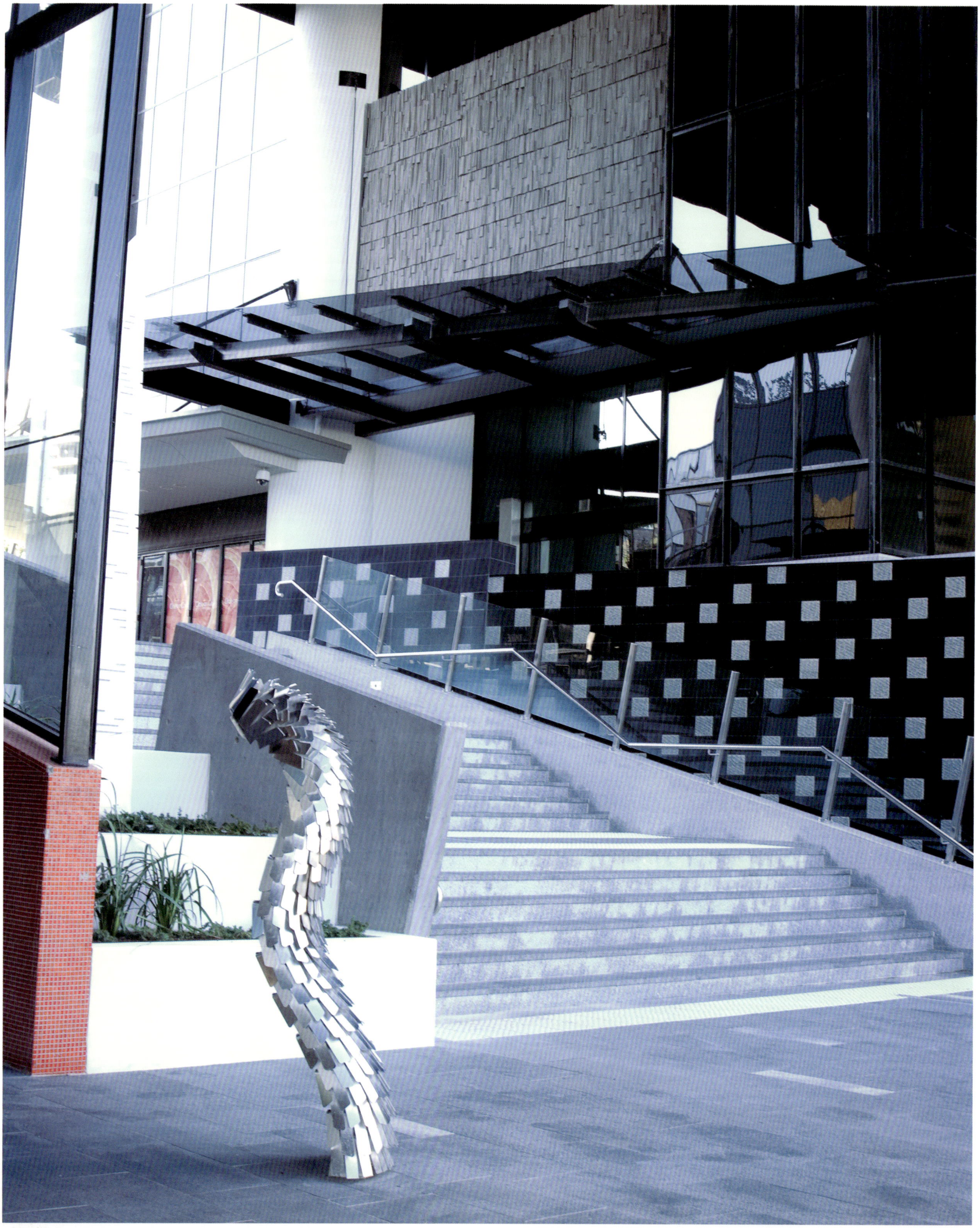

Left: Public art and stairs to central plaza
Upper right: A corner of central plaza
Lower right: Detail of public art

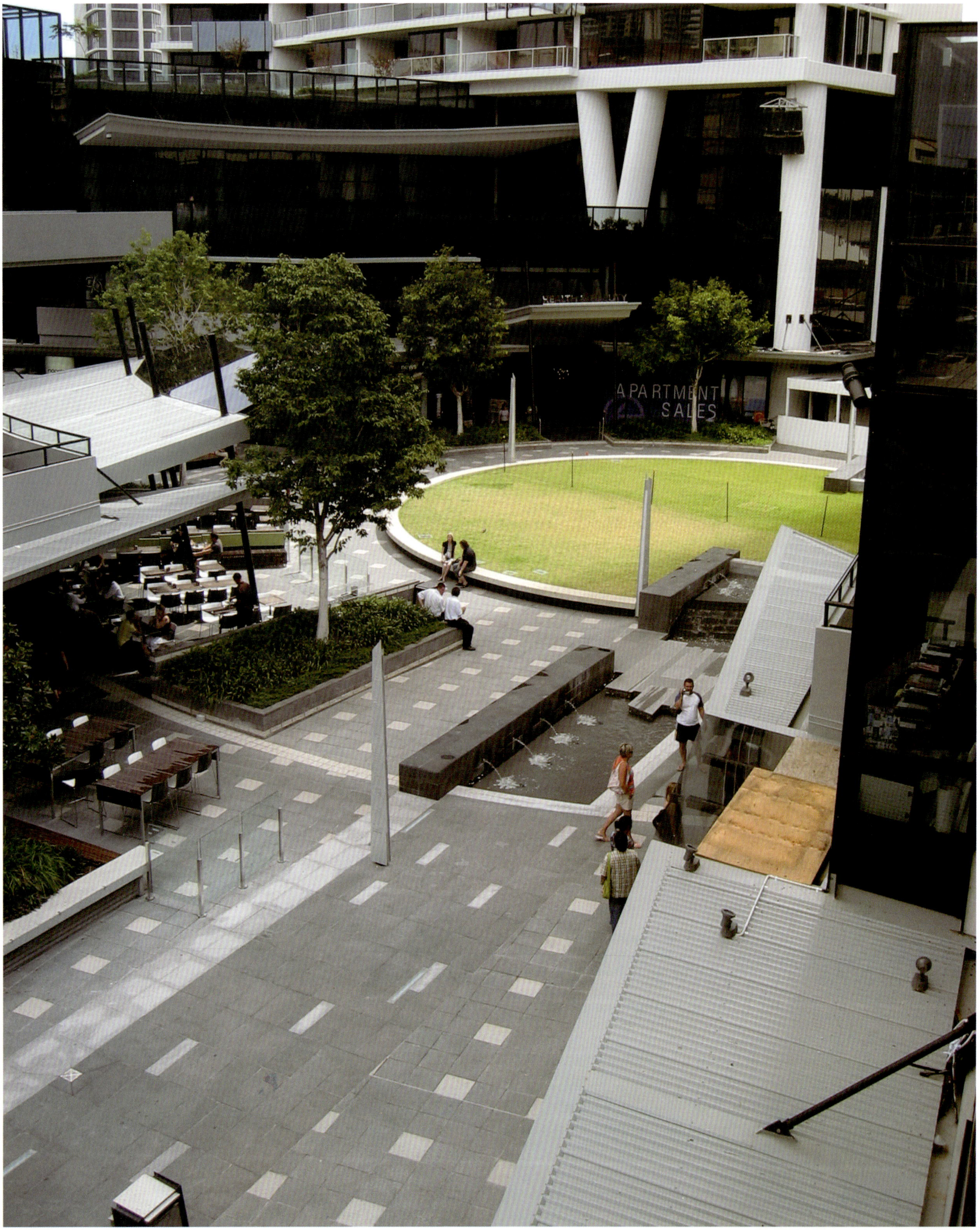
APARTMENT
SALES

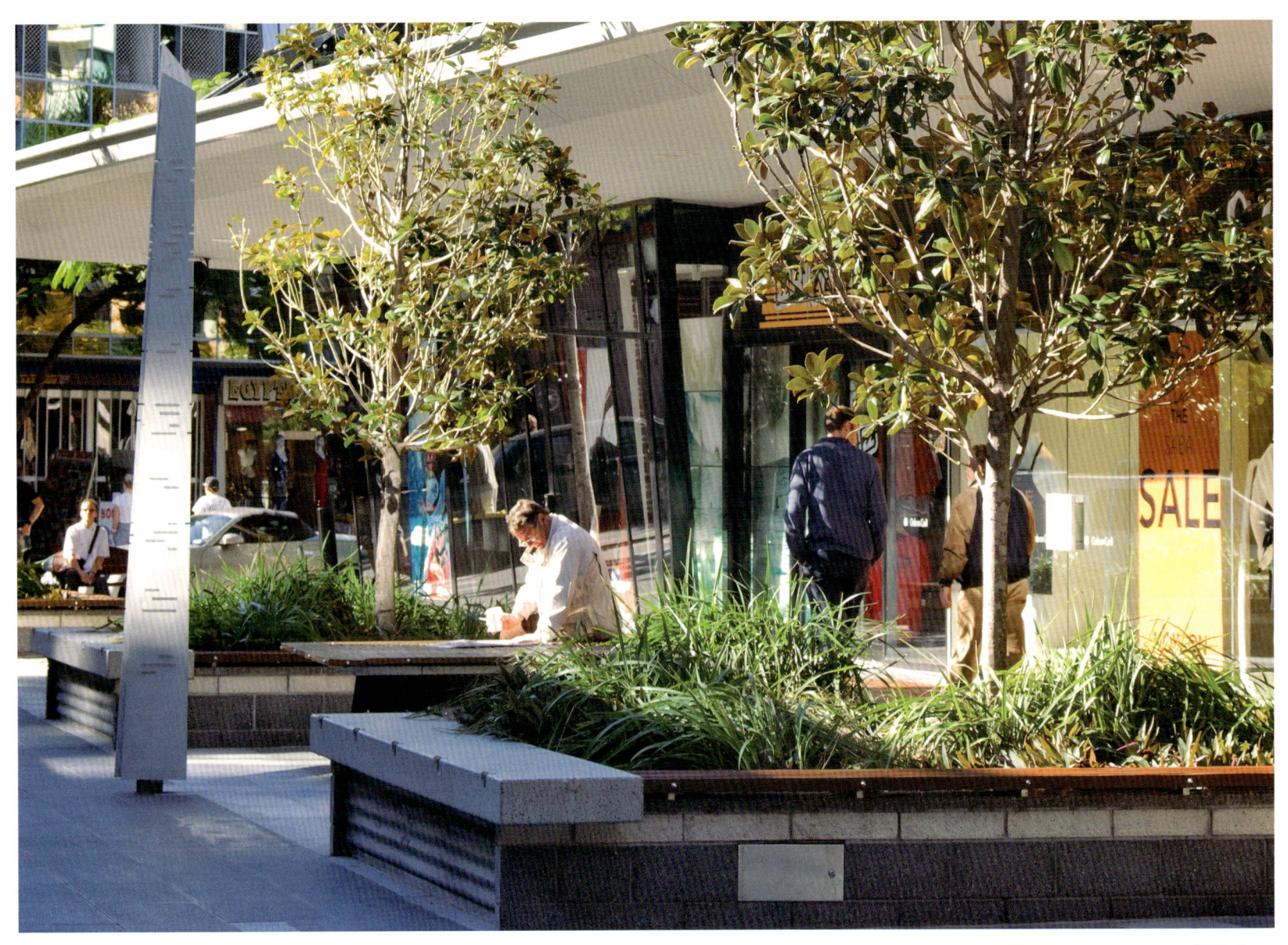

Left: Central plaza
Upper right: Planters in central plaza
Lower right: Detail of stair handrail

Santa Monica Place

Location: Santa Monica, USA **Designer:** The Jerde Partnership, Inc.
Photographer: Macerich, The Jerde Partnership, Inc. **Completion date:** 2010
Site area: 40,468 sqm

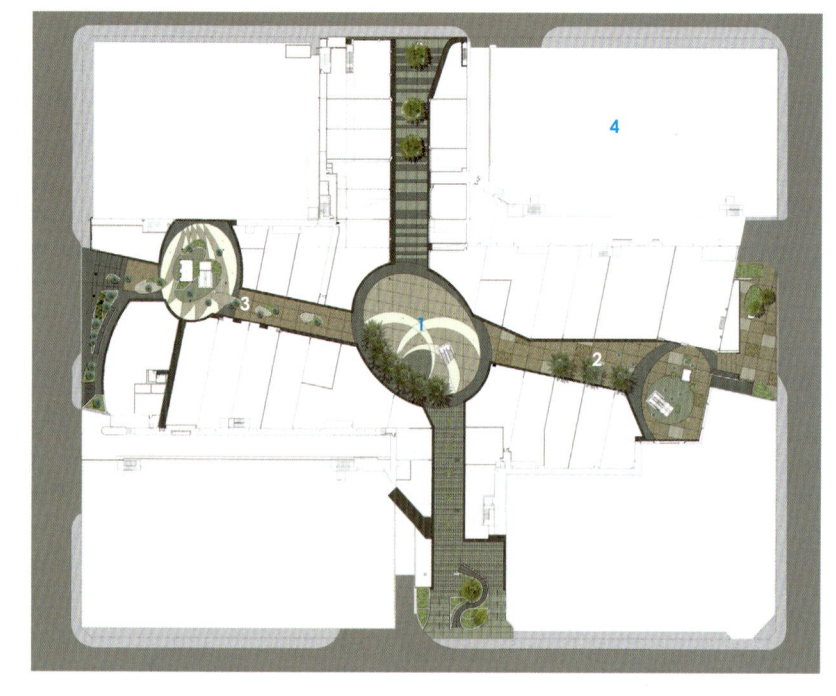

The new Santa Monica Place changes an obsolete, enclosed, multi-level mall into a dynamic urban heart that celebrates the cultural and geographic openness that makes Santa Monica a great place to live, work, play and visit.

Commissioned by Macerich to renovate the outdated mall, The Jerde Partnership set out to create a vibrant and intimate public setting rather than a shopping center. Blending timeless urban principles that predate conventional malls with its organic approach to retail design, Jerde carefully and intricately wove the project into the existing city fabric. The firm opened up the mall by removing the roof, creating generous open spaces, and establishing pedestrian connections that extend the famous Third Street Promenade and strengthen the surrounding city core. By incorporating forms, materials, and landscaping that are found throughout the city, Jerde enhanced the projects natural fit, both aesthetically and functionally, in the seaside village of Santa Monica.

The new Santa Monica Place replaces a dead mall with a vibrant, open-air district that fills in a vital missing piece within thriving downtown Santa Monica. By seamlessly connecting its popular and diverse surrounding uses, creating new public spaces, and attracting a new caliber of retail tenants, including new department store anchor concepts, it will become the hub of Santa Monica and create a new destination in greater Los Angeles.

Award description:
Southern California Development Forum 2010 Design Award – Commercial category

1. Plaza
2. East Galleria
3. West Galleria
4. Parking Structure

Right: Street promenade view

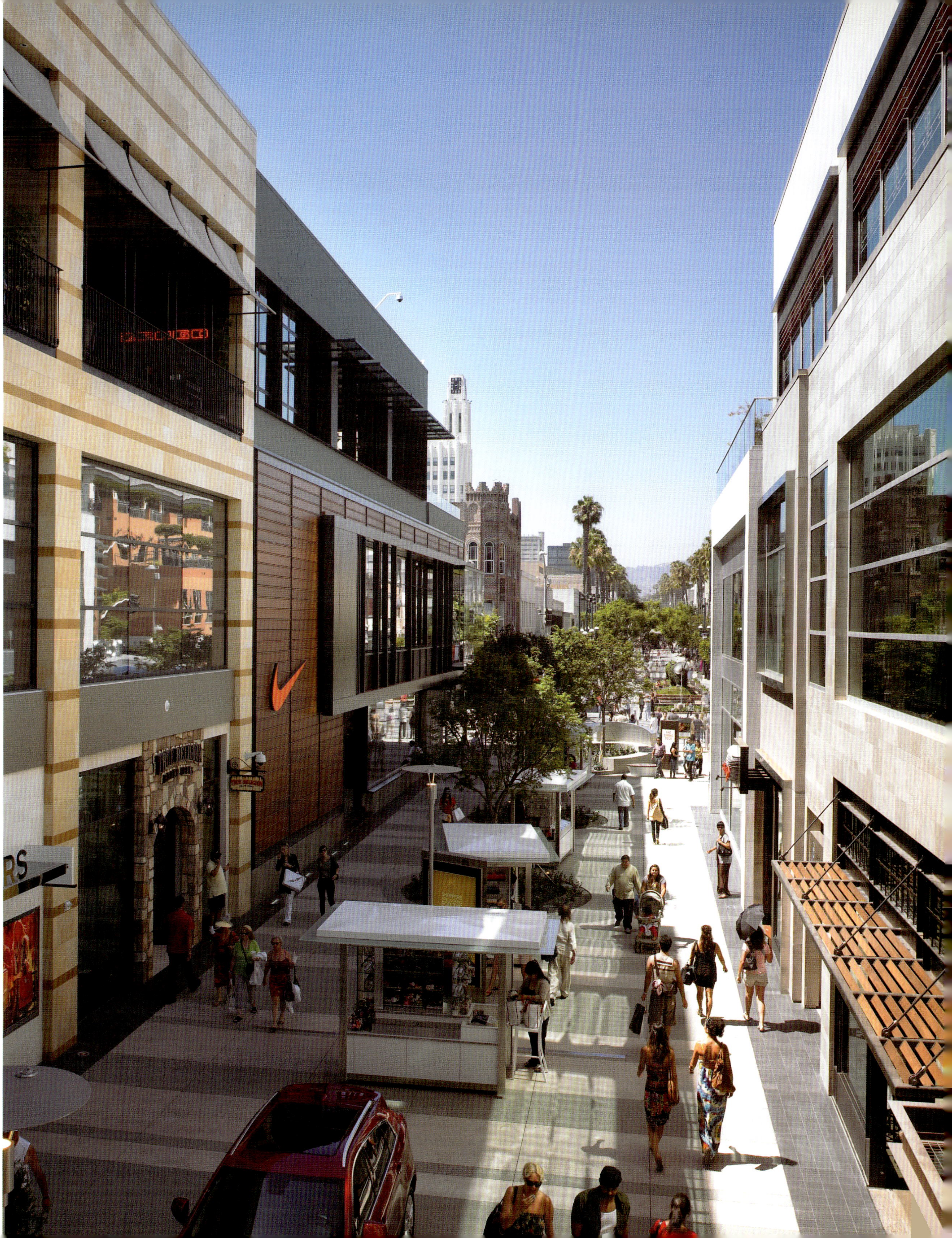

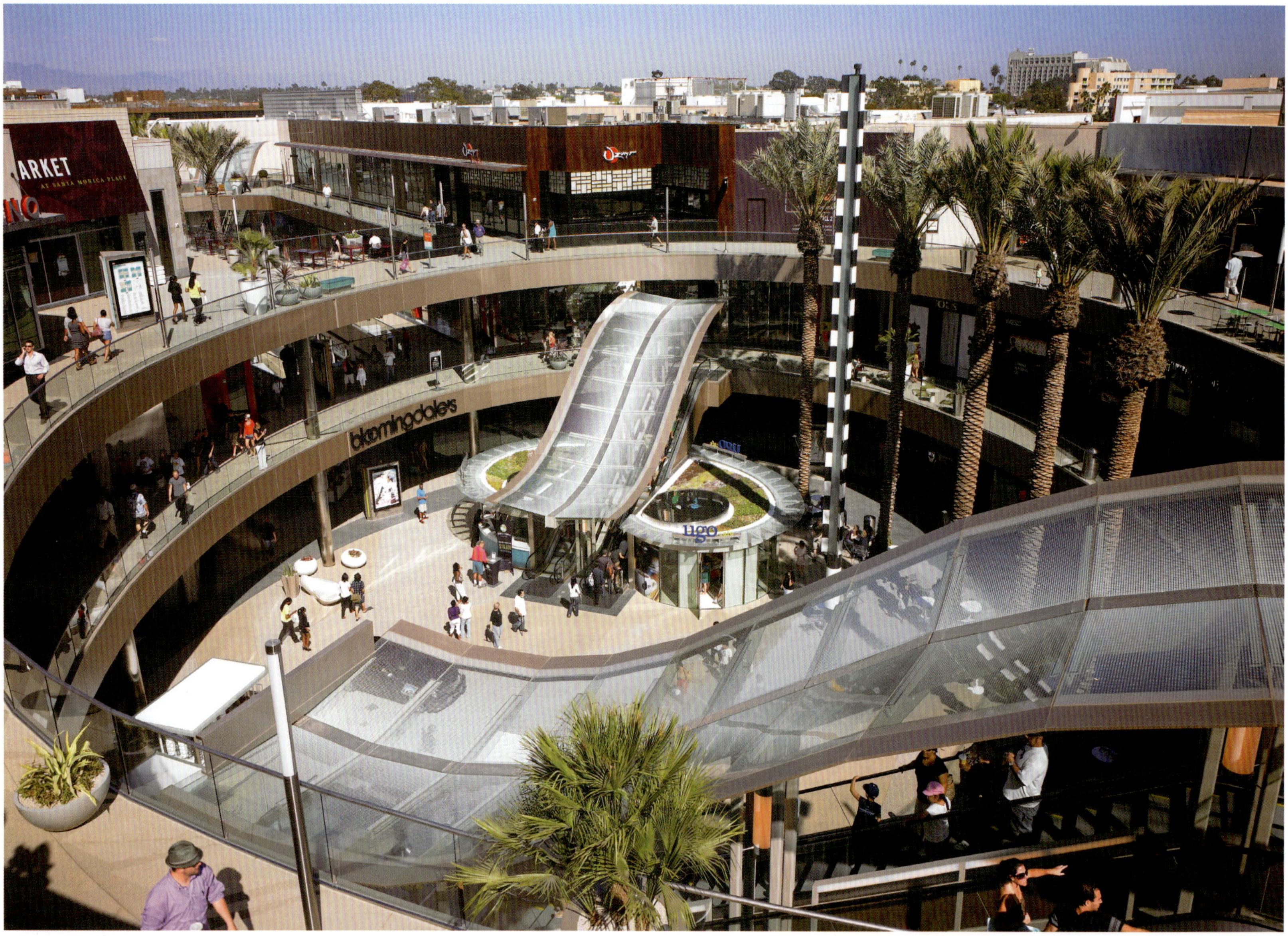
ARKET
bloomingdale's

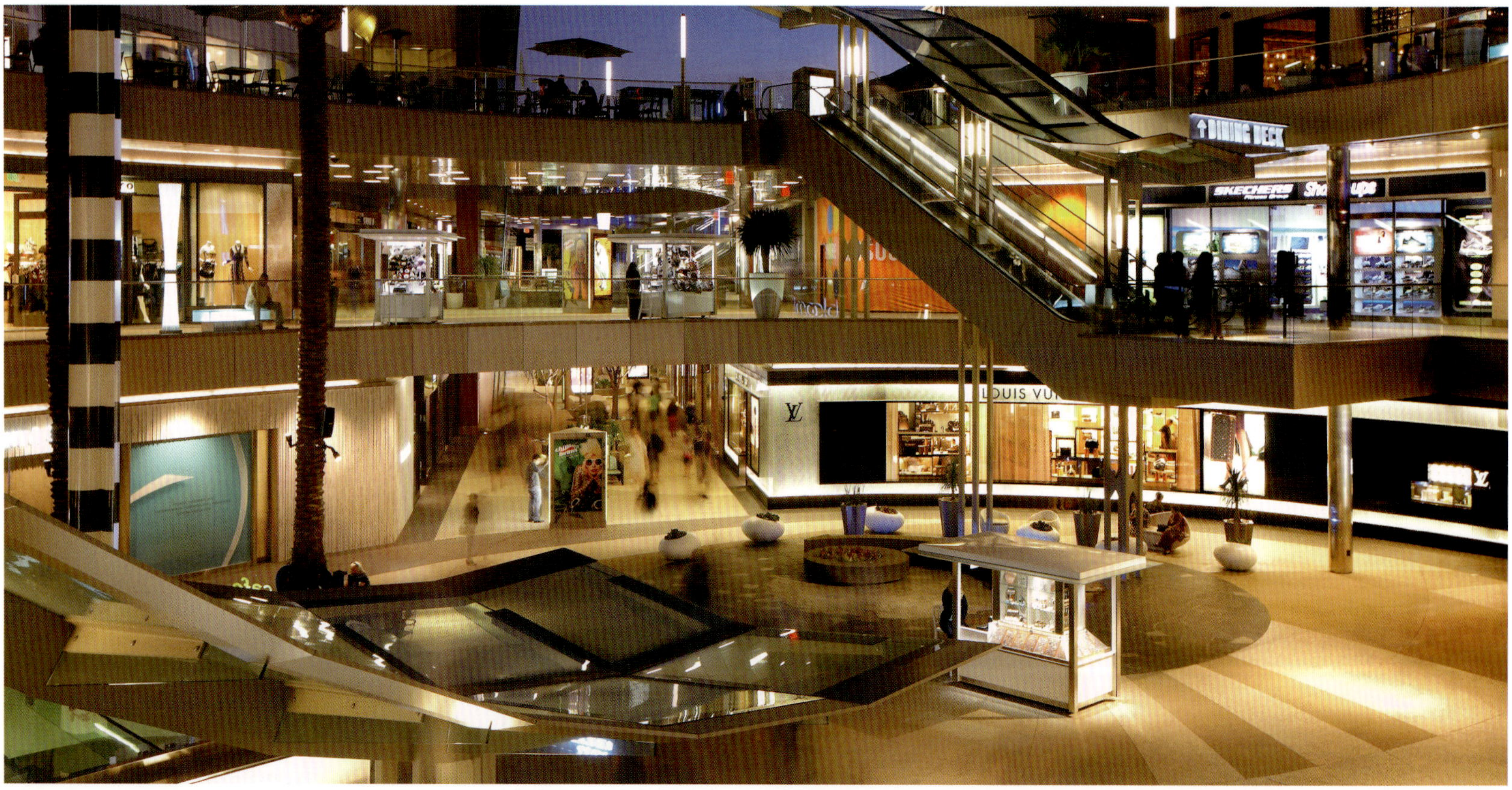
DINING DECK
SKECHERS
LOUIS VU

142~143

Upper left: Central court from roof
Lower left: Night view of the central court
Lower Right: Dining deck view

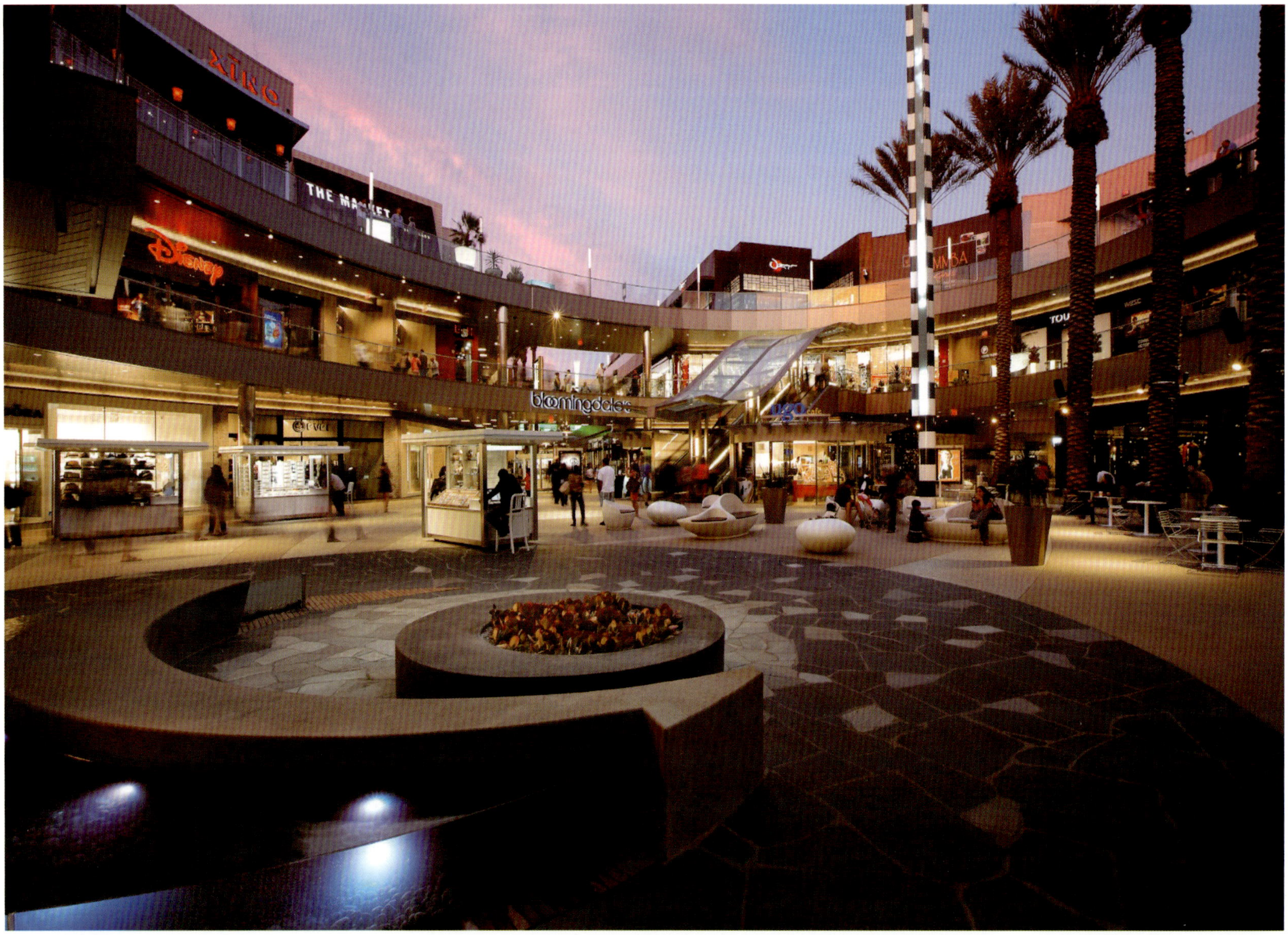
Disney
bloomingdale's
ugo

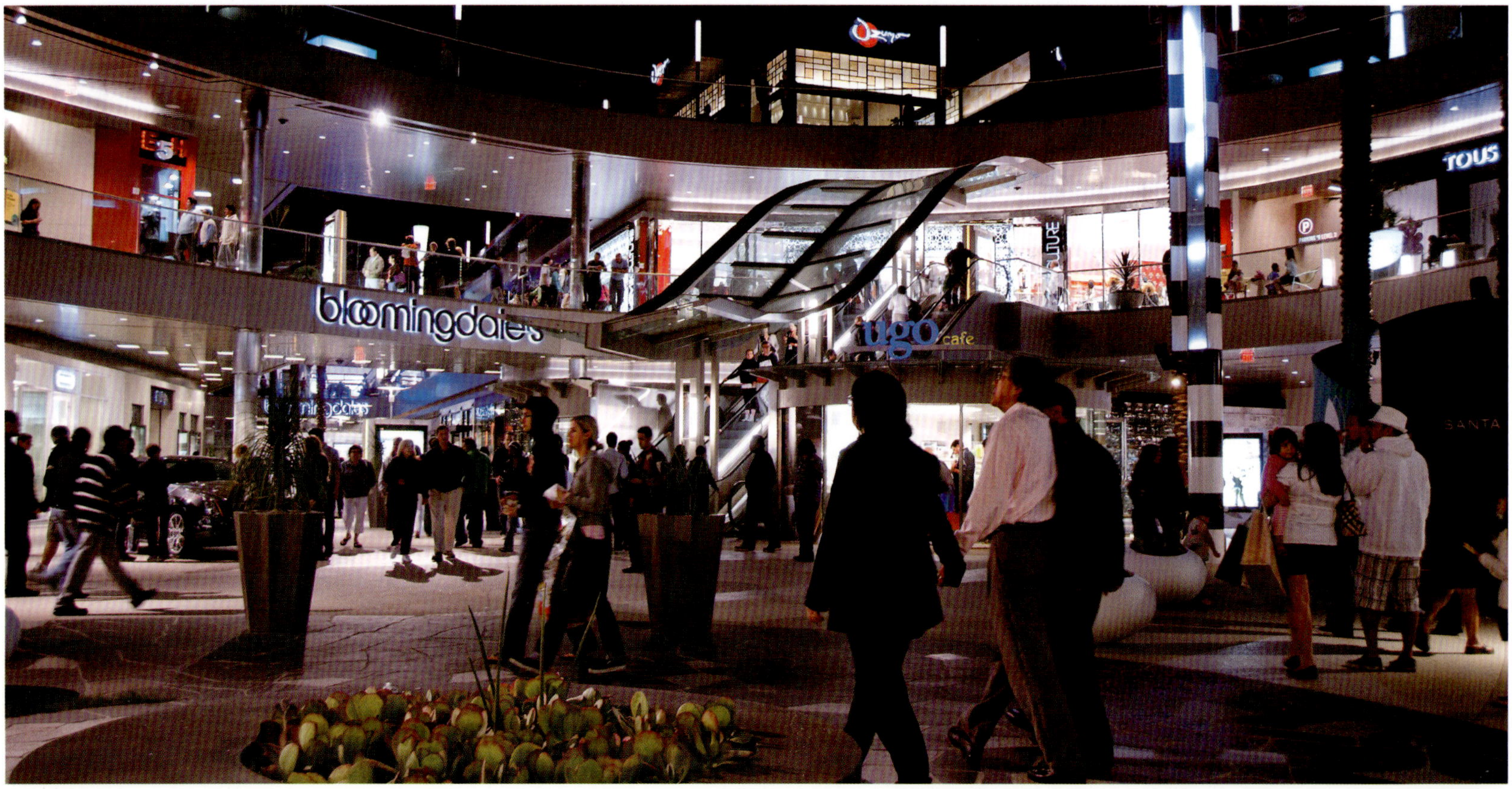
bloomingdale's
ugo cafe
TOUS

Upper left: Central court from ground at night
Upper right: Aerial view of central court

Southport Central

Location: Queensland, Australia **Designer:** PLACE Design Group **Photographer:** Aperture Photography, Denise Yates **Completion date:** 2008 **Site area:** 18,900 sqm

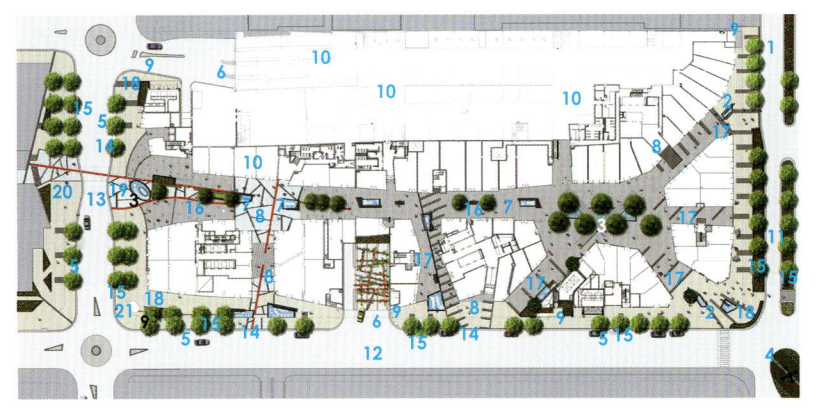

Southport Central is a multi-purpose development located at the corner of Scarborough and Lawson Streets Southport, Queensland, Australia, the business 'hub' of the Gold Coast.

This three-stage project consists of residential apartment towers located above an integrated commercial and retail shopping precinct in Southport. The design marries the development with the three surrounding streetscape and the creation of a linear walkway connecting the city block from one side to the other was an integral part of the overall planning. Extensive recreational facilities were incorporated on the upper podium level to complement the mixed-use development.

The incorporation of landscape planting in public spaces can enhance the urban environment and contribute to Southport's identity as a usable and pleasant place. The planting of trees and vegetation is an effective measure to implement the subtropical character and provide shade and thermal comfort for the users of the space. The use of native trees and vegetation in parks, street revitalization schemes and other public places will provide native habitat for native fauna and contribute to the environmental sustainability of Southport.

The implementation of high quality urban furniture and materials, such as seats, lighting and ground surface treatment are essential in determining the aesthetic quality and functionality of the place.

1. Bus Stop Zone
2. Major Visual Attraction Water Feature
3. Water Feature at Plaza
4. Roundabout with Directional Planting
5. Loading Zone/Carparking
6. Carpark Access Ramp
7. Linear Water Features
8. Feature Pavement Highlights Residential Tower & Commercial Entries
9. Property Boundary
10. Level 3 Recreation Area
11. Scarborough Street Streetscape
12. Lawson Street Streetscape
13. Garden Street Streetscape
14. Set Down Zones
15. Street Tree Continuation
16. Internal Pedestrian Street/Plaza
17. Pedestrian Linkages to Plaza
18. Open Sightlines through Street Corners
19. Public Plaza Addressing Library Civic Space
20. Upgraded Pavement and Plaza to Library
21. Artwork/Sculpture

Right: Podium gardens throughout the plaza

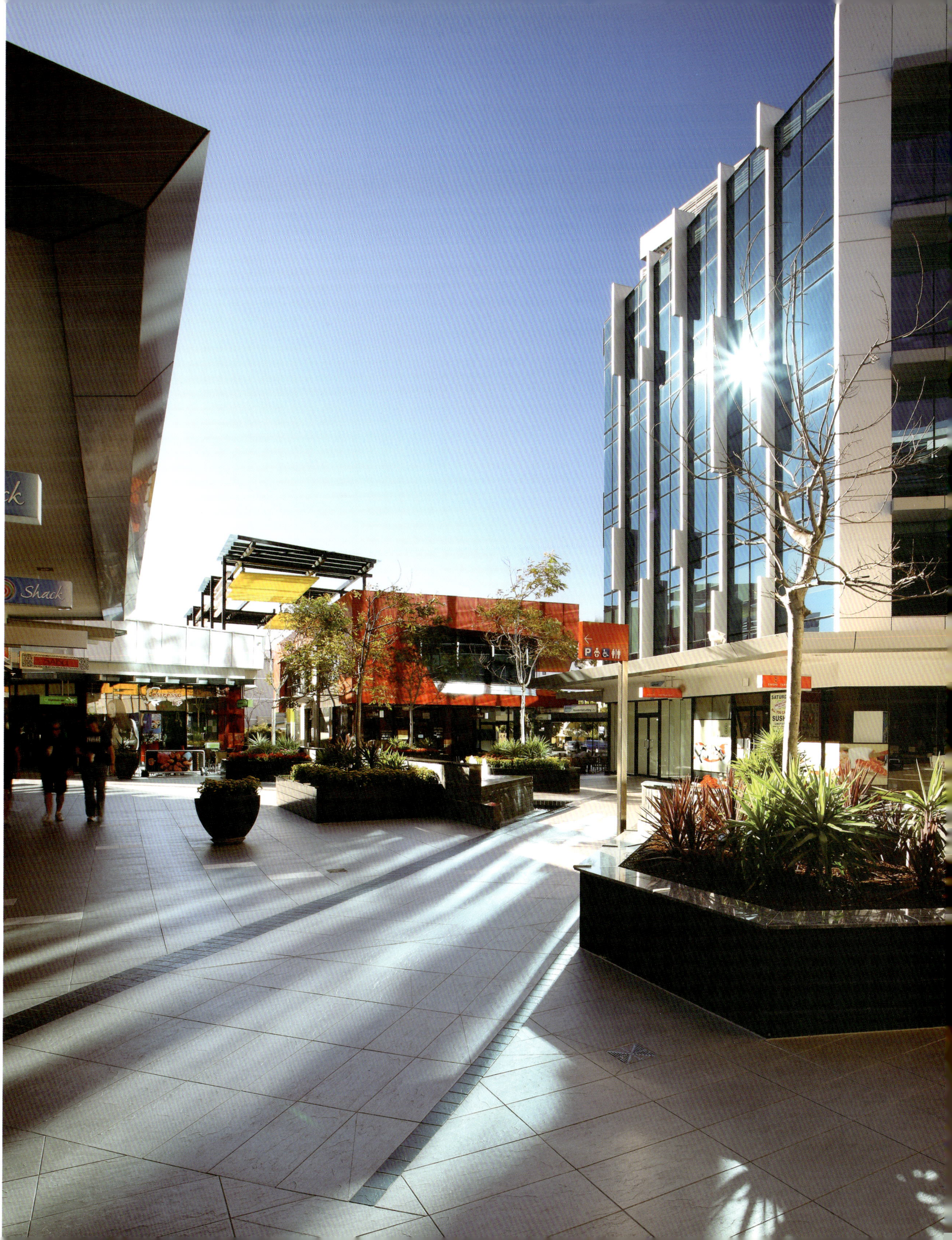
Shack

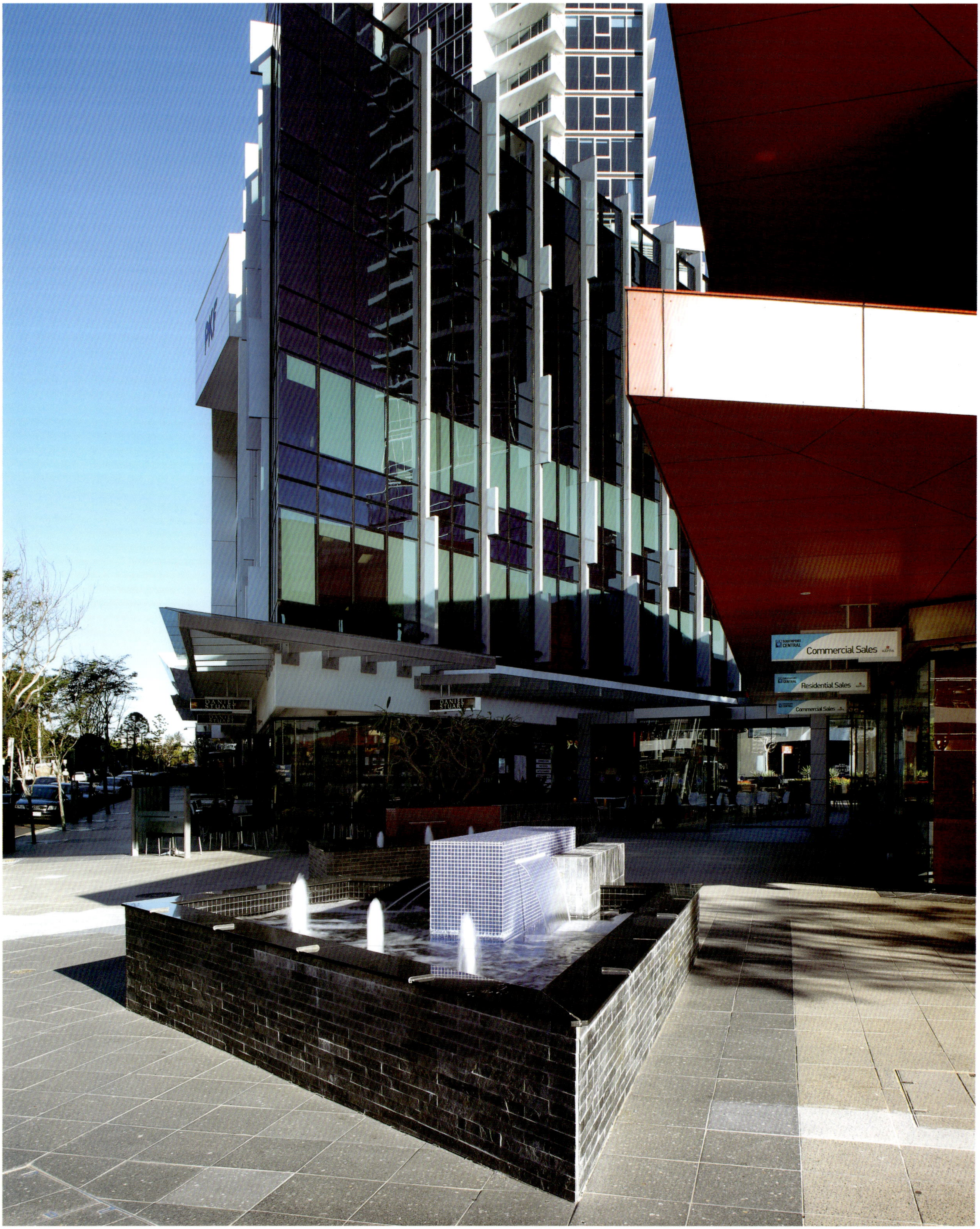
Commercial Sales
Residential Sales

Left: Southport Central entrance
Upper right: Upper residents' level water feature
Lower right: Detail of water feature

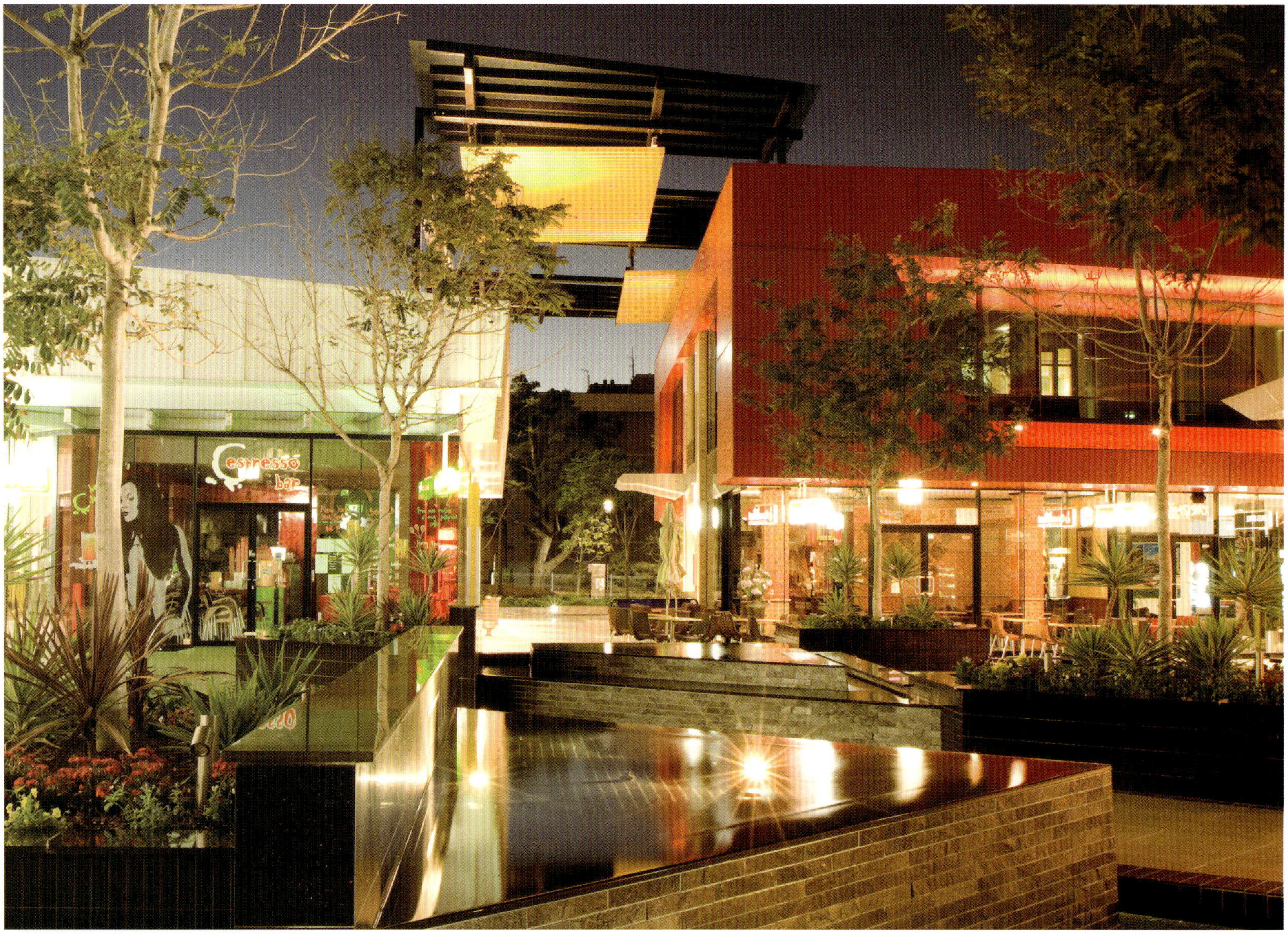
espresso
bar

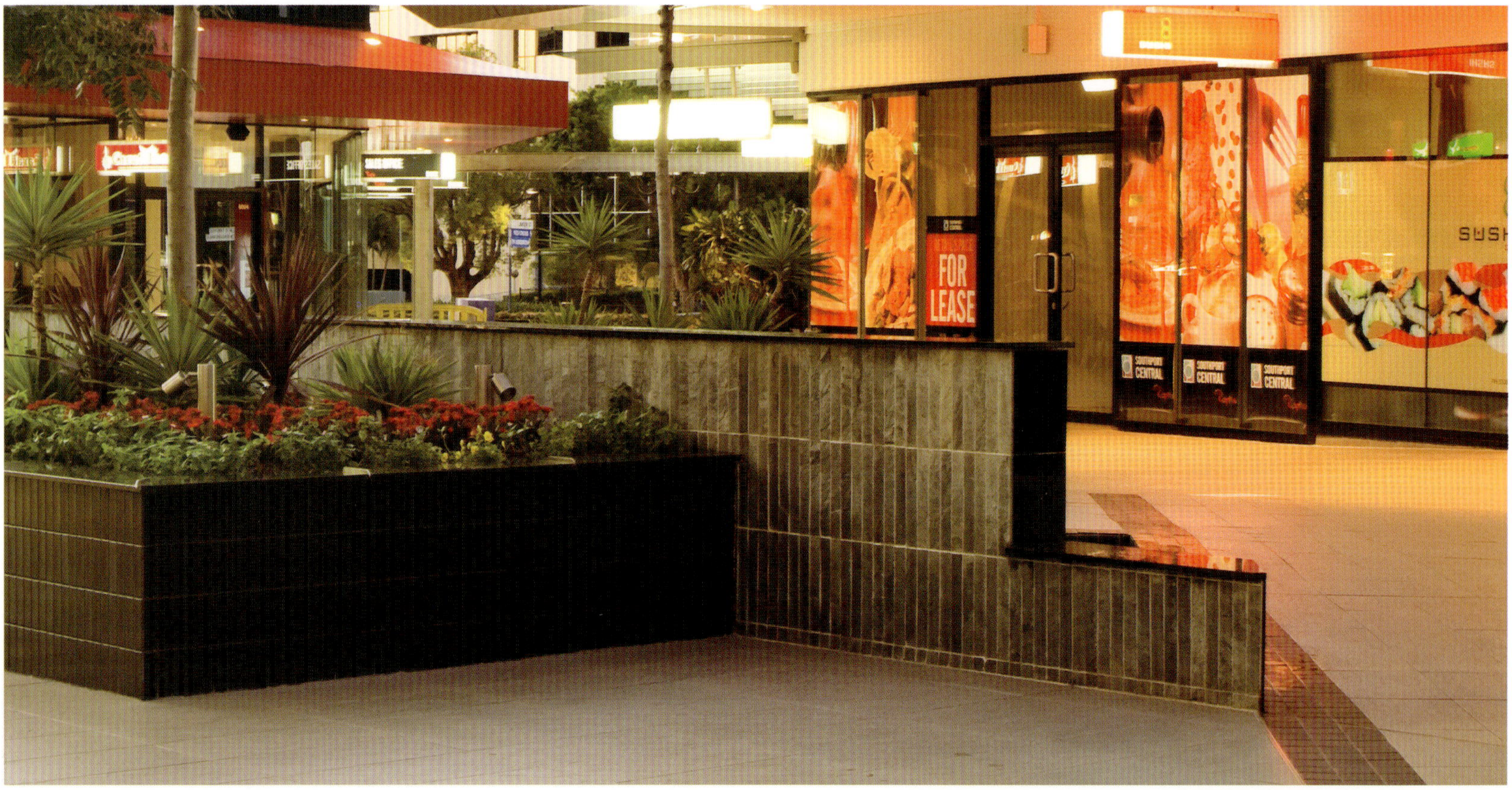
FOR
LEASE

Upper left: Central retail plaza
Lower left: Podium gardens in central retail plaza
Upper right: Streetscape planting
Lower right: Seating and lighting features throughout the plaza

Fukuoka Bank

Location: Fukuoka, Japan **Designer:** EARTHSCAPE, Inc. **Photographer:** EARTHSCAPE, Inc. **Completion date:** 2008 **Site area:** 27,500 sqm

The new head office of Fukuoka Bank is located in the center of Fukuoka. Its development and relationship with Fukuoka were well considered in the planning. Designer took the Hakata-ori (a famous fabric of Japan) as the designer's idea and created a unique streetscape by plants, details of seats and mosaic title. Earthscape expected the head office could be well integrated with the landscape to embrace a bright future.

In this project, the designer combined landscape design with architecture and landscape art to invoke both the city of Fukuoka and the Fukuoka Bank. The basis of the landscape, which draws from the word 'weave', is a floor embellished like a weave with fine designs inspired by hakataori, a traditional textile of Fukuoka City. The design created five axis lines using the geography and environment of Fukuoka, the five presentation colors of hakataori, as well as the management principles of Fukuoka Bank, and wove them together as special threads into the piece of cloth (the landscape), in order to construct the identity of this location.

This landscape is a space of rich greenery designed to beckon the neighboring Ohori Park into the city, through the entrance plaza that, through various programs, serves as a point of communication with the region. At the same time, it has become an index for Fukuoka, stored with information to help visitors learn a little more about Fukuoka.

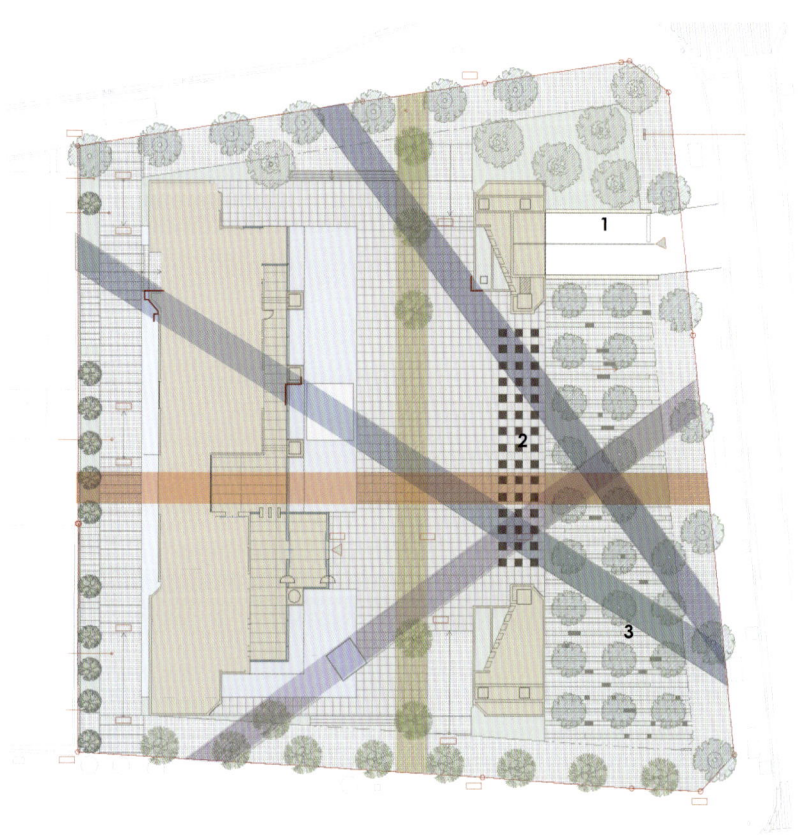

1. The Entrance Landscape
2. The Plaza
3. Resting Area

Right: Detail of the bench

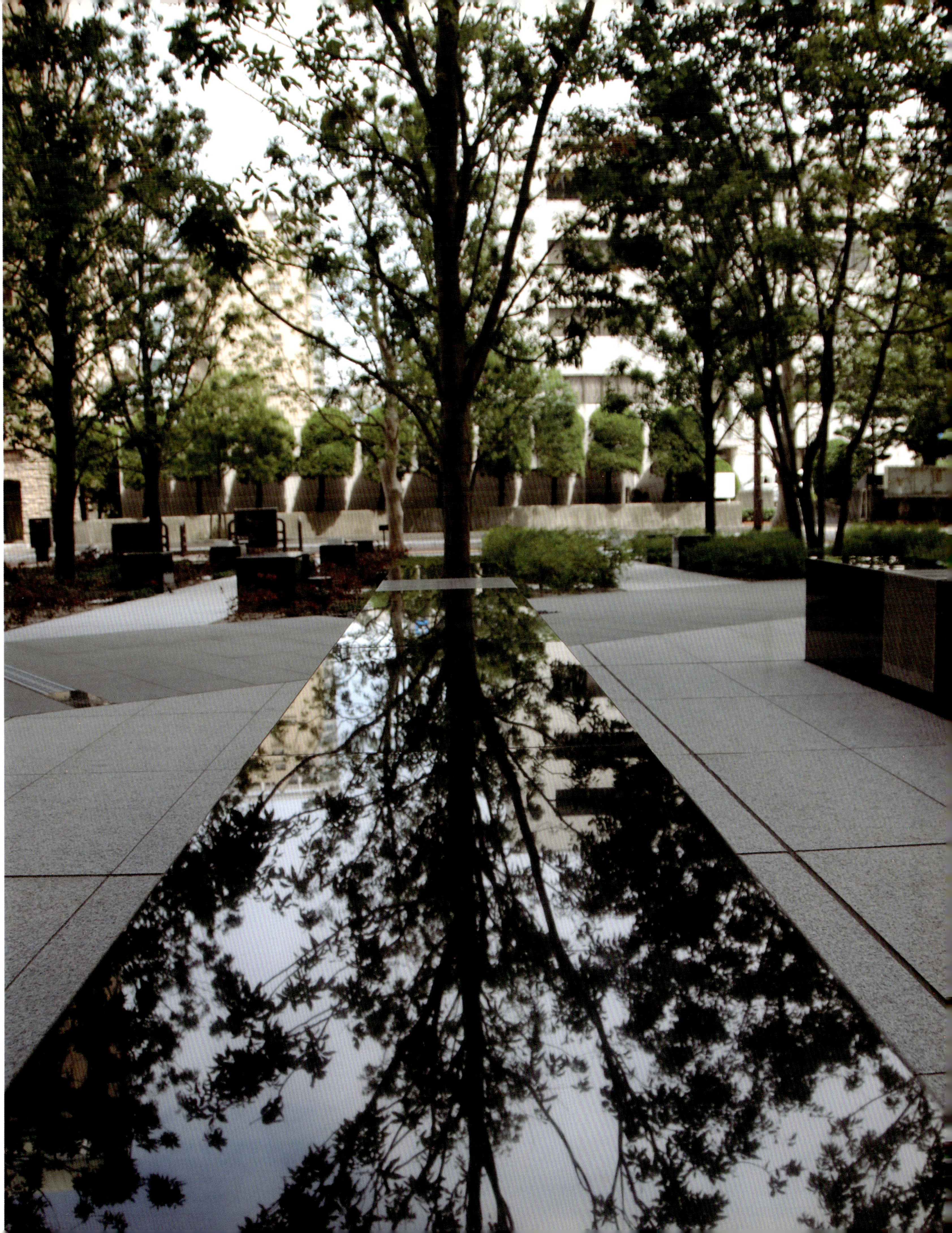

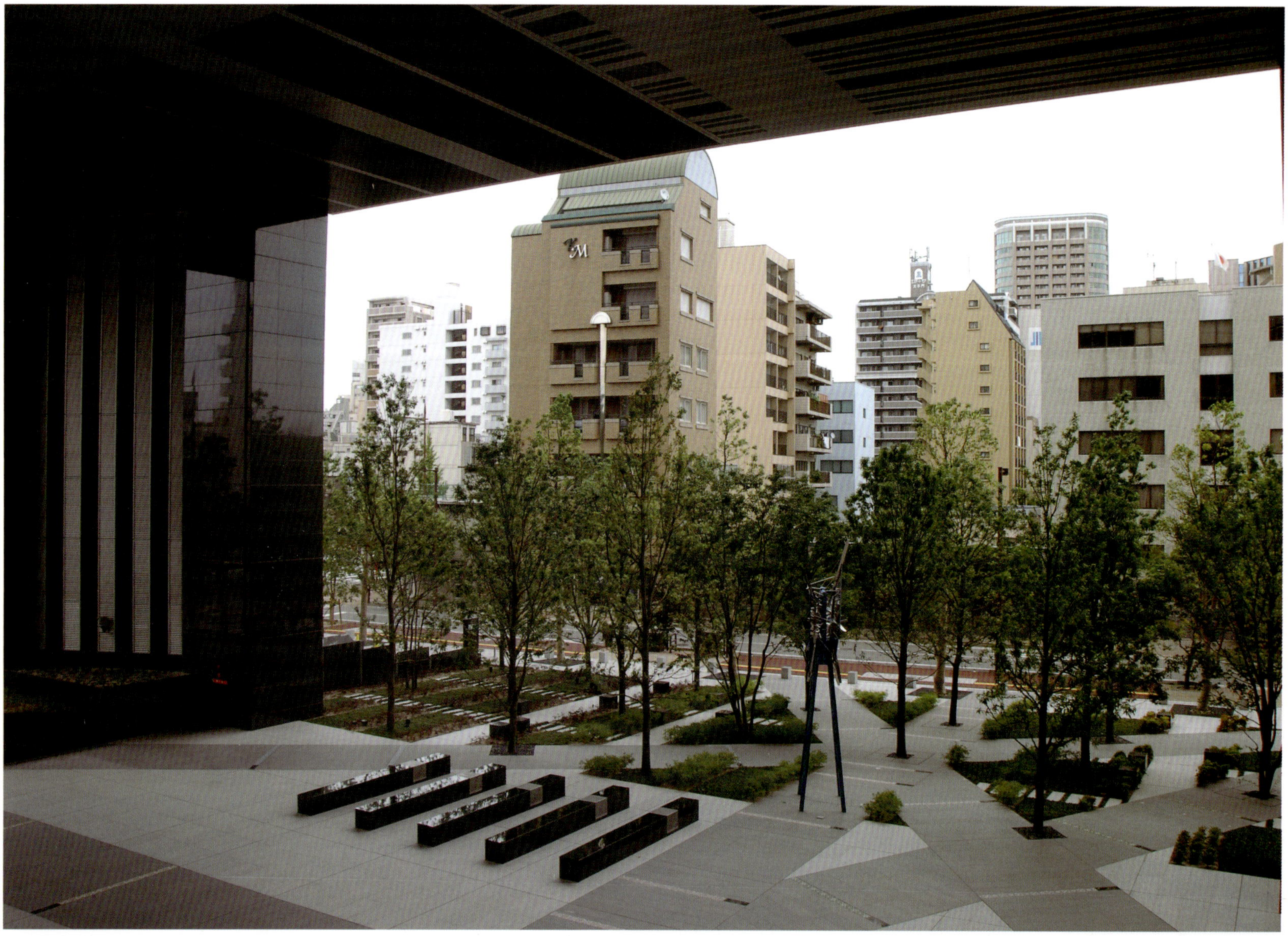

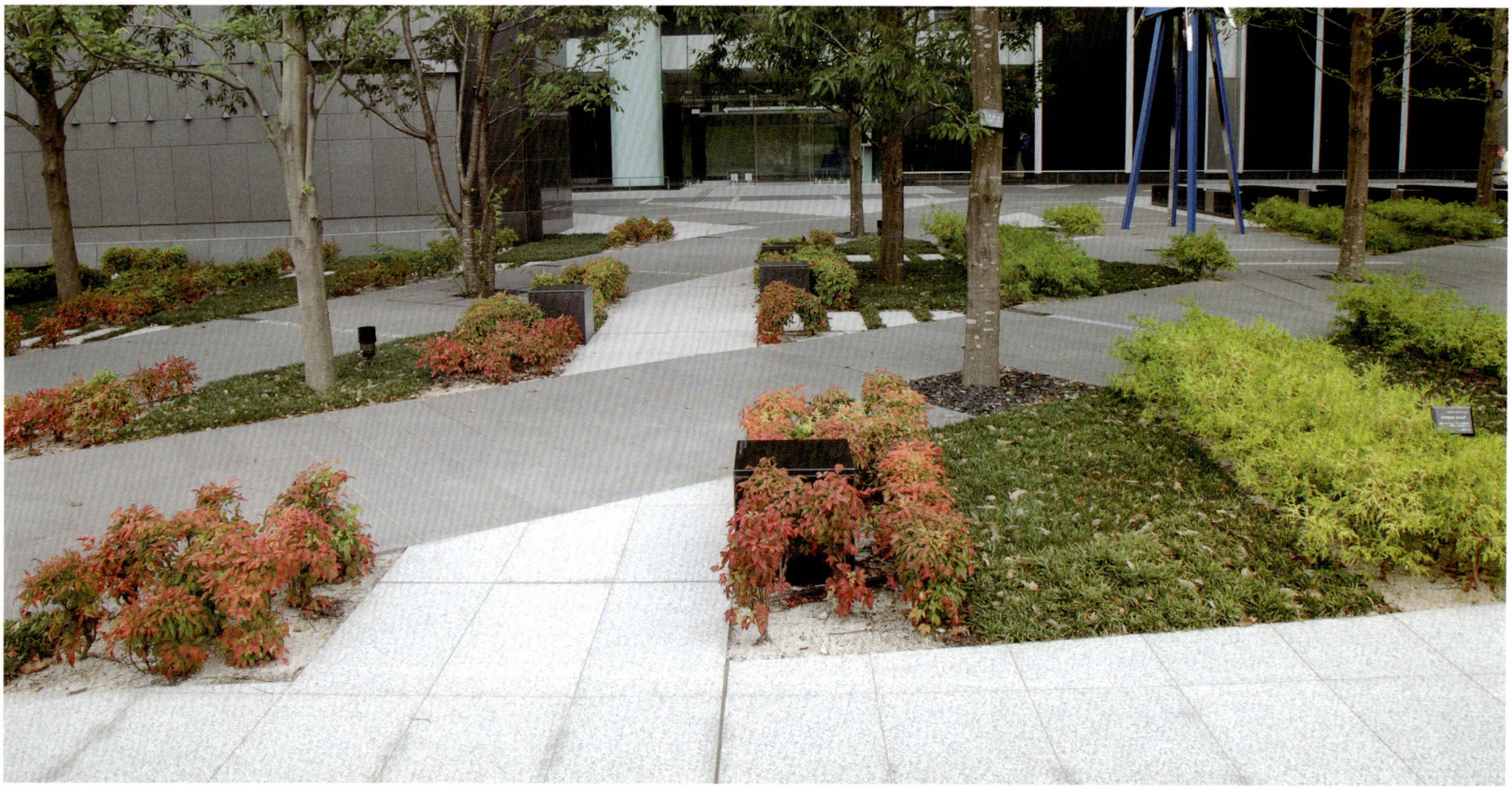

Upper left: Aerial view
Lower left: Hardscape and walkway pavement
Upper right: Entrance area
Lower right: Benches with lightings

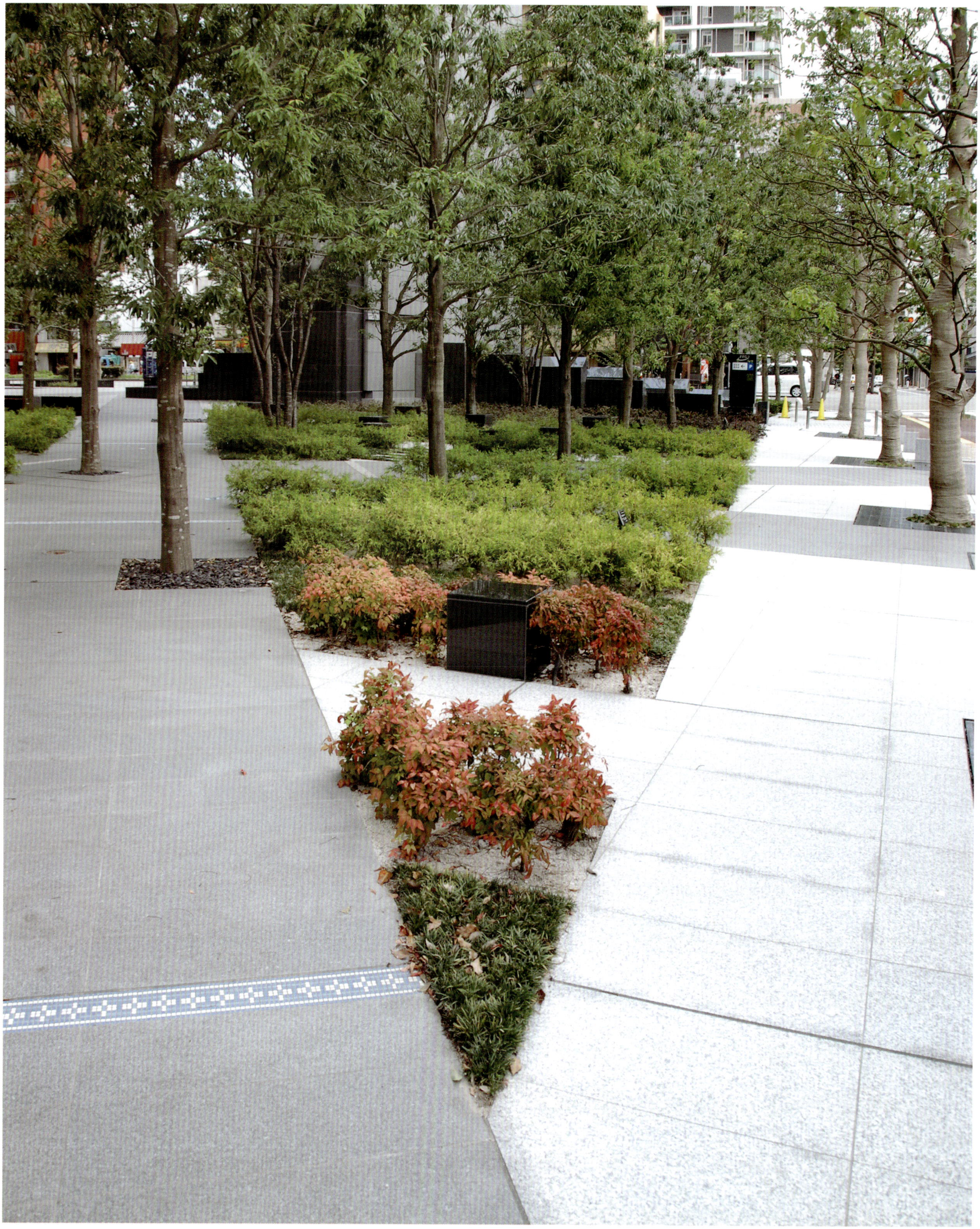

Upper right: Entrance plaza
Lower right: Detail of the pavement pattern

EnBW City

Location: Stuttgart, Germany **Designer:** Gnuechtel Triebswetter Landscape Architects **Photographer:** Tim Corvin Kraus **Completion date:** 2008 **Site area:** 35,000 sqm

Integration and design of the outside grounds is an important factor for quality and acceptance of the design proposal for the entire facility. The envisaged concept for the outdoor areas provides a flowing transition from urban structure and space formation into a valuable nature reserve area. This is achieved by terracing of the urban piazza and courtyards toward the gardens in the rear area, and by integrating a transition zone covered with trees toward the forest, while at the same time considering the spatial situation of the city.

The stone piazza at the foot of the multi-story building becomes the public center of the quarter. The line of road trees is interrupted at the piazza area, creating a clear gesture of opening toward the city. The area invites to linger and may be either used for public events or as outdoor area for the adjoining restaurants as well. The representative character of the three courtyards is supported by classic landscape-design elements. As a concept, the natural elements of water, wind and sun were picked out as a central theme.

1. Entrance Plaza
2. Water Thematic Garden
3. Wind Thematic Garden
4. Light Thematic Ggarden
5. Garden

Right: Aerial view

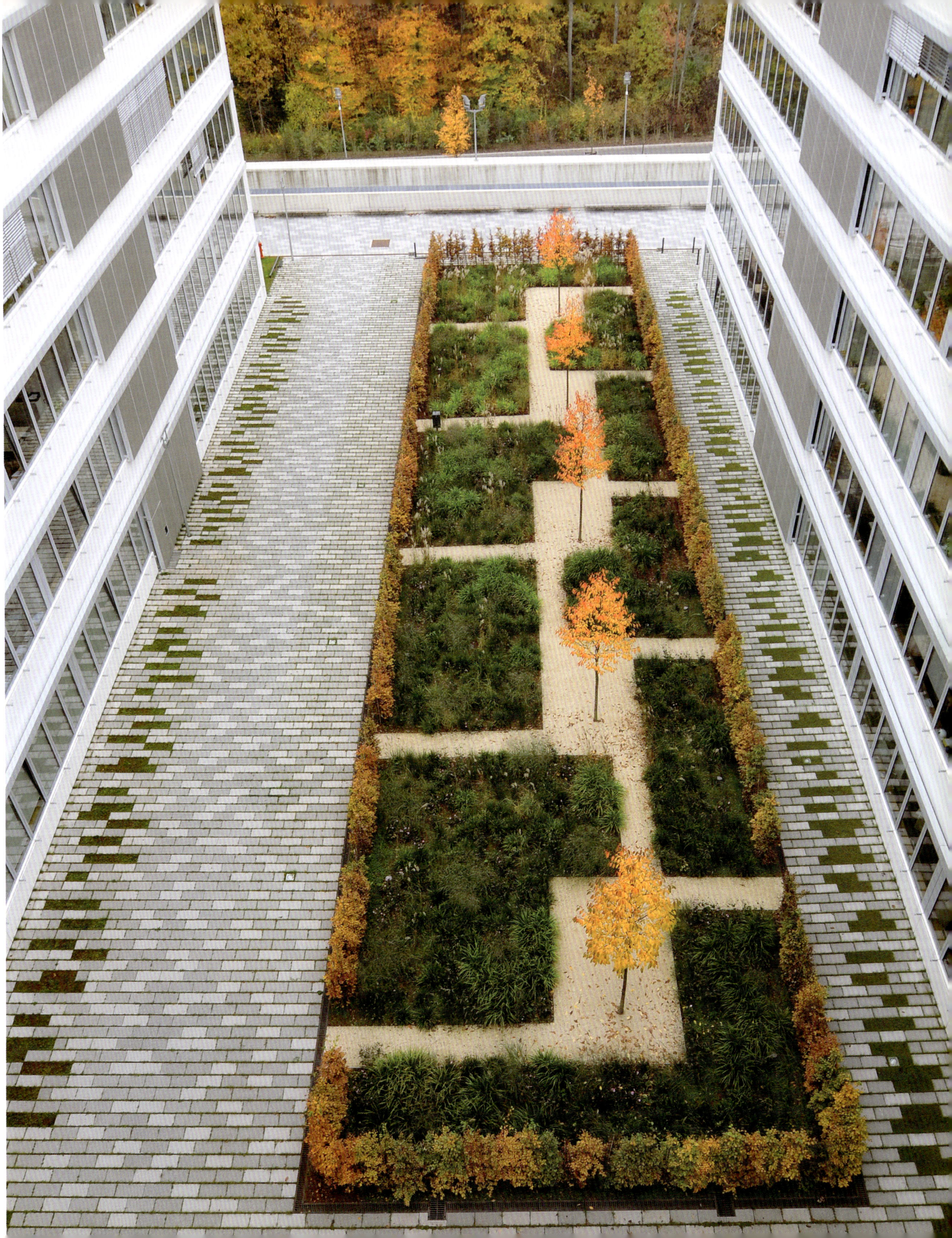

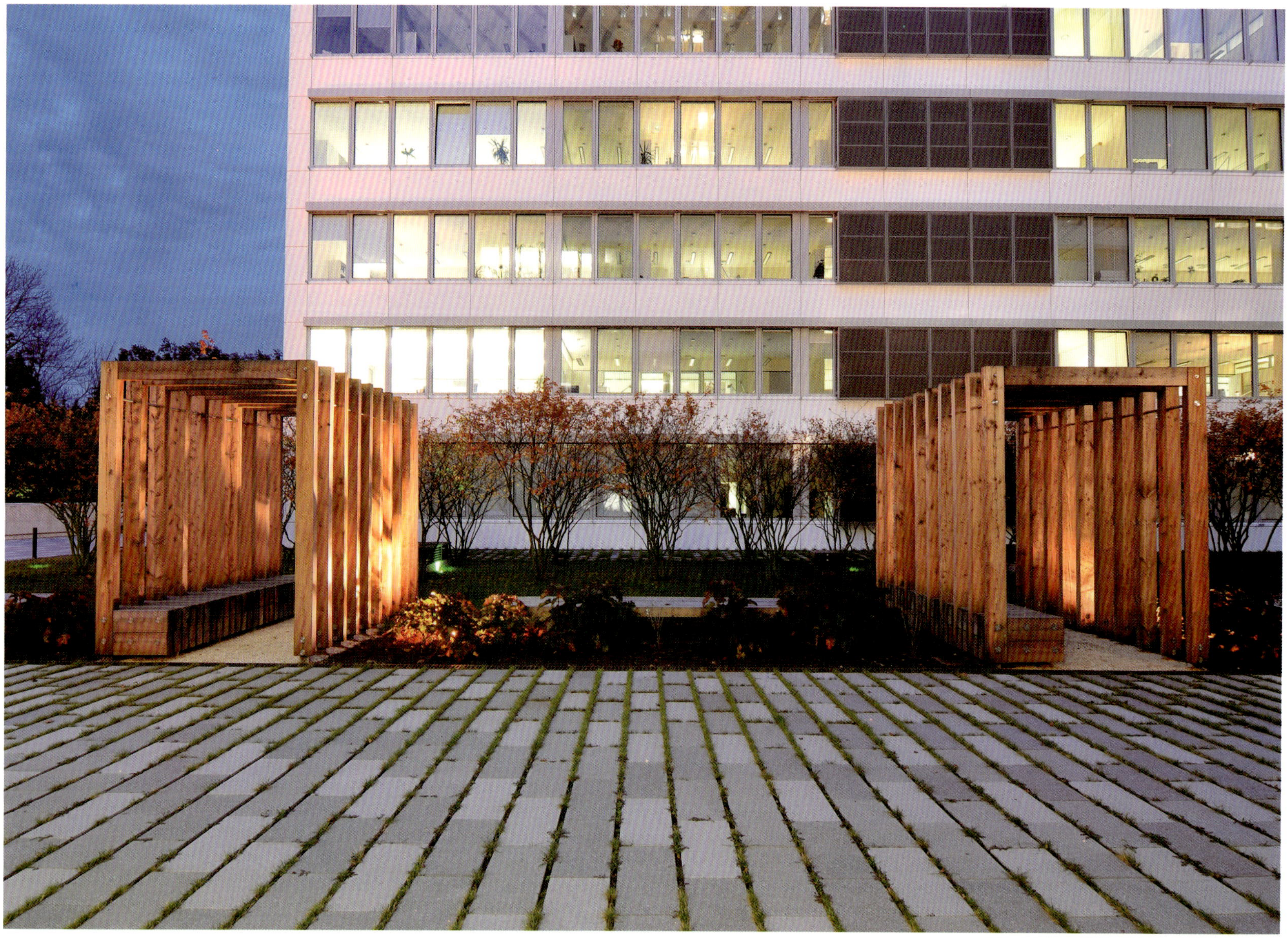

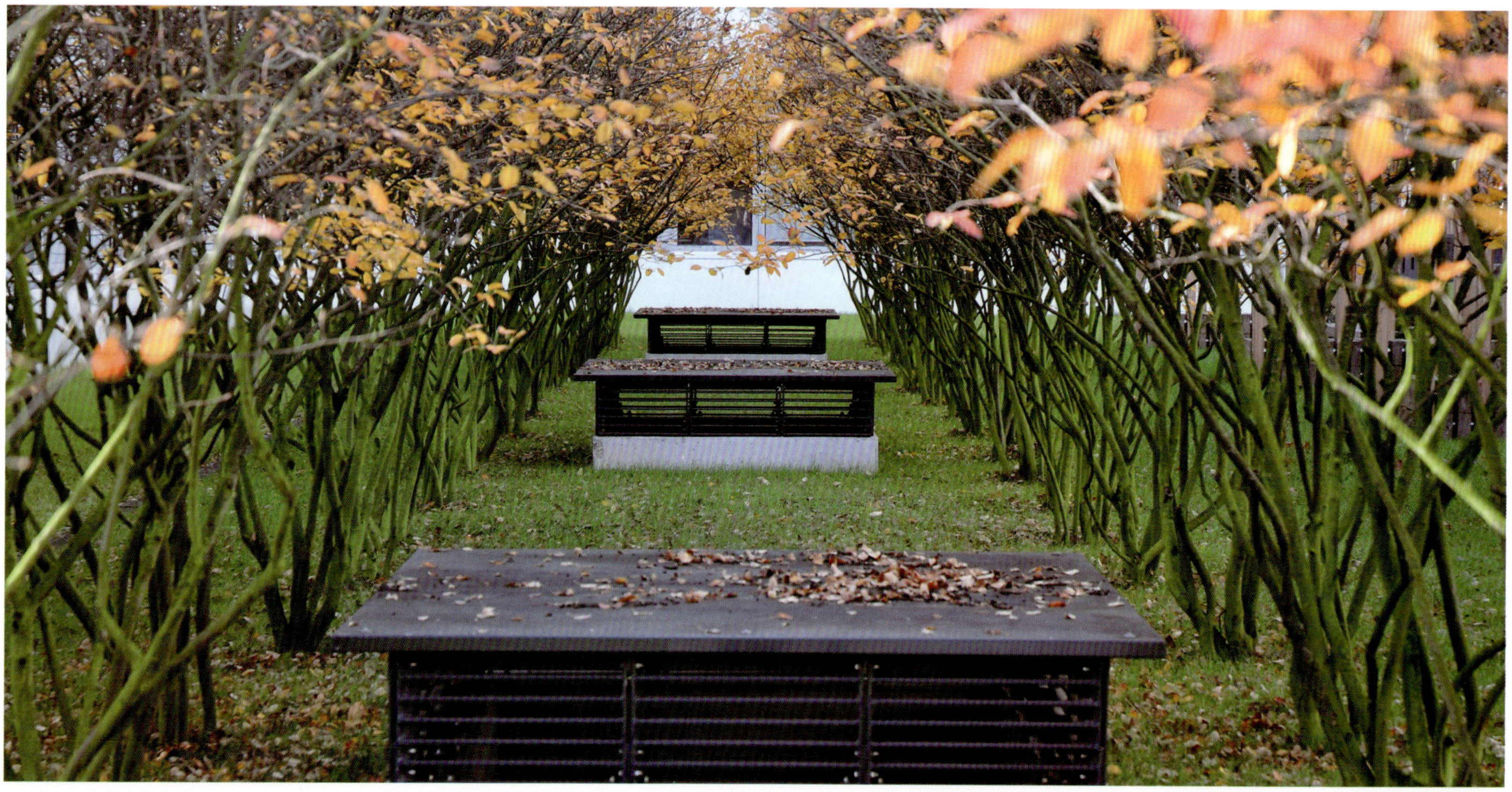

Upper left: Recreational pergola
Lower right: Close-up of stone pavement

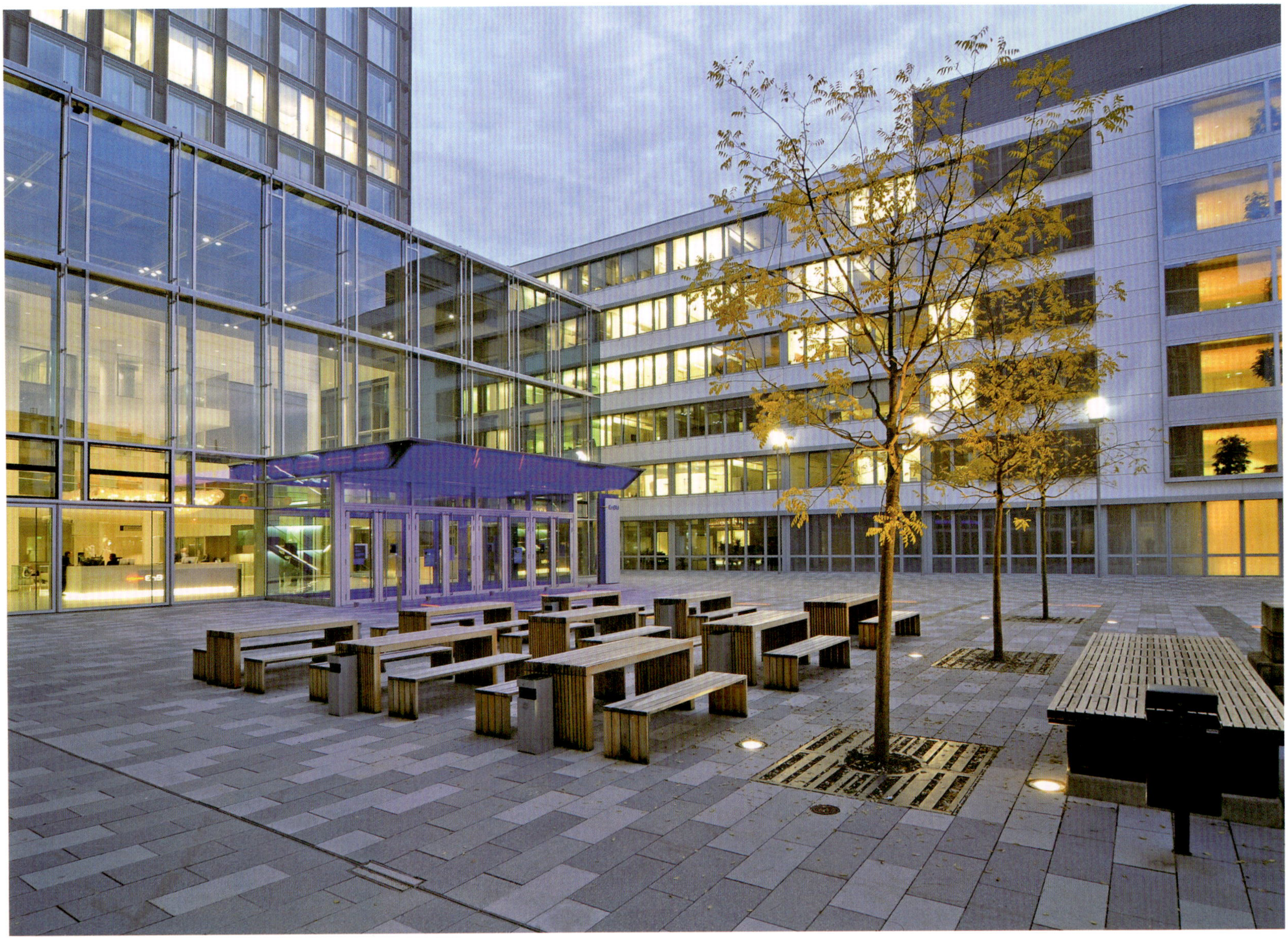

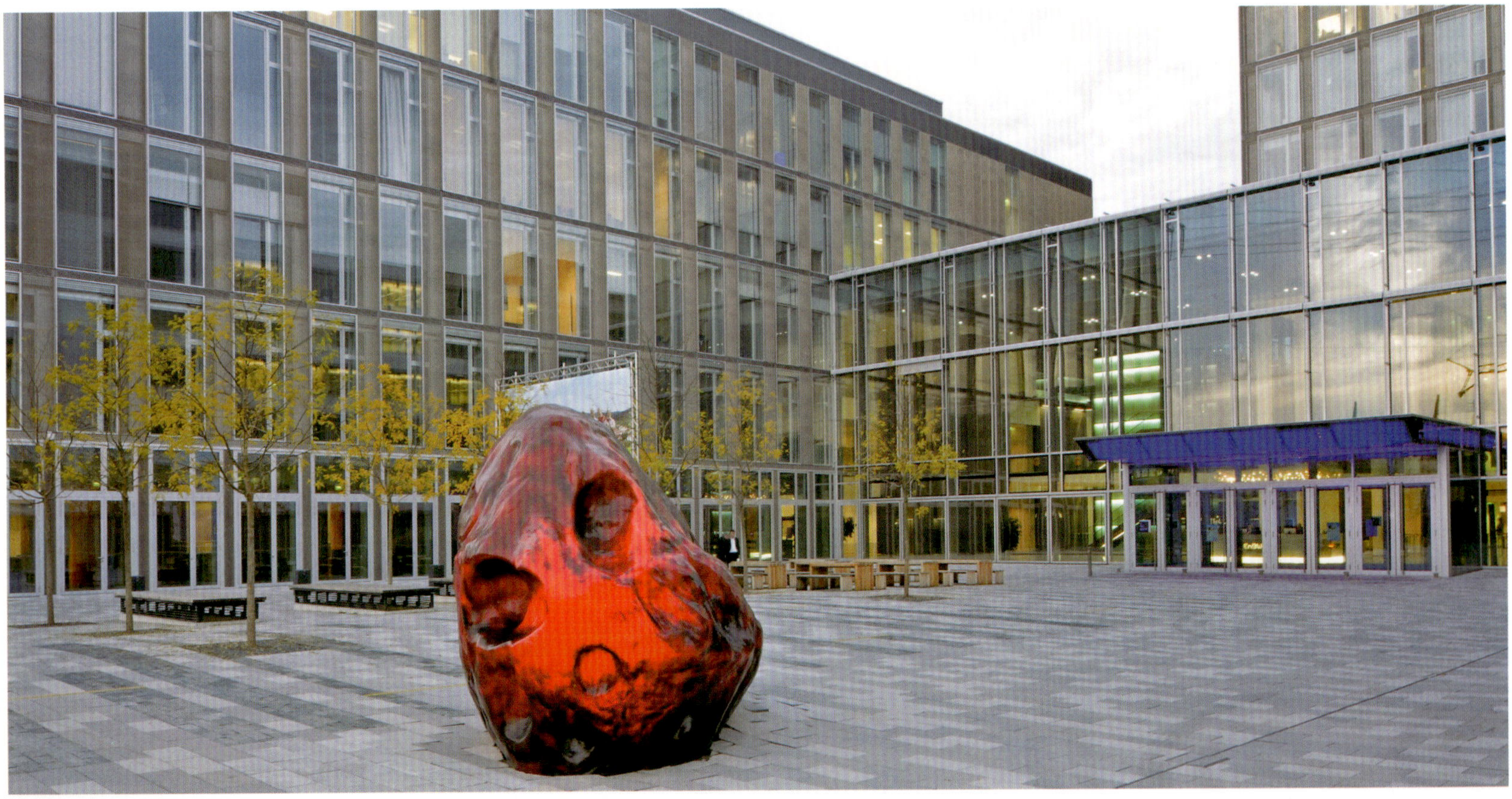

Upper left: Entrance plaza
Lower left: Sculpture at the entrance
Upper right: Thematic garden

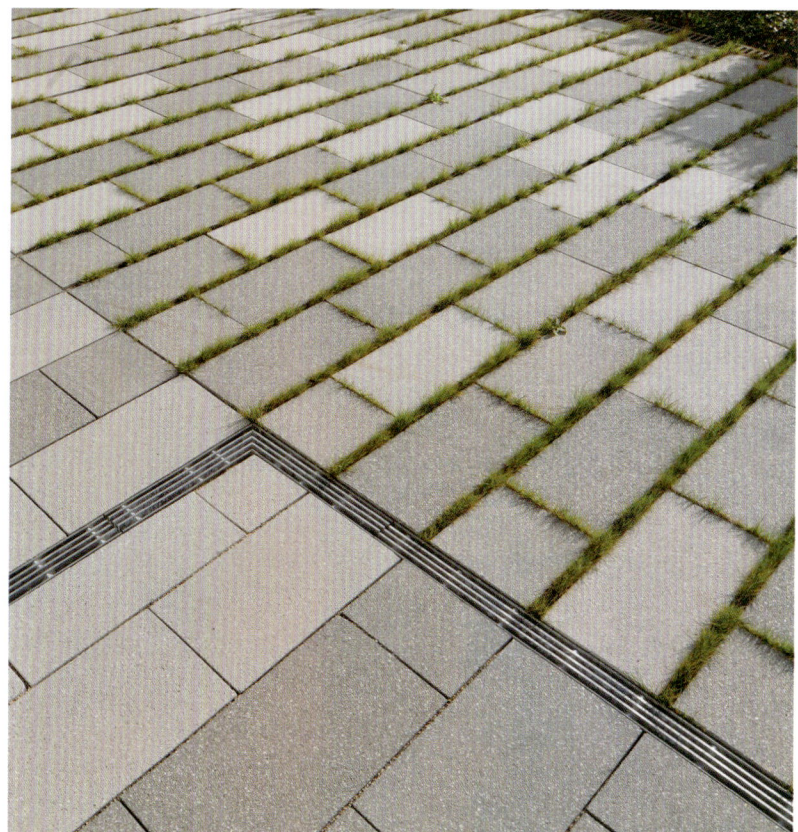

Enterprise Plaza at 1100 Louisiana

Location: Houston, USA **Designer:** The Office of James Burnett **Photographer:** Hester + Hardaway **Completion date:** 2009 **Site area:** 1,394 sqm

The plaza welcomes visitors and tenants through the creation of an outdoor gathering space with canopy shade trees, cooling water features, comfortable furniture and fascinating plantings. Because the plaza is located above an existing parking structure, and the design also faced significant technical challenges.

A large elliptical fountain basin defines both the primary function space and the primary pedestrian path to the entry. The fountain features a series of overflowing basins, concentric rings of bubblers and a focal with a choreographed display of jets shooting up to six meters in the air.

To further mitigate the environment in the newly formed spaces, Water Oaks were introduced on the plaza. The trees serve to act as a wind break and to provide shade in the warmer parts of the year. Given the structural considerations of the existing plaza, the trees needed to be in raised planters. The circular planometric shape of the tree planters and water jet fountain was then repeated playfully throughout the entire composition as a reinforcing element in the paving.

The design team then introduced movable tables and chairs into the plaza to allow the public to utilize the space. The building management maintains the furniture and moves it in and out on a daily basis. The movable furniture has proved very successful in bringing people into the plaza.

Award description:
2010 Texas Chapter ASLA Merit Awards

1. City Sidewalk
2. Seating Lawn, Typical
3. Terraced Water Feature
4. Feature Fountain
5. Outdoor Seating & Movable Furniture
6. Topiary Domes & Raised Tree Planters

Right: Overall view of the plaza from an adjacent building showing the trees in topiary mounds, fountain, and lawn disks

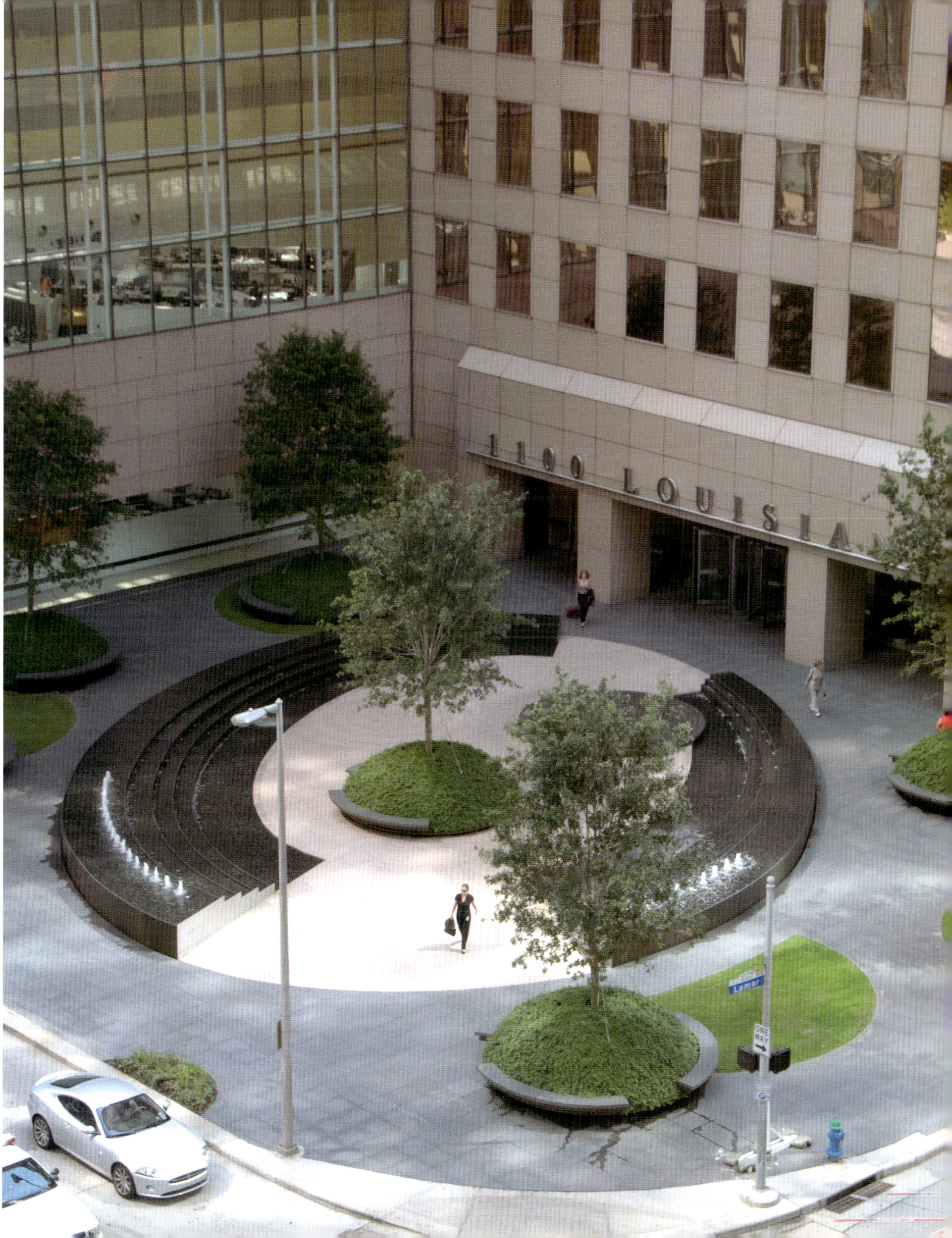
1100 LOUISIAN
Lamar
ONE WAY

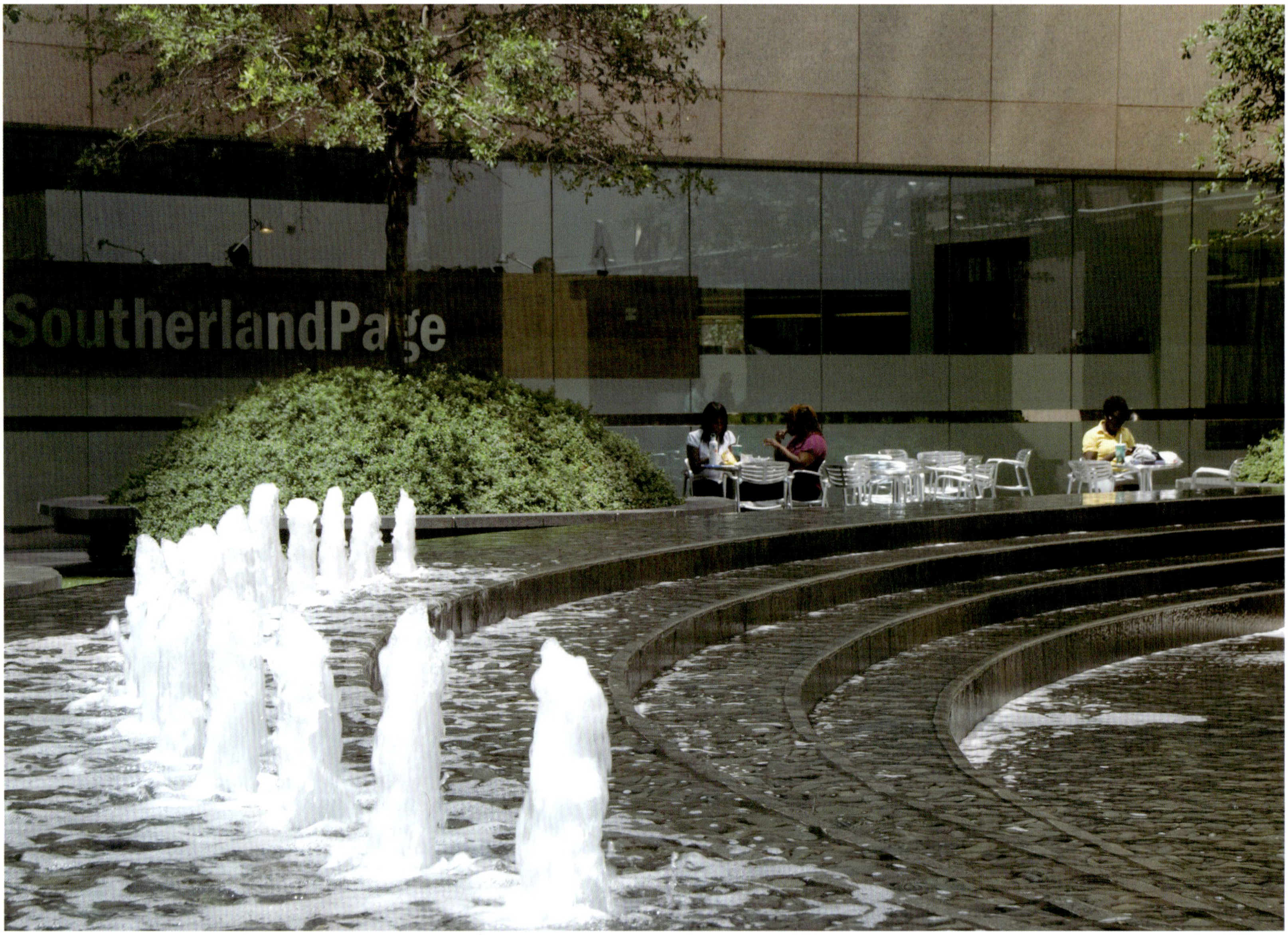
SoutherlandPage

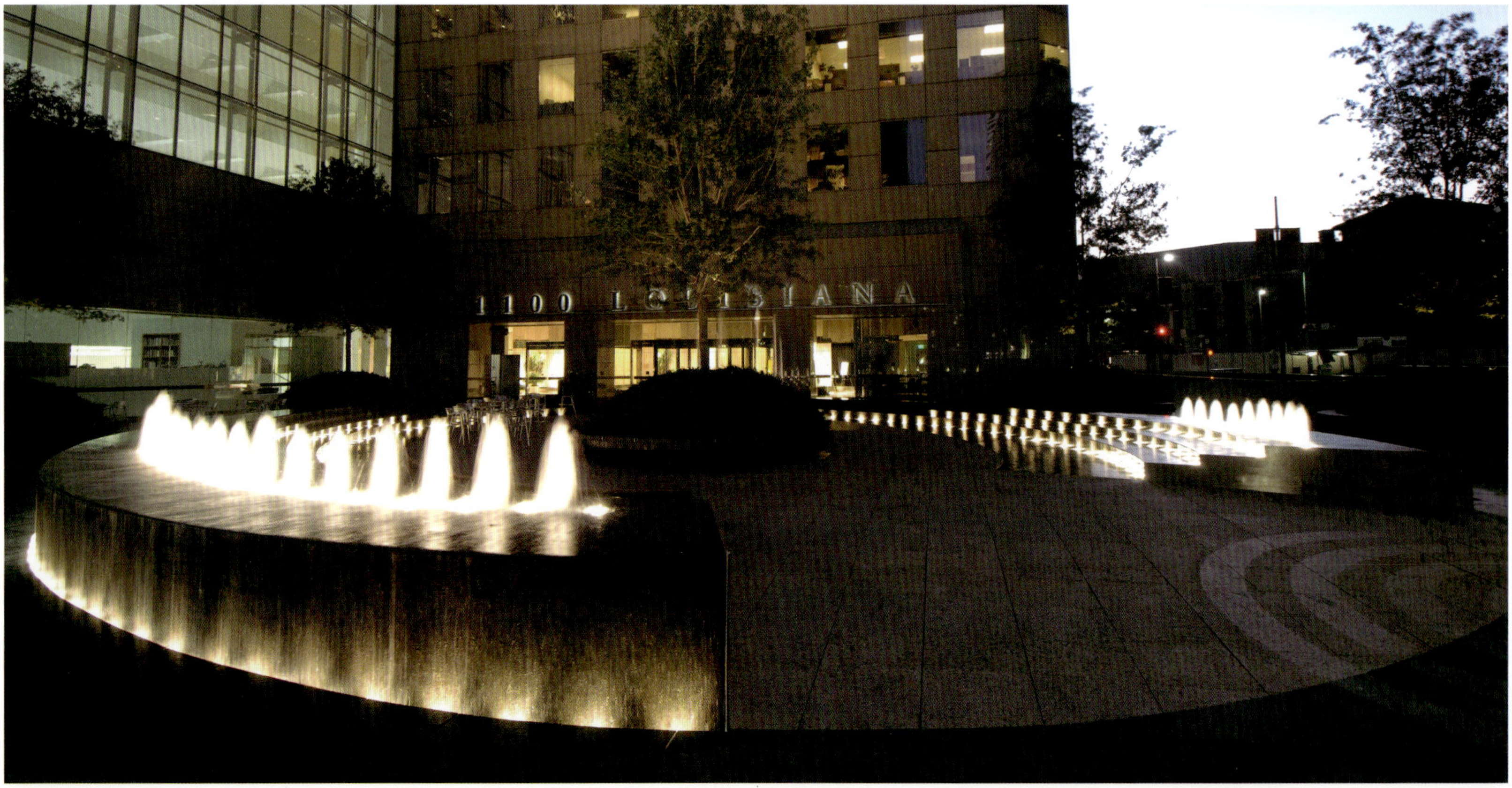
1100

Upper left: View across the fountain basin cascade to the terrace
Lower left: View looking from fountain toward the building lobby, displaying the bubblers at the outer edge of the basin and the central topiary mound
Upper right: View from the lobby of 1100 Louisiana looking across the plaza to the downtown skyline
Lower right: Details of the concrete

Red Soils Plaza

Location: Oregon, USA **Designer:** Atlas Landscape Architecture **Photographer:** Nick Wilson **Completion date:** 2008 **Site area:** 4,000 sqm

The Red Soils Plaza is the central open space of the 55-acre Clackamas County Red Soils Campus. It was constructed according to a master plan that will consolidate most of Clackamas County's government services and facilities into an efficient campus setting. The master plan anticipates a courthouse to be constructed the west of the plaza in the future. The plaza is intended to be used by the County employees as well as visitors to the campus.

The plaza is organized around an elliptical lawn area. The major axis of the ellipse points toward Mount Hood, the highest point in Oregon and a beacon for pioneers on the Oregon trail as they neared the end their arduous 2,000-mile journey from Independence, Missouri. A water feature on the sunny side of the plaza is the primary focal point. Tables and other seating opportunities have been integrated into the fountain. The water feature is reminiscent of nearby Willamette Falls. The water feature has a face cast in a basalt pattern and basalt columns have been incorporated in and around the fountain. A mosaic entitled 'Granite Rug' by artist Brian Goldbloom has been incorporated into the paving at the northeast corner of the Plaza. A stainless steel sculpture entitled 'Periennial' by artist Aaron Hussey, has been located at the terminus of the major axis. The central oval lawn is intended to be used for events including performances, weddings and exhibits.

1. Oval Lawn
2. Water Feature
3. Granite Rug Mosaic
4. Perennial Sculpture
5. Development Services Building
6. Public Services Building
7. Future Courthouse Site

Right: Early morning view of cascade face with lights

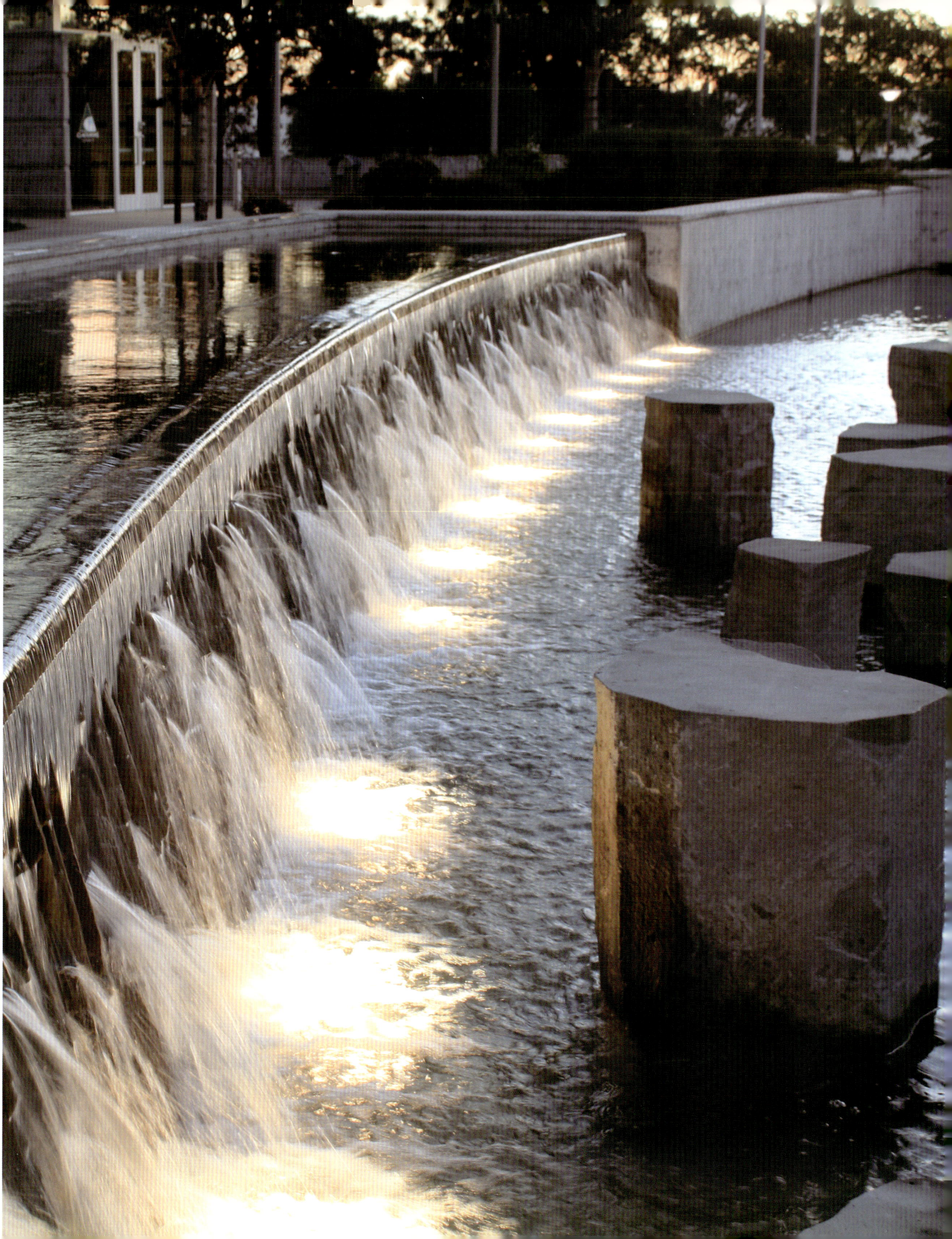

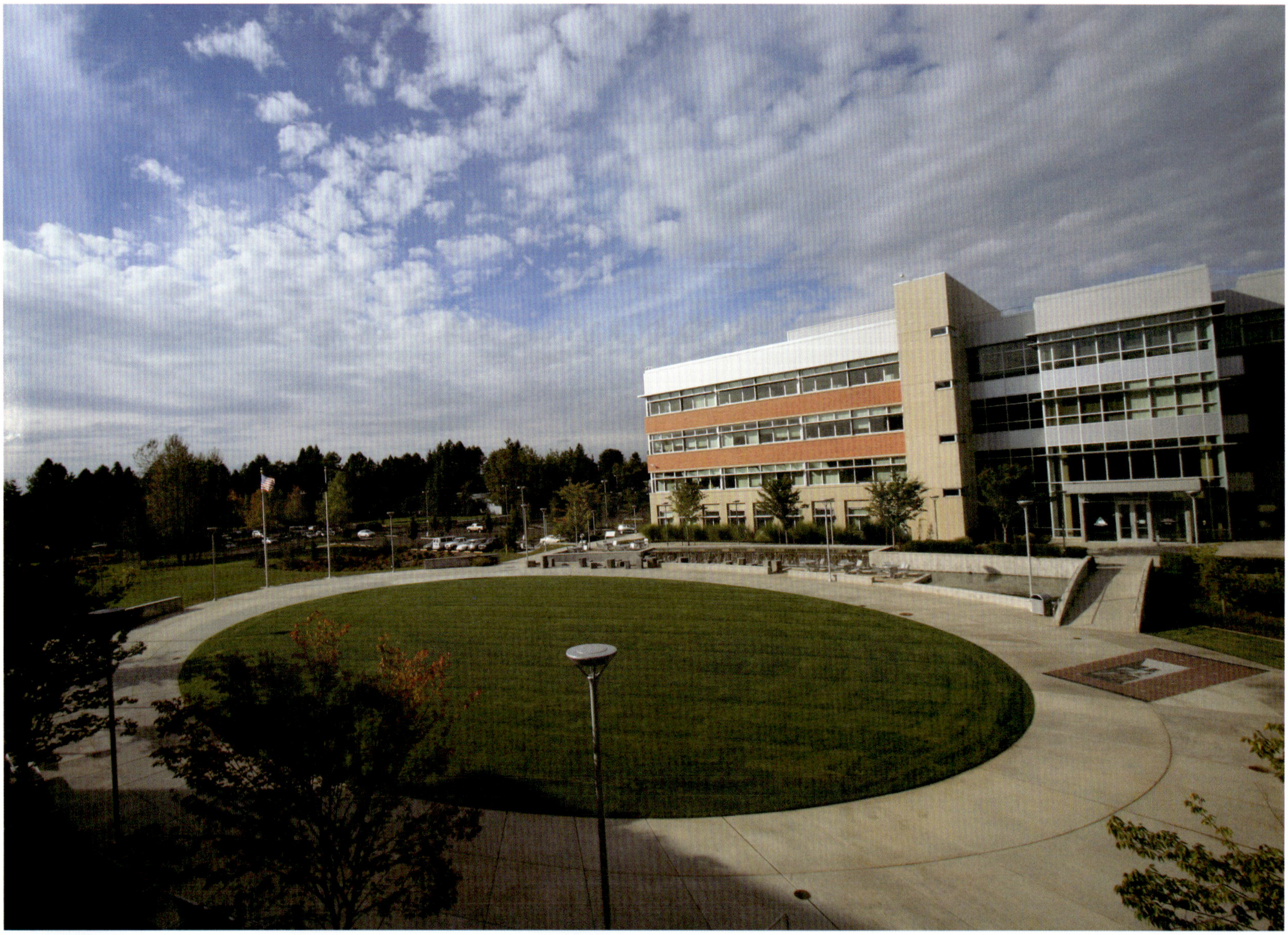

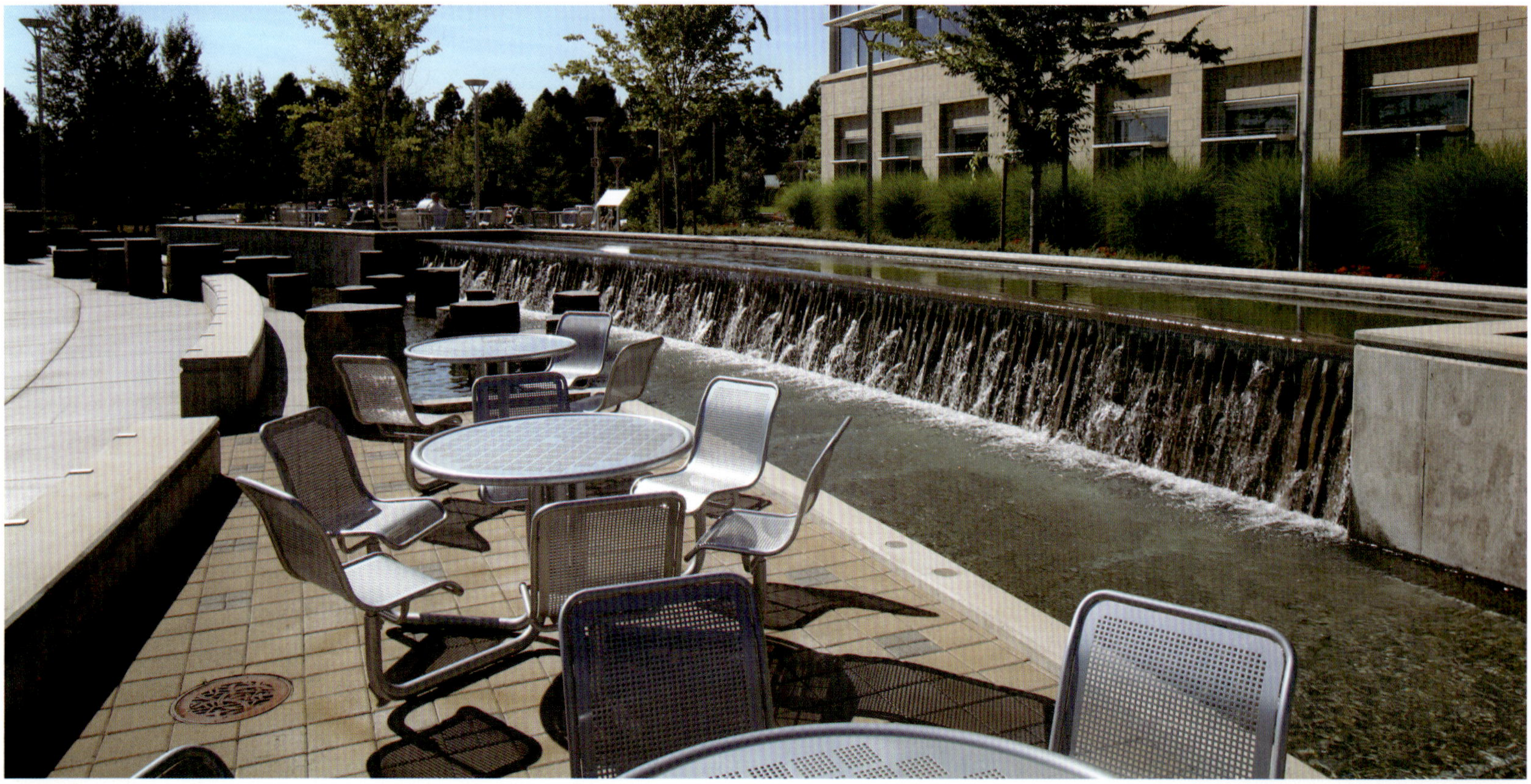

Upper left: View of plaza from southeast, and development services building in background
Lower left: Seating area at lower pool
Upper right: Seating area at upper pool
Lower right: 'Perennial' by sculptor Aaron Hussey

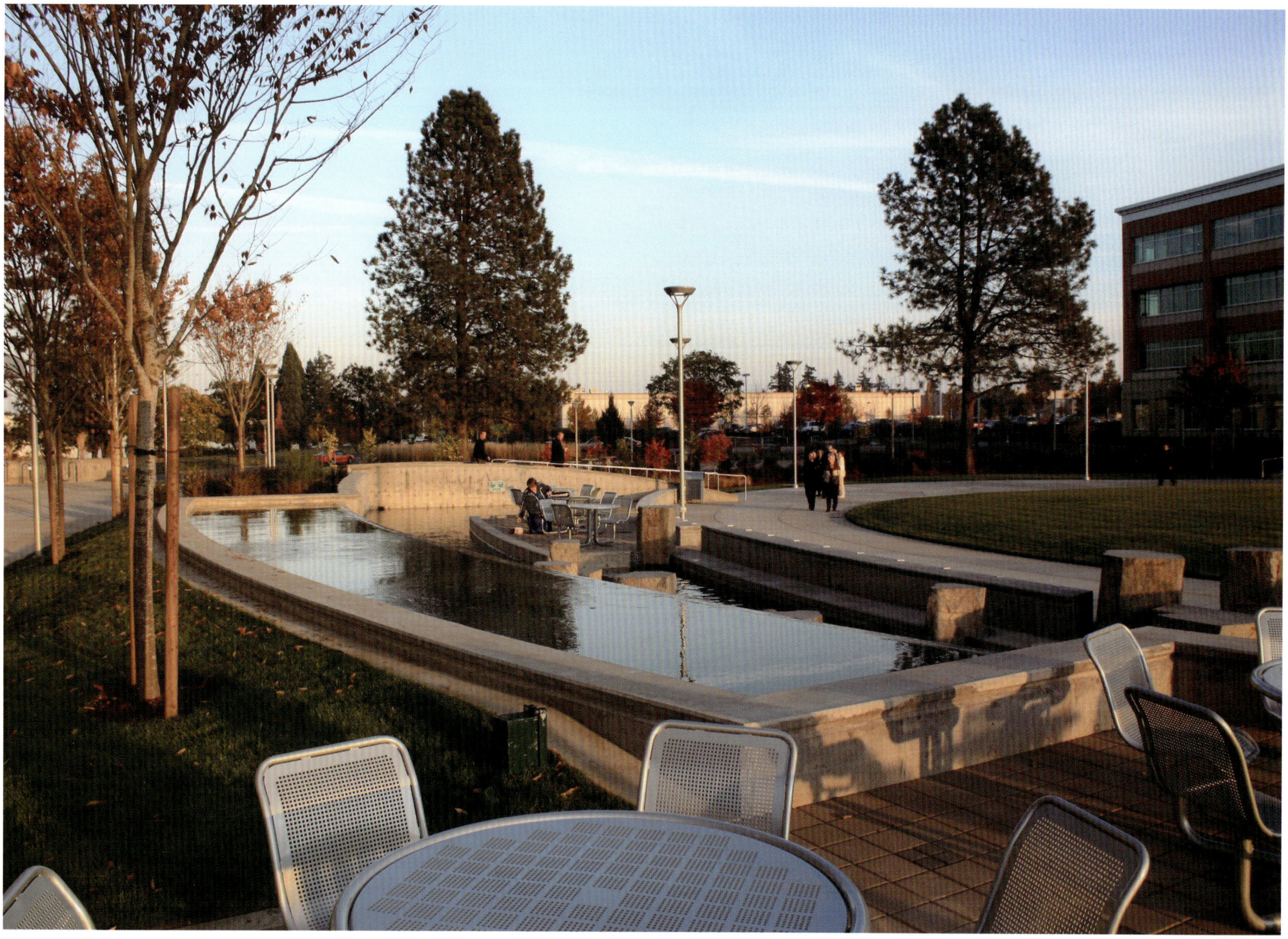

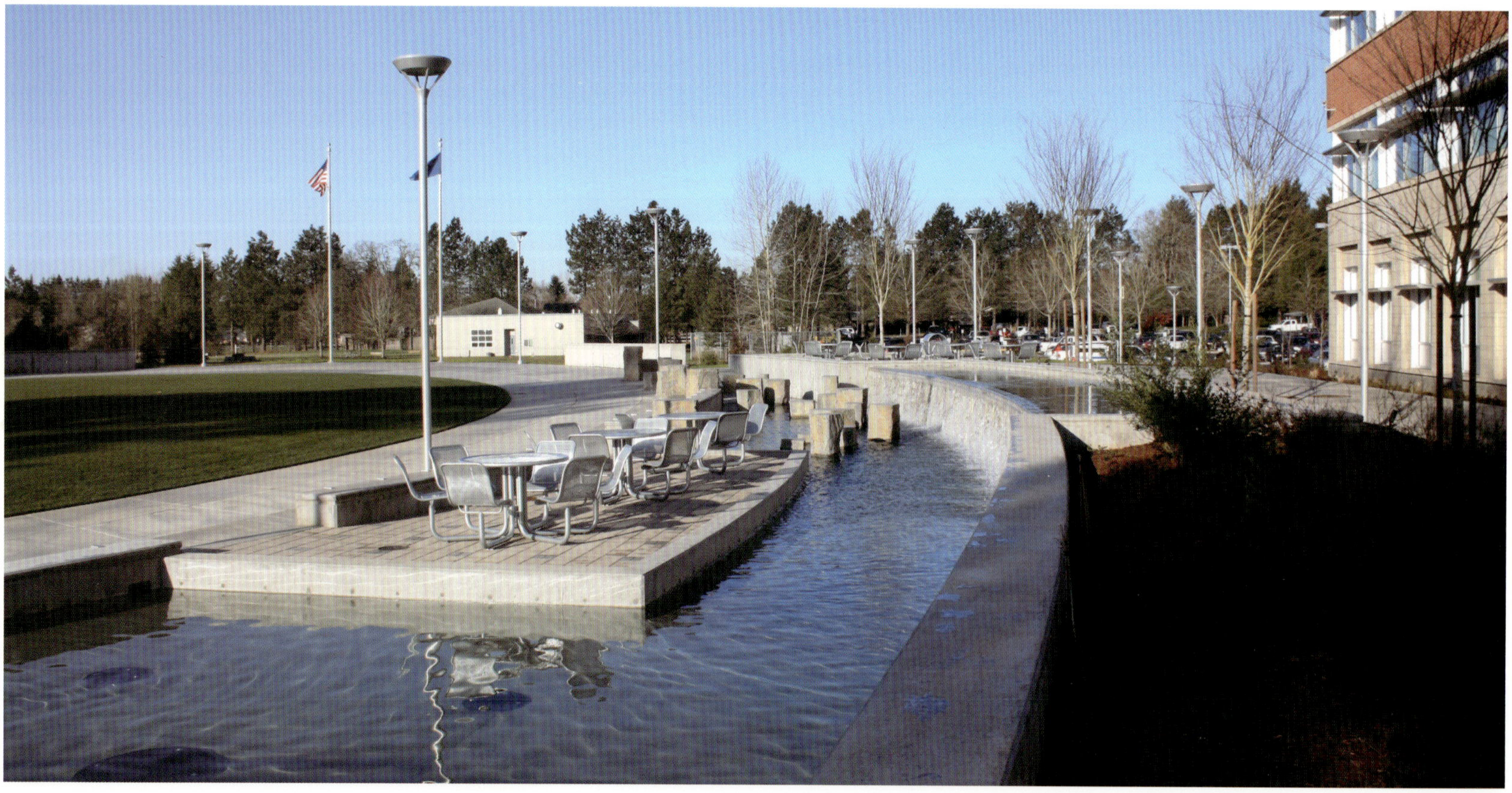

Upper left: Seating area at lower pool at dusk
Lower left: Seating area at lower pool
Upper right: Early morning view of water feature with lights
Lower right: Close-up of water feature cascade with basalt columns

Solingen Townhall Square

Location: Solingen, Germany **Designer:** Scape Landschaftsarchitekten **Photographer:** fotoatelier 2, Gereon Hofschneider, Scape Landschaftsarchitekten, Rainer Sachse **Completion date:** 2008 **Site area:** 21,000 sqm **Plants:** Japanese Pagodatree, Yoshino Cherry

For the designers the objective was to create the town hall district as a public space for all citizens, a place to meet and to stay. A network of squares and promenades connects the scheme to the surrounding and creates an exiting space.

To build a coherent area, a pattern of black and white lines traces the whole public open space. Like a marquetry, a connecting concrete carpet integrates various functional elements and provides zones with different characters and uses. The entrance to the new quarter is formed by a wide square. Its design is inspired by the movement of people. Along the edge it offers enough space for walking, seating and events. In the center three huge, organically shaped benches along with a group of flowering trees establish an area to pause and communicate.

Four courtyards within the quarter are a counterpart to this open, lively square. The courtyards are arranged as abstract gardens, as green, quiet places. Here the black and white pavement was transformed into strips of gravel, perennials, bulbs and grasses. Wooden platforms serve as seats and contain the ventilation of the underground parking.

The center of the town hall square was designed as a linear pocket park: two footpaths frame a mounded grass strip, planted with multi-stem cherry trees. The park provides areas for playing and relaxation; it acts as a green boulevard and links all parts of the project.

1. Pavement
2. Asphalt/Bus Lane
3. Courtyard Garden
4. Public Green/Playground
5. Seating Elements
6. Wooden Deck
7. Circular Bench

Right: Bird's-eye view of the Square

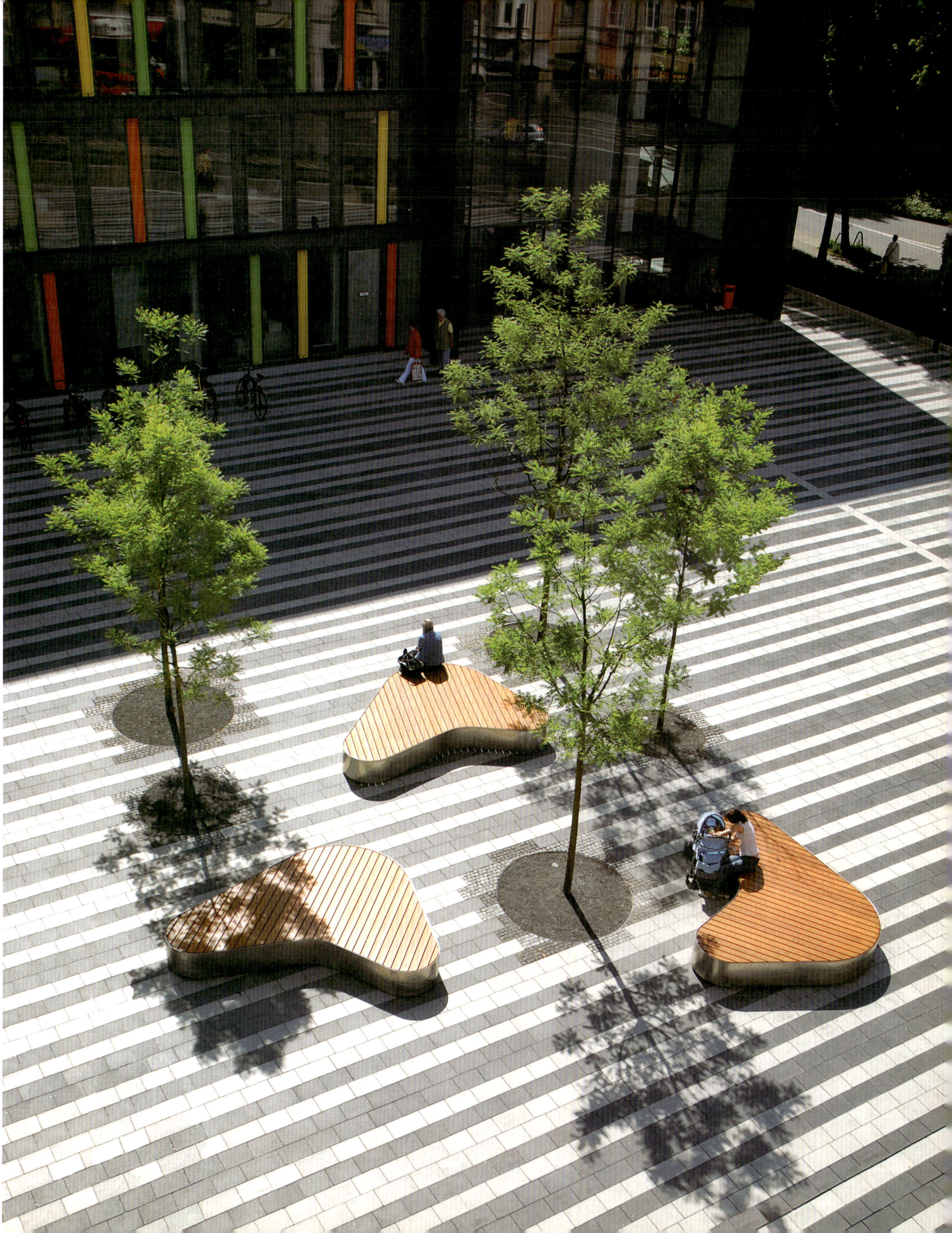

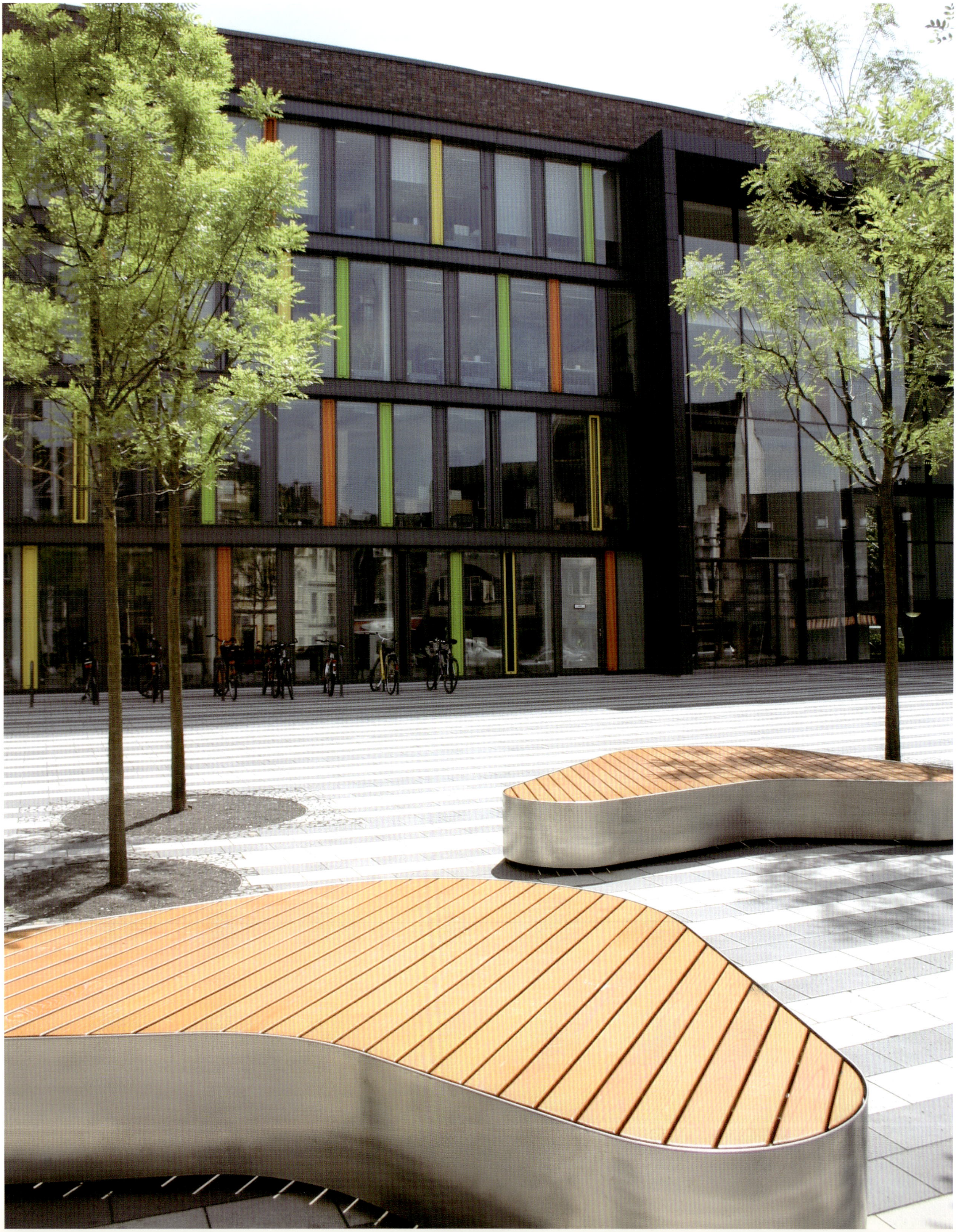

Left: Organic benches
Upper right: Courtyard
Lower right: The black and white pavement

Location: Apeldoorn, The Netherlands **Designer:** LODEWIJK BALJON Landscape Architects **Photographer:** Rik Klein Grotink, Lodewijk Baljon, Daniel Nicolas **Completion date:** 2009 **Site area:** 10,000 sqm

Station Square Apeldoorn, The Netherlands

The public space integrates different modes of transportation (bus terminal, railway station, major bicycle and pedestrian route under passing the tracks, ride and taxi stand). At the center is an underpass for bicycles and pedestrians, both linked with the railway station and platforms. A large bicycle parking is combined with the underpass. The storage is underground but, through the concaved shell shape of the square, at the same time presenting itself with a facade and is well accessible.

The shell-shaped floor radiates calm and exclusive simplicity. Yellow Portuguese granite continues throughout and up until the tree trunks. In the pattern of craquelure-like cracks, line drains, tree grates and light poles have been effortlessly integrated. The unique tree grates are a culmination of the characteristic paving pattern.

Pine trees were selected from a nursery, as if picked from the regional forest. They stand in a loose arrangement that moves with the Crescent, denser along the edge of the square and giving way to openness toward the center.

The simple light poles stand loosely spread amongst the stems of the pines. The emphasis is on the spectacle of the glass wall. The 1.3 millions LED lights in the glass wall picture a continually changing reference of 'traveling sand' that refers to a sand drift, a phenomenon of the regional landscape.

Award description:
Dutch Design Award 2009
German Design Prize 2010

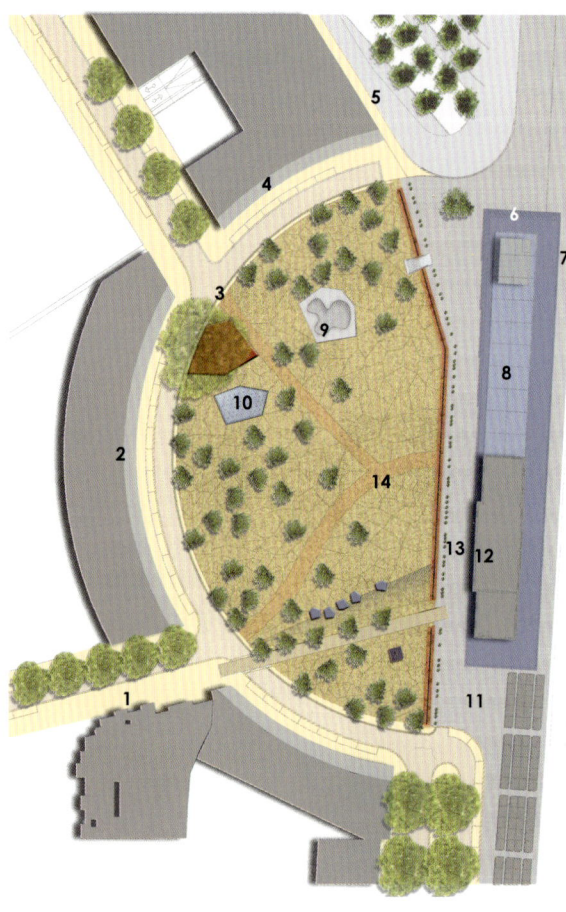

1. Road to Inner City
2. Crescent Housing + Shops
3. Platanus
4. Office
5. Bus Terminal
6. New Pavilion
7. Tracks
8. Bike Parking
9. Skate Pool
10. Water Table
11. Taxi / Drop-off
12. Historical Station Building
13. Glass Wall
14. Road to Underpass

Right: The large red metal box protects the roots of the existing plane tree, and also serves as an iconic seating element

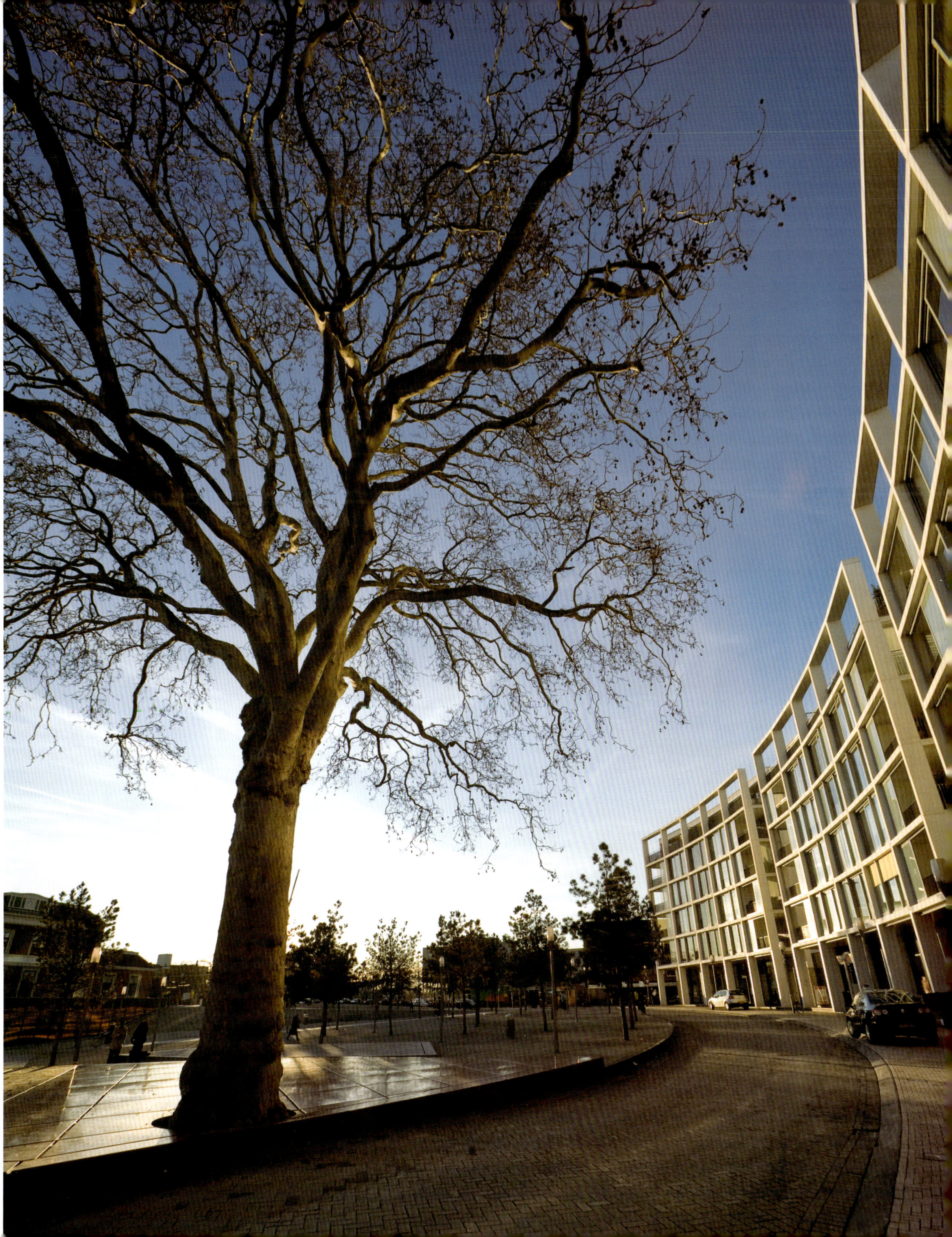

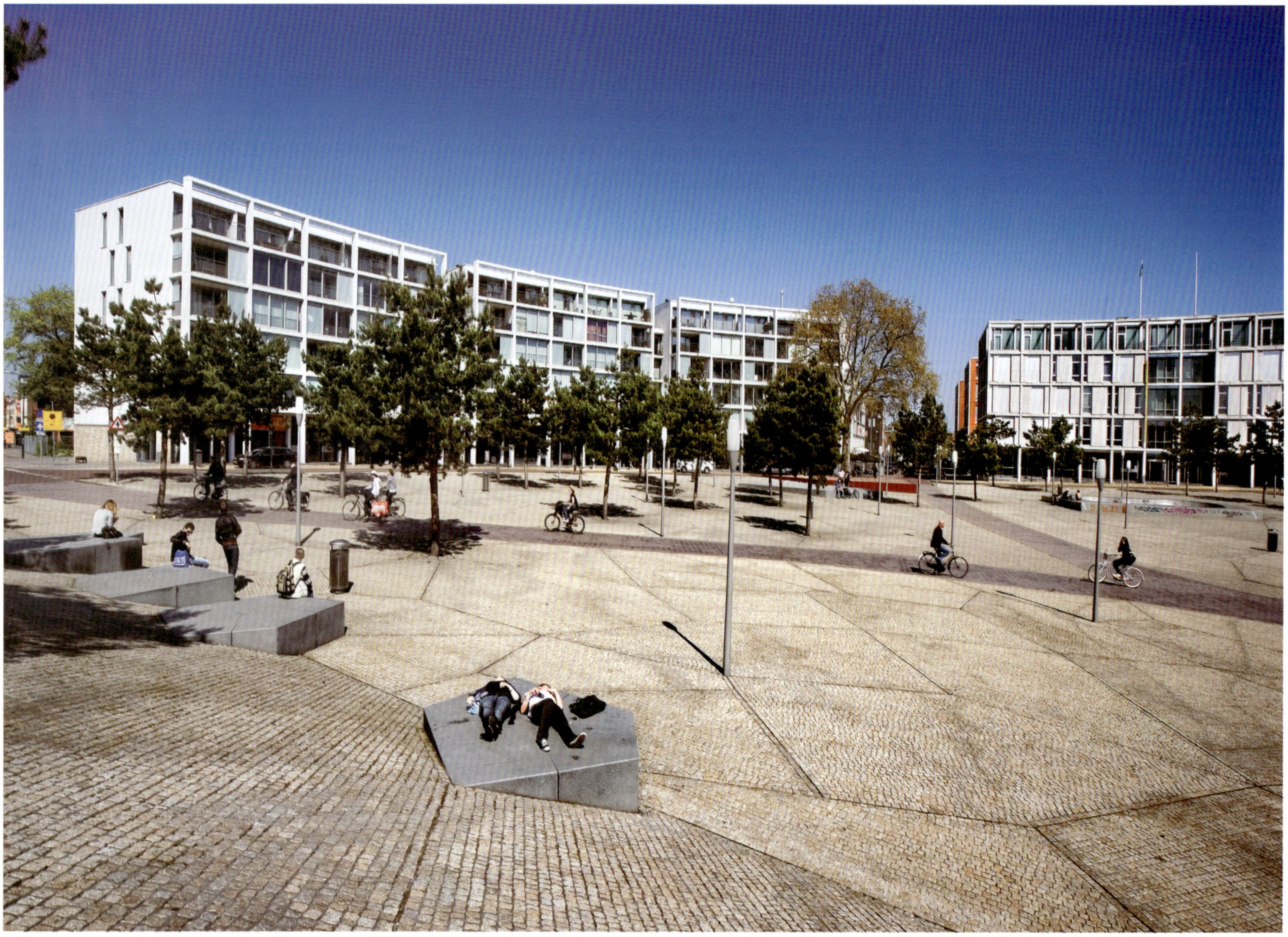

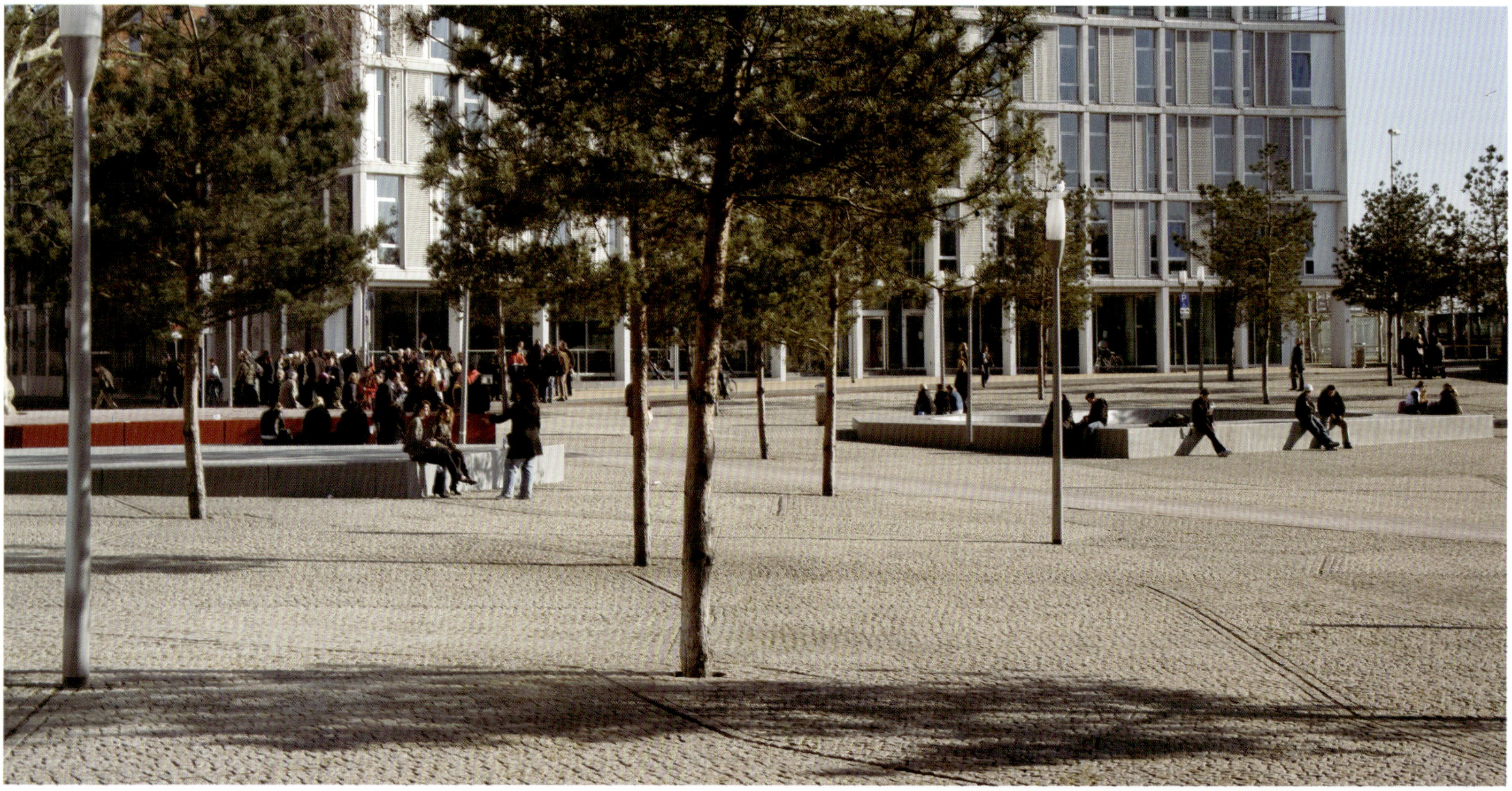

Upper left: The edge of the square expands to the crescent-shaped buildings
Lower left: The station square serves as a link for the two sides of Apeldoorn as well as from the train station to the city
Upper right: Large sitting elements express the characteristic of the craquelure pattern of the floor
Lower right: The craquelure pattern of expansion joints and line drains continues into the tree grates

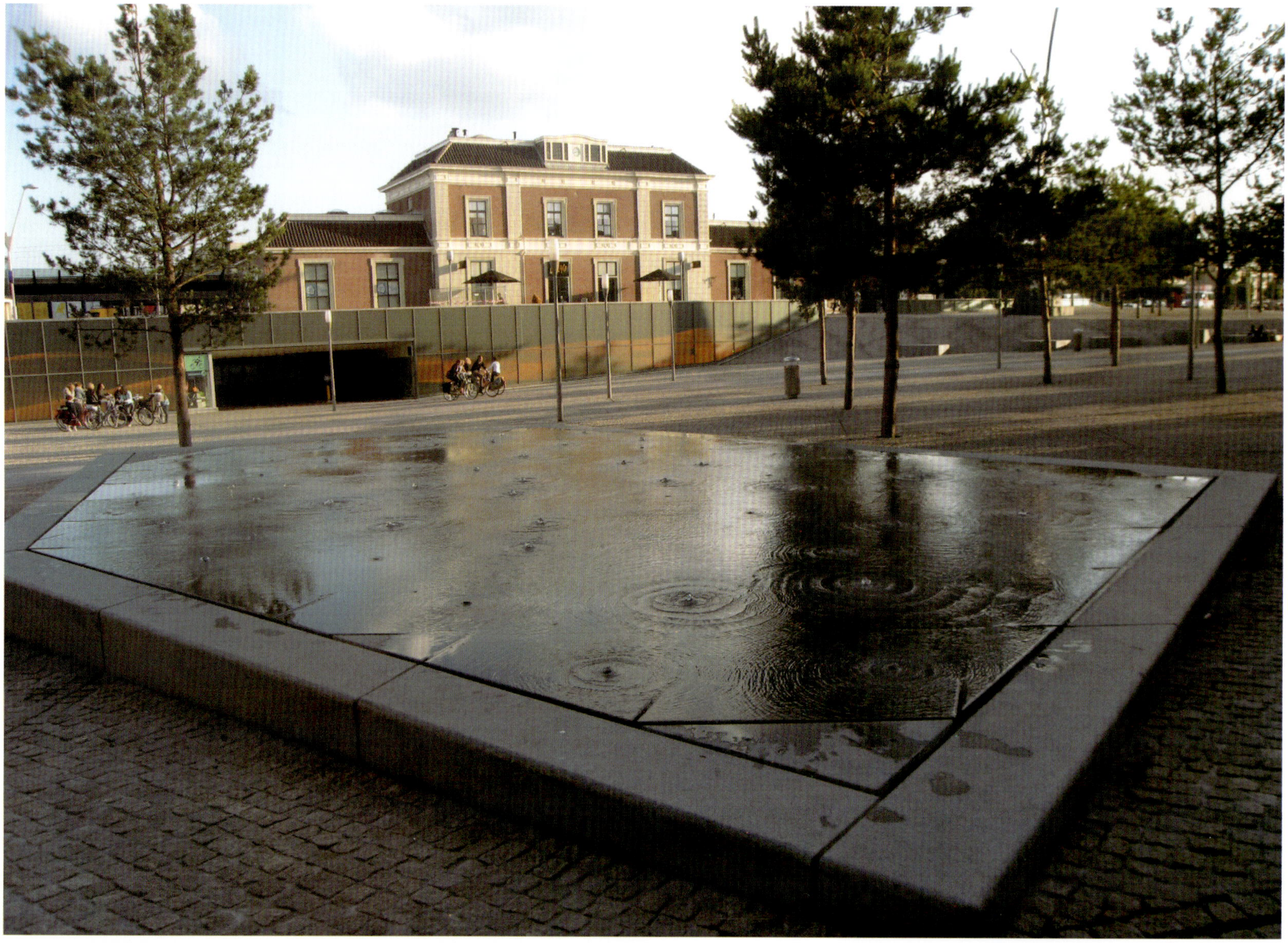
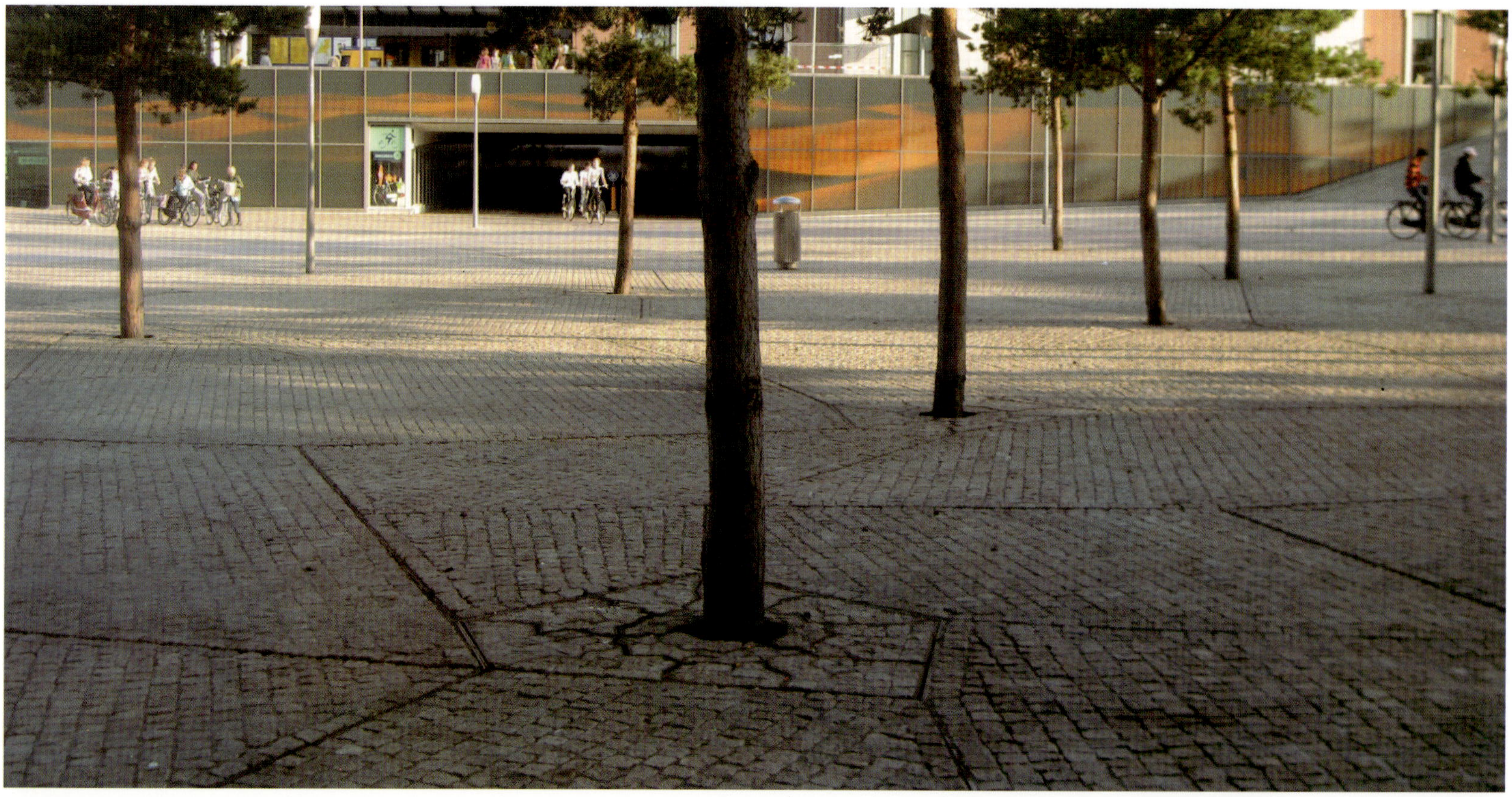

Upper left: The granite water table reflecting the sky
Lower left: Local pine trees are reference to the characteristic forest of the region
Upper right: The skate pool is a source of liveliness and diversity in activity of the square
Lower right: The irregular bubble pattern of the granite water table

ULAP-Square Berlin

Location: Berlin, Germany **Designer:** Rehwaldt Landschaftsarchitekten
Photographer: Rehwaldt Landschaftsarchitekten **Completion date:** 2008 **Site area:** 13,000 sqm

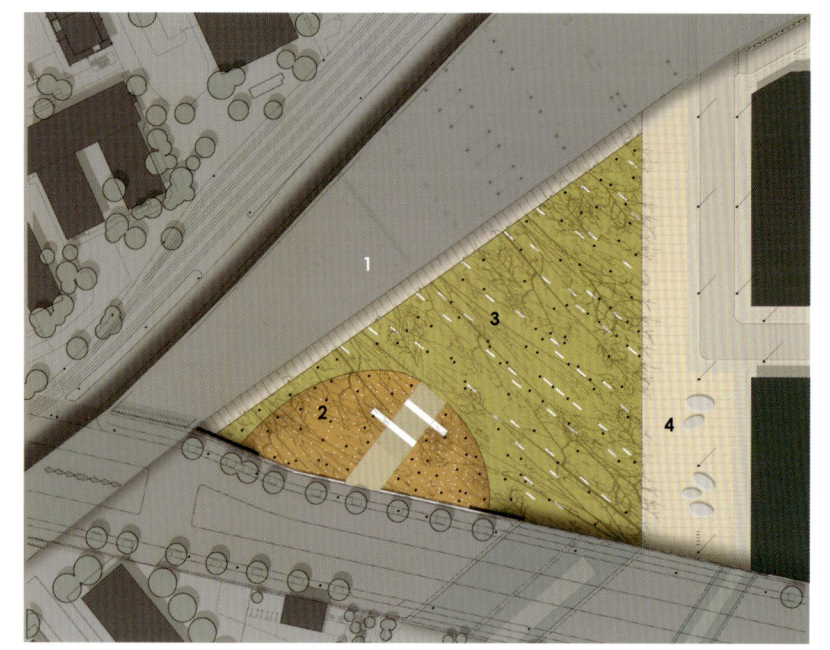

After the implementation of the new design in 2008 the triangle of the ULAP-Square became a prominent urban space which gives the new quarter a self-contained identity.

The large number of existing trees gave the reason to develop a closed green space. The picturesque developed tree population was saved consistently and dominates the space furthermore. Through pruning and removal of rank growth a 'green hall' has been formed which characterizes the square as a public open space by its atmosphere and communicative potentials. The slope at the former exhibition entrance was formed to a self-contained figure. The historic references were respected but not presented dominantly, because the utilization has totally been changed nowadays. The still existing exhibition entrance staircase at Mont-ULAP, meanwhile populated with trees, was gently integrated and in one segment adjusted to modern standards.

The urban square gives space for a wide variety of activities. The flanking building's ground-floor zones at ULAP-plaza and areas at the train track offer the opportunity of utilizing these outdoor spaces as outdoor dining zones or venue spaces. The green hall with its water-bounded surface is a flexible zone, responding in various ways to the multiple uses and activities of its surroundings. Prominent seating furniture accentuates the self-contained character of ULAP-Square. The benches which were purpose-designed and built for the site describe the space in its depth. At night they give the space a self-contained atmosphere by turning into a swarm of elegant light sculptures.

Award description:
German Landscape Prize 2009

1. Viaduct
2. Mont-ULAP
3. Green Hall
4. ULAP-Plaza

Right: Triangular square

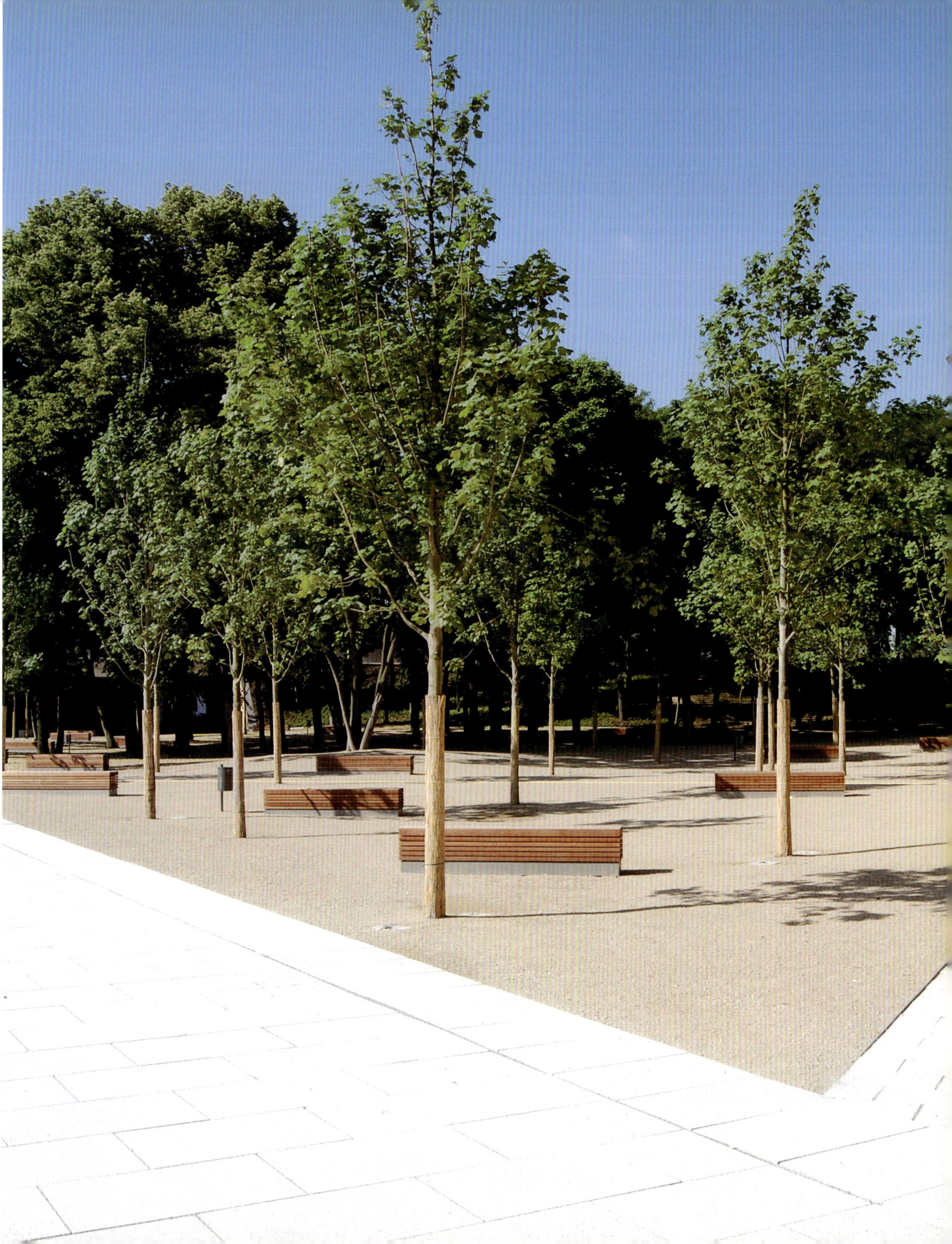

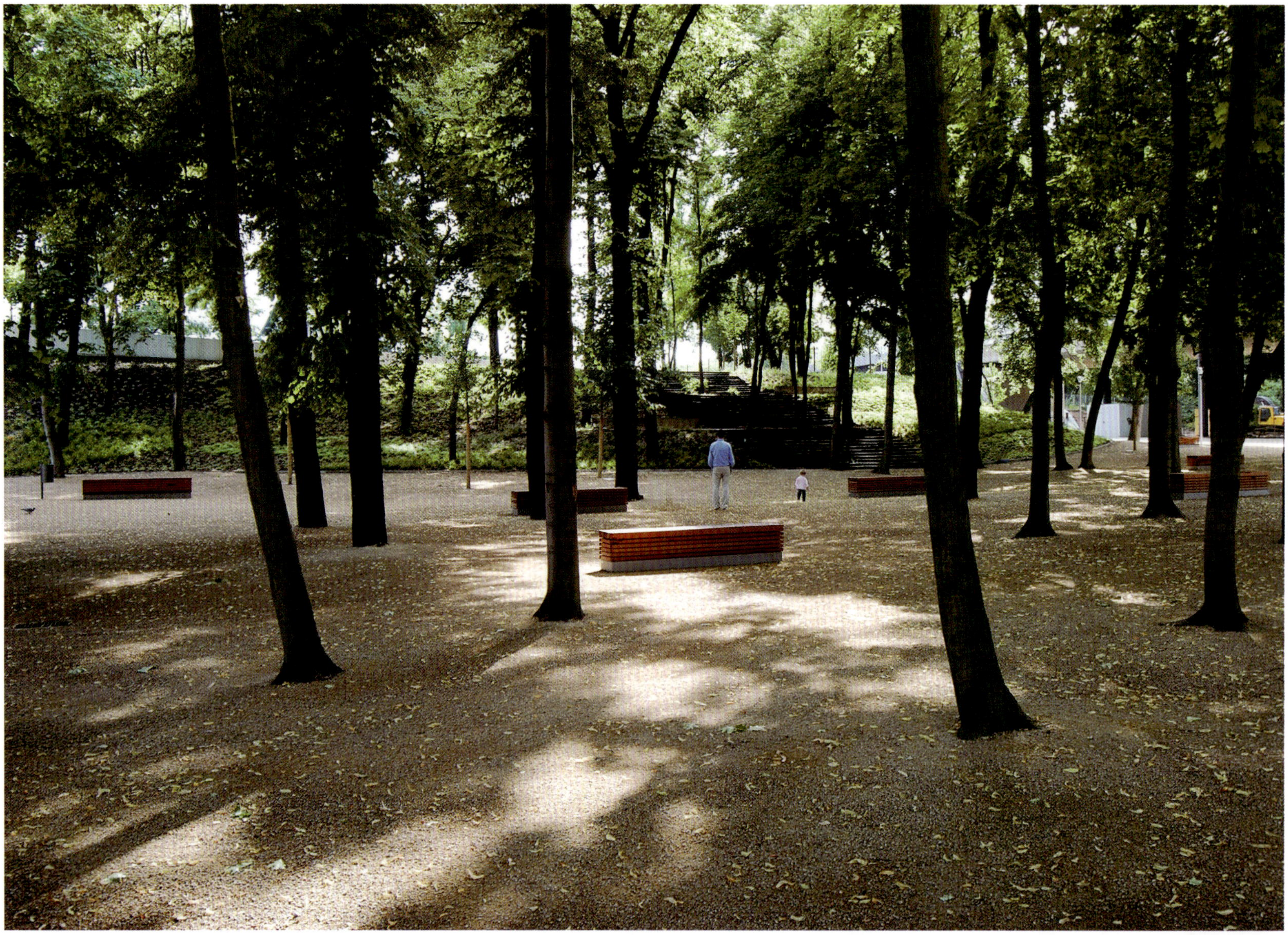

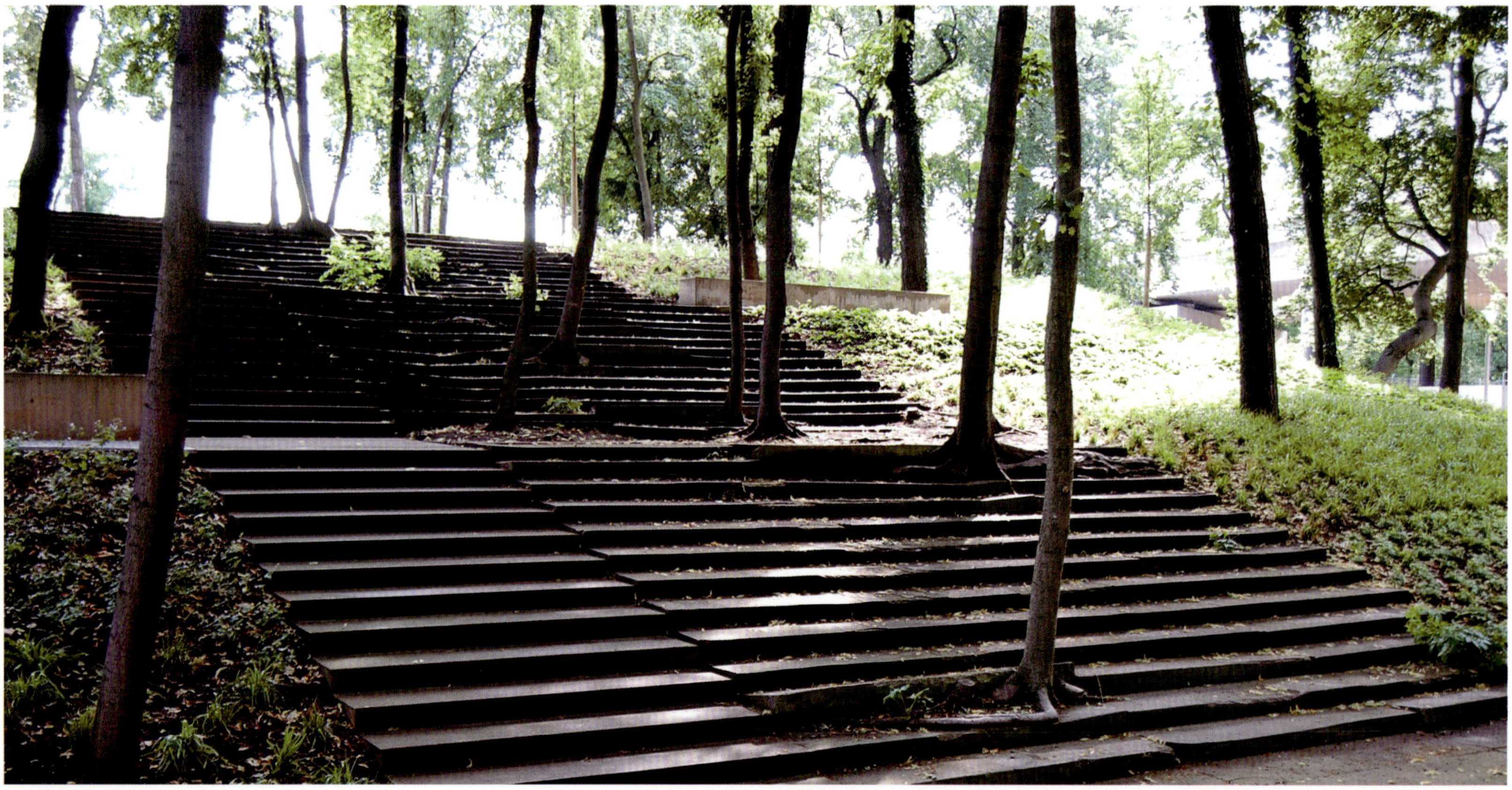

Upper left: Green hall
Lower left: Ancient and modern staircase
Upper right: View to Berlin main station
Lower right: Detail of the bench

Ursulines Square

Location: Brussels, Belgium **Designer:** L'Escaut Architectures **Photographer:** Filip Dujardin **Completion date:** 2006 **Site area:** 4,000 sqm

The project as a whole became a process of reappropriating urban space. Given the low budget, meddling with existing structure was out of question, as was overcharging it. To ensure maximum lightness, the embankment was thus inspired by techniques used in mountain highways.

Different zones occupy the whole square, according to what happens underground. Over the tunnel a mineral environment offers natural slopes and long ramps up to 45° for skating. Even before being completed, the bowl had gained international reputation as a great skating spot, as well as a welcoming space where skaters can share their culture as a testimony of art and social behavior. You will feel relaxed and comfortable when you have a walk on this square.

The lack of depth of the soil induced low vegetation, combined with wooden furniture. Tall trees and a low vegetation mattress cover the slope leading to the street side. The huge screen works as a window on the social, cultural and economical context.

Award description:
Les Règles d'Or de l'Urbanisme 2008: Public Space Award

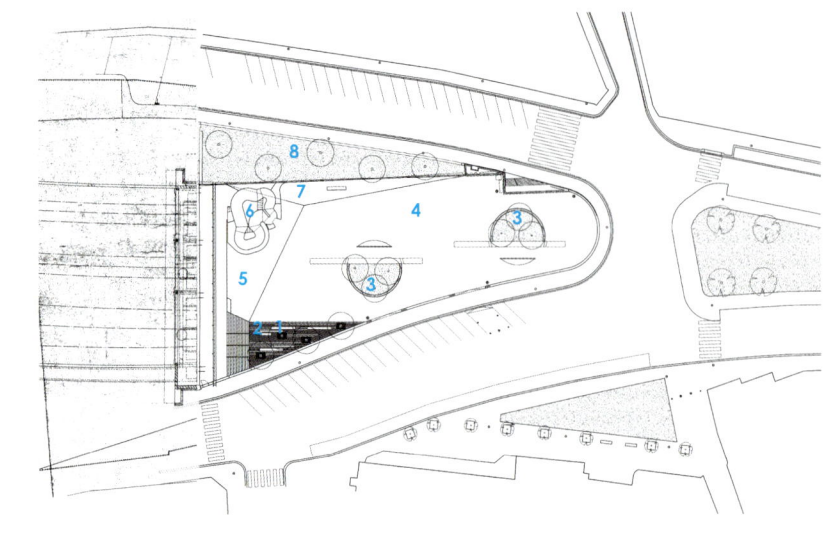

1. Rest Area
2. Drinking Water Fountain
3. Low Vegetation Bordered with Benches
4. Skate Square
5. Big Ramp (Variable Slope)
6. Bowl
7. Ursulines Ramp
8. Earth Berm

Right: Skating bowl

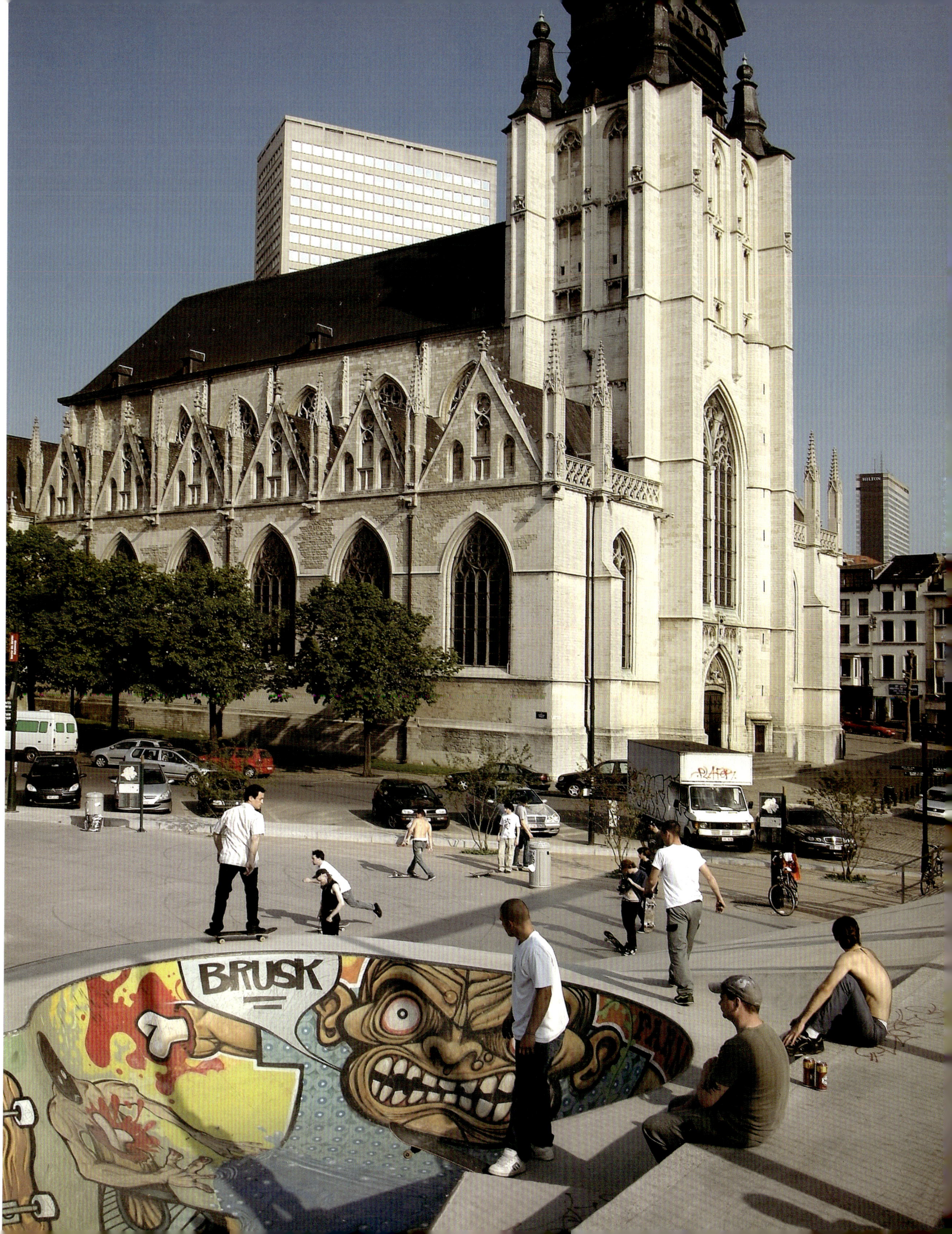
BRUSK
HILTON

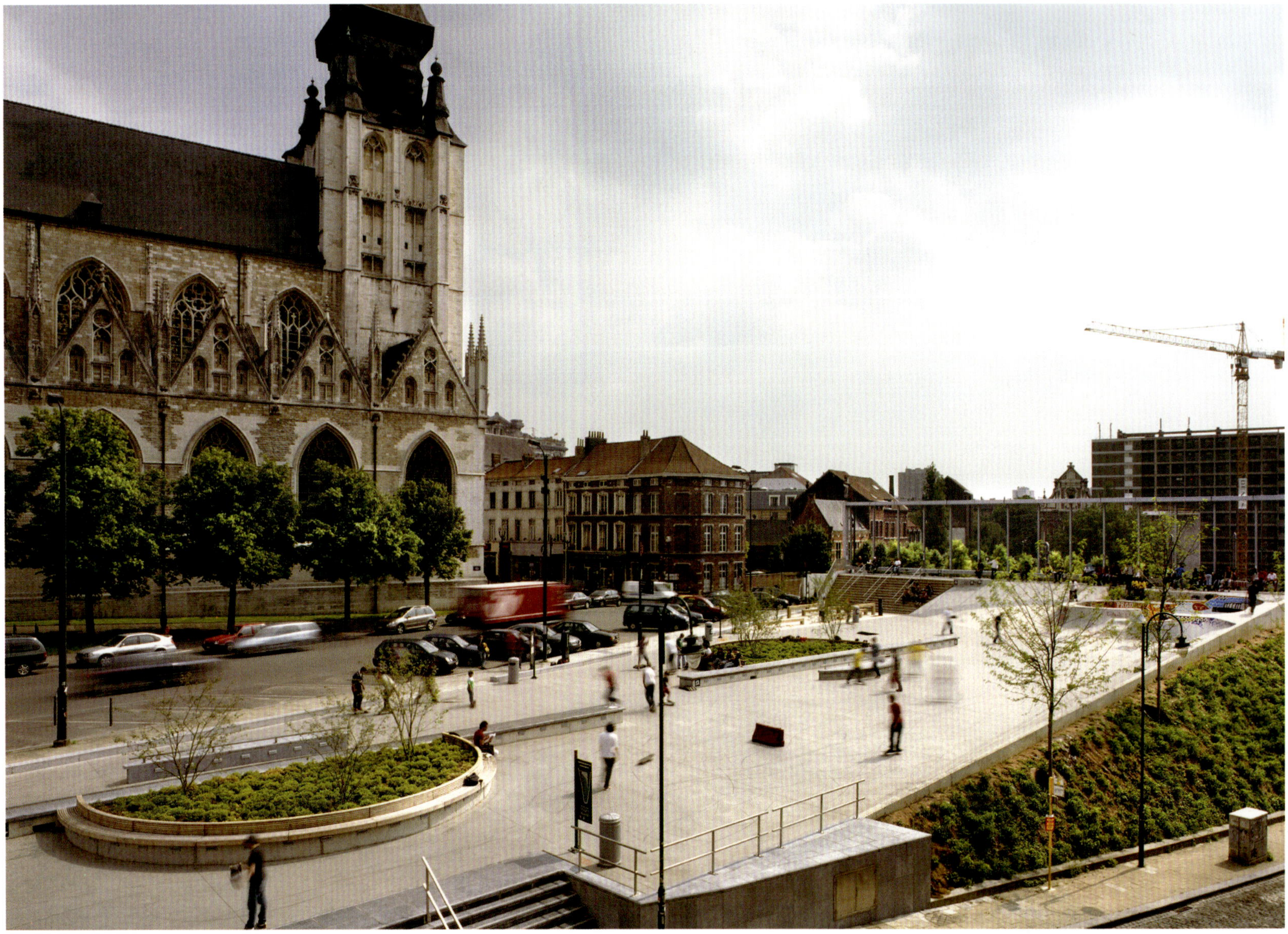

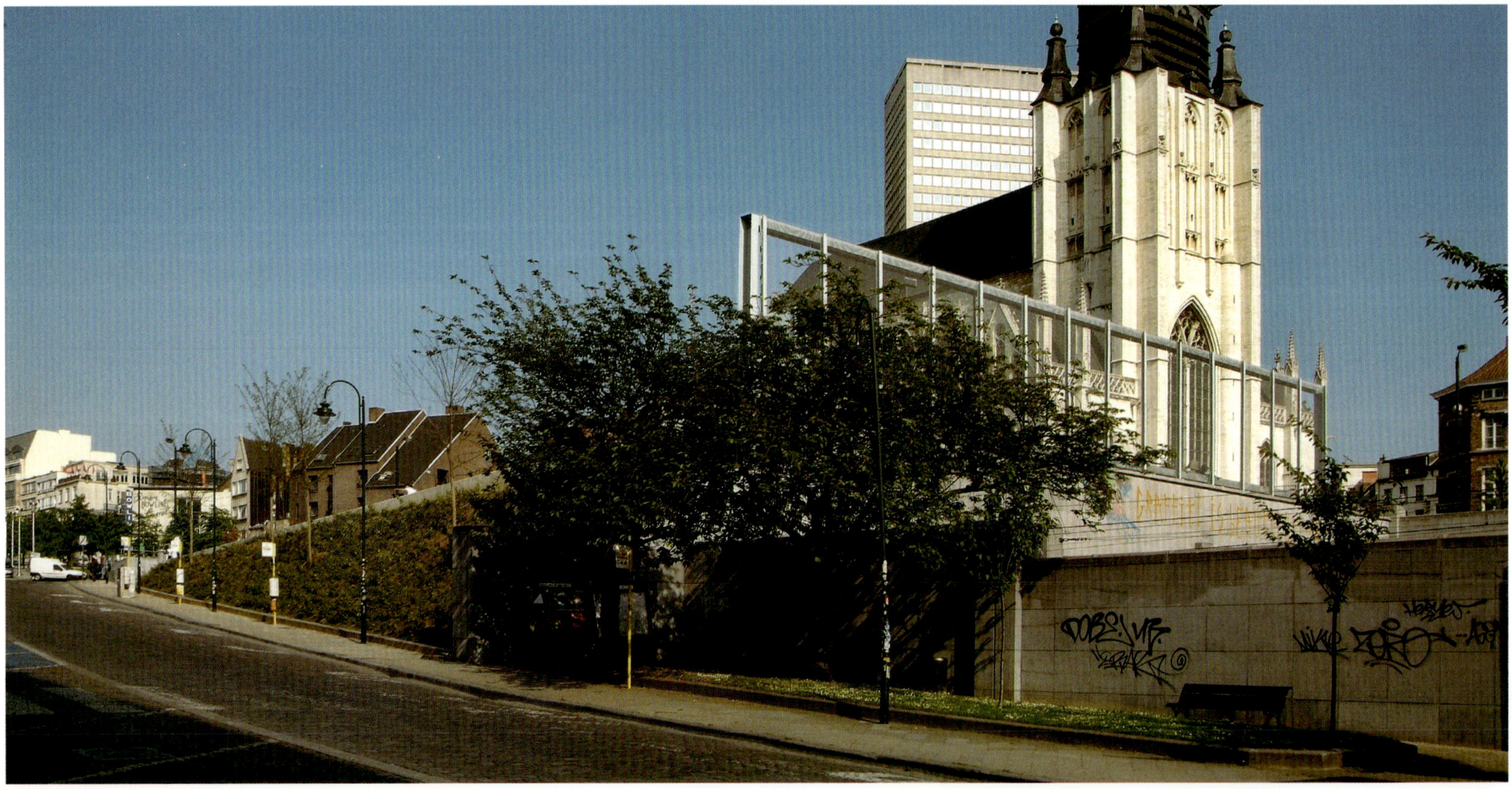

Upper left: General view
Lower left: Pathway
Upper right: Central square
Lower right: Featured skating pathway

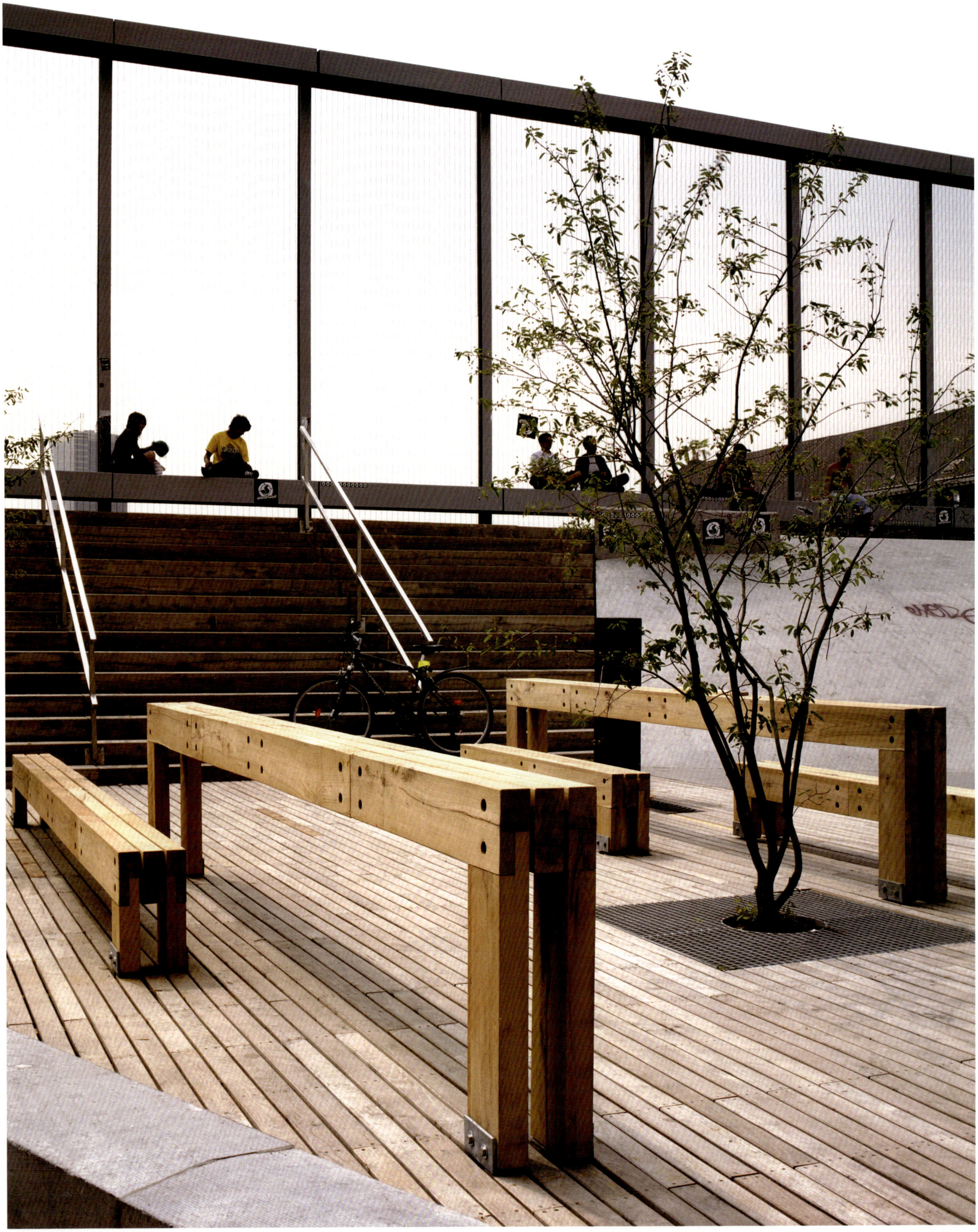

Left: Relaxing area
Right: Skating place

Koelnmesse Nord

Location: Cologne, Germany **Designer:** FSWLA Landschaftsarchitektur GmbH
Completion date: 2005 **Site area:** 88,500 sqm

The designer understands the design of the new trade fair area from a holistic perspective. The main target was to communicate the positive, friendly image of Koelnmesse to visitors within the exterior spaces. Tree and shrub plantings are set as a demarcation against the heritage-listed Arcor high rise building resembling the original character of the site. Along the boulevards between the trade fair halls column-shaped trees organize the space in a rhythmic patter. Lush groups of trees dominate the western area. They interweave the Cologne trade fair with the adjacent green spaces.

The opening square is outlined by a consistent and significant design idea – linearity. Rhythmic stripes cover the entire surface thus creating unity. The design consists of few elements – hardscape, green and furniture. Logical traffic organization across the square helped creating generous pedestrian areas of high recreational value. Column-shaped trees accentuate the third dimension of the site while an array of multi-trunk shrubs in bizarre shapes stabilize the main axis. An interesting play of light and shade shows as a result. The hardscape is structured and brought to life by three different colors. Along the main axis linear stripes of planting and seating are alternating. Hedges add extra support to the spatial structure by coating the square. A stretched-out circular bench is located in front of the building entrance. Little rooms created by column-shaped trees, hedges and flowering planting beds offer opportunities to communicate and relax.

1. Traffic and Logistics
2. Recreation and Leisure Area

Right: Overlooking the north entrance from the road

Eingang Nord Entrance North
spoga
gafa
Congress-Centrum Nord

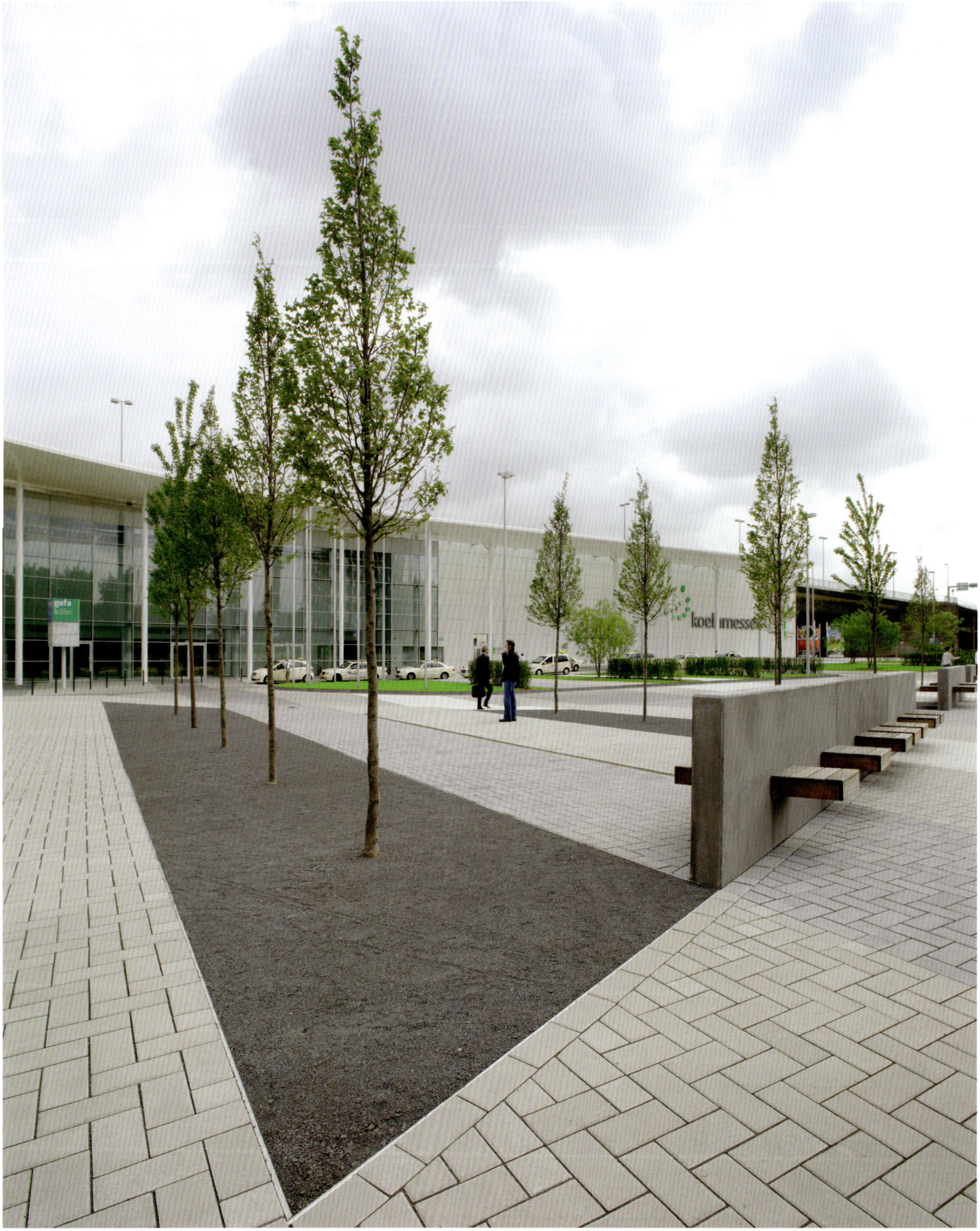
gafa
köln

Left: Close-up of resting area
Upper right: Aerial view of the north entrance
Lower right: Deliveries area

Ausstellereingang
Exhibitors' Entrance

Eingang Nord Entrance North

Upper left: Tree planting by exhibitors' entrance
Lower left: View across the site toward the north entrance
Upper right: Resting area facing the entrance
Lower right: Planting bed by the entrance

Target Plaza at Target Field

Location: Minnesota, USA **Designer:** Oslund.and.Assoc. **Photographer:** Paul Crosby, Oslund.and.Assoc, George Heinrich **Completion date:** 2010 **Site area:** 28,327 sqm

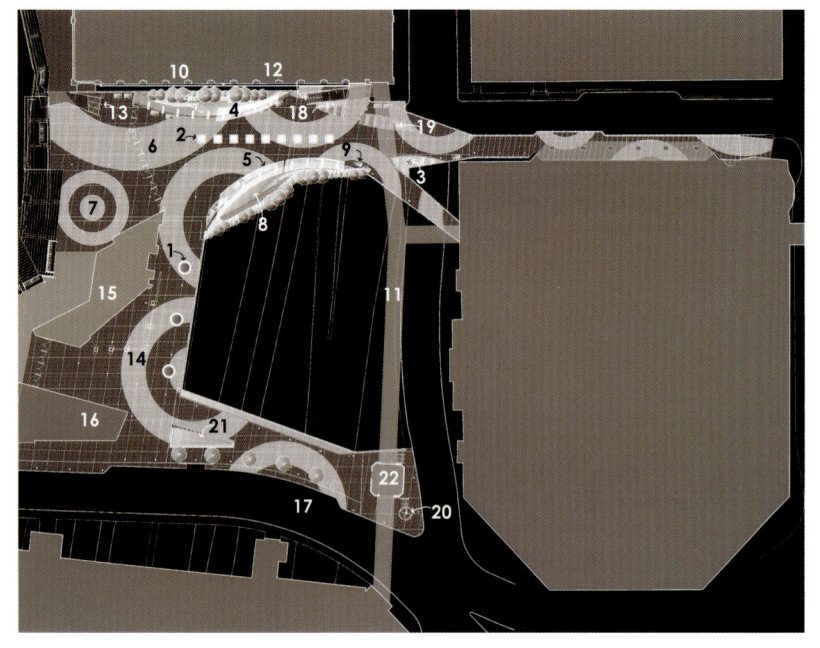

The intent was to create a dynamic urban space that offers enjoyment on multiple levels, both on game days and when the field is quiet.

Moving into the plaza from the Sixth Street, fans pass by a custom-designed sculpture of Rod Carew and nearby stands another sculpture of Kirby Puckett. Vendor carts line the edges of the space, adjacent to extensive bench seating placed under metal shade canopies. Lining the main axis into Target Field is a line of topiaries that recall baseball bats, planted with hops. Integral bench seating surrounds the base of each topiary, complimenting the seating found on either side of the walkway.

Covering the entire facade of the 'B' Ramp is a kinetic wind sculpture by artist Ned Kahn. A mesmerizing compilation of baseball-sized aluminum discs that move like liquid as the wind blows across its face. Immediately below, and across the walkway from the wind sculpture are large planted green spaces with canopy trees, flowering trees, perennials, shrubs, and turf. An oversized bronze baseball glove sculpture is located on the ramp side – allowing many opportunities for improvised pictures. Small 'pitcher's mound' planters are found adjacent to the ticket office – also with integral seating surrounding them.

1. Mound Planters
2. Topiary Frames
3. Target Logo
4. Bronze Glove
5. Shade Canopies (Visors)
6. Entry Canopy
7. Target Logo Paving Pattern
8. Raised Turf Areas
9. Vending Cart Locations
10. Wind Veil
11. Skyway
12. Stairs to Plaza from Skyway
13. Stairs to Outfield Upper Deck Seating
14. Ticketing Area
15. Ticket Office
16. Pro-Shop
17. Drop-Off Area
18. Kirby Puckett Statute
19. Rod Carew Sculpture
20. Harmon Killebrew Sculpture
21. Wedge Planter
22. Skyway Tower

Right: This curved, low-walled planting and seating area provides scale to the 27-meter-wide deck

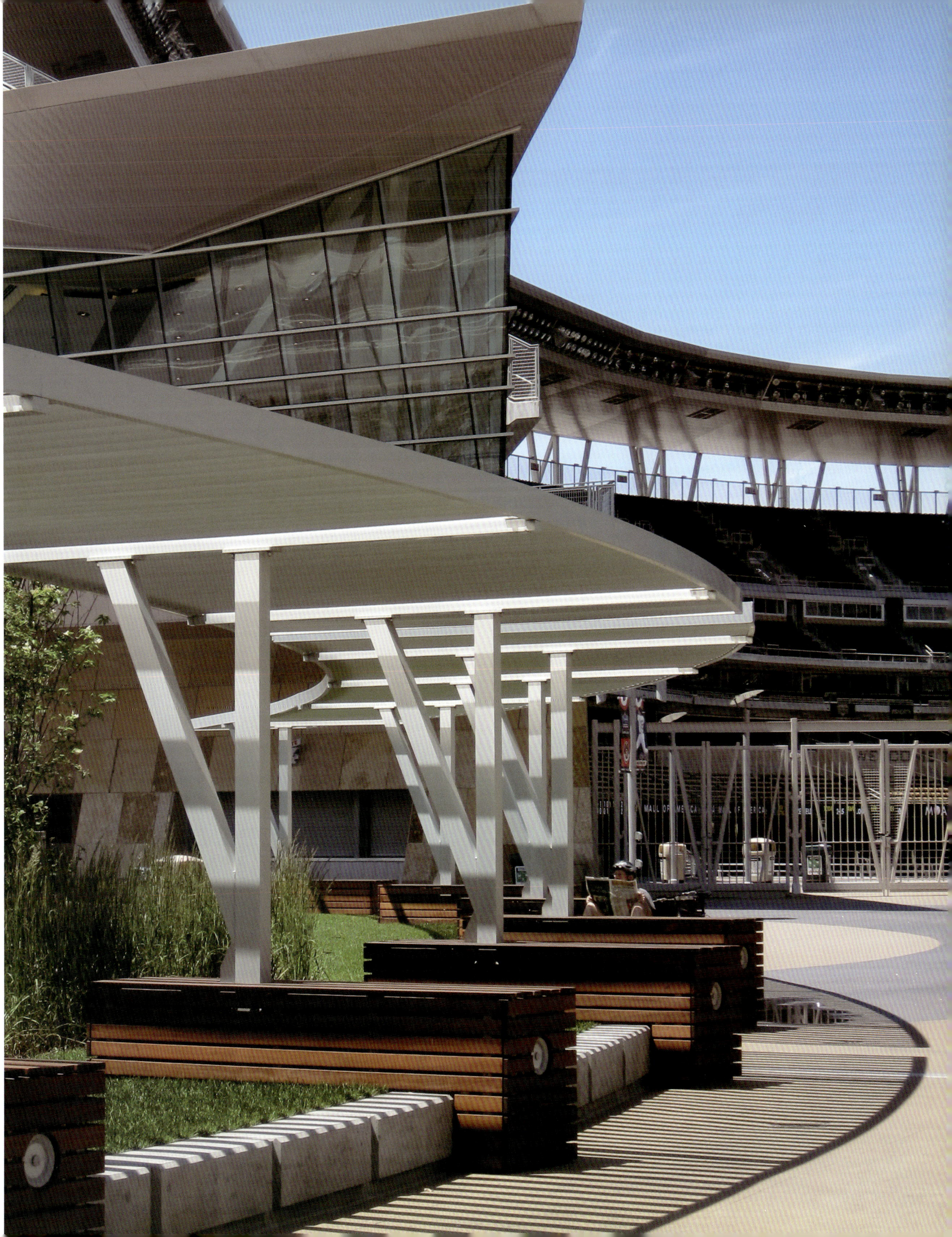
MALL OF AMERICA
MOA

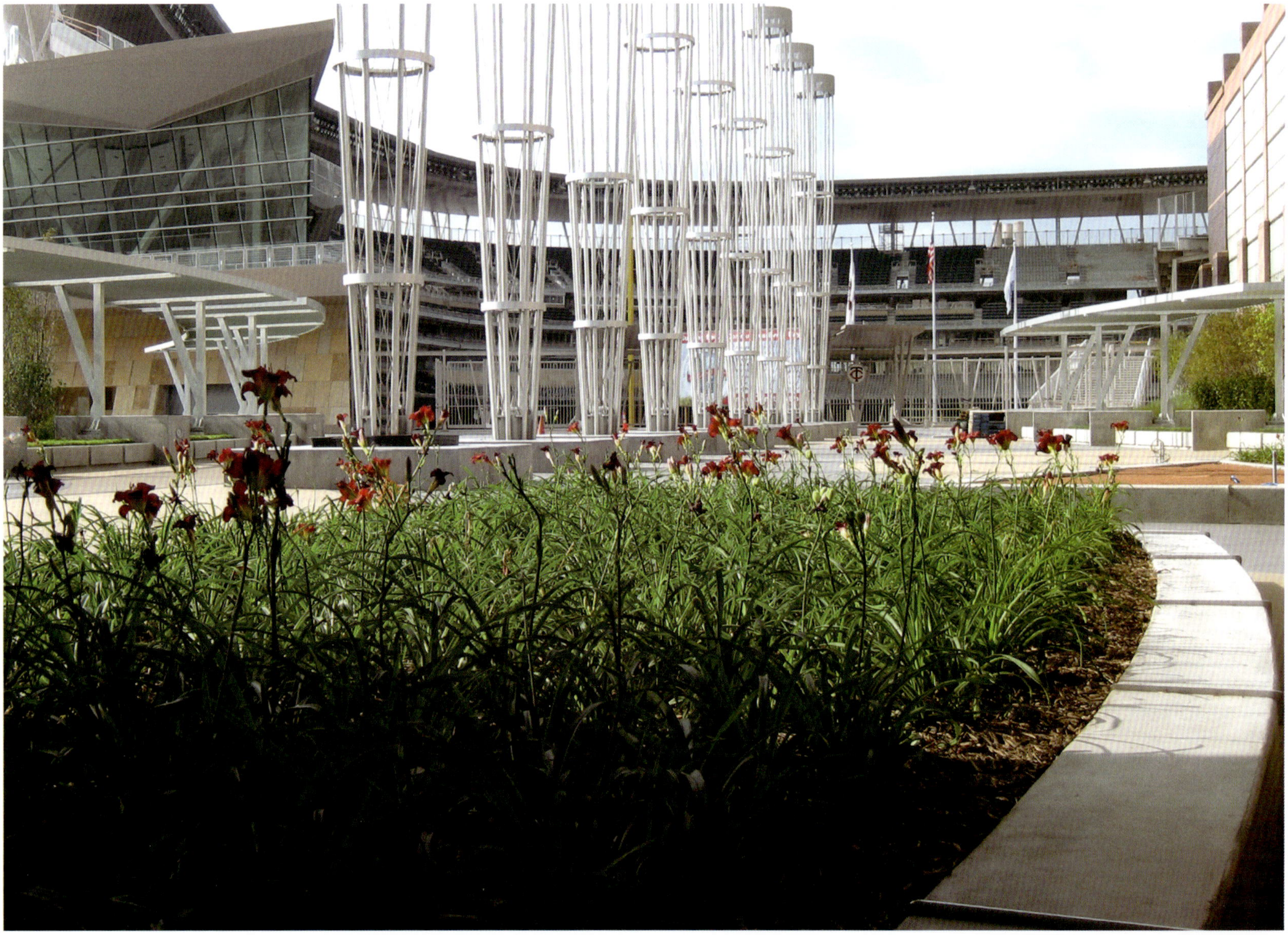

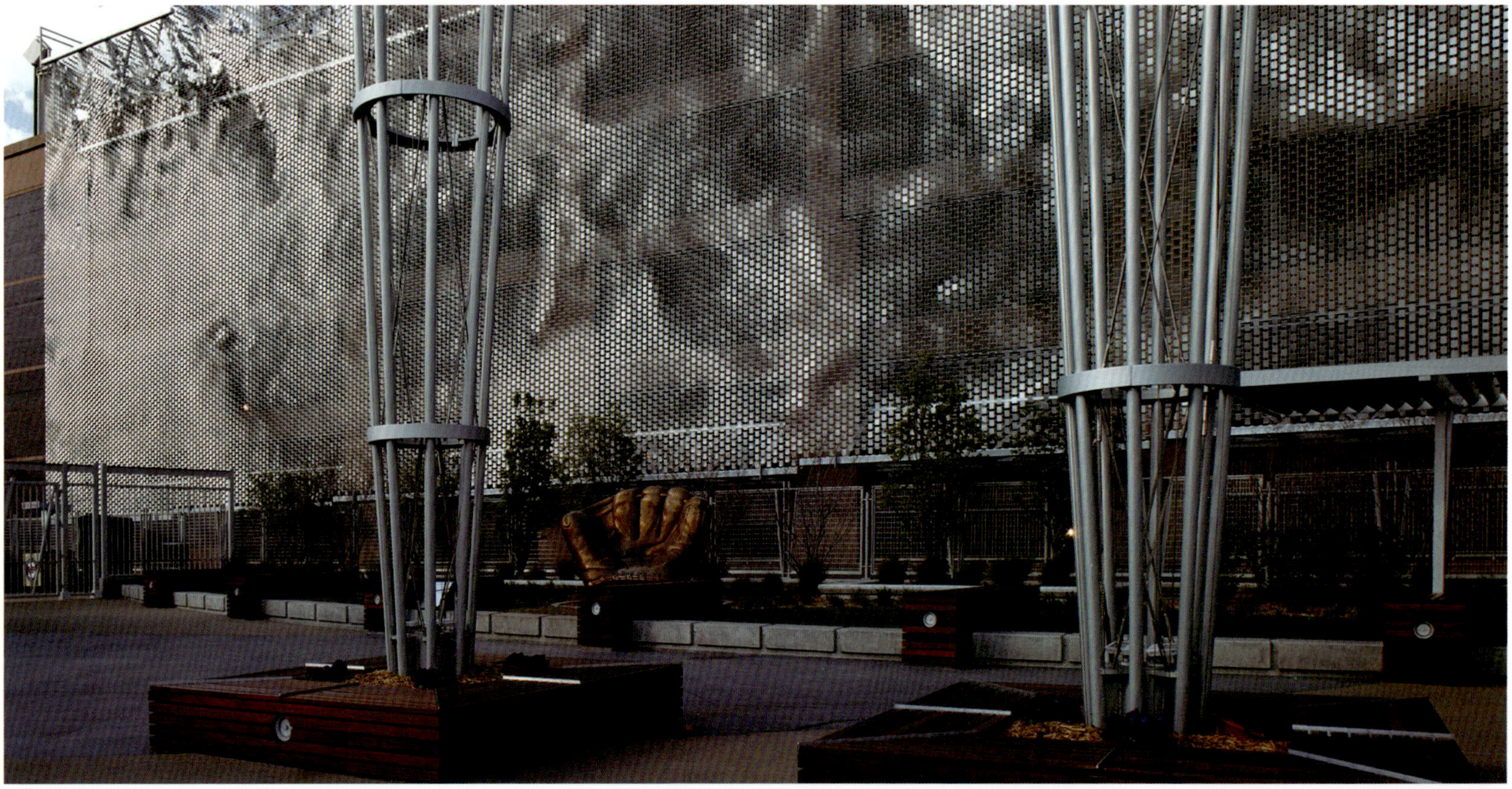

Lower left: The 'wind veil' masks the parking-ramp facade that edges one side of the plaza
Upper right: Evening reveals the subtle details of paving on the plaza, the one bat per inning that is lit, and the life-sized bronze of Twin's great, Kirby Puckett
Lower right: Harmon Killebrew bronze statue

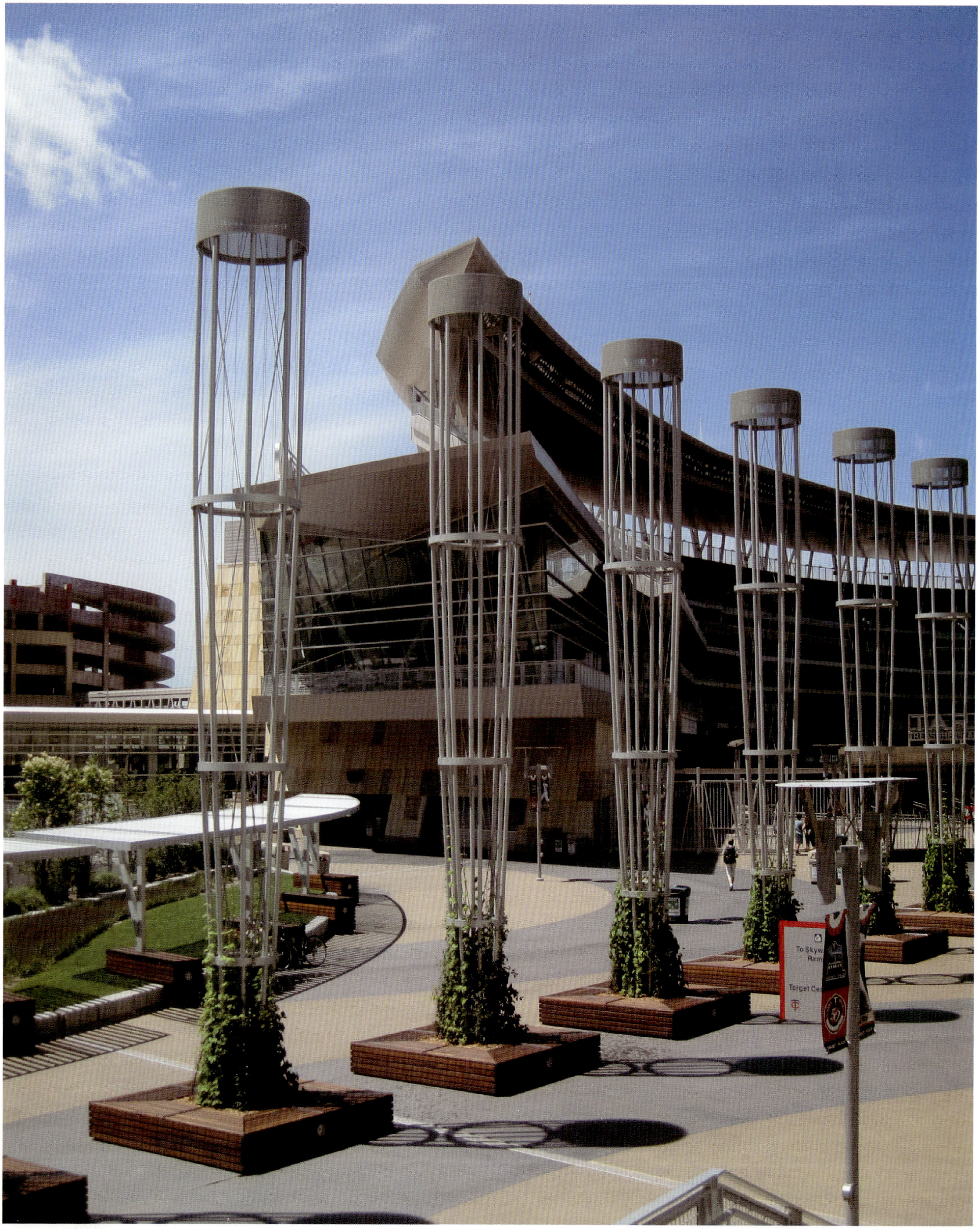

Left: Lining the main axis into Target Field is a line of topiaries that recall baseball bats
Upper right: Crowds descend upon Target Plaza on opening day for the Twins 2010 season
Lower right: Ipe bench detail, of the Mound Planter

Plaza Indautxu

Location: Bilbao, Spain **Designer:** Ander Marquet Ryan (JAAM Architecture Partnership) **Photographer:** Elker Azqueta **Completion date:** 2006 **Site area:** 18,500 sqm

When creating the social space, the designers opted for a big central circle with a diameter of 40 meters. This circle would be used to celebrate fairs of the arts, of books and of local gastronomical products. To support all of these activities, the designers built a translucent glass and wooden canopy more than four meters wide which goes along the entire perimeter of the large circle.

The remaining space between the squared perimeter of the plaza and the central circle would become a peaceful space. It shouldn't be an open space but filled with vegetation and suitable for walking. Therefore, the designer created circular gardens with a tree in its center, of different diameters imitating the central space, and sprinkled throughout the square. Between them there are many picturesque paths for walking that, on the other hand, allow those who are passing through to cross the square in any direction.

This possibility to cross the square in all directions was another important goal that affected its definition: its urban quality. This goal presented a problem because there was more than three meters of difference in height from one extreme to the other, and the designers didn't want to use steps or ramps that would affect the walking paths. The solution was to develop a continuous surface with changing inclinations generated from the union of the square's center with the perimeter through straight lines.

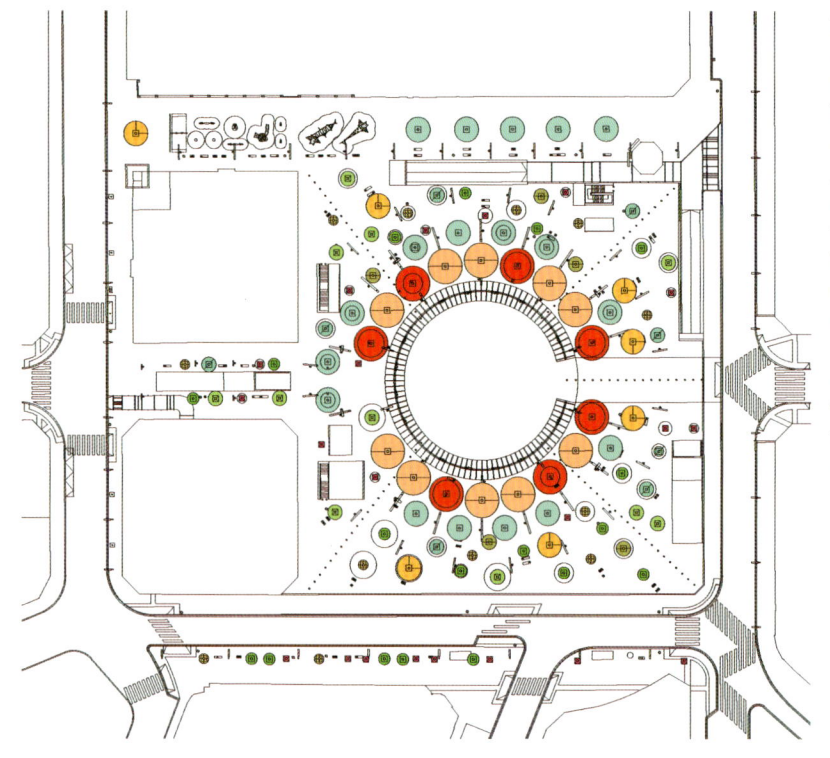

1. Liquidambar Styraciflua 'Worplesdon'
2. Acer X Freemani 'Jeffersred'
3. Betula Utilis 'Jacquemotii'
4. Porrotia Persica
5. Taxus Baccata Fastigiata Aurea
6. Thuja Orientalis 'Pyramidalis Aurea'
7. Prunus Serrulata 'Amanogawa'
8. Laurus Nobius
9. Nandina Domestica
10. Photinia Fraseri 'Red Robin'

Right: General view of the plaza

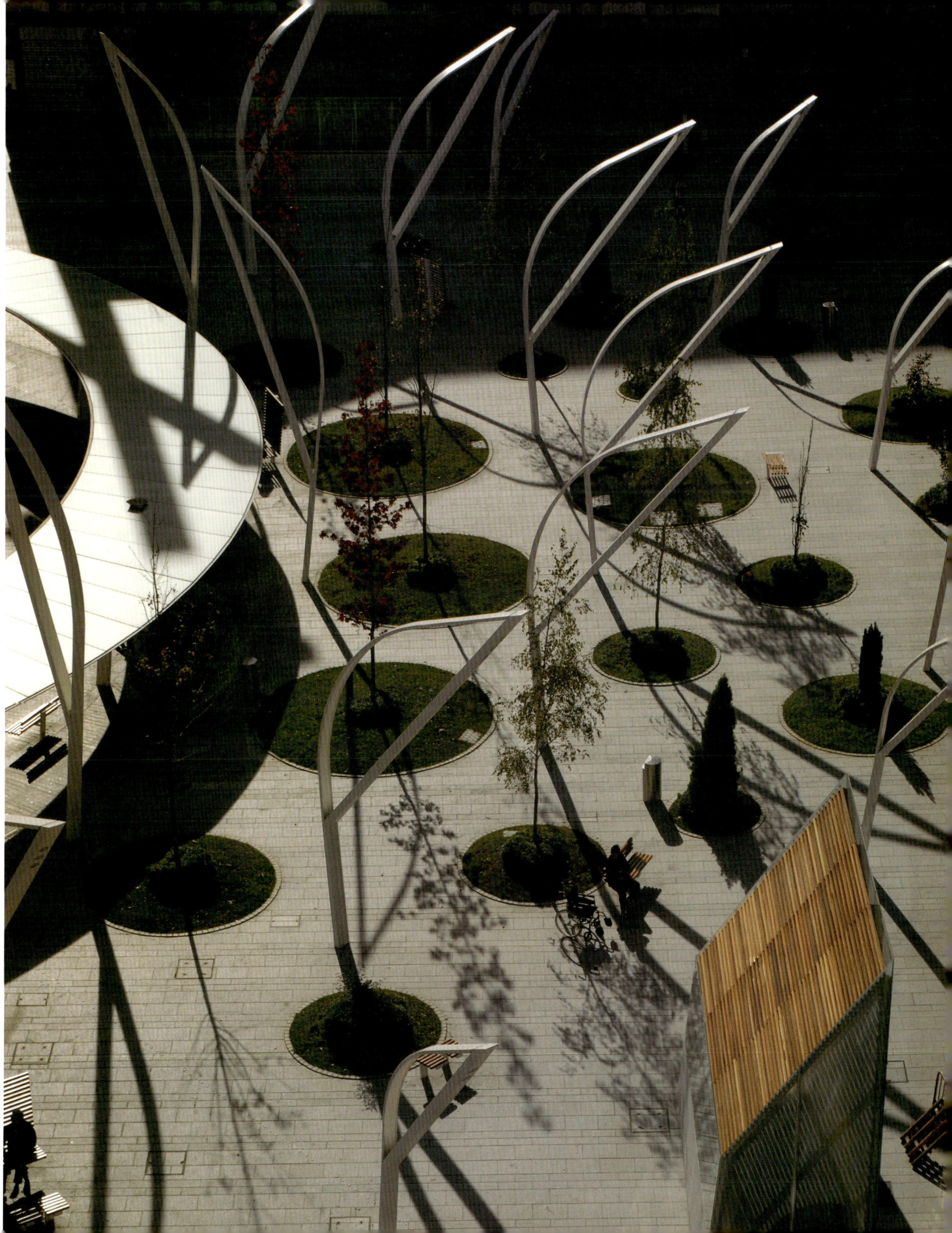

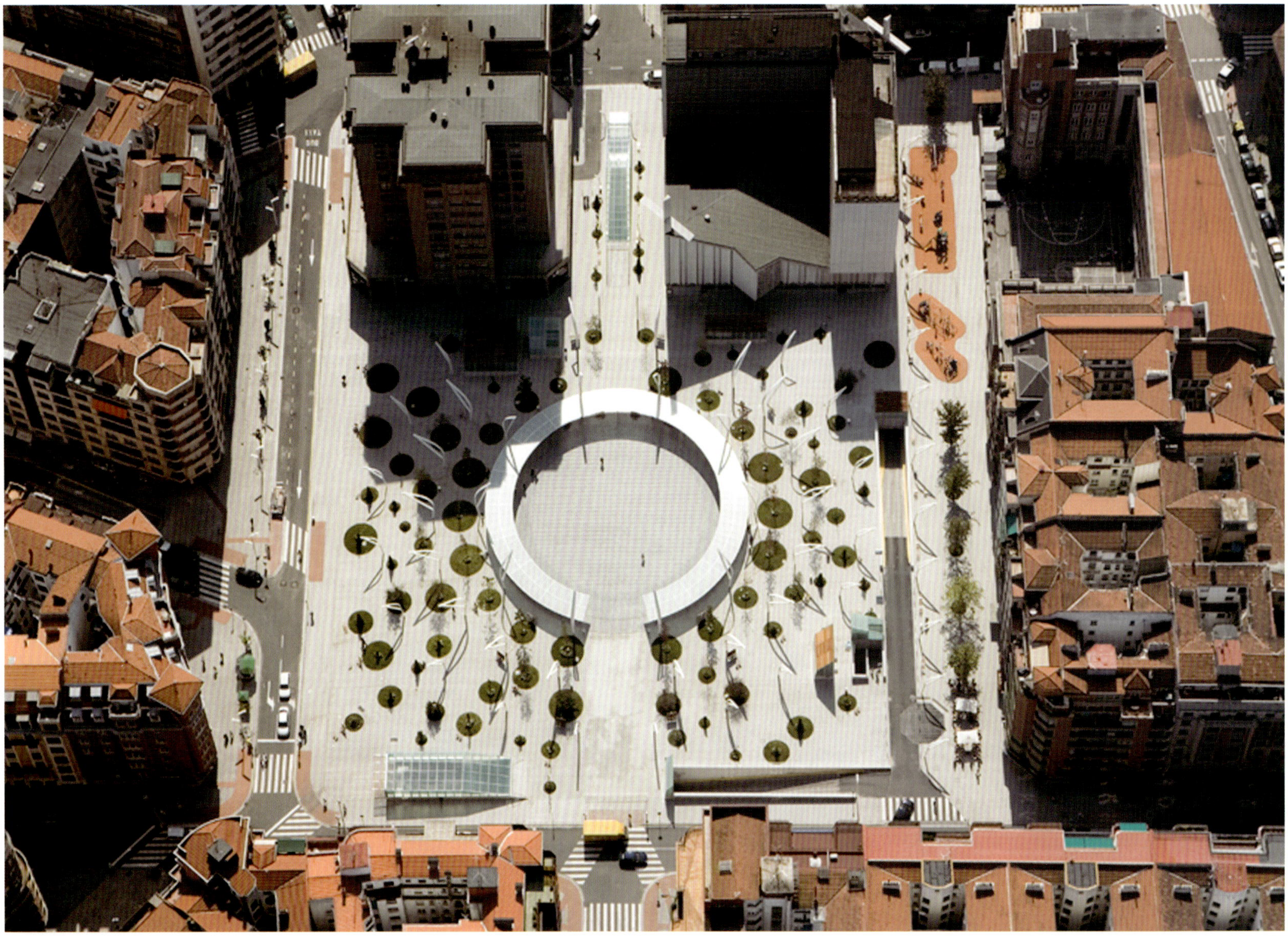

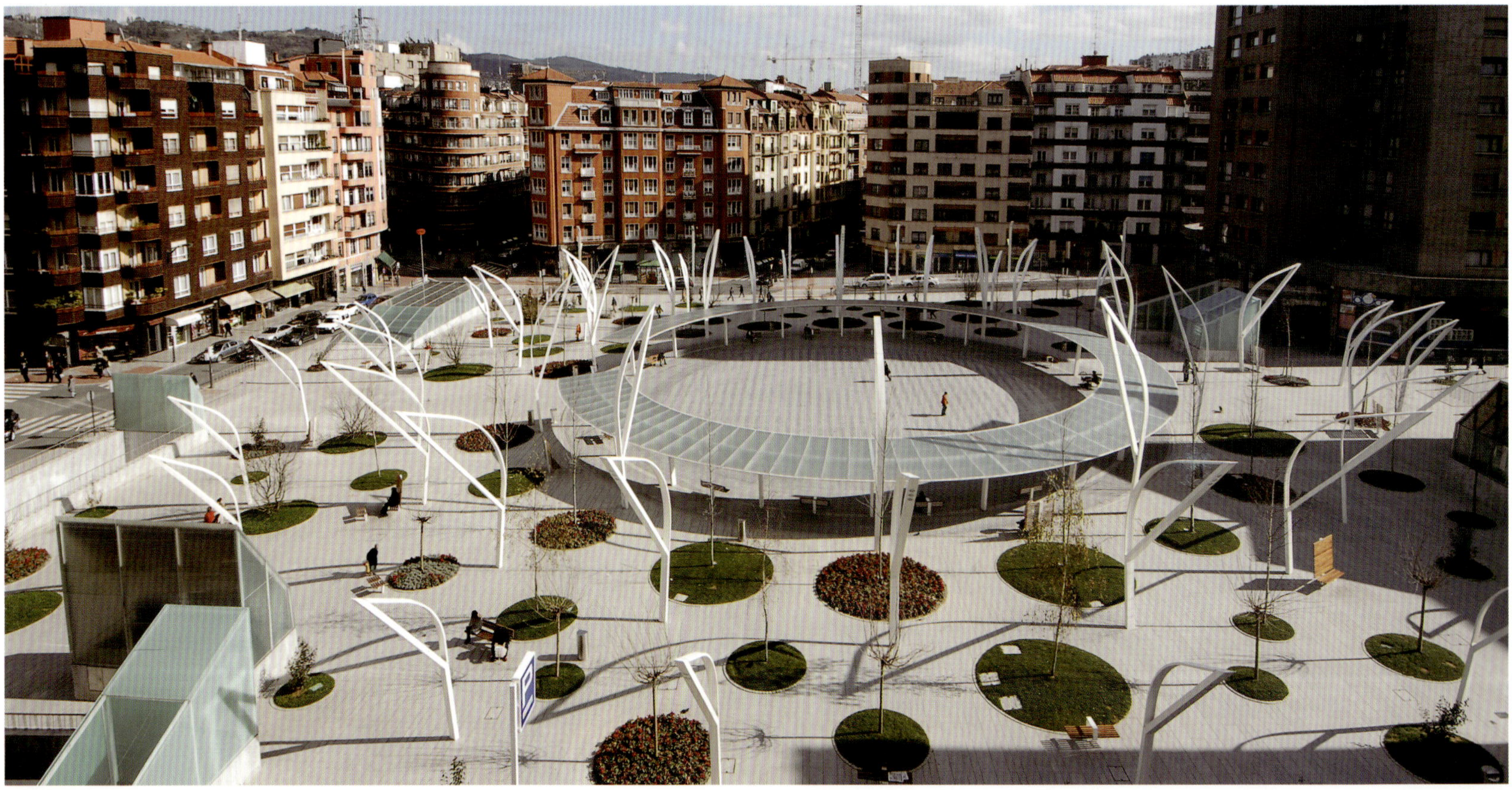

Upper left: The possibility to cross the square in all directions was another important goal that affected its definition

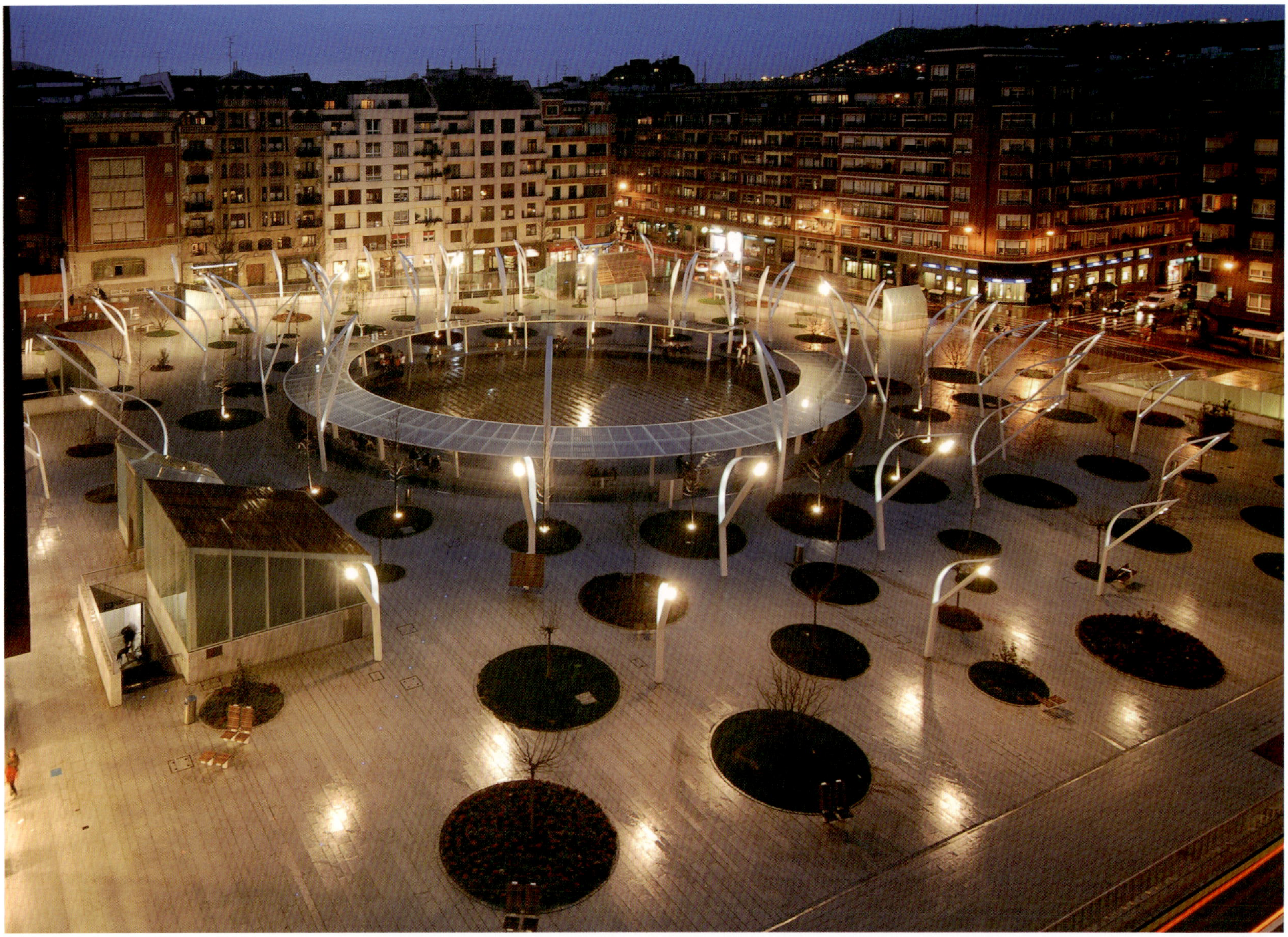

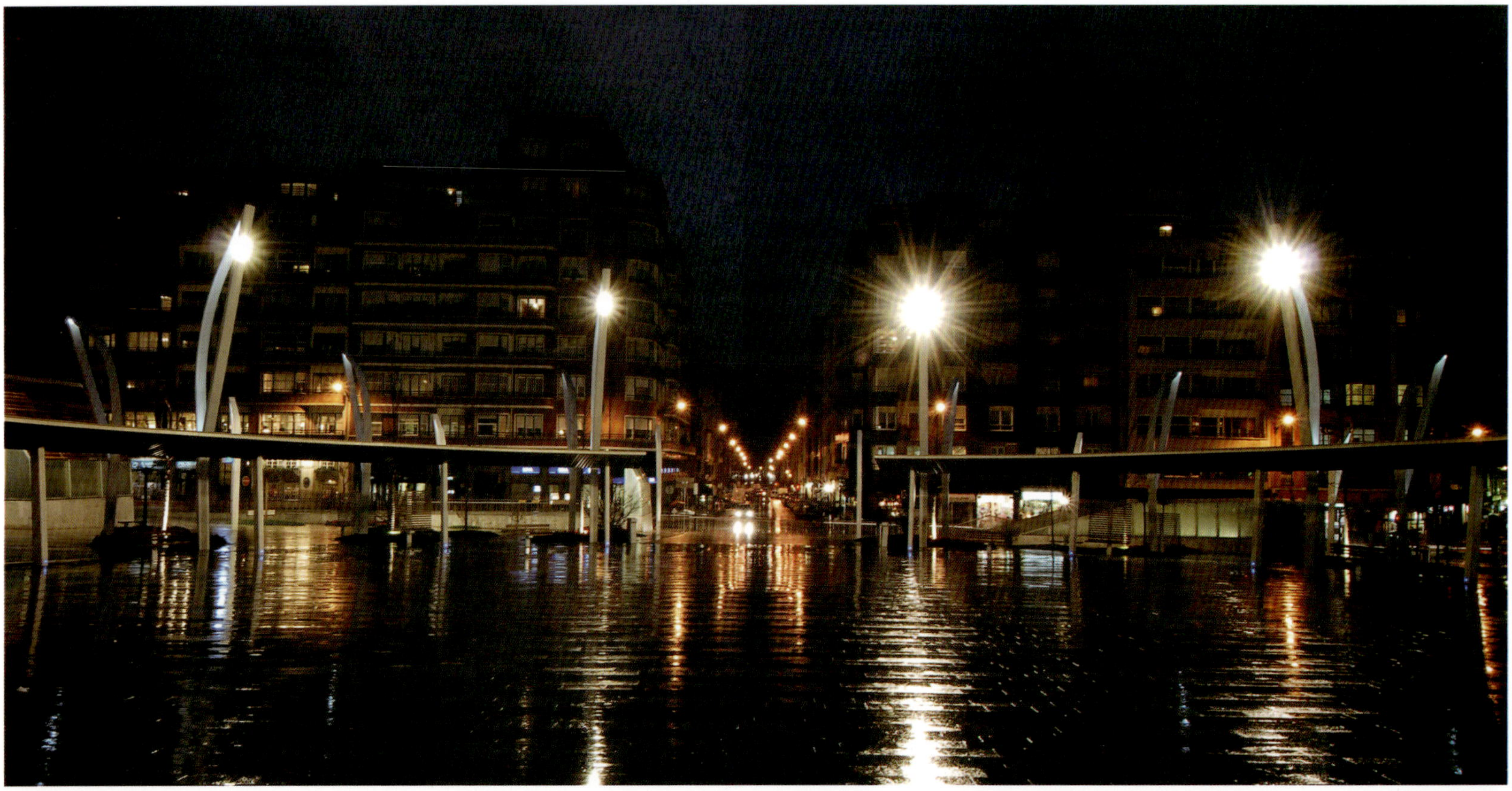

Upper left: Night view of the plaza
Lower right: Sculptural light pole as a decorative streetscape

Vancouver Convention Center Expansion Project

Location: Vancouver, Canada **Designer:** PWL Partnership Landscape Architects Inc. **Photographer:** PWL Partnership Landscape Architects Inc.
Completion date: 2009 **Site area:** 24,000 sqm

The landscape architects contributed solutions to two major design challenges in the overall project. First, for a structure entirely on marine deck and 40% over water, conventional planting approaches were not possible. The plaza, designed to hold up to 8,000 people, did not offer the depth or structural support for tree plantings. Instead, smaller peripheral spaces defined by planters moderate the scale of the plaza and create intimate, comfortable and flexible areas. The landscape architects also worked with the structural engineers to modify the viaduct truss structure to facilitate tree planting. With these modifications, the trusses now contain enough growing medium to provide continuous trenches for street trees along the south edge of the project.

The second design challenge was to mediate disparate architectural forms. The original Convention Center and the new expansion feature strikingly different architecture and a 12-meter grade change at the west end. The landscape architects used paving patterns and furnishings as wayfinding devices and unifying elements. Working with the architects, the landscape architects created a grand staircase, complete with fully accessible ramps, between the existing Harbor Green Park and the plaza.

The vocabulary of regional and sustainable materials includes locally sourced growing medium, plants, railings, concrete and basalt pavers and permeable pavers. Rainwater runnels run throughout the plaza and articulate the district markers at the street ends, celebrating this defining West Coast characteristic. Treated blackwater from the building irrigates both the living roof and the plaza plantings.

1. Coal Harbor Lookout
2. Jack Poole Plaza
3. Living Roof
4. Grass Slopes
5. Living Roof

Right: Plaza from roof

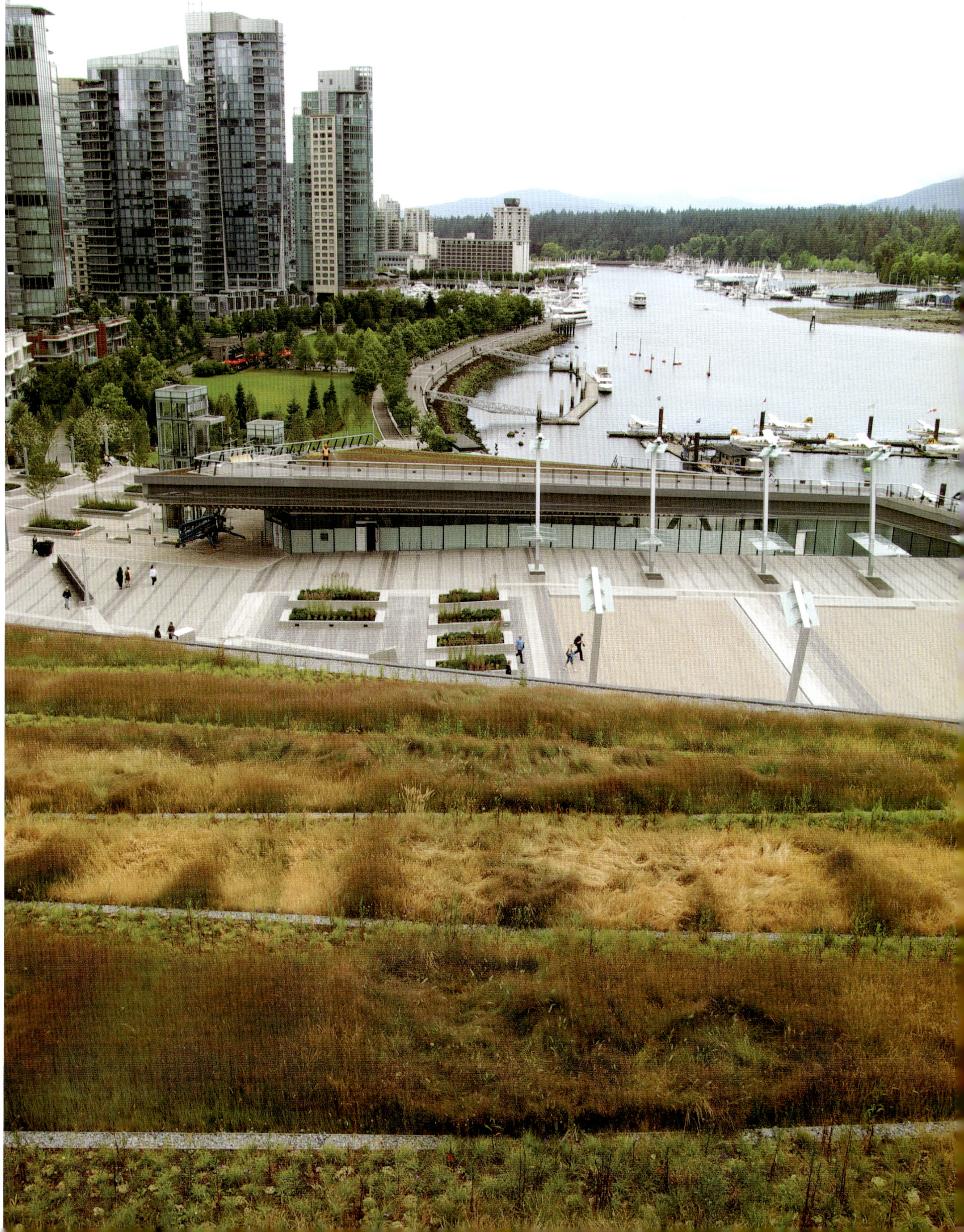

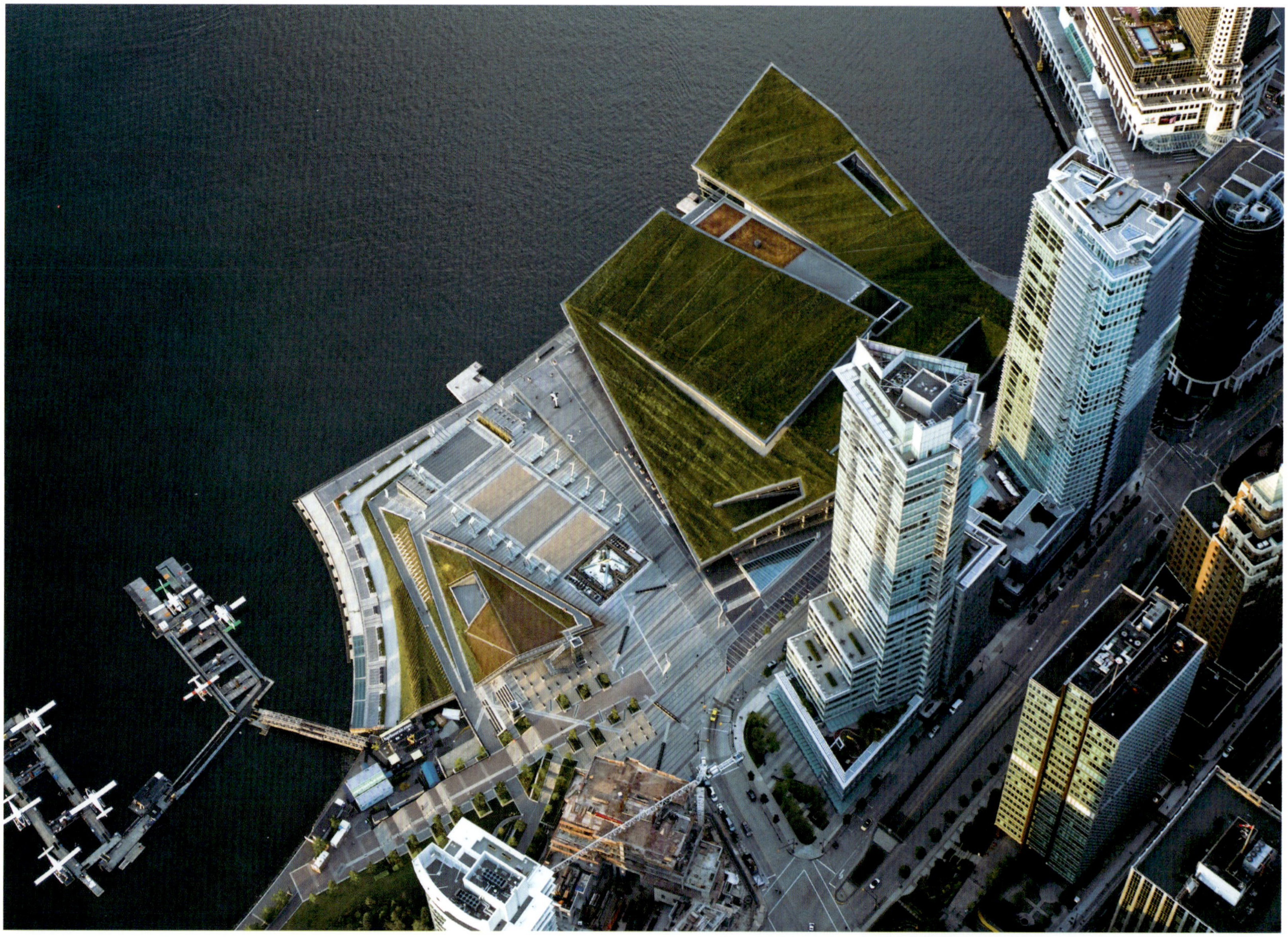

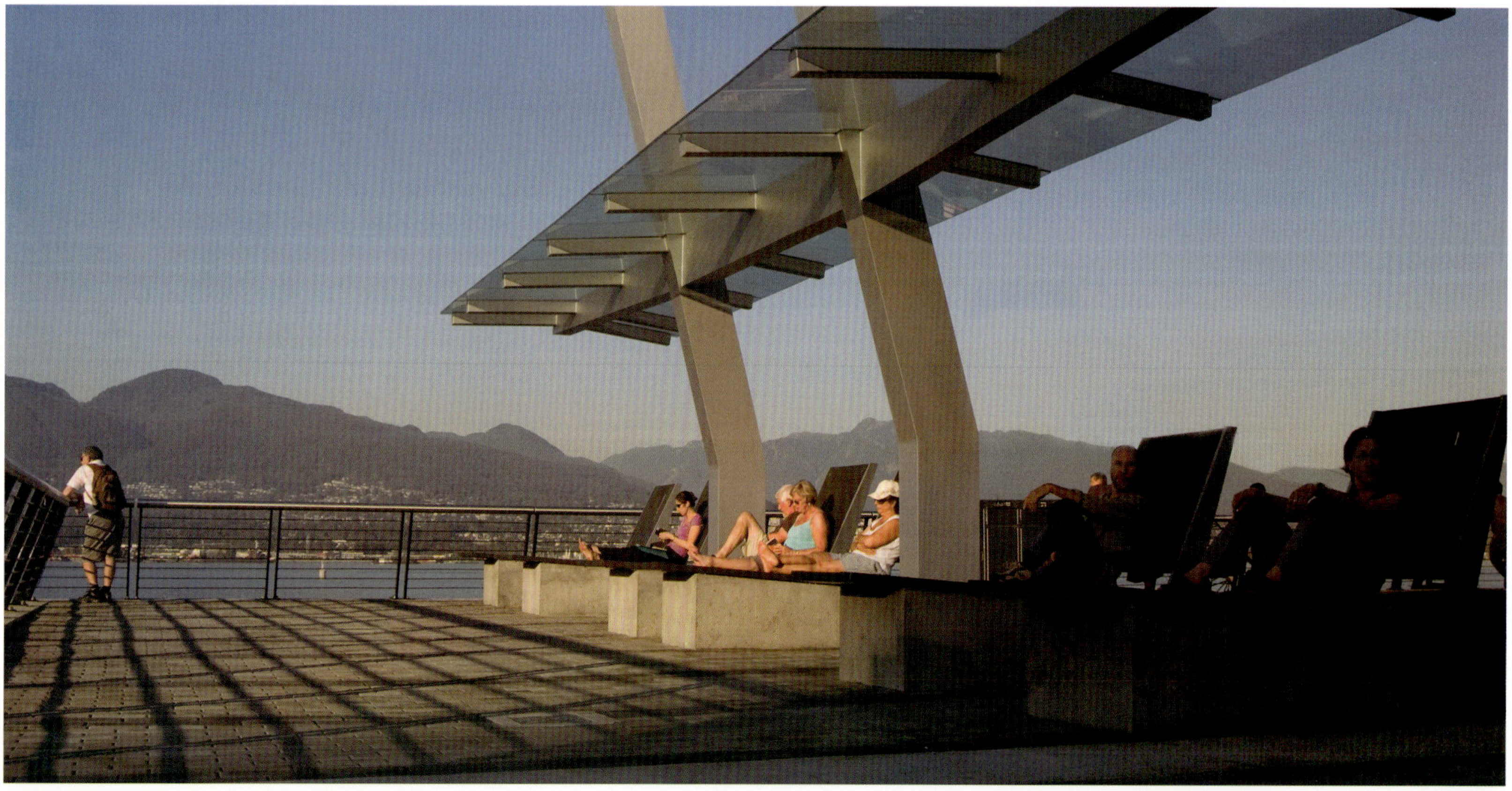

Upper left: Aerial view
Lower left: Plaza seating
Upper right: North view of the plaza
Lower right: Public art

Frederiksberg New Urban Spaces

Location: Copenhagen, Danmark **Designer:** SLA **Photographer:** Jens Lindhe, Torben Petersen, SLA **Completion date:** 2005 **Site area:** 20,000 sqm

The center of Frederiksberg is the most densely populated area of Copenhagen. It lacked, however, quality public spaces for the over 30,000 visitors that each day passed through the area. The Municipality of Frederiksberg turned to SLA to create new urban spaces bustling with life.

The Frederiksberg City Center is a 20,000-square-meter public space dominated by large, introvert buildings. The 'normal' method in creating life between buildings, opening up the buildings to the surrounding area, was therefore not an option.

SLA reversed the relation between the inside and the outside. Instead of creating urban spaces that were subordinated to the buildings, SLA created five urban spaces that in themselves were 'rooms' in their own right, using the surrounding buildings as facades. Using a method borrowed from soap bubbles, the five separate urban spaces were wedged intimately together, while at the same time providing each urban space with its own, distinctive feel and expression.

Moving through the different urban spaces, the visitors will experience radically different sensations: trees, fragrances, colors, surfaces, sounds (even the temperature and climate) will change from one urban space to the next. The only common denominator between the five urban spaces is that they are all extremely dependant on the weather, changing feel and expression with the rain, sun and the wind.

As a result, Frederiksberg City Center has evolved from an introvert place for transit to a bustling urban space rich in expression and atmosphere.

1. The Solberg Pinet
2. Solberg Plaza
3. Falkoner Square
4. Solbjerg Square
5. Holger Tornoes Passage

Right: Solbjerg Square between high school and Frederiksbergcenteret

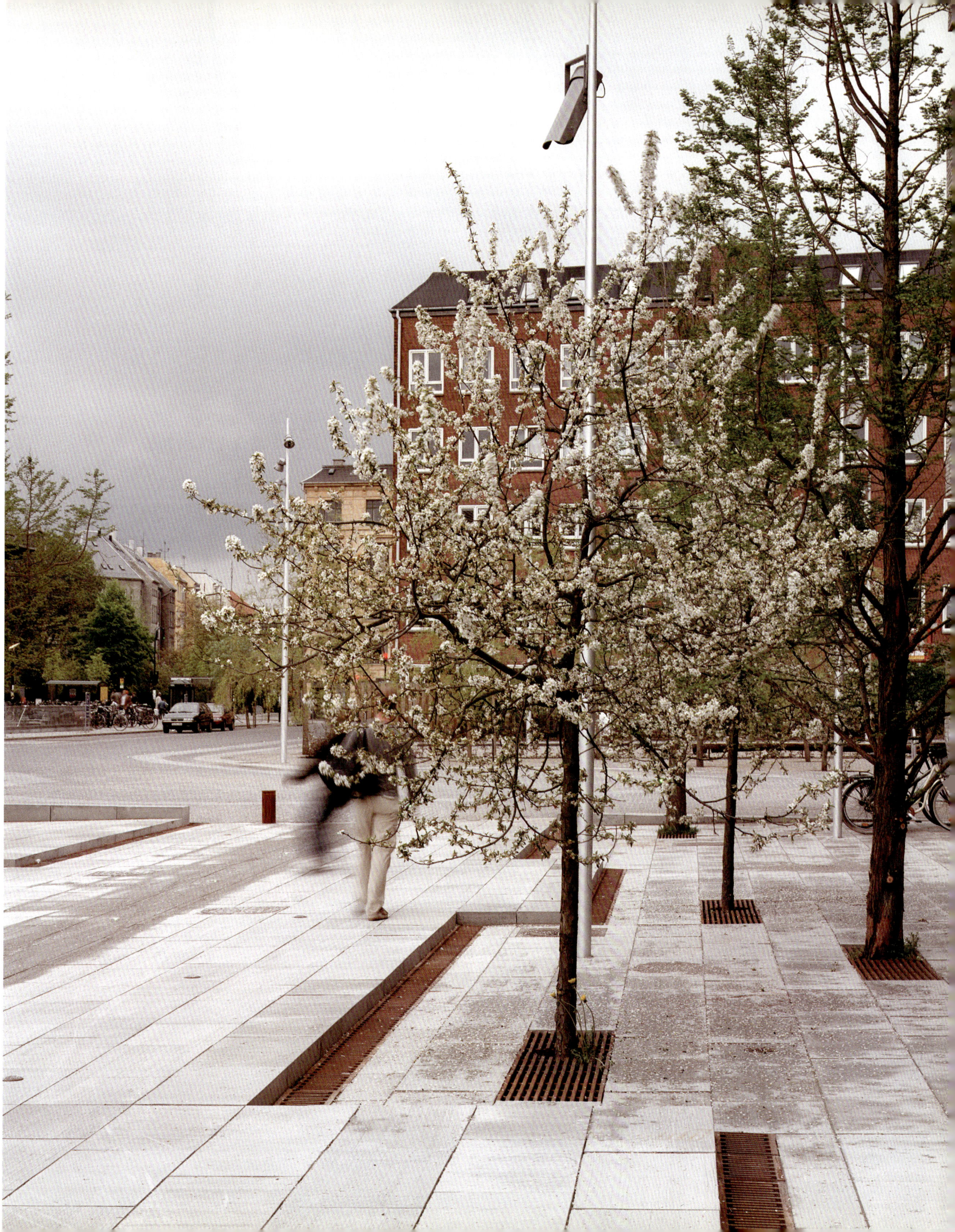

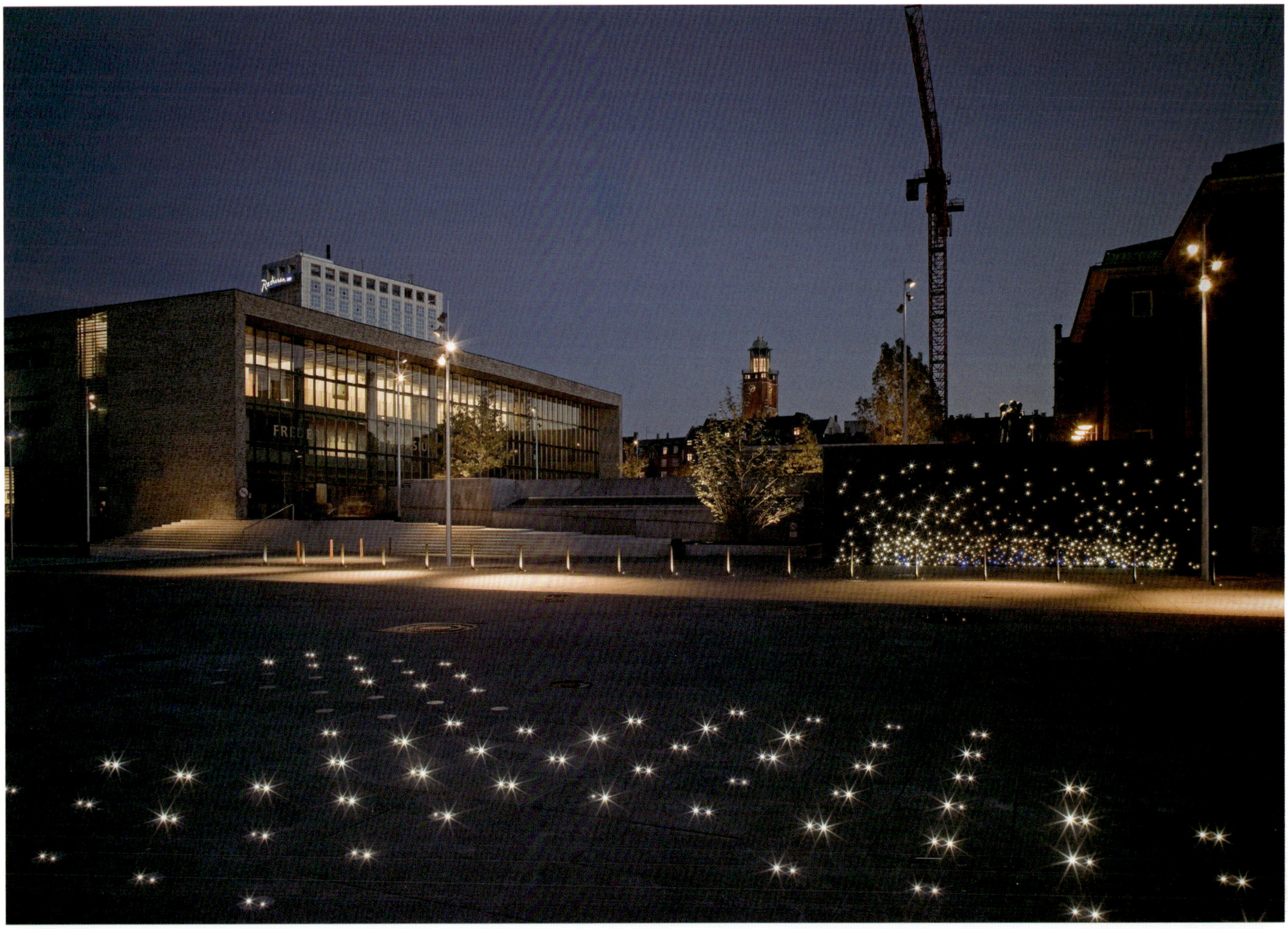

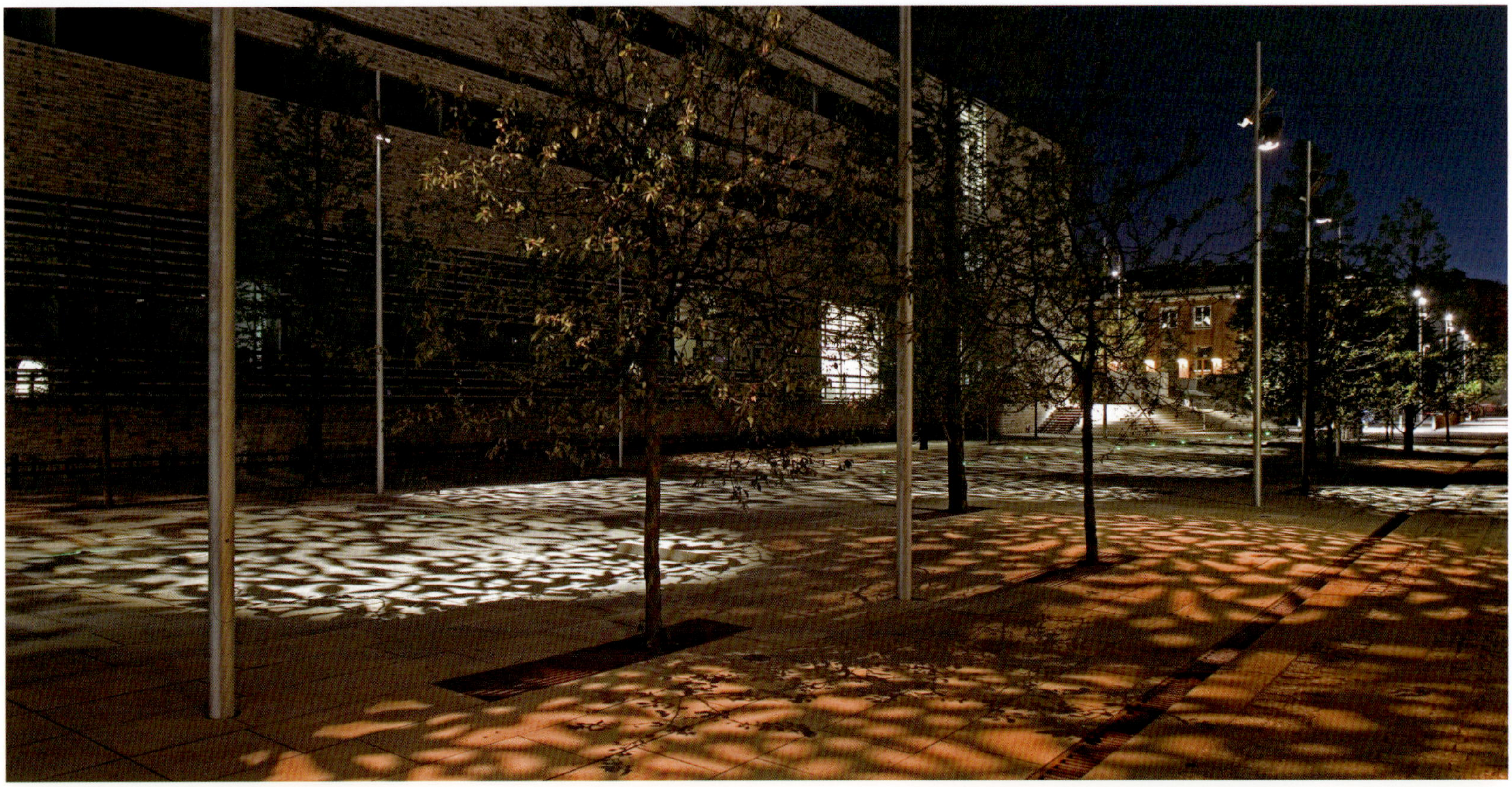

Upper left: View toward high school
Lower left: Solberg Square view toward high school
Upper right: Water atomizers with view toward Frederiksbergcenteret
Lower right: Shadows at Falkoner Square between high school and library

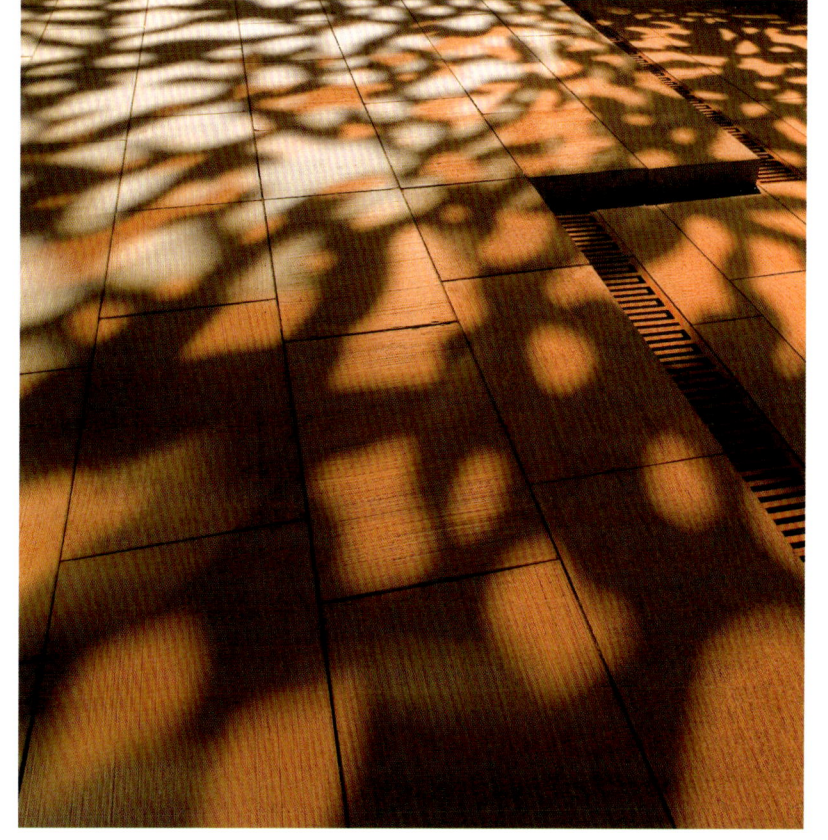

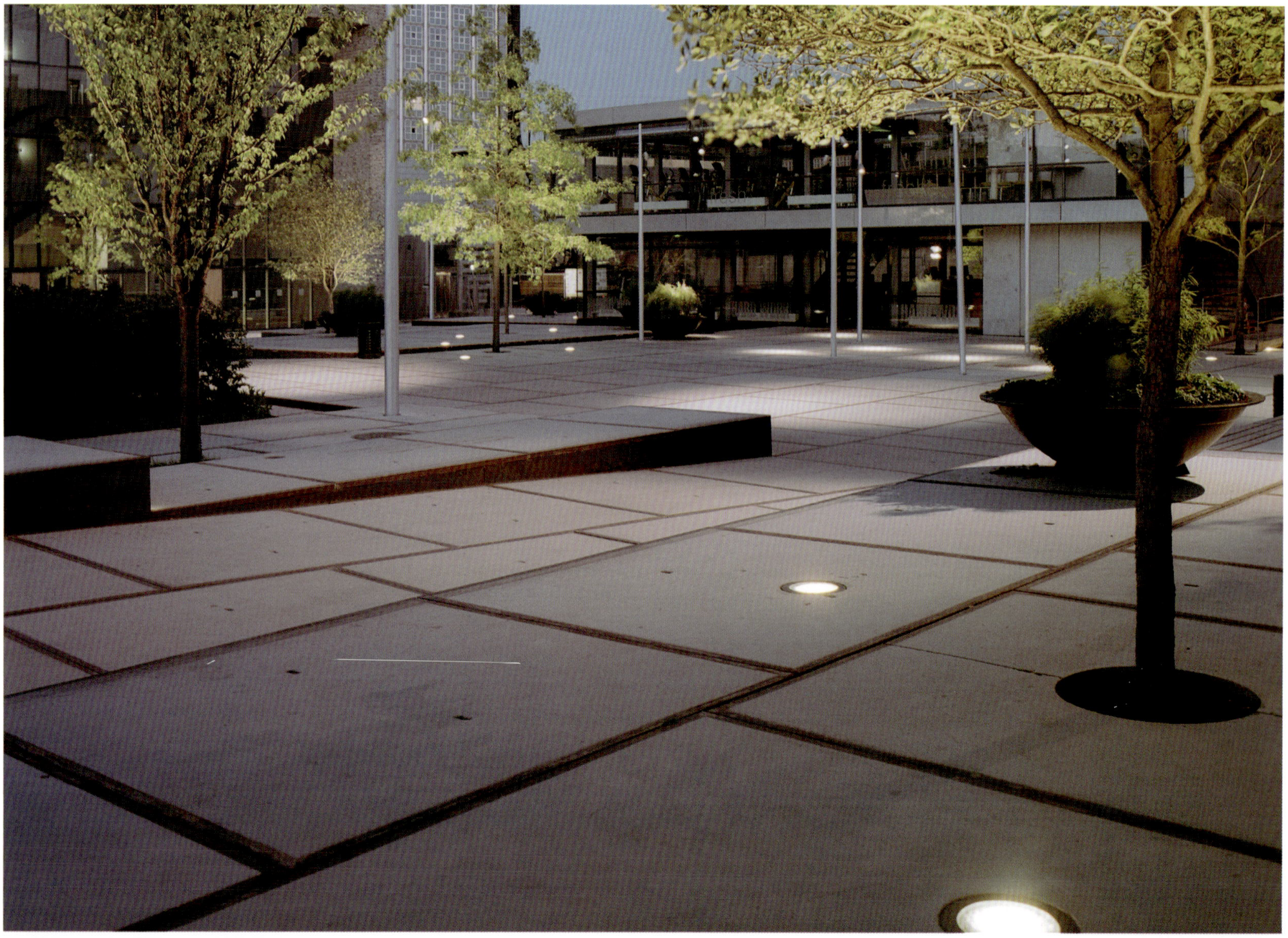

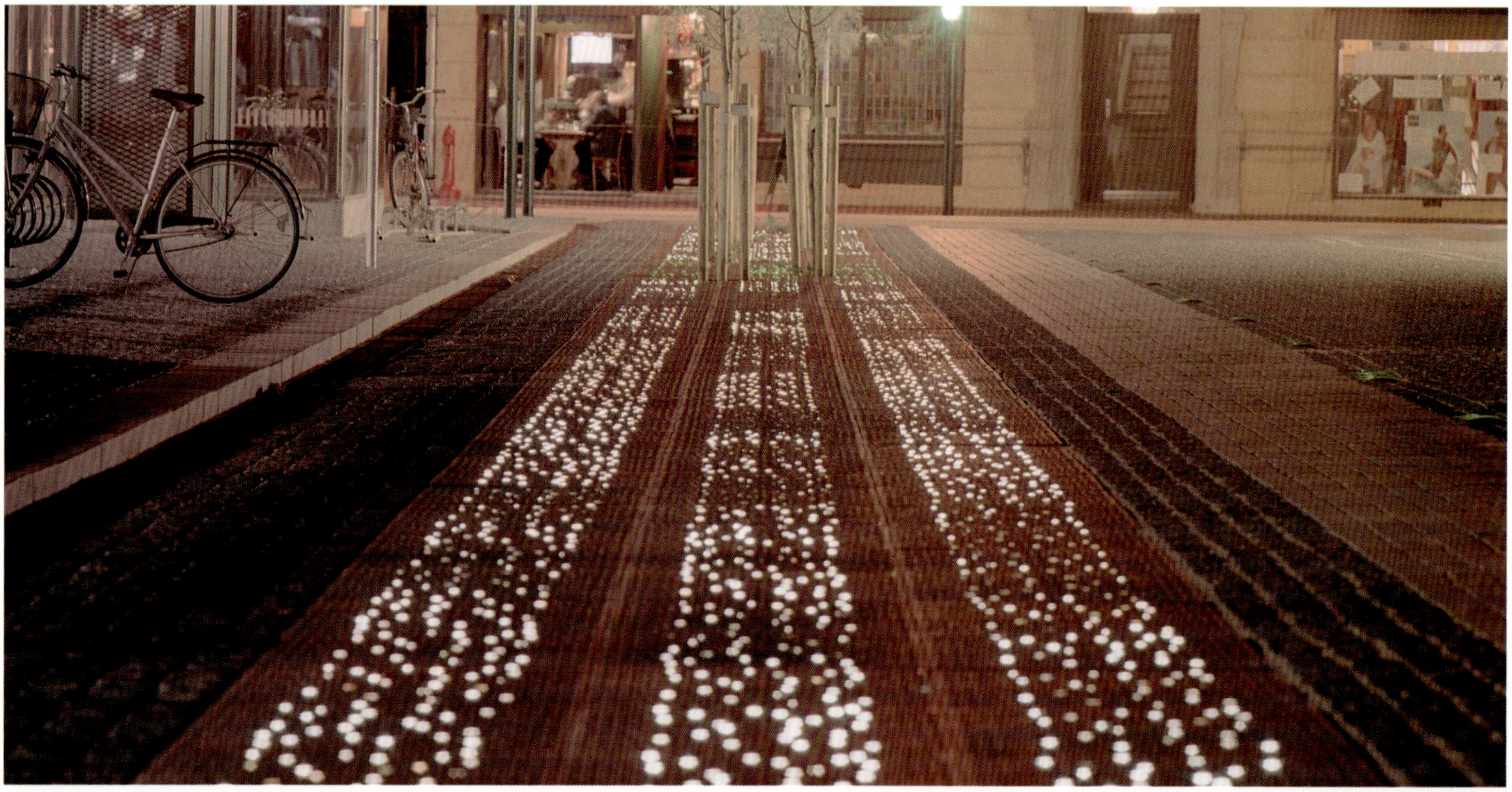

Upper left: Falkoner Square
Upper right: Trees and flowers collection in Solberg Plaza with furniture
Lower right: Water curtain on Solbjerg Square

Place des Festivals

Location: Montreal, Canada **Designer:** DAOUST LESTAGE Inc. Architecture Design Urbain **Photographer:** Marc Cramer **Completion date:** 2009 **Site area:** 12,000 sqm

Historically home to Montreal's red light district, theaters and museums, the project demonstrates the ability of cultural momentum to shape an urban redevelopment.

Reawakening Montreal's theater district, this first step in a multi-phase urban regeneration project brings people back to the urban core; revitalizing an eroded area of the city, and creating a permanent setting for festivals and cultural events such as Montreal's International Jazz Festival and the Just for Laughs Festival.

The Place des Festivals captures the transient nature of the festival, drawing the playfulness of nightlife into the daily experience of the city.

The new urban plateau of 12,000 square meters, capable of hosting 25,000 people, functions as a formal setting for festivals, equipped with lights, wiring and cabling, and as a stage for public life throughout the remainder of the year.

The largest interactive fountain in Canada, the theatrical curtains of water and light are composed of 235 jets and 470 lights, the focal point of the plateau is the central fountain that rises 12 meters above the surface of the Place. Red and white curtains of water rise 2.2 meters creating an experiential light and soundscape. The fountains, programmed to respond to movement, light and sound, invite and showcase public interaction.

Signature lighting elements, the mega-structures form the walls and ceiling of the urban stage, illuminating the space below and acting as festive, urban markers confirming the presence of le Quartier des Spectacles within the city's urban fabric.

Award description:
2011 - Winner - Award of Excellence - Quebec Association of Architects - Urban Design Category
2009 - Winner - Silver Medal - National Post Design Exchange - Urban Design Category

1. Place des Festivals
2. Mayor Terracing Steps
3. Sainte Catherine Terracing Steps
4. Promenade
5. Vitrines Habitées
6. Montreal Museum of Contemporary Art

Right: The new urban plateau

QUARTIER DES SPECTACLES
DESIGN
HUMOUR
CINÉMA
ARTS TECHNOLOGIQUES
EXPOSITIONS
CONFÉRENCES
IMPROVISATION
JEUNESSE
THÉÂTRE
LITTÉRATURE
DANSE
FESTIVALS
ARTS VISUELS
MUSIQUE
OPÉRA

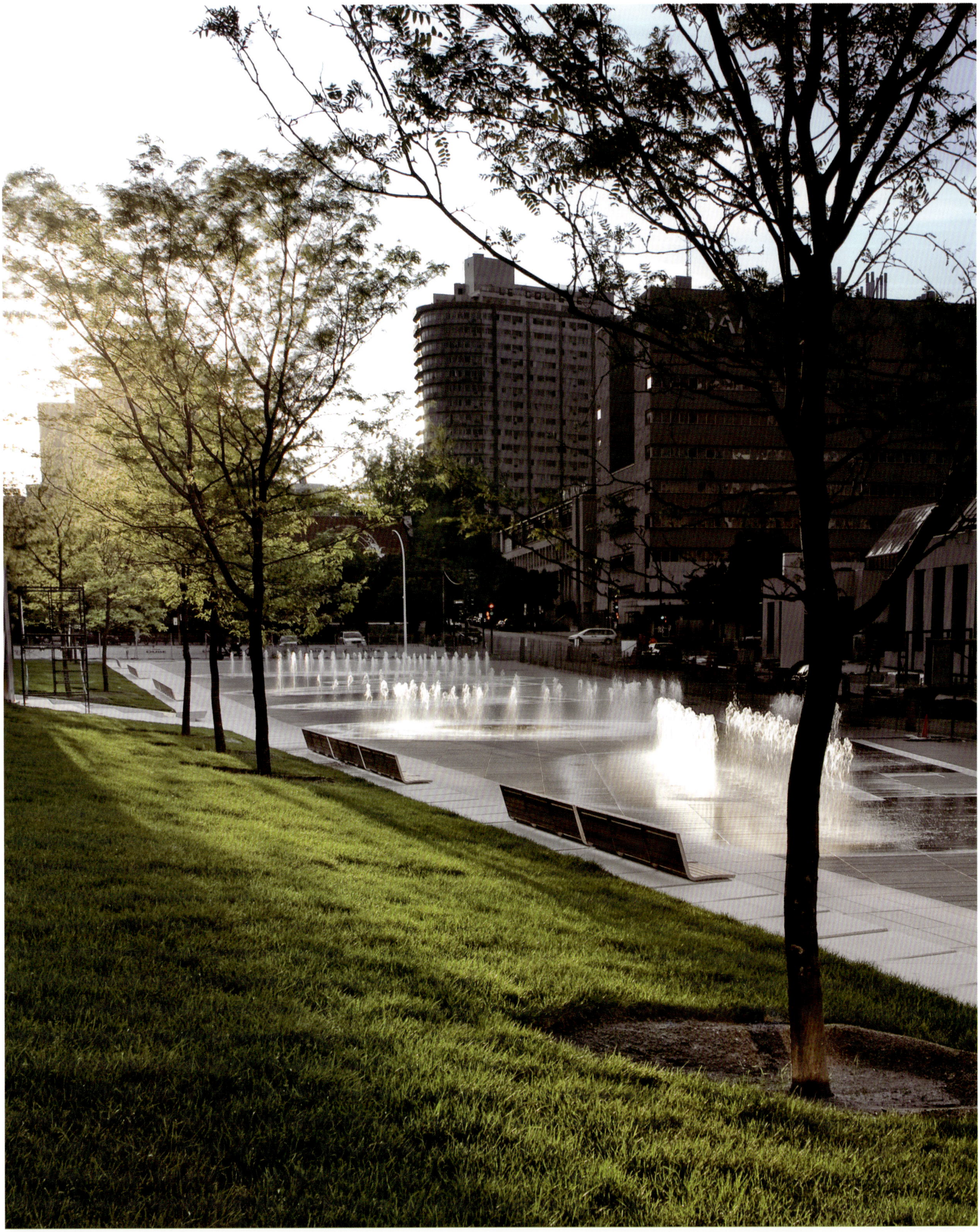

Left: The green landscape and the fountains
Upper right: The black and white granite surface
Lower right: Urban furniture

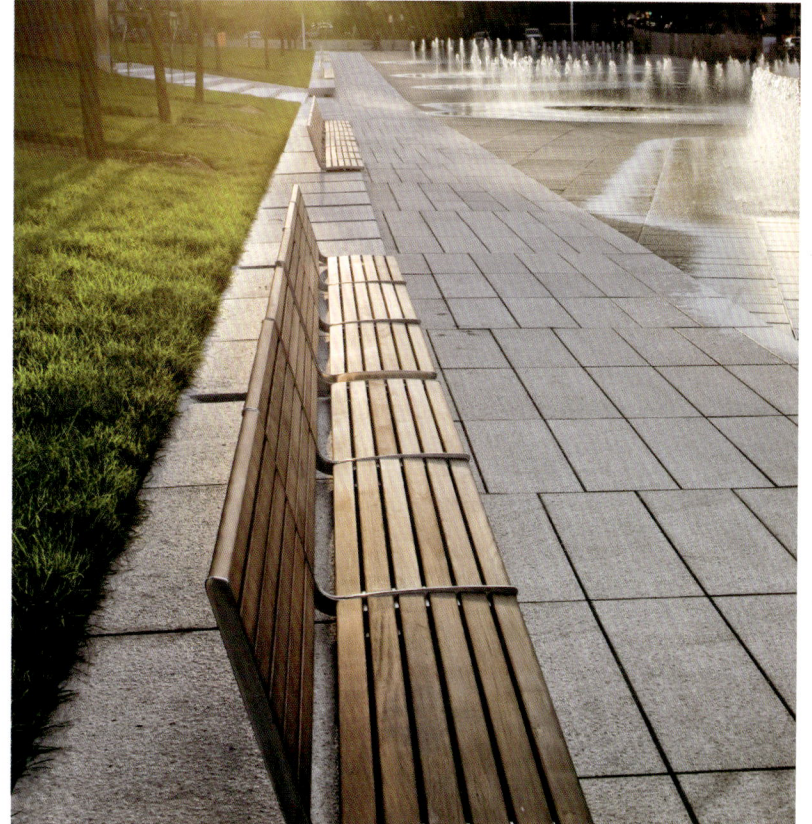

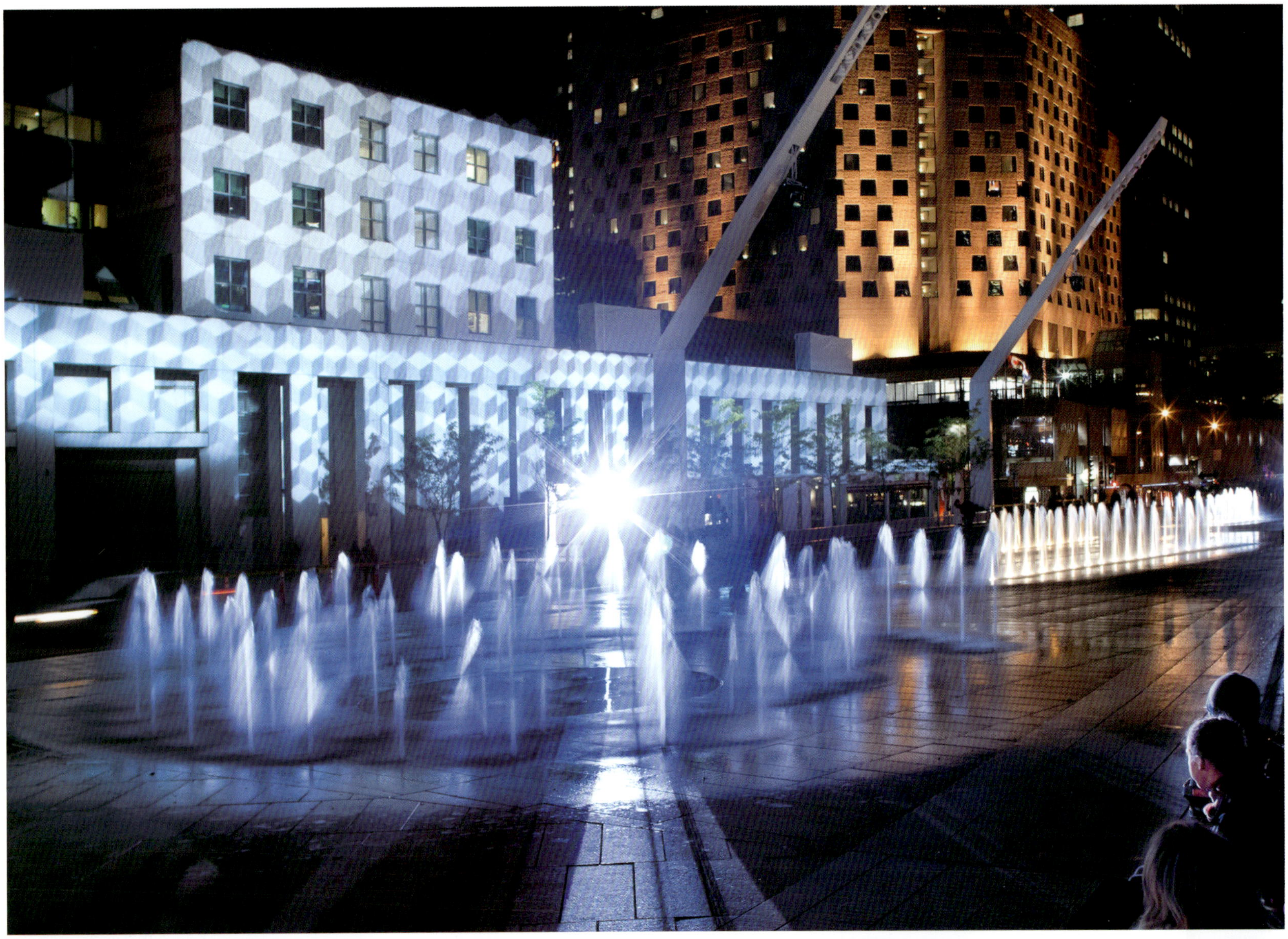

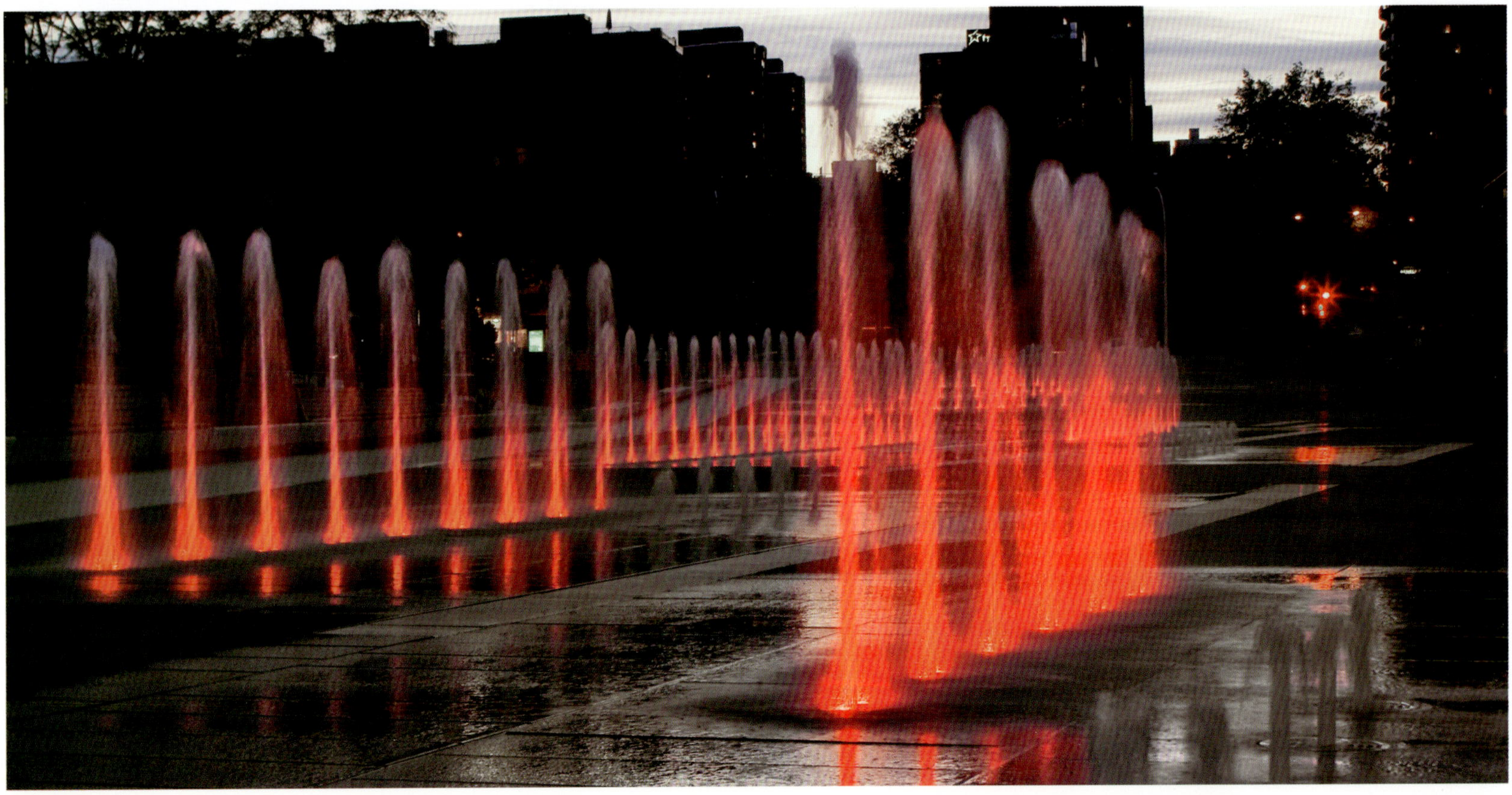

Upper left: Theatrical effect
Lower left: Red water curtains
Upper right: Aerial view of Place des Festivals
Lower right: Red and white fountain

Mathilde Square

Location: Eindhoven, The Netherlands **Designer:** Buro Lubbers **Photographer:** Buro Lubbers **Completion date:** 2009 **Site area:** 55,000 sqm

Versatility guided the principles for the Mathilde Square. The square had to add value to the series of public squares and places in Eindhoven's inner city. Besides, the monumental Light Tower deserved to be showcased by means of an outdoor space. Furthermore, the semi-public square needed to host different functions: an entrance to the homes and businesses in the tower and a drive in for the hotel, terraces and bicycle sheds. Above all, it had to become an attractive place for both residents and passersby.

The amorphous form of the planning area demanded an exacting structure that brings serenity and also guarantees an optimal view of the Light Tower. The design concept was therefore based on rigid lines that run counter to the building.

The unity of the design was accomplished by using consistent shapes and materials. Thus the surface was paved with just one material: a dark gray concrete slab. This gray carpet is laid in a rigid, complex pattern and is surrounded by a plinth that distinguishes the square from the building and also highlights the difference in level between the parking deck and the environment. The difference in level distinguishes between on the one hand the hectic city life and on the other the intimate and green area of the square. These divergent worlds are also emphasised by the fence around the square, which serves mainly as a security measure. Wisteria and roses overgrow the adjacent pergola and create a transparent barrier, offering passersby a glimpse of the green atmosphere and the terraces.

1. Fence
2. Stripe Pattern of Corten Steel Planters
3. Terraces
4. Benches
5. Hotel
6. Light Tower

Right: The terrace

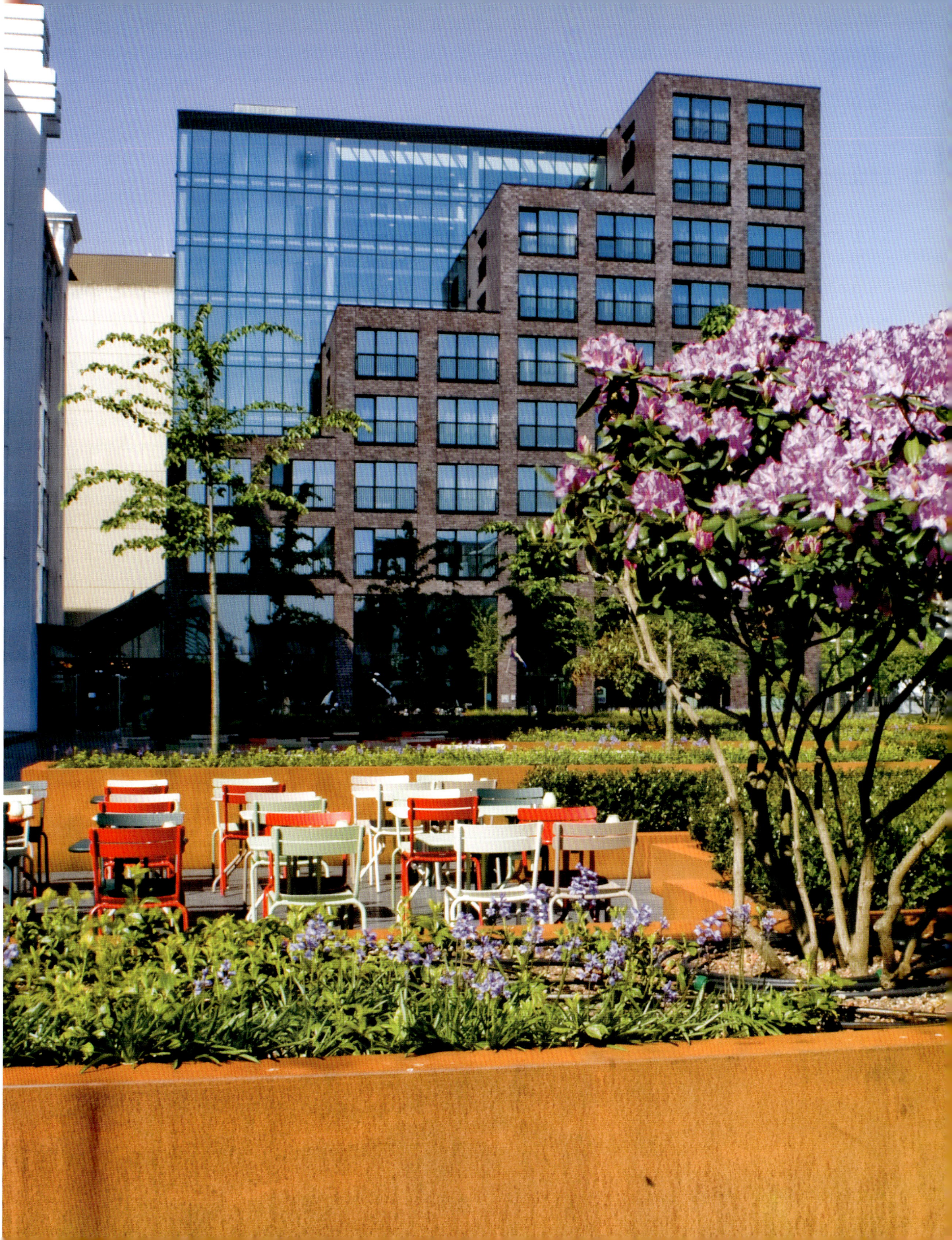

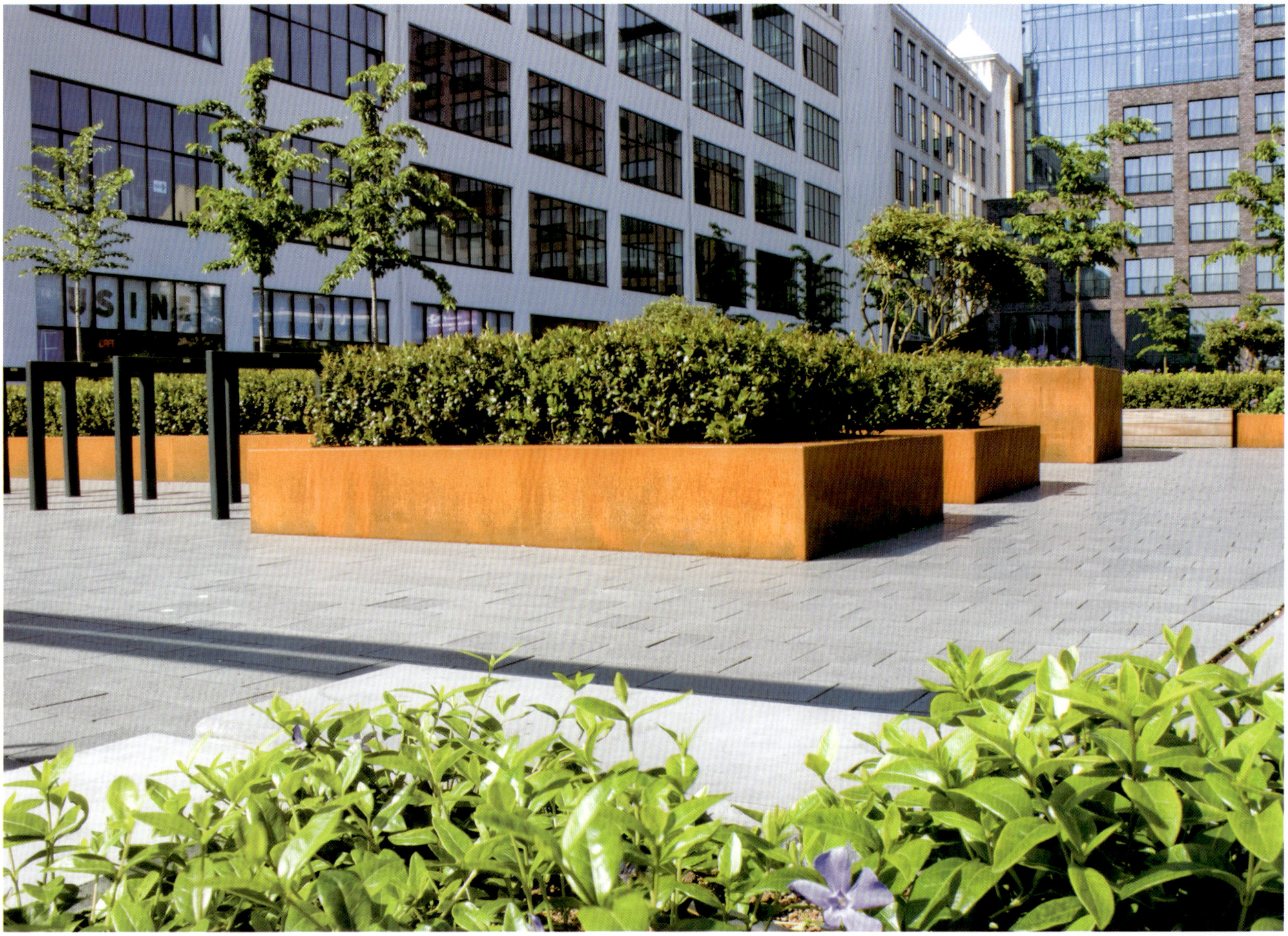
USINE

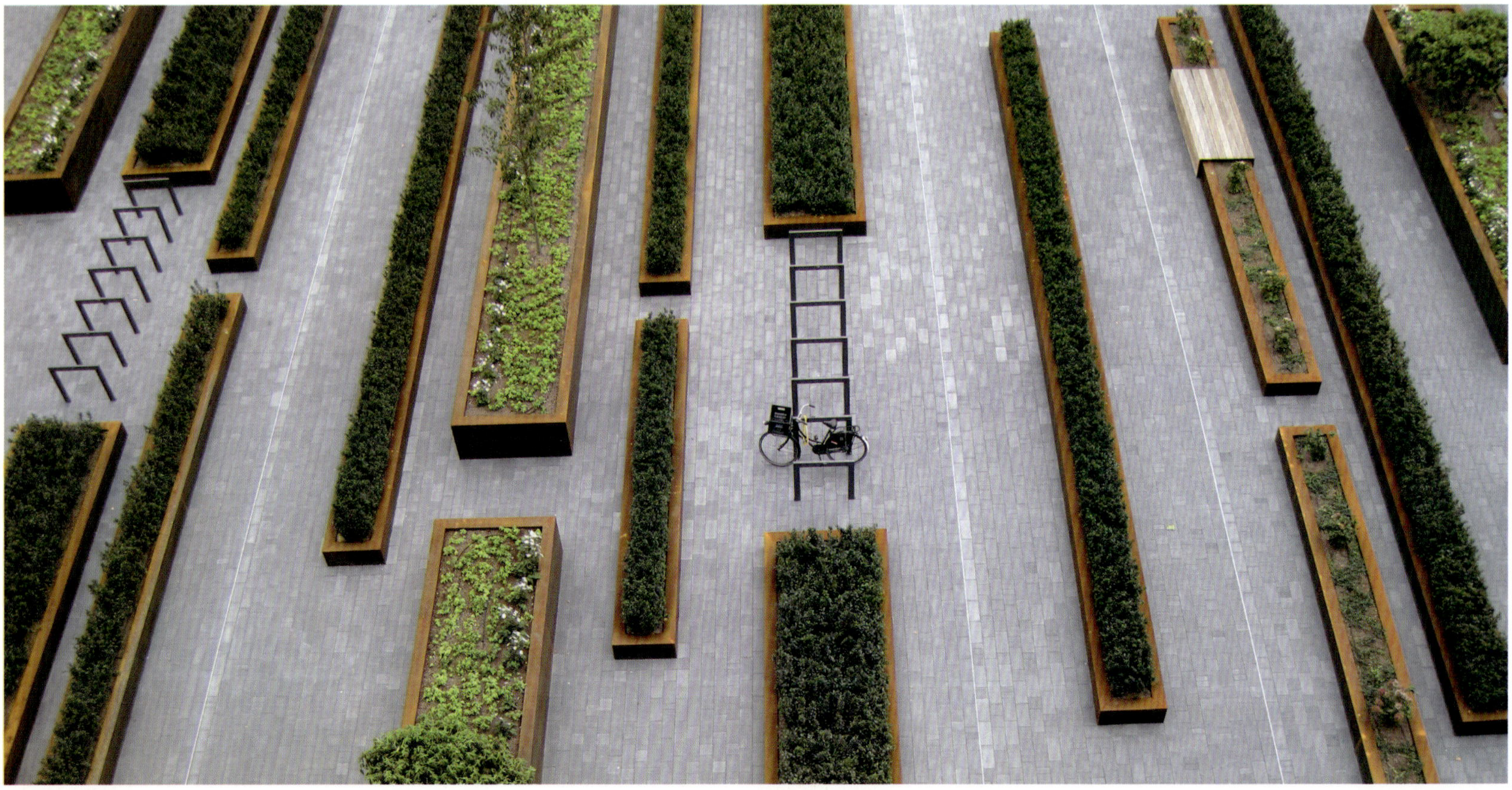

230~231

Upper left: Cast iron planting bed
Upper right: Overview of the terraces, benches and plants
Lower right: Detail of the bench

Town Hall Square

Location: Toronto, Canada **Designer:** Janet Rosenberg + Associates (JRA)
Photographer: JRA **Completion date:** 2006 **Site area:** 2,428 sqm

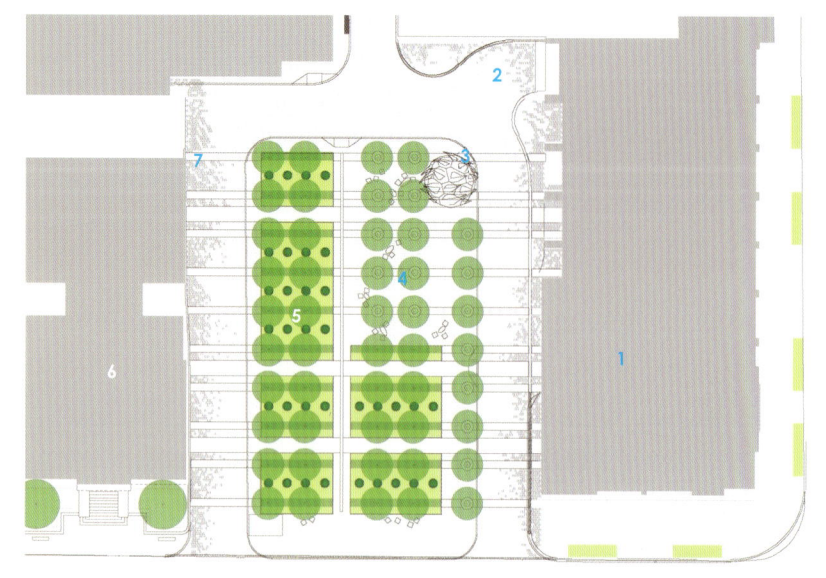

Inspired by the French Parterre, the intent of the park design was to create a pedestrian plaza and a flexible public space. Town Hall Square is elegant and inviting, a unique space where people can sit under tree canopies. A planting palette of rich greens give the space vibrancy and texture. The plant material was specifically chosen to withstand harsh urban conditions. Large precast concrete pots with custom tint and hand rubbed finish house boxwood balls while precast concrete tree disks and wood benches provide flexible seating. An eight-meter cortan and aluminum sculptural piece entitled 'Piercing a Cloud' by Canadian artist Jean-Pierre Morin is a focal point, drawing people to the park.

Continuous tree pits and structural soils were used to effectively maximize tree and plant growth but at the same time provide necessary levels of compaction for hard paving surfaces. The park is also equipped with an irrigation system, which is connected to a remote computer. Daily rainfall levels are recorded and irrigation levels adjusted accordingly.

Town Hall Square is a successful urban space that accommodates pedestrian movement and allows for a variety of events such as Yorkville Public Library's outdoor book readings. Town Hall Square works perfectly with Yorkville's historical identity and reputation for being an international gathering place for celebrities and a bustling shopping area.

Award description:
2006 CSLA Award, Regional Honor

1. 18 Yorkville Condominium
2. Entrance to Underground Parking Garage
3. Art Sculpture by Jean Pierre Morin
4. Ginkgos in Precast Concrete Disks
5. Boxwood Balls in Large Pots
6. Yorkville Library
7. Dispersing Paving Pattern

Right: Aerial view of the square

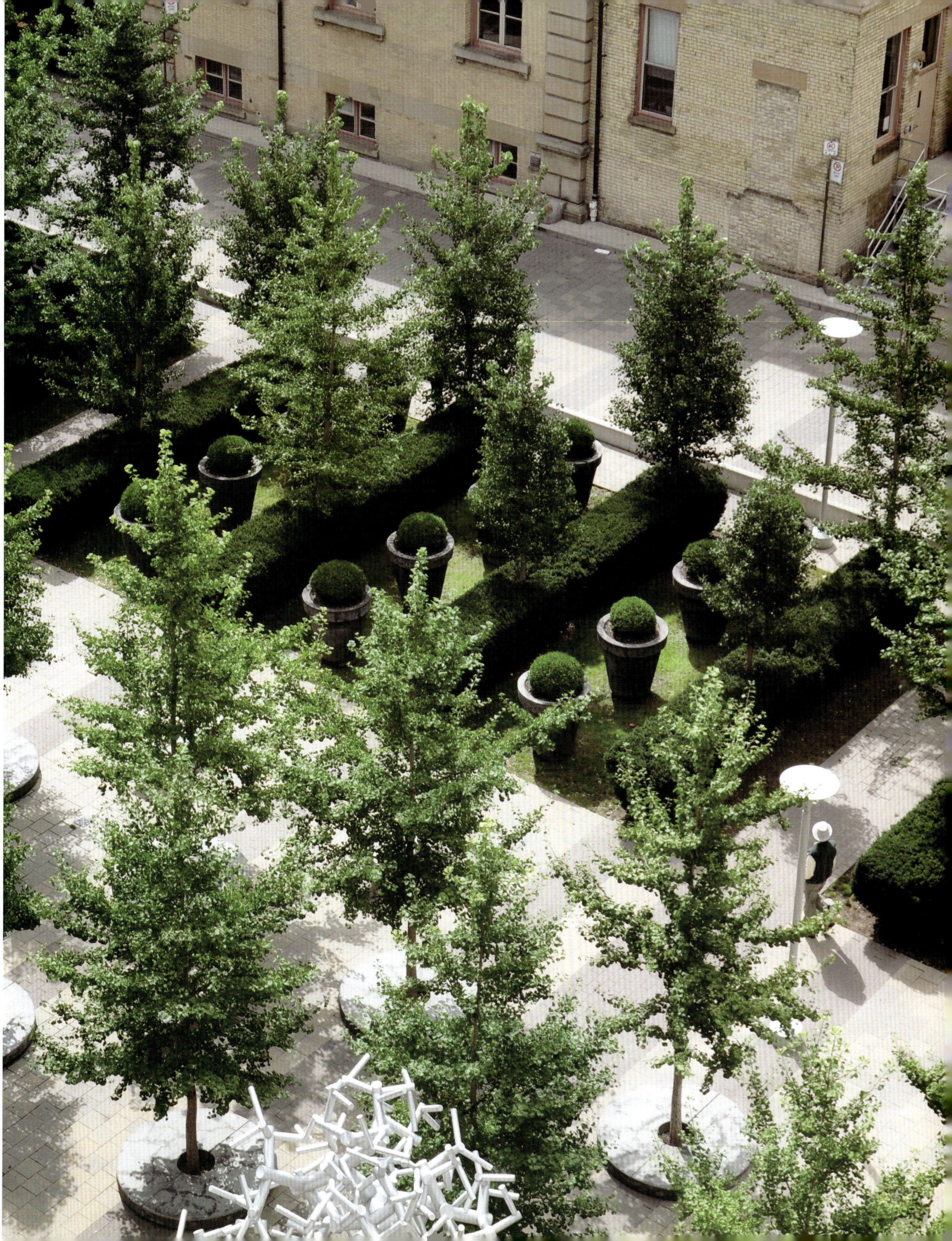

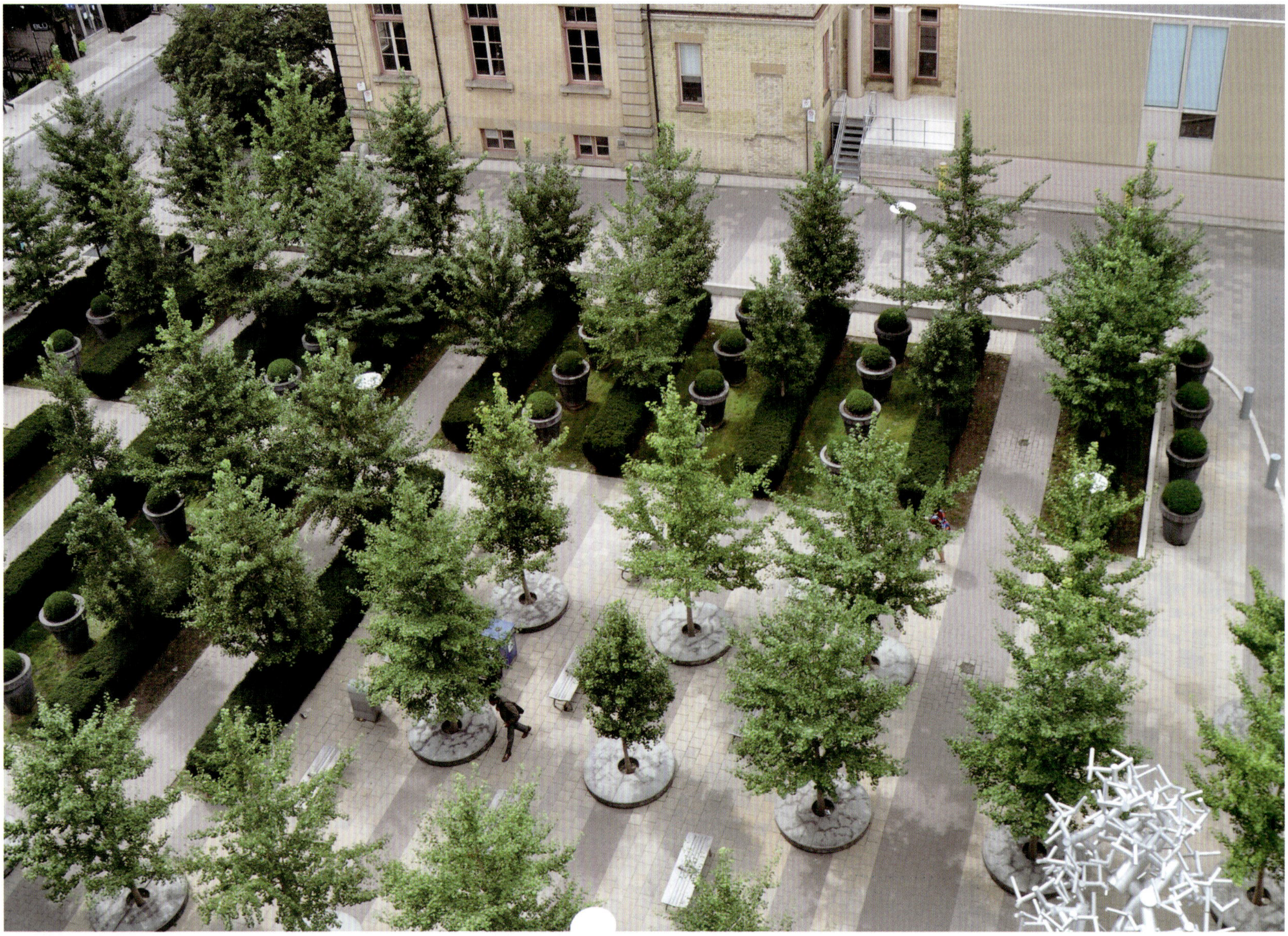

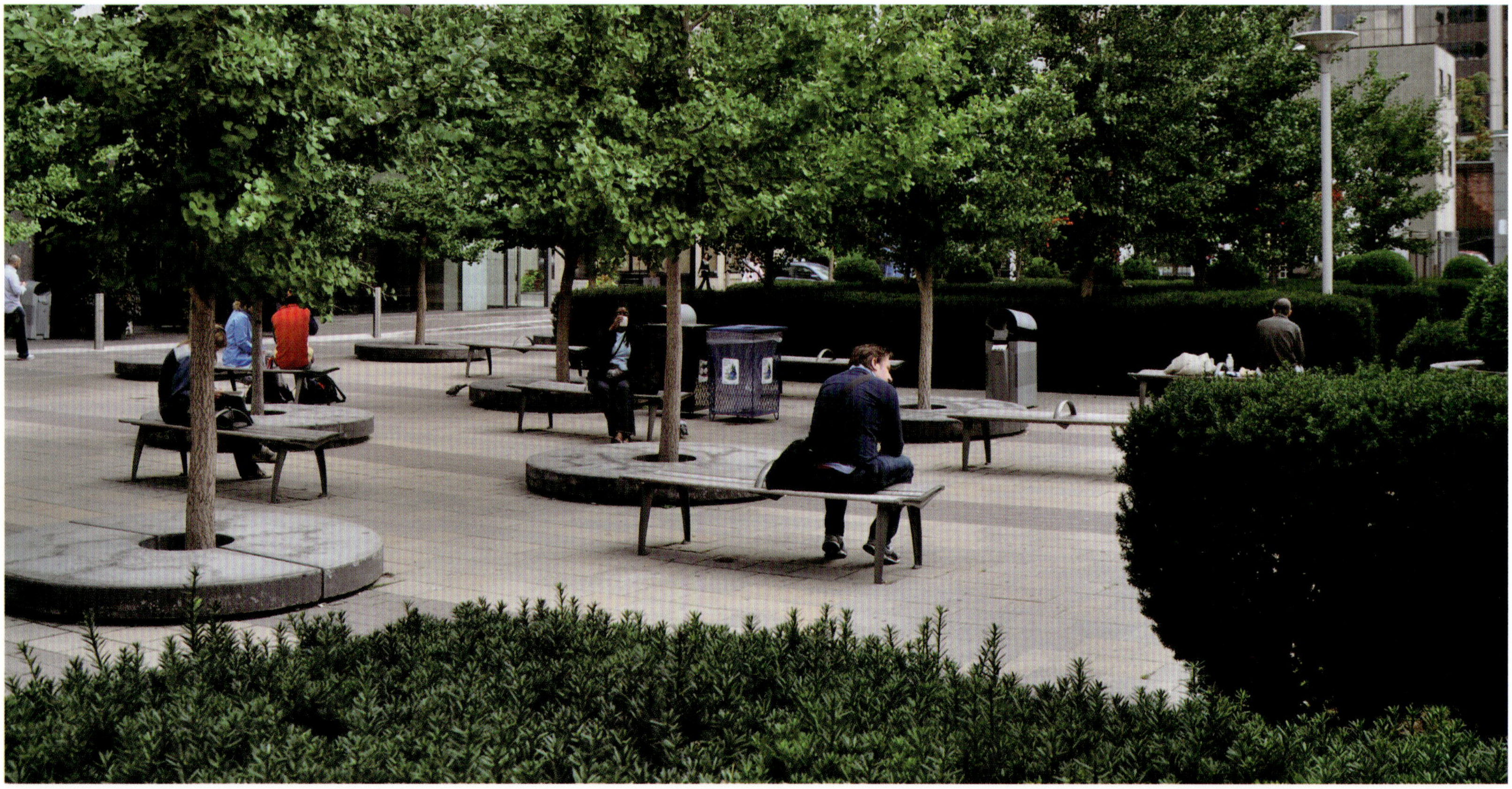

234~235

Lower left: Close-up view of tree disks
Upper right: View of the square facing south
Lower right: Close-up view of pots

Piazza Municipio, Povegliano

Location: Povegliano, Italy **Designer:** MICROSCAPE Architecture_Urban Design
Photographer: Francesco Castagna & MICROSCAPE **Completion date:** 2009
Site area: 5,986 sqm

The design methodology on which the project is based makes the system flow relational its backbone. The green areas allow access from the new square's 'public area' to the private residential area (north). The different space conformations create both continuity and give a special mark to the area. The architectural-scale elements, working by repetition, have been interpreted as analog 'figures' relying both of the site's specific memory references and archetypes of public urban space.

The floor plan of the square area to the north becomes 'active' thanks to the ever-changing LED lighting RGB signal, which by randomly inserting slabs of stone generates a continuous light surface. The eastern boundary of public space is delegated to a metamorphosis system that is transformed from concrete reinforced shaved curtain into hedges, ending up in the fountain of green marble Issorie. The entrance walkway houses the Public Bulletin Board and is covered by a system of horizontal photovoltaic panels which are highly efficient. This gives public area an independent energy source. The flooring of the entrance is in Ipè wood, suitable for outdoors, and within the flooring there are white LED spotlights. The designers have paid special attention to the balance between light sources and radiation, while avoiding any problem of light pollution through a system of control developed with iGuzzini.

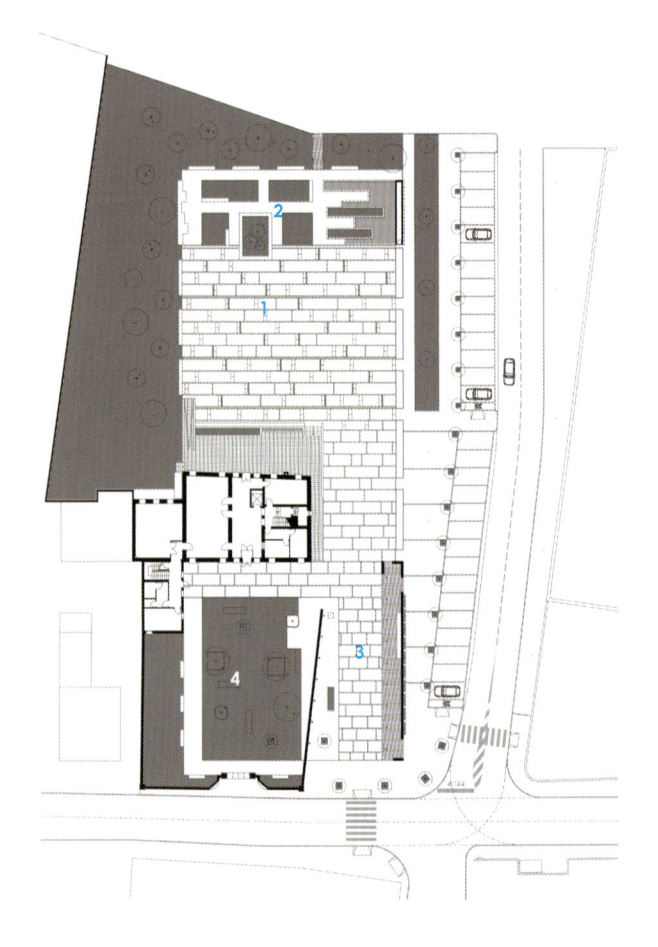

1. Central Plaza
2. Planting Area
3. Pathway from South to North
4. City Hall Building

Right: Night view of the fountain

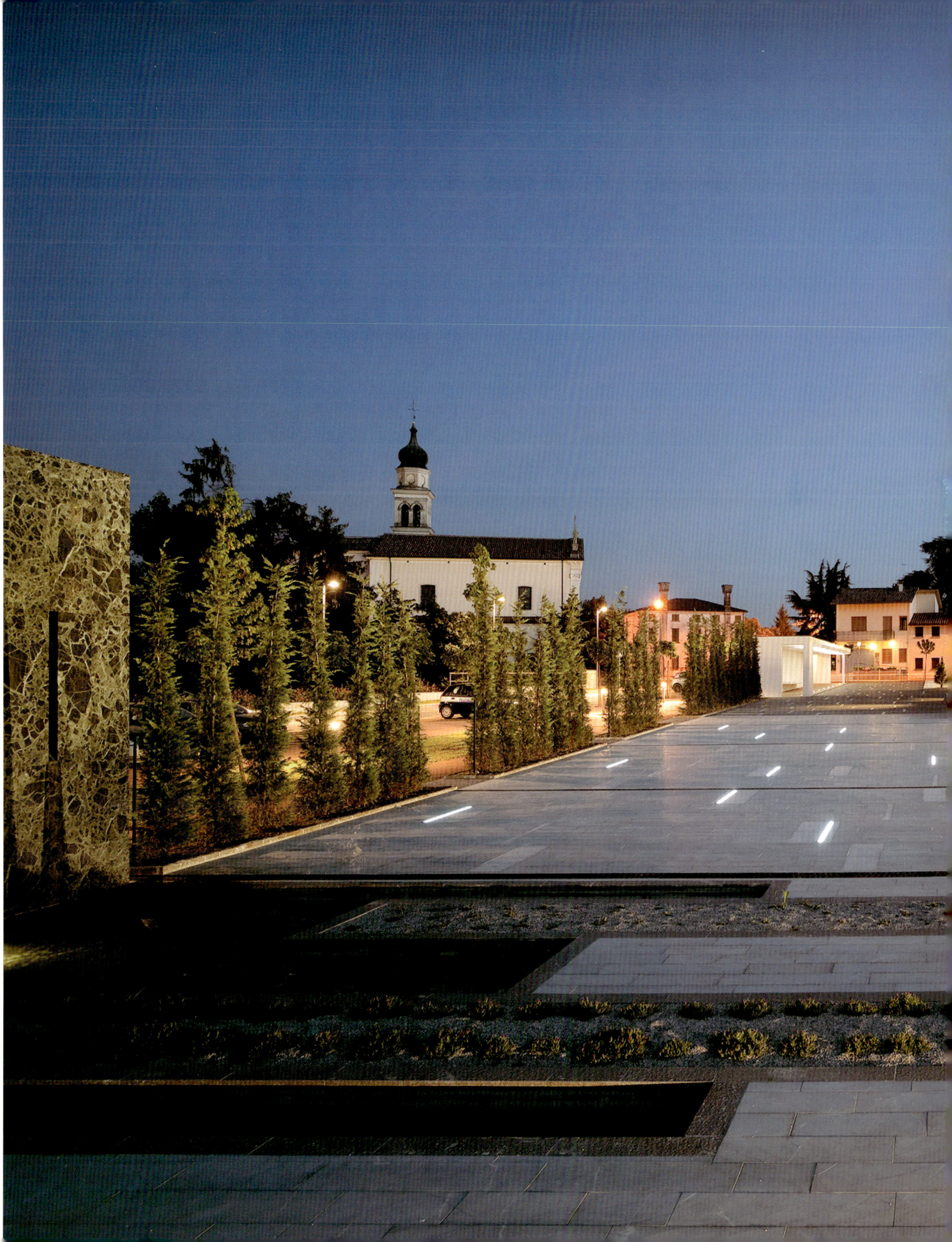

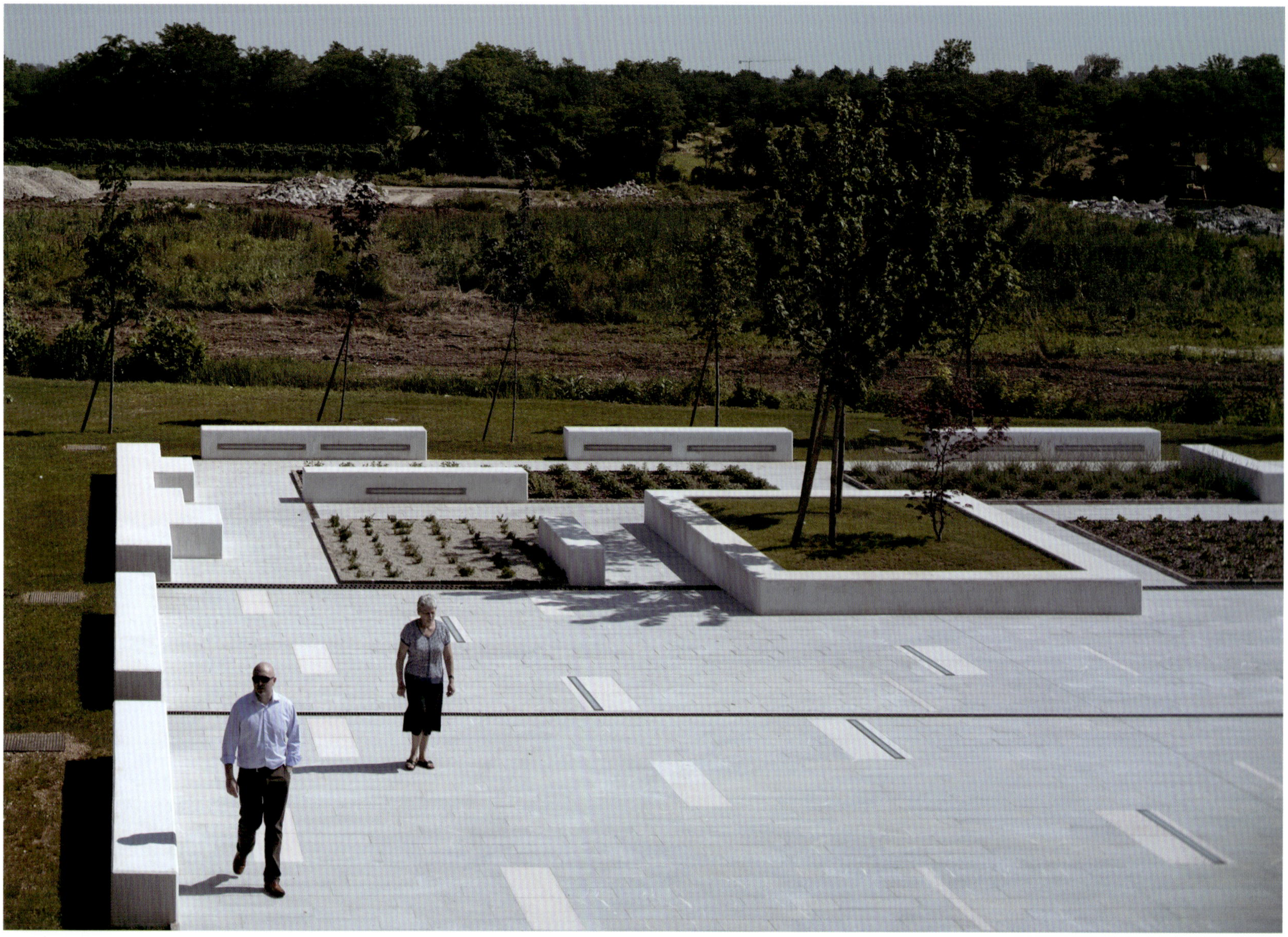

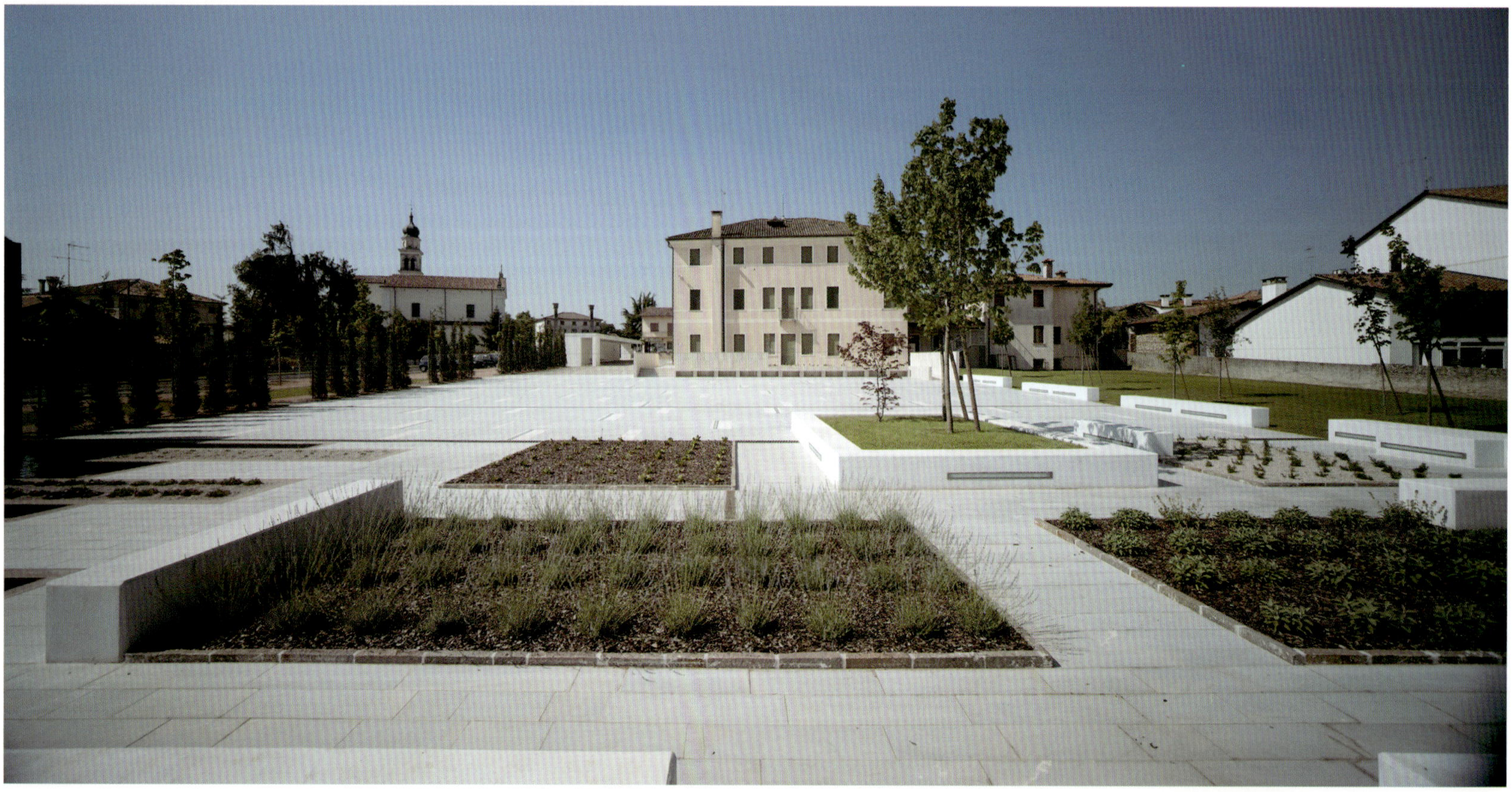

Upper left: Central plaza
Lower left: Planting area
Upper right: Resting area on the central plaza
Lower right: Pathway from south to north

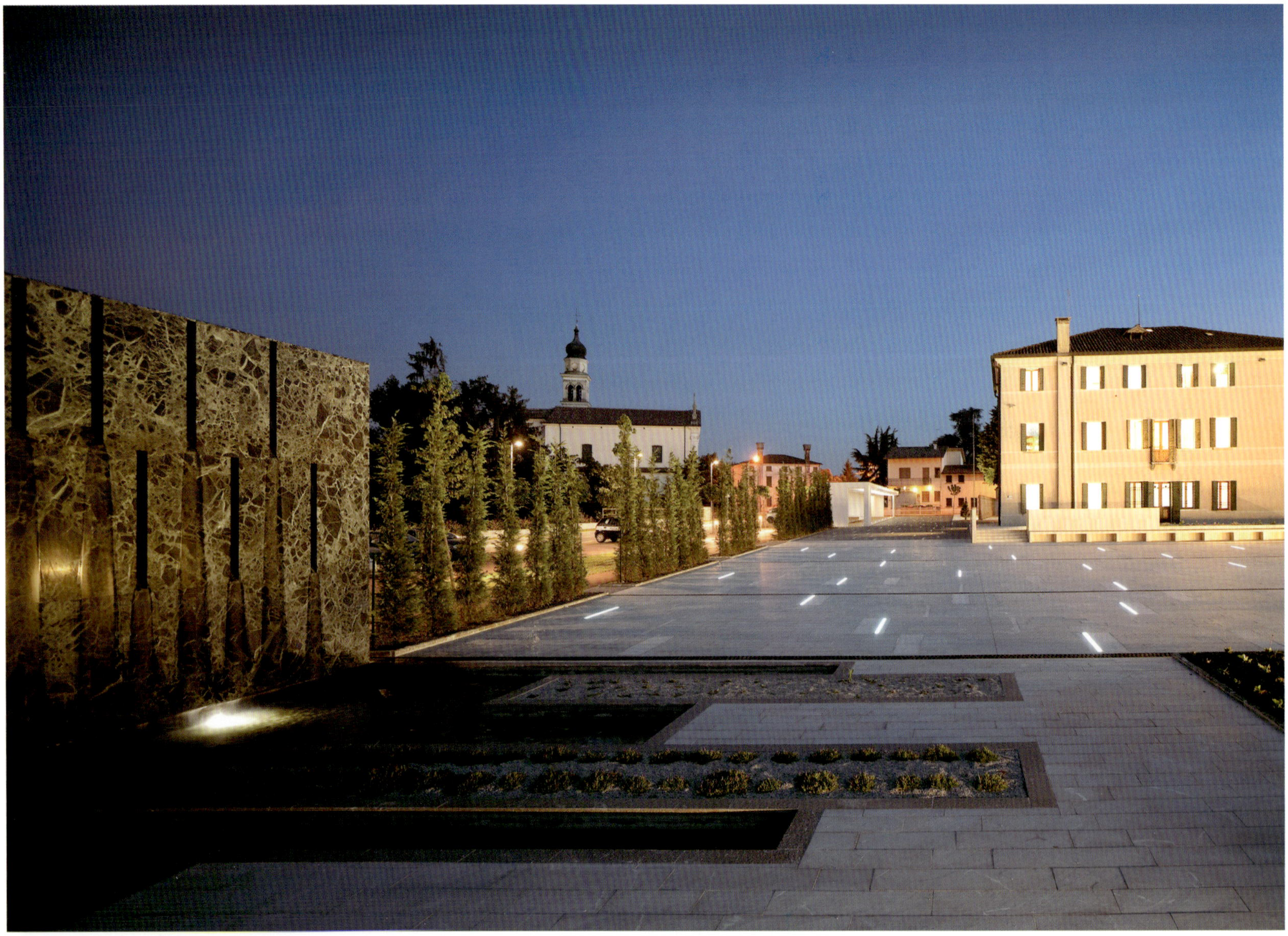

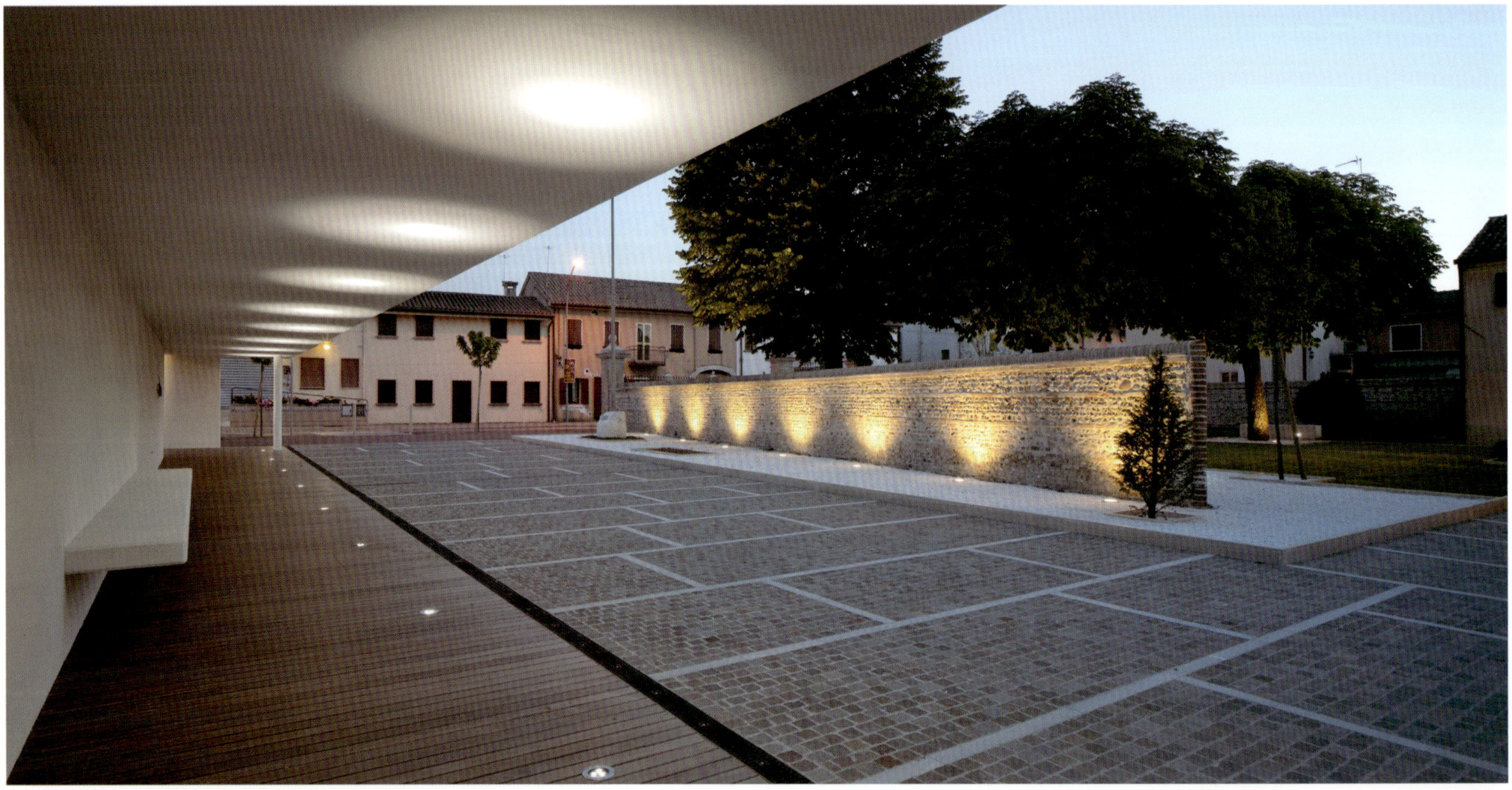

240~241

Upper left: Night view of the plaza
Lower left: Night view of the pathway from south to north
Upper right: Night view of the central plaza
Lower right: Detail of the planting

Location: Califonia, USA **Designer:** SQLA Inc. **Photographer:** Kenneth Katich & SQLA Inc. **Completion date:** 2009 **Site area:** 323,749 sqm **Plants:** California Sycamore, White Alder, California Pepper Tree

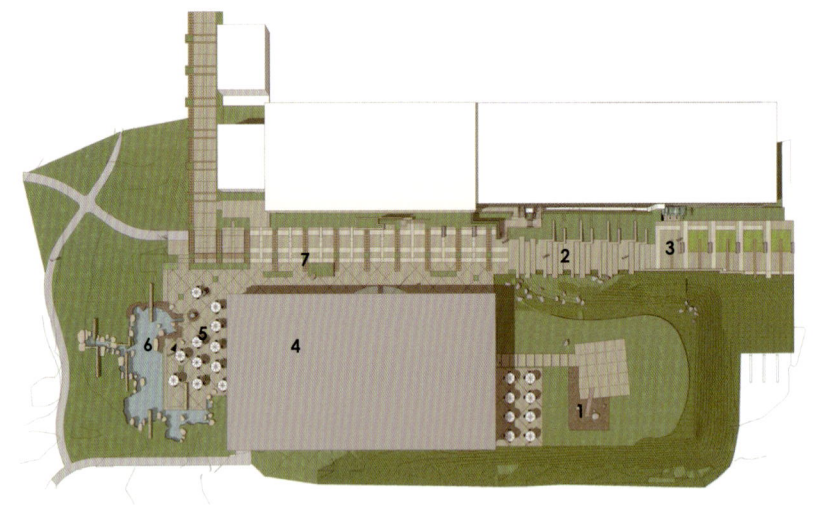

West Hills Corporate Pointe Cafe and Conference Center

The new West Hills Corporate Pointe Cafe patios, promenade and gardens have given new life to the Campus of West Hills. It has become the central destination in the campus to come and eat, relax, enjoy and play.

The outdoor dining patio unfolds to an inviting and lush water garden with cascading waterfalls, pond and a bountiful backdrop of landscaping on a mound that screens out the parking lot beyond. Naturally strewn boulders add to the drama of water and landscaping, as an extension of Santa Susana Mountains beyond.

The pedestrian promenade provides connection from the new parking structure at north-east corner of campus via the cafe to the central green open space of the campus. The grand steps straddle the knoll garden bringing pedestrians to the cafe plaza. The promenade is modulated with articulate paving, benches and allee of Tipu trees, water veil feature help to define the main plaza area and entrance to the cafe.

It is a continuous garden experience along the promenade; however, the Knoll Garden, on the east side of cafe building is an expansive patio, lawn and gravel garden that can accommodate multiple uses. The mature stand of existing Eucalyptus Grove gives the garden character and stature.

This project has been awarded LEED Gold Certification. As part of the Gold Certification, the landscape design has qualified for Water efficient landscaping, Restore habitat, Maximize open space and Low heat island effect.

The fruition of this project testify to the power of good design in transformation of our environments for living, work and play; but most of all, communion with nature that enhance the quality of life.

1. Knoll Garden
2. Grand Steps
3. Promenade
4. Cafe Building
5. Cafe Patio
6. Water Garden
7. Promenade Plaza

Right: Cafe patio and water garden

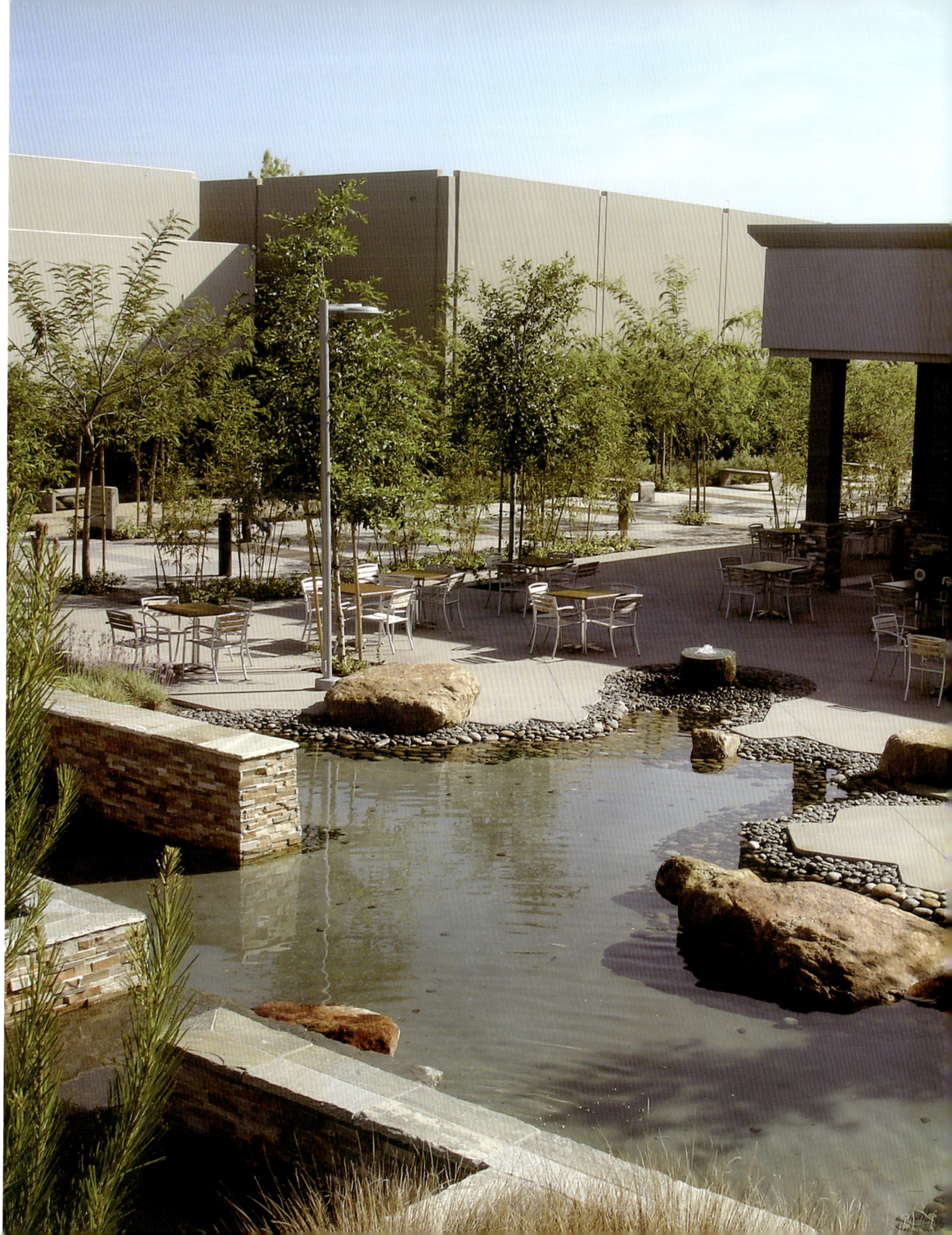

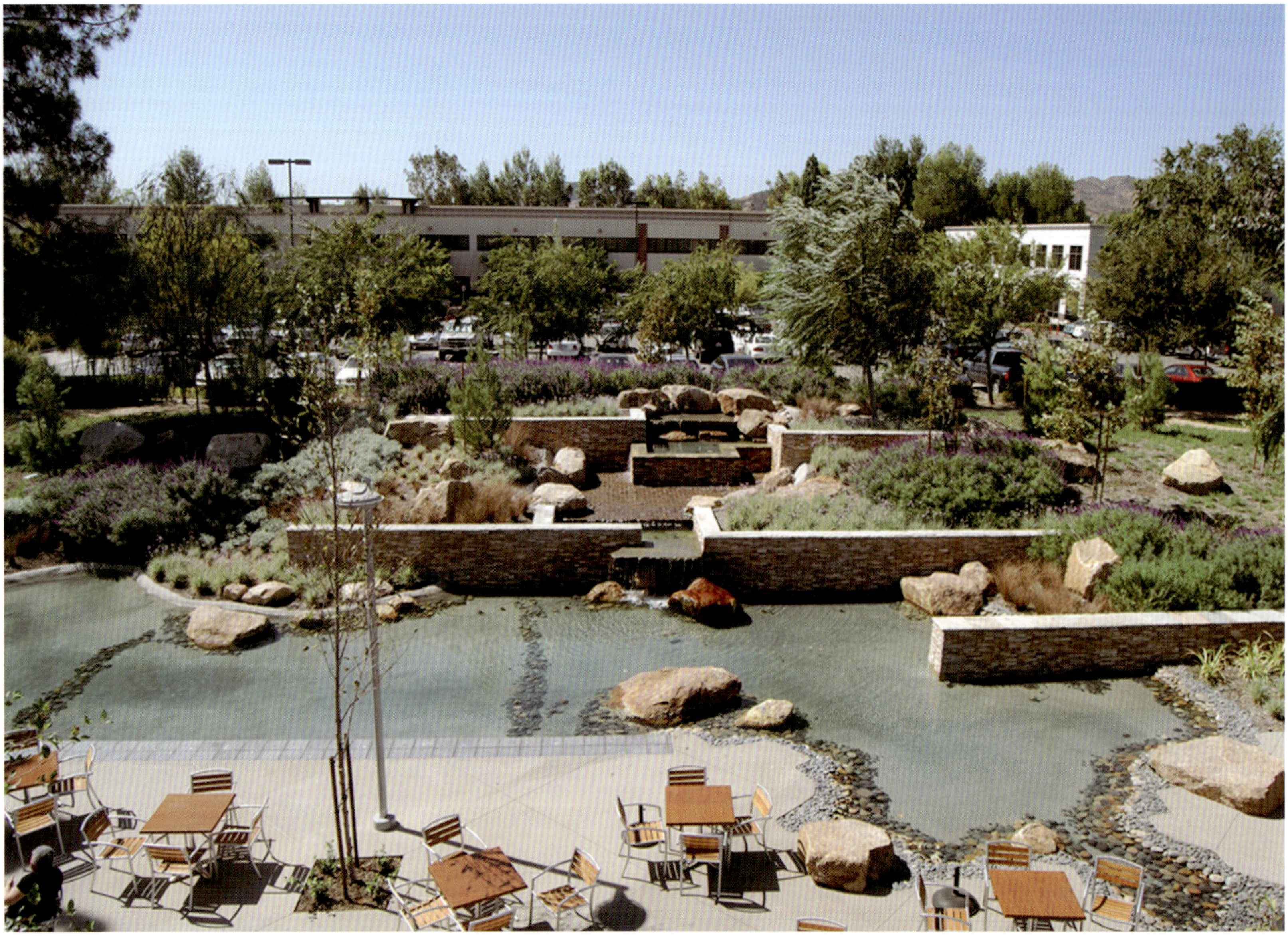

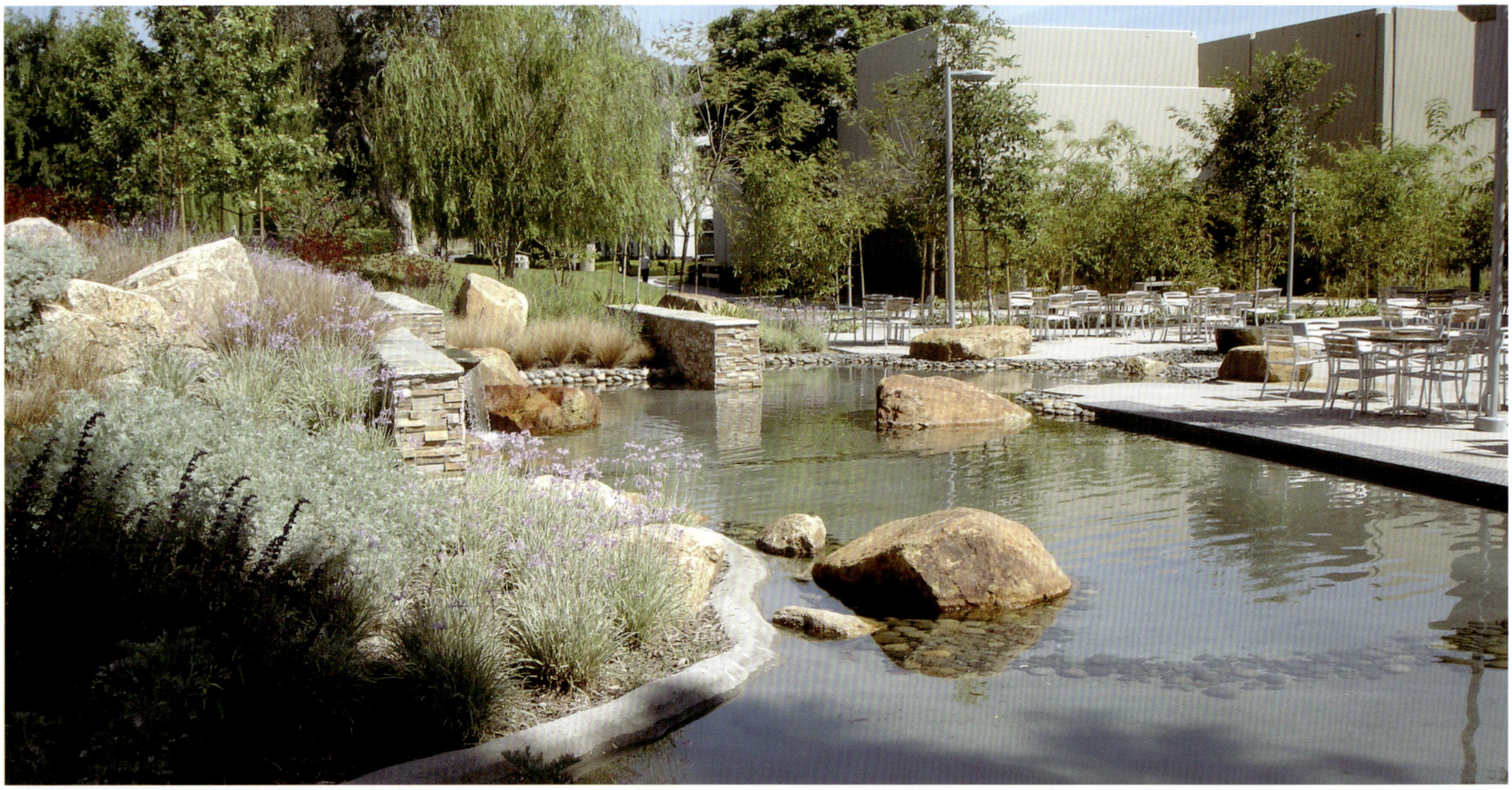

Upper left: Overview of the water garden

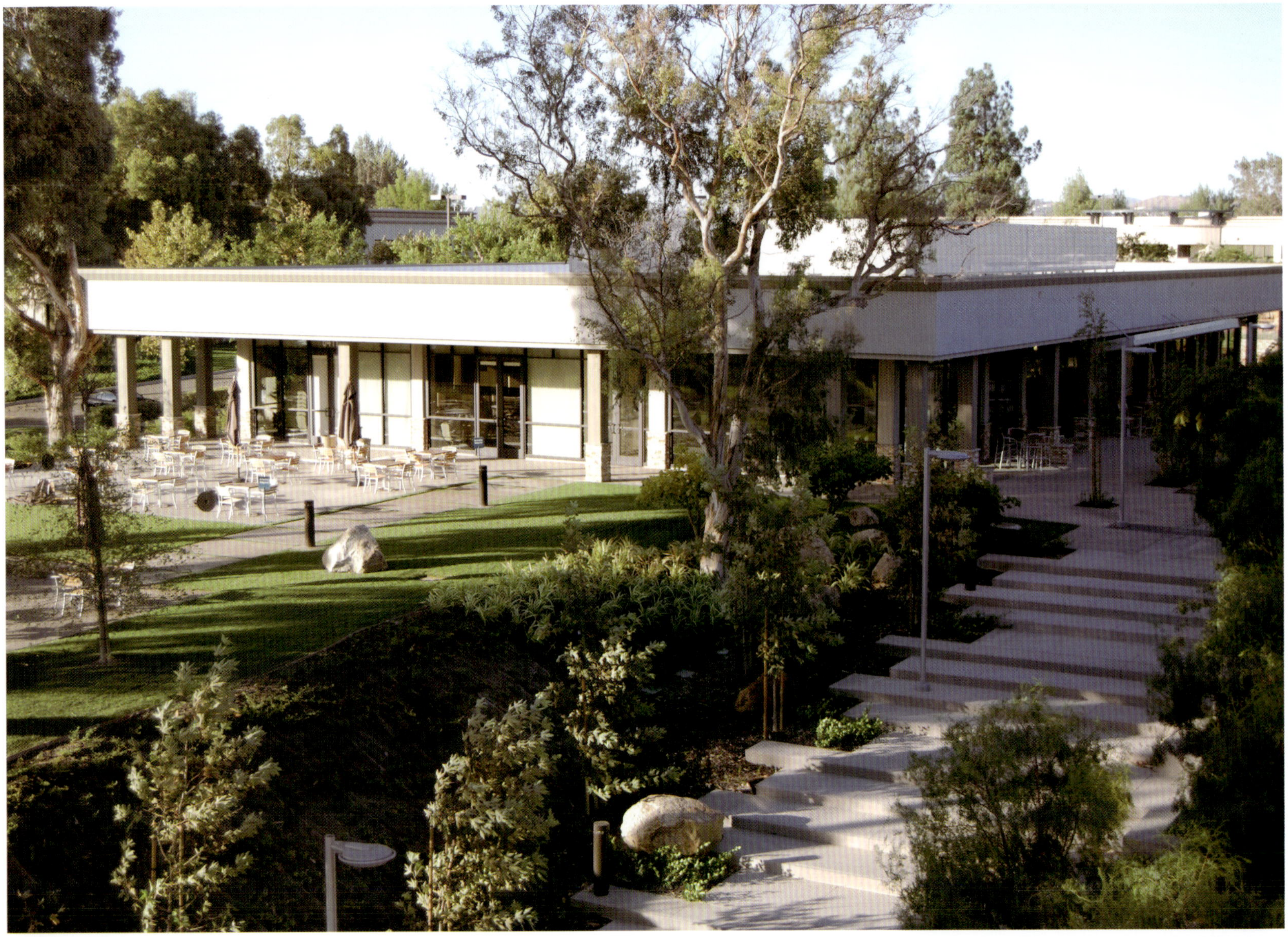

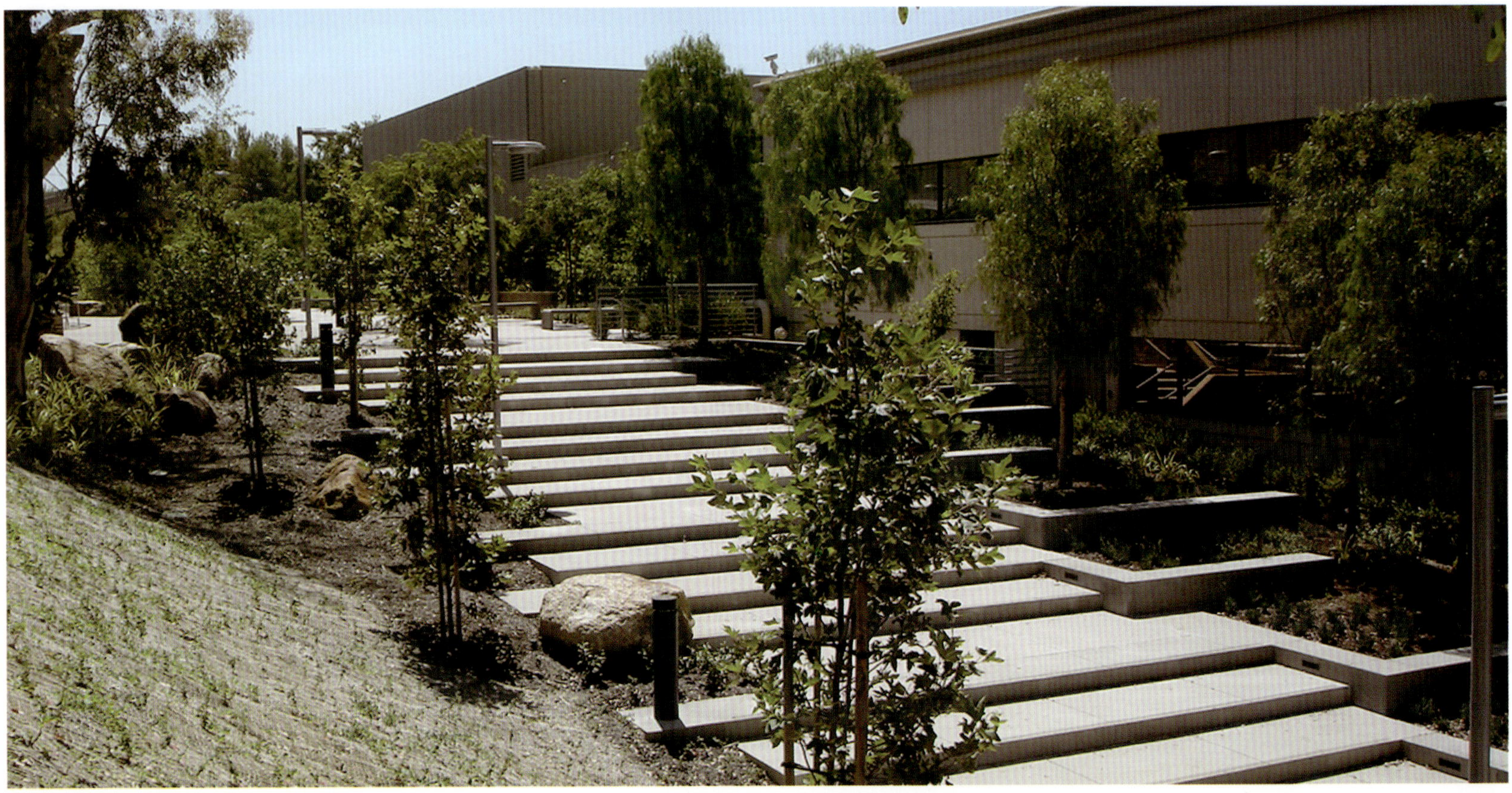

Upper left: Promenade
Upper right: Knoll garden

Tecnoparque

Location: Mexico City, Mexico Republic **Designer:** Mario Schjetnan / Grupo de Diseño Urbano **Photographer:** Francisco Gómez Sosa, Pedro Hiriart, Jorge Almanza **Completion date:** 2007 **Site area:** 155,000 sqm **Collaborators:** José Luis Gómez/ Grupo de Diseño Urbano **Office Buildings' Architecture:** G+A Arquitectos; Alberto Askenazi, Humberto Gloria **Sculpture-Symbol:** Mario Schjetnan, José Luis Pérez, Enrique Espinoza **Exterior Illumination Design:** Luis Lozoya, Luz + Forma

The Tecnoparque located in Azcapotzalco, the northern area of the Mexico City, the United States of Mexico, is a 155,000-square-meter complex geared to satisfy new leisure space requirements in the city. In conjunction with authorities, the objective is to improve the area, creating new jobs in the tertiary sector, integrating energy saving systems, rain water collection and infiltration, recycling of vital resources such as water.

The intention is to reactivate a post-industrial area in continuing transformation with existing infrastructure, roads, public transportation (metro); housing and near-by higher education institutions in order to establish a new high-tech leisure complex (meeting centers, cafe bar and landscape architecture, etc.) with international standards.

The complex incorporates the landscape architecture through contemporary green open spaces, plazas, gardens and water features which help provide areas for workers to relax and communicate in a high quality leisure environment.

The ecological concepts which were adopted incorporate through technology: rain water collection from roofs and plazas, on-site water harvesting cells, re-infiltration of storm water into the aquifer by a system of deep wells and the treatment of gray and toilet waters on-site incorporating the effluent into a series of landscape pools and into the irrigation of planted and forested areas.

The Tecnoparque represents an interesting participation of private area in conjunction with urban strategies to reactivate Mexico City in its post-industrial role, within an ecological vision and ethic.

P1. Plaza 1
P2. Plaza 2
P3. Plaza 3
4. Comercial Area
5. Restaurant

Right: General view of plaza

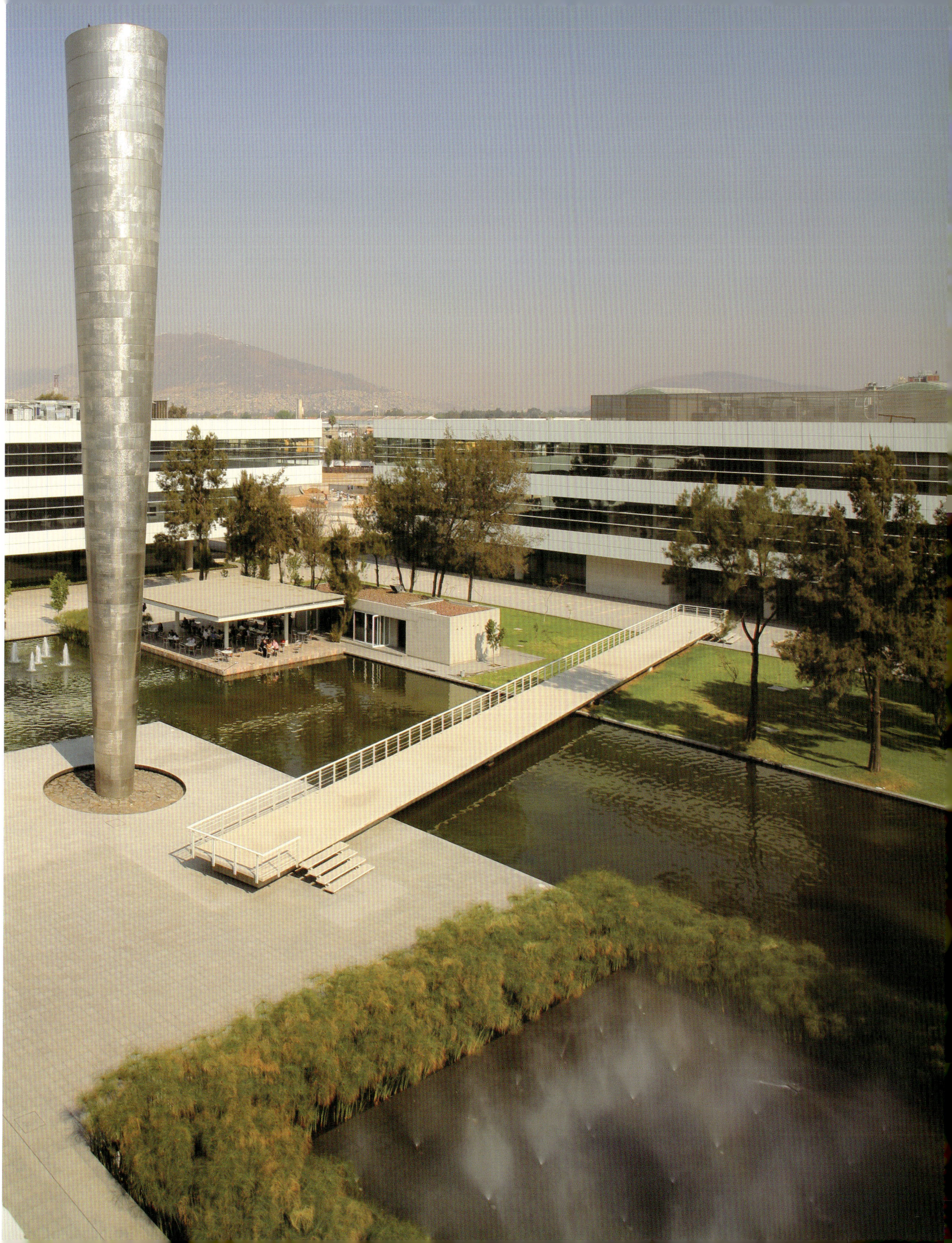

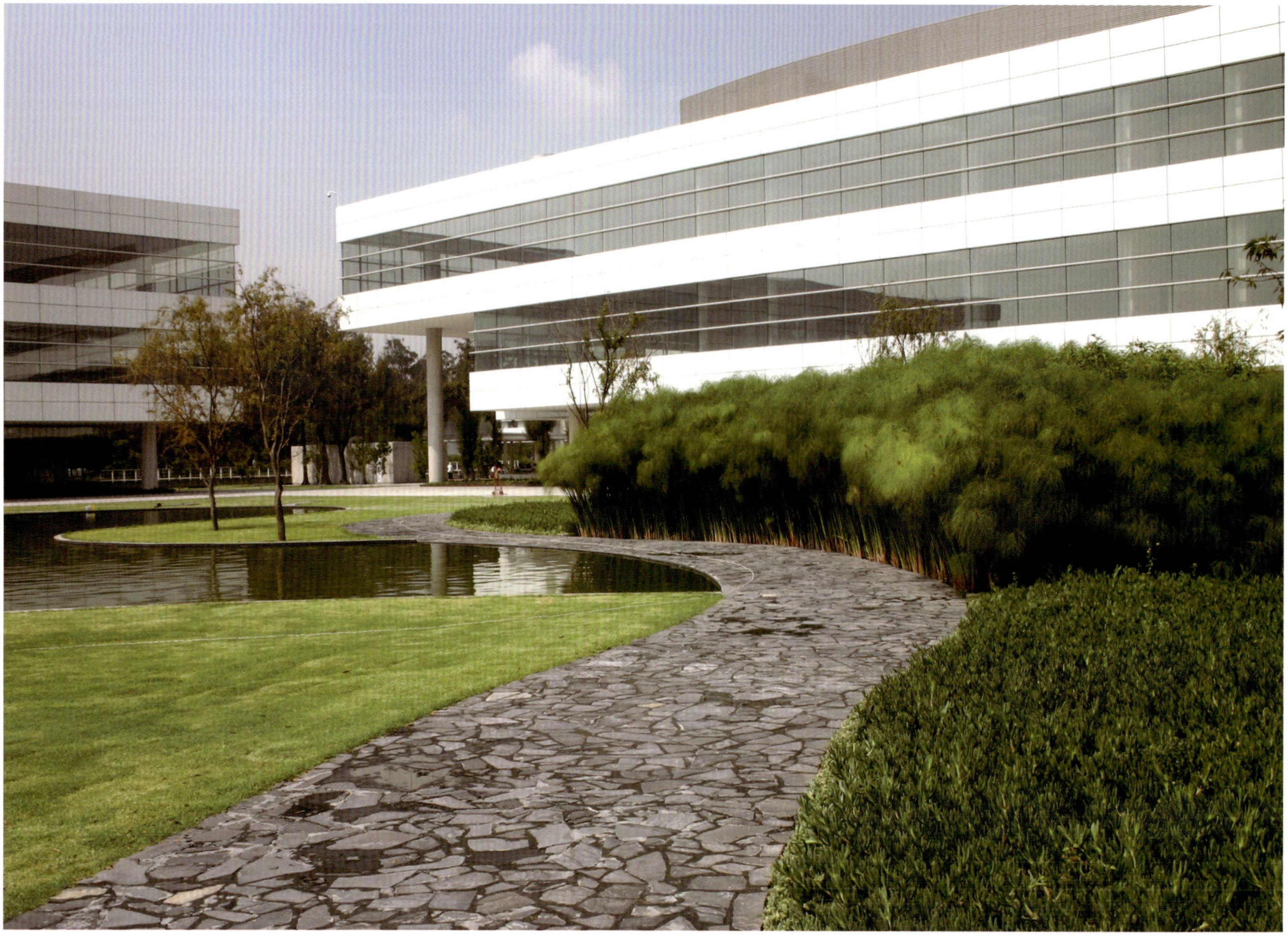

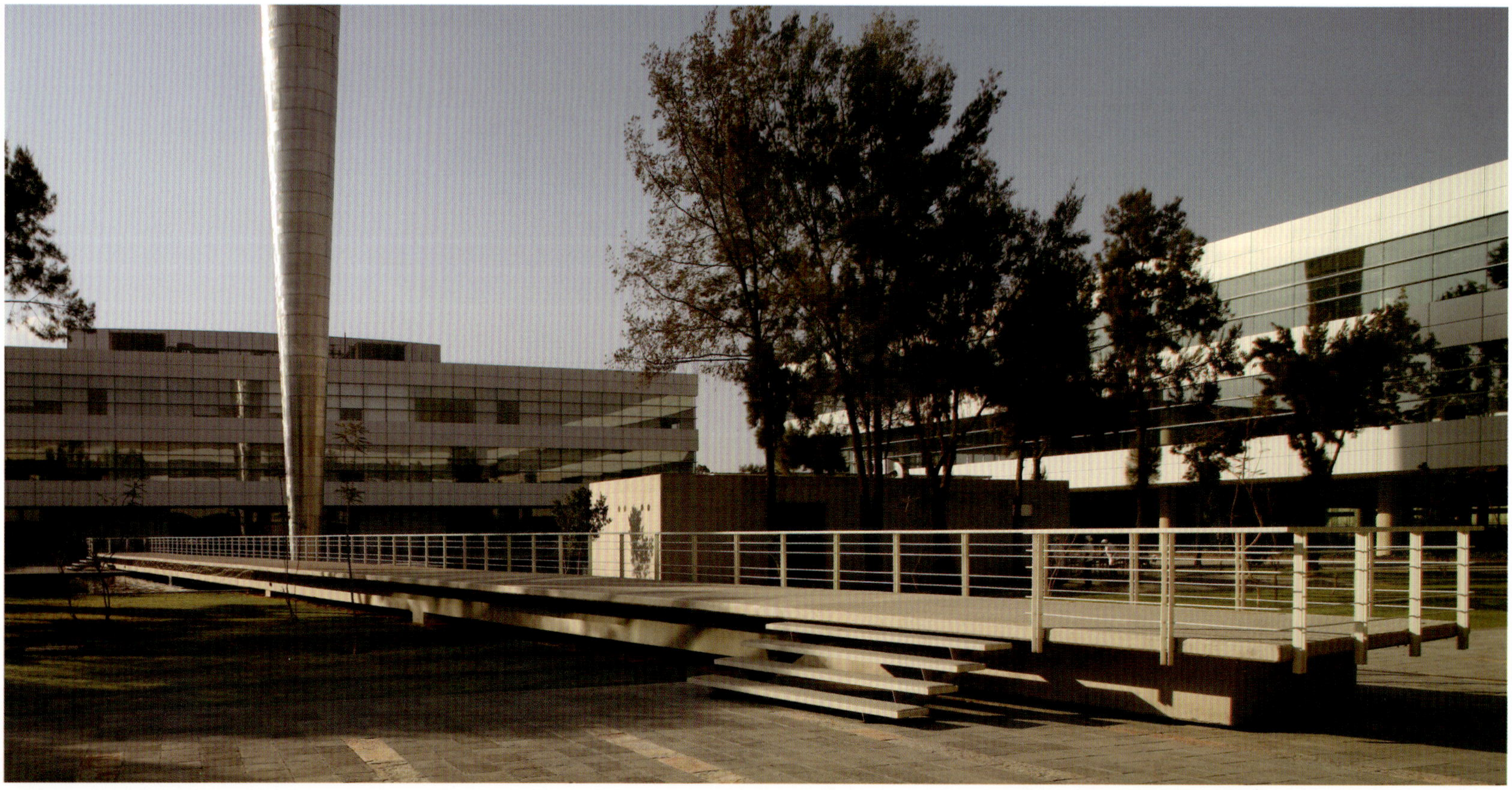

Upper left: Pathway on the plaza
Lower left: Plaza and tower
Upper right: Overview of the pool

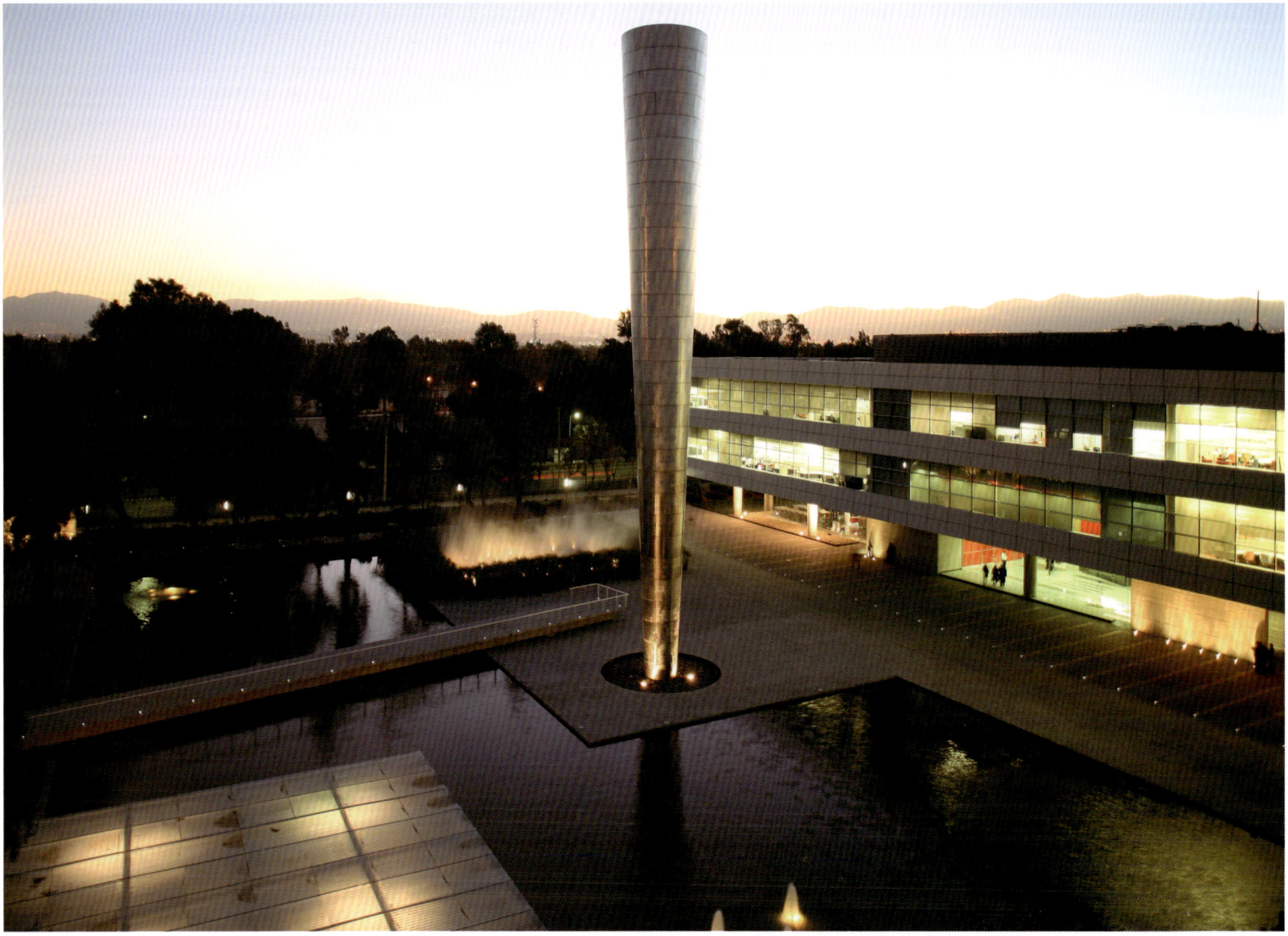

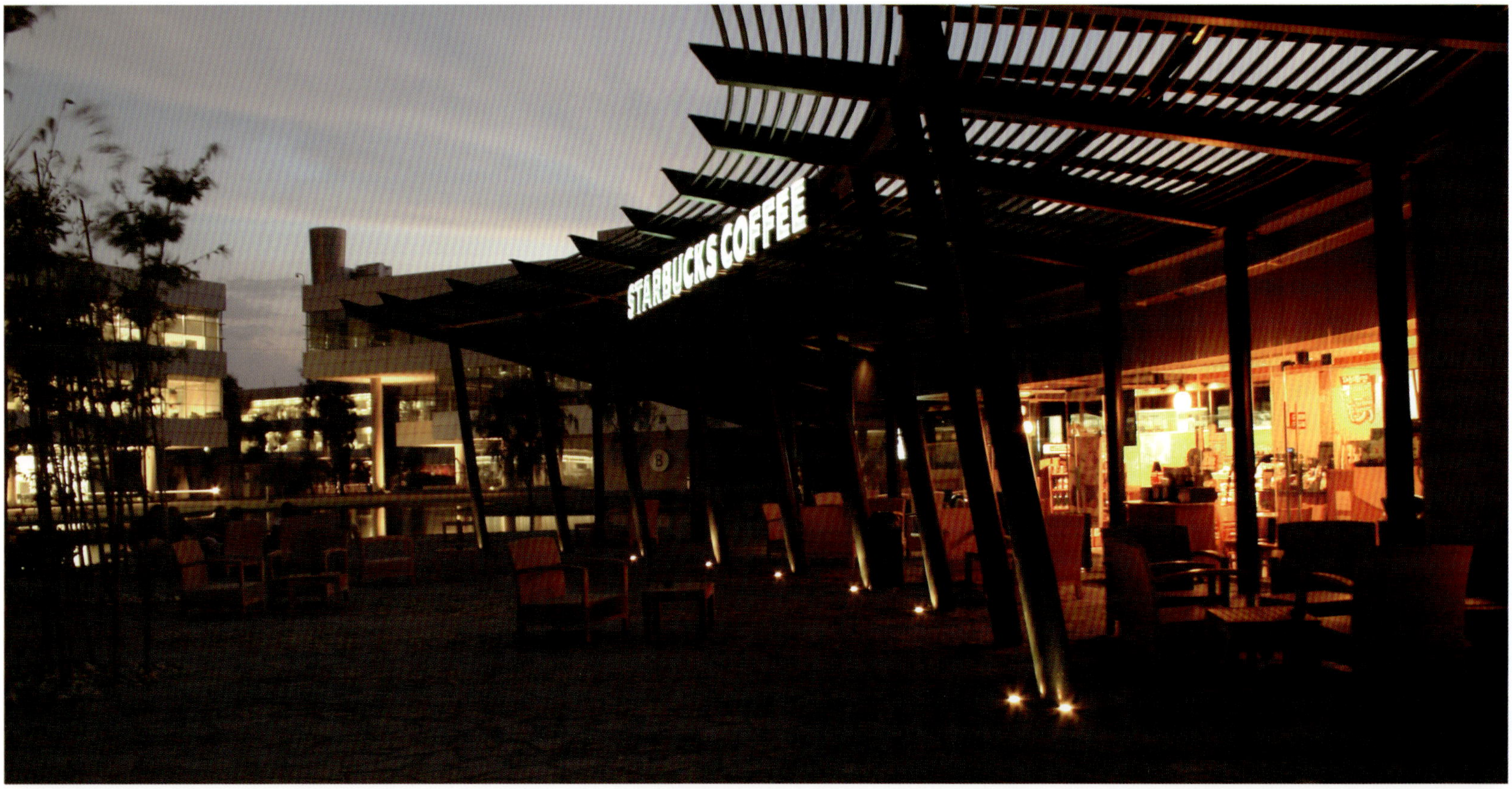
STARBUCKS COFFEE

Upper left: Night view of plaza
Lower right: Cafe zone

Furtwängler Garden

Location: Salzburg, Austria **Designer:** Auböck + Kárász **Photographer:** Andrew Phelps **Completion date:** 2009 **Site area:** 5,000 sqm

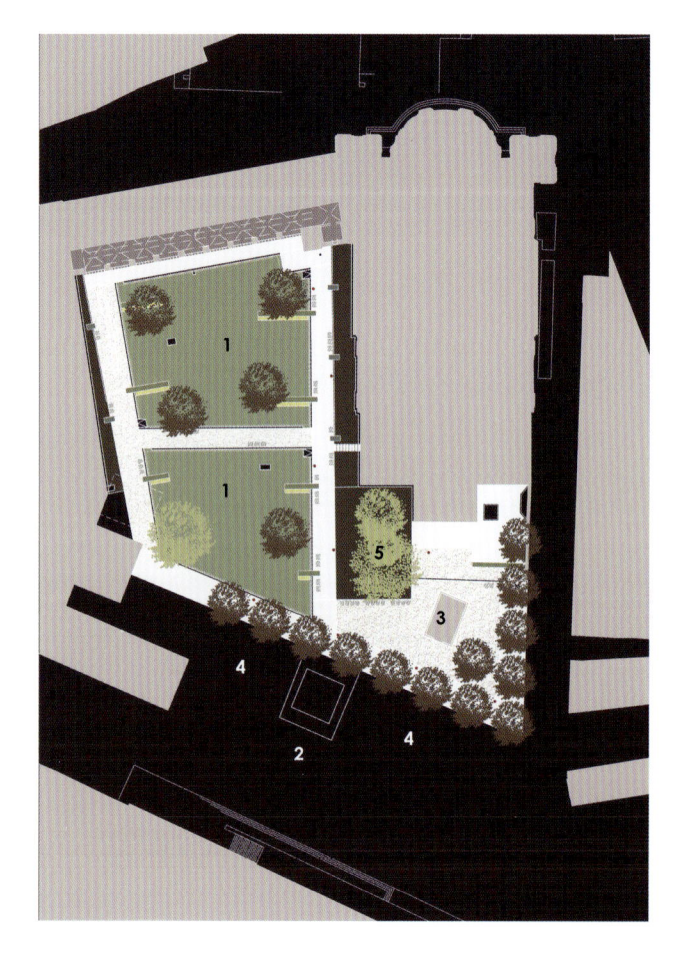

Since mediaeval times the public spaces of Salzburg merge from streets, squares, courtyards and passages to a unique urban setting. The redesign of the Furtwängler Garden adds an interesting new element: a contemporary garden-square in the city center.

The project unfolds as a modern interpretation of Salzburg's inner gardens of the 17th and 18th century bordered by walls: A wide framelike path – partly in light green quartzite, partly in white gravel – constitutes the enclosure for two sunken lawn fields. A broad of lime trees form an edge toward the bordering square creating a new outline in the urban fabric. This net of promenades serves as a relax area as well. The deepened lawns planted with sophora trees are linked to the boarding promenades by scenographically shaped hedges of hornbeams. The fringe along the buildings was planted with Ivy, accentuated by strips of Hydrangea overlapping into the framing paths.

Visitors can relax on garden chairs like on a veranda deck, looking toward the green fields, which invite for a more casual, easygoing stay. Art works of Fritz Wotruba, Emilio Greco, Giacomo Manzù and Anselm Kiefer complete the ensemble.

1. Sunken Lawn
2. Max-Reinhardt-Plaza
3. Kiefer Pavilion
4. Line of Lime Trees
5. Ginkgo

Right: Night view of the plaza

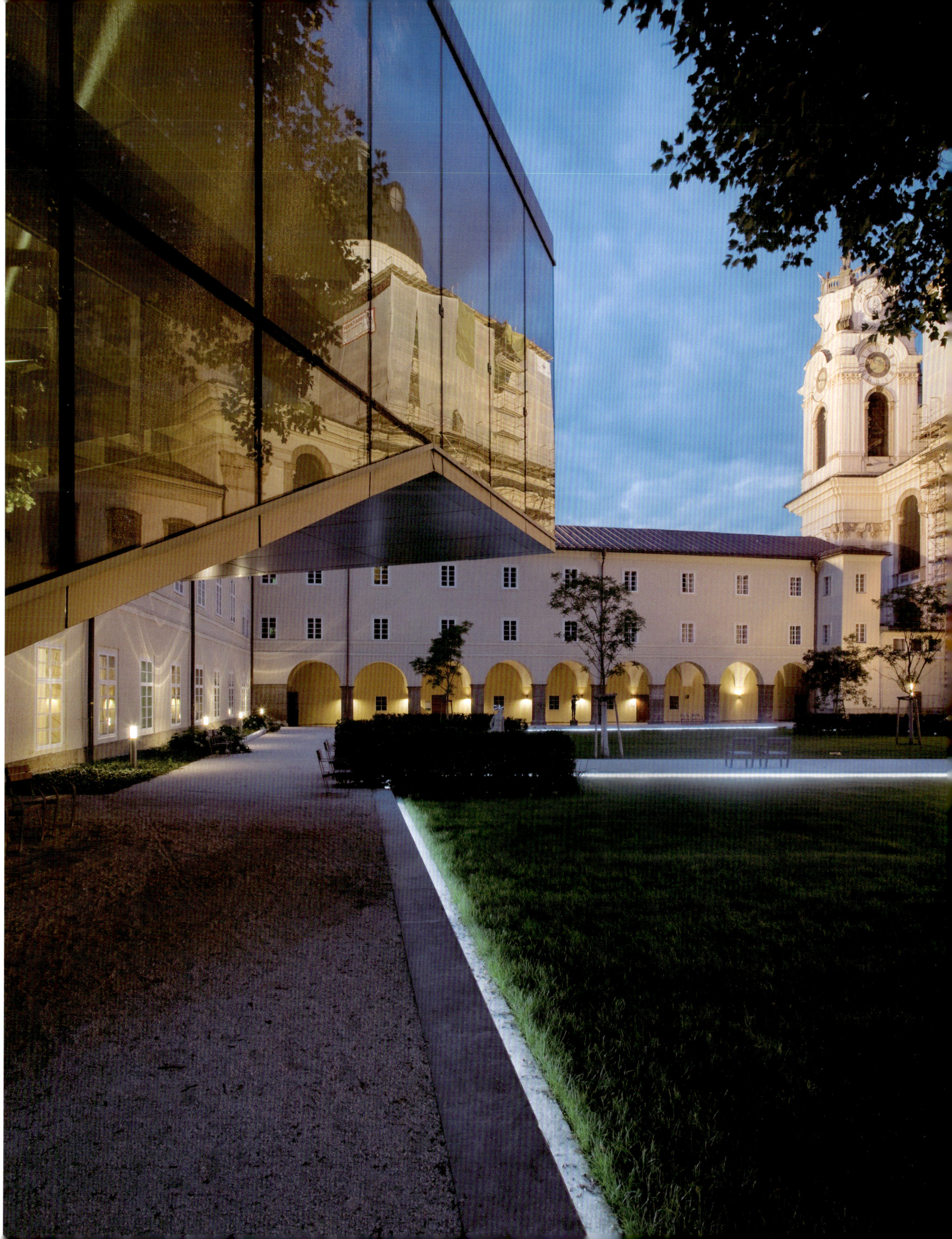

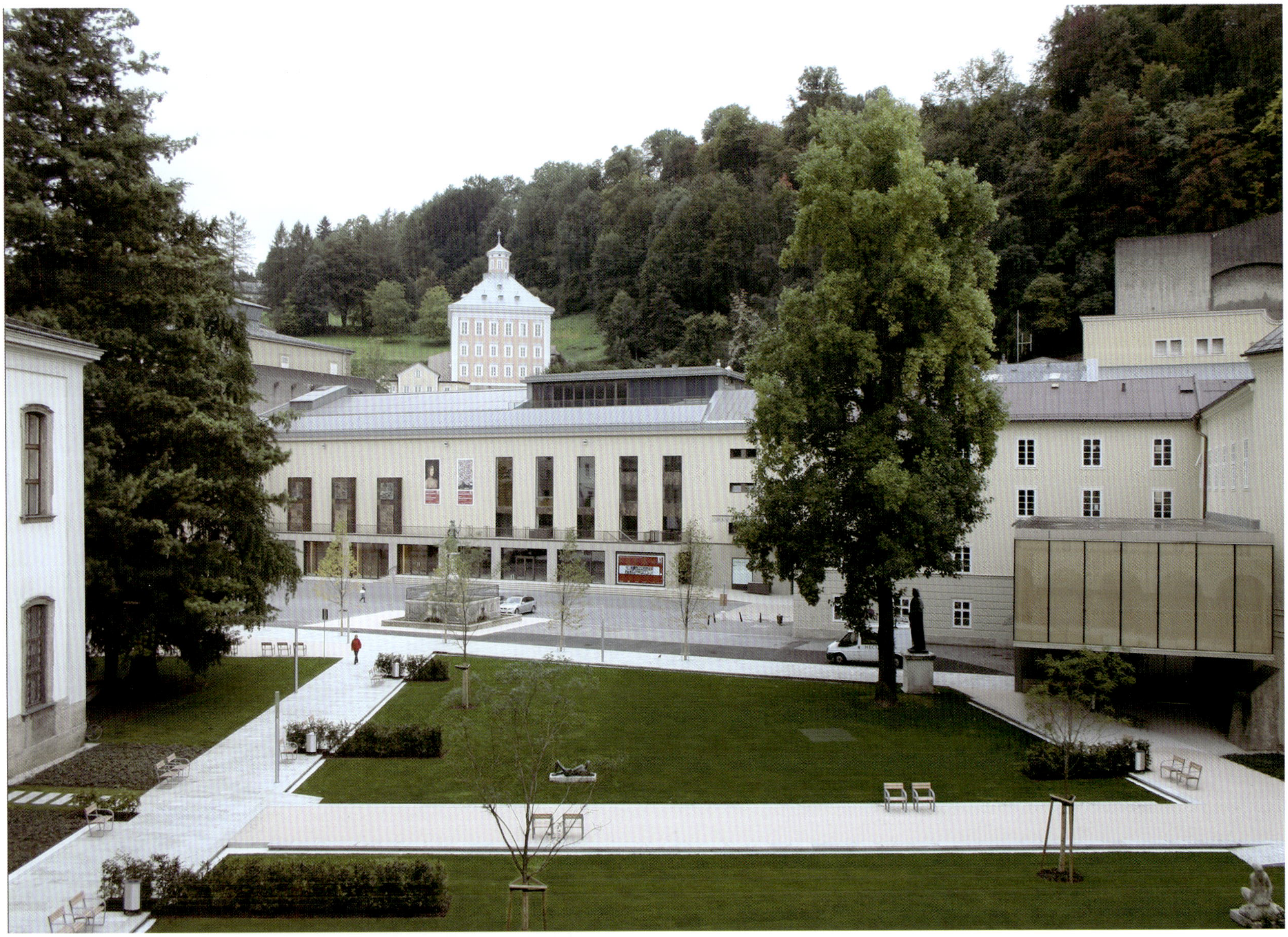

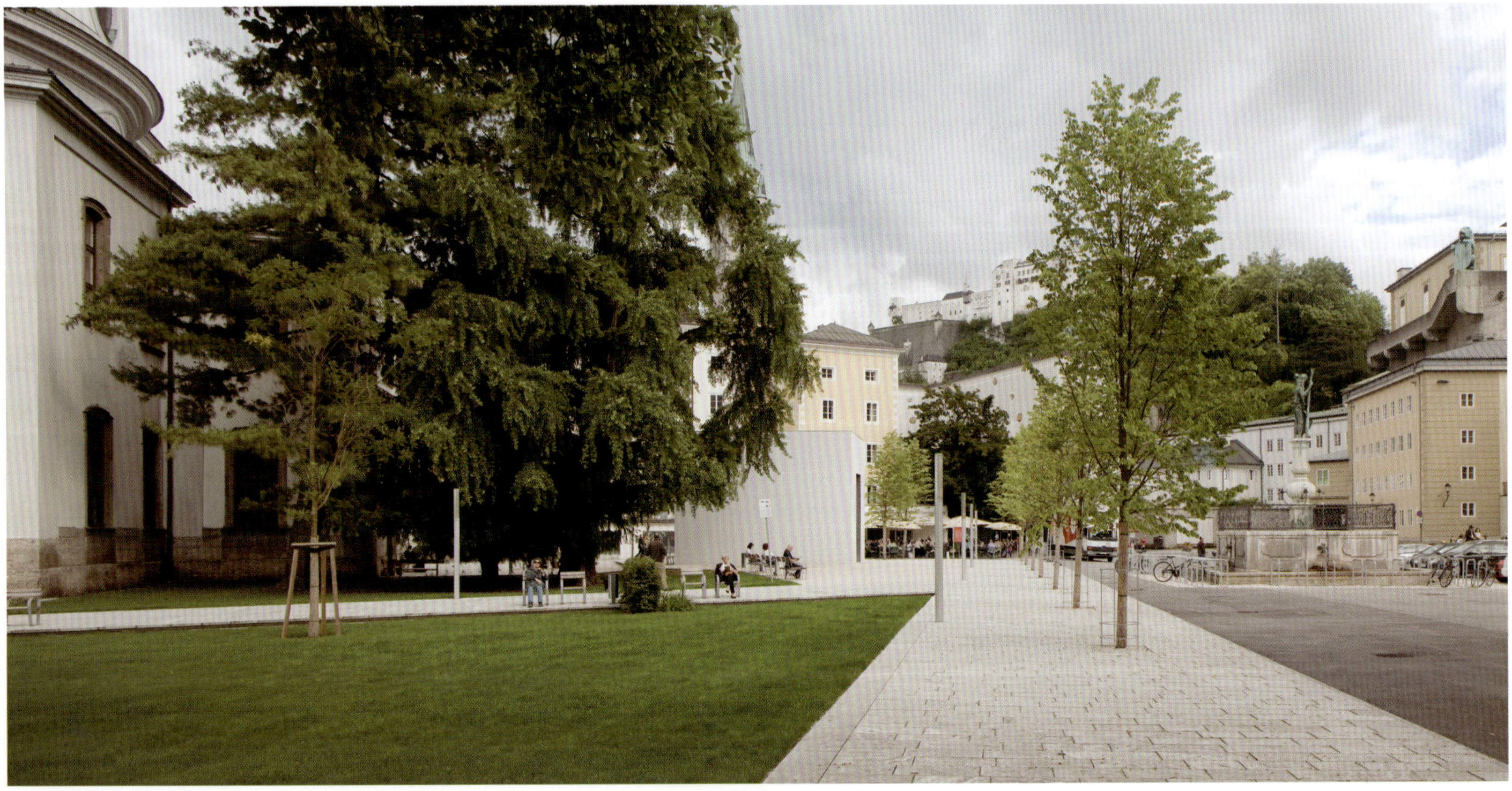

Upper left: View to festival hall
Lower left: View to Salzburg Castle
Upper right: View toward university
Lower right: Aerial view

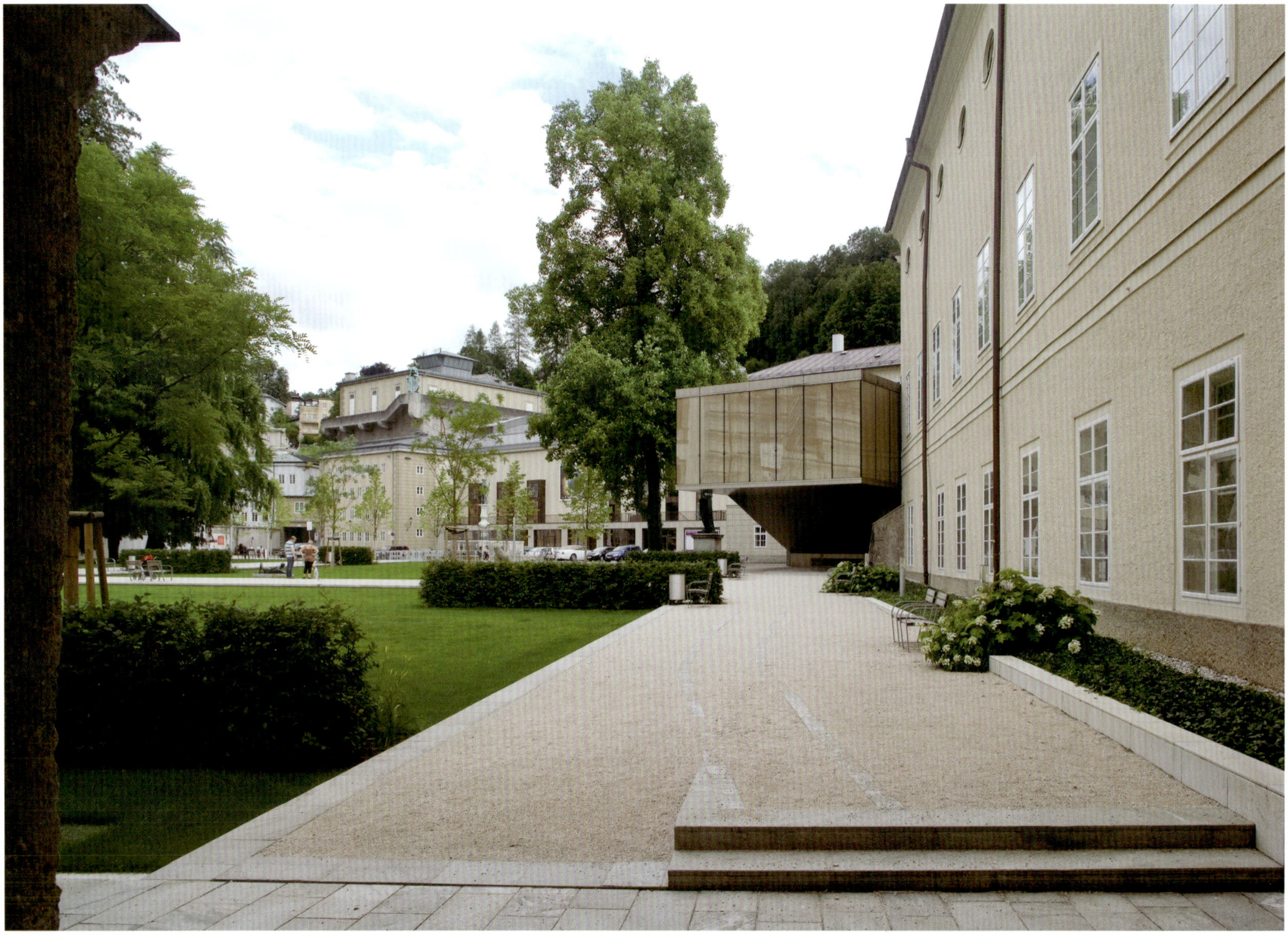

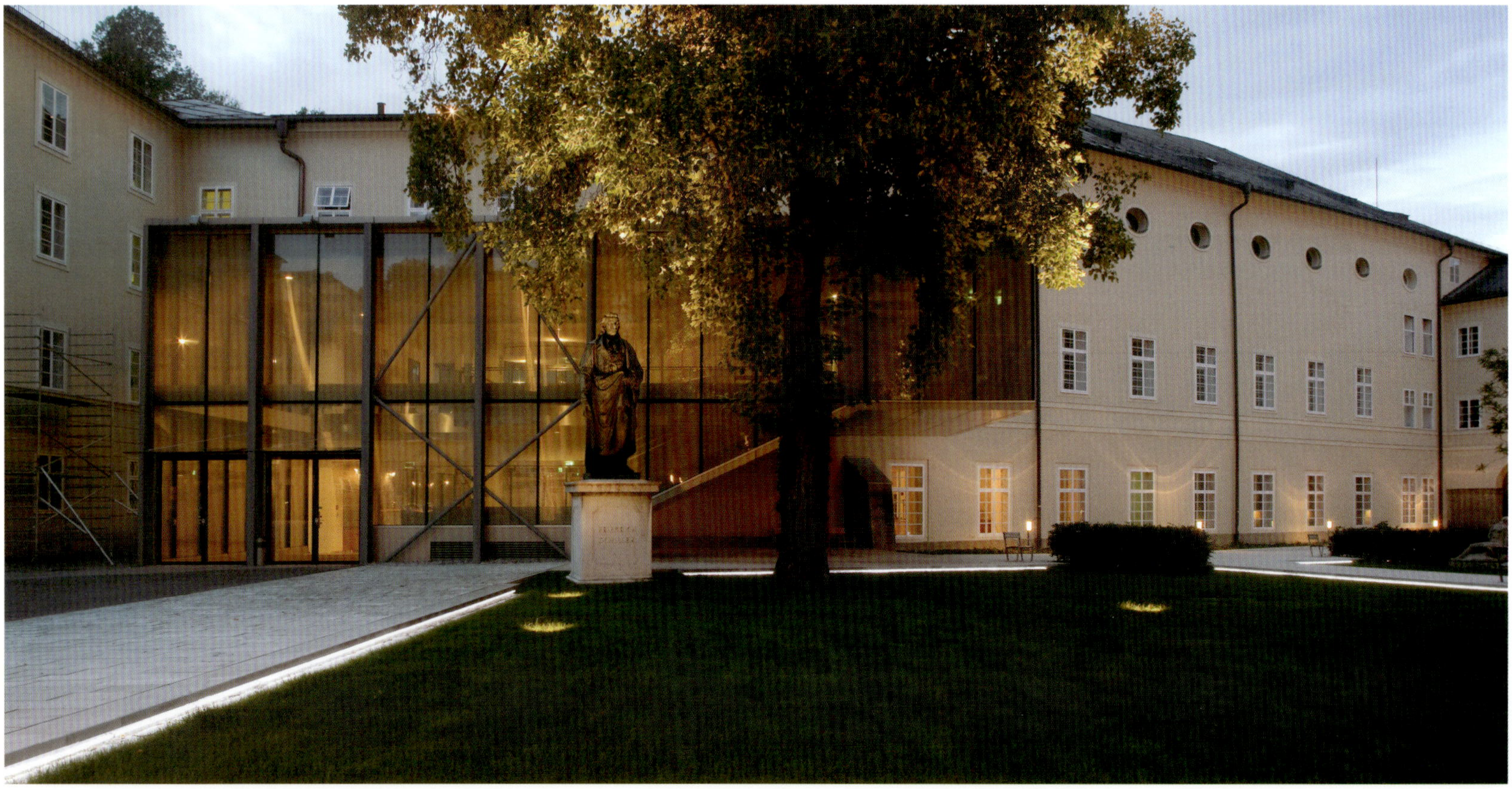

Upper left: Promenade along library
Lower right: Sculpture

Southeast False Creek Plaza

Location: Vancouver, Canada **Designer:** Phillips Farevaag Smallenberg
Photographer: Scott Massey **Completion date:** 2010 **Site area:** 4,100 sqm

The Southeast False Creek Plaza is designed to integrate many layers of meaning and function into a rich and engaging social space for its community. Key themes are 'Recollection of History, Crossroads, Social Gathering and Appreciation of Water'.

The history of Southeast False Creek as a place of heavy industry has inspired the design of the Plaza in myriad ways. Shipbuilding was a dominant activity that is referenced in abstractions of the traditional skill of lofting – scaling drawing to make full-size patterns – and of ship components – bulkheads, masts and transoms.

The Plaza is located at the intersections of many paths through the Southeast False Creek neighborhood. The design facilitates freedom to move along direct routes among destinations and invites people to co-exist with vehicles on the adjacent streets.

The Plaza is intended as the place where the community gathers for holidays and celebrations as well as where people go every day to eat, read, play, and observe each other.

The design responds to many of the sustainable practices that have been established for the Southeast False Creek community from use of local materials to promote of local agriculture. Foremost among the sustainable objectives is the fostering of an appreciation of the importance and value of water through the collection and use of stormwater in ways that are easily understood, educational and highly visible.

1. Community Space
2. The Transom
3. The Yard
4. The Fair Curve
5. The Lofting Floor

Right: Overview of the plaza at night with light

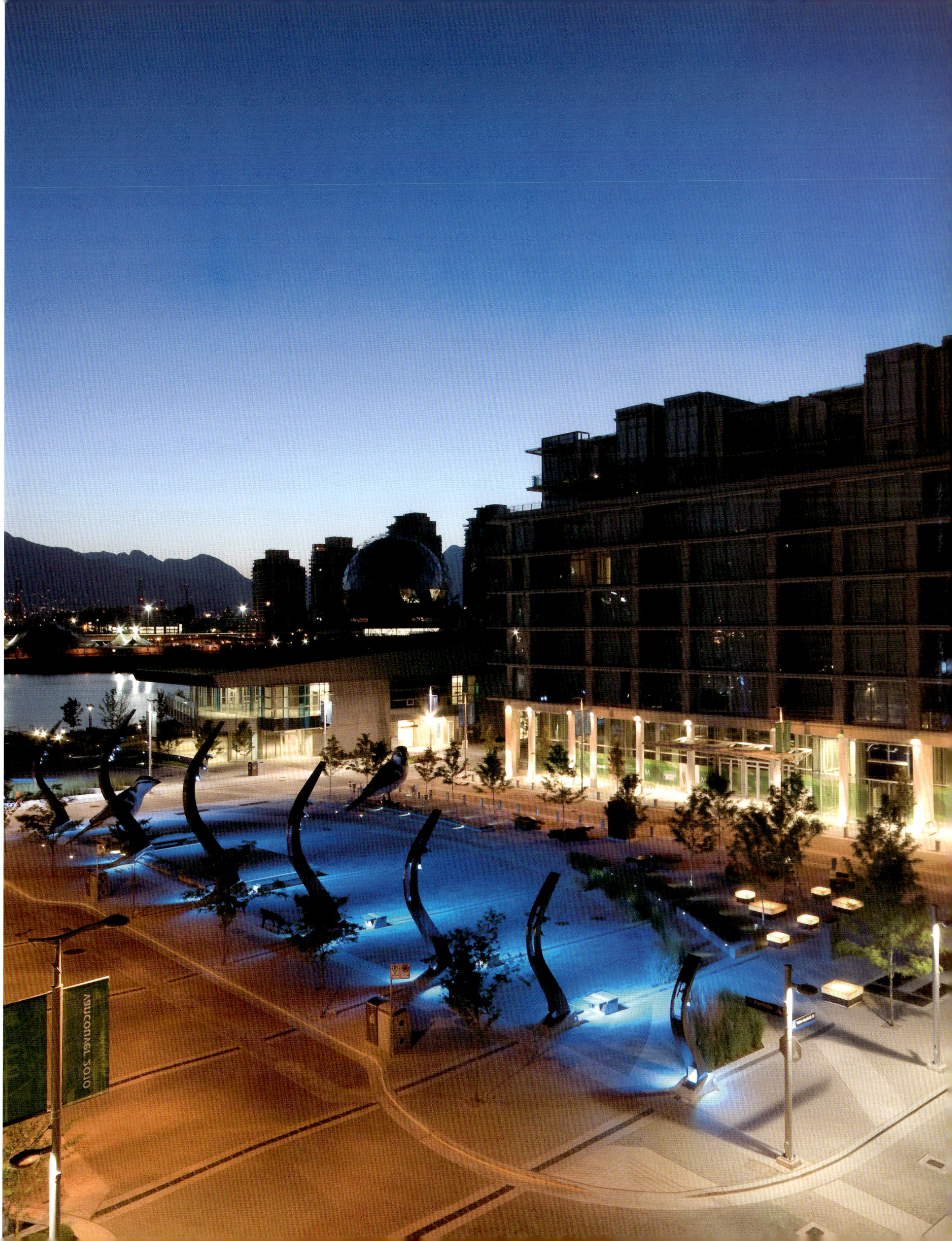

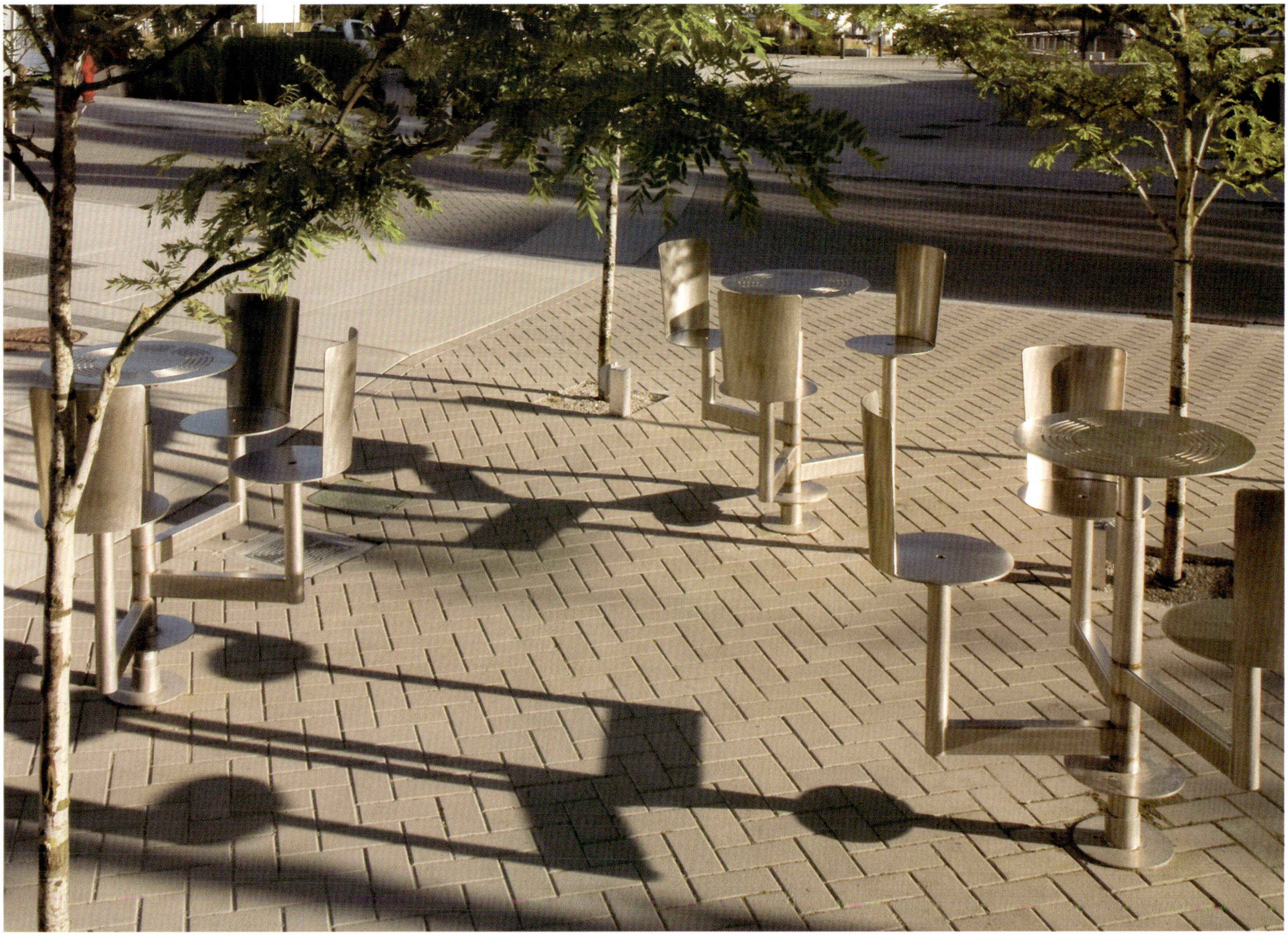

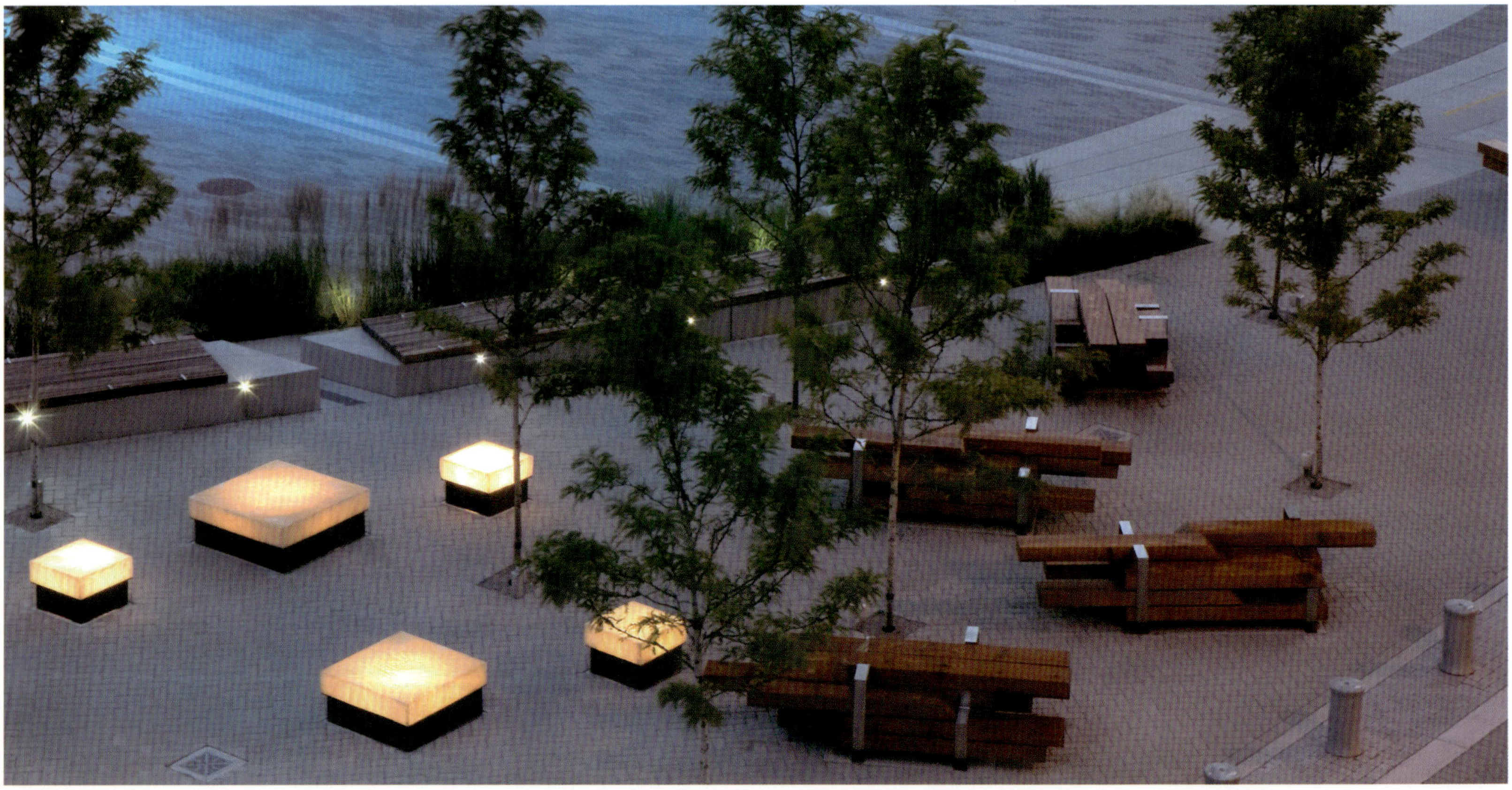

Upper left: Rest place
Lower left: Bird's view of the site furniture
Upper right: Bird's view of the plaza
Lower right: Details of the benches

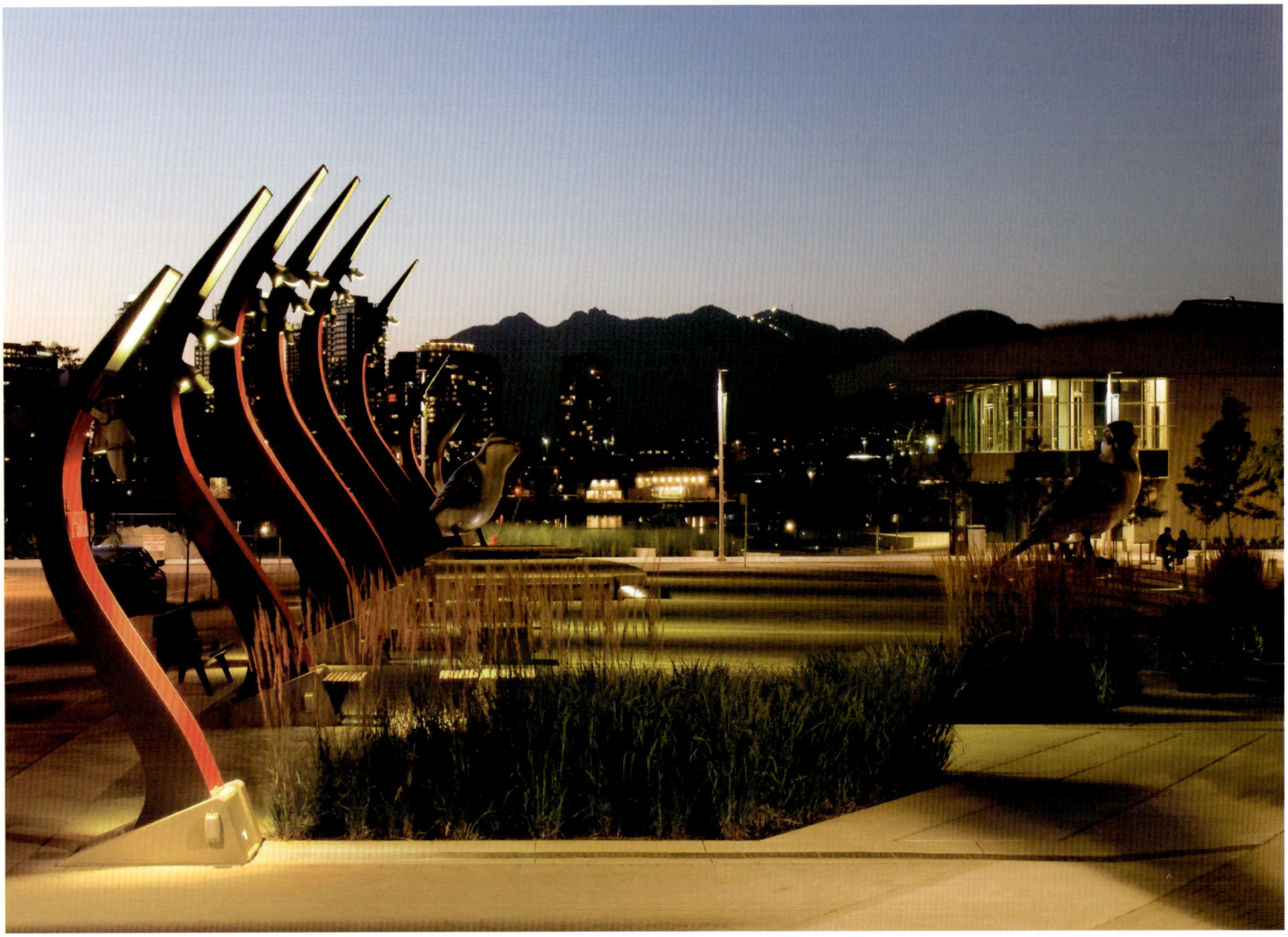

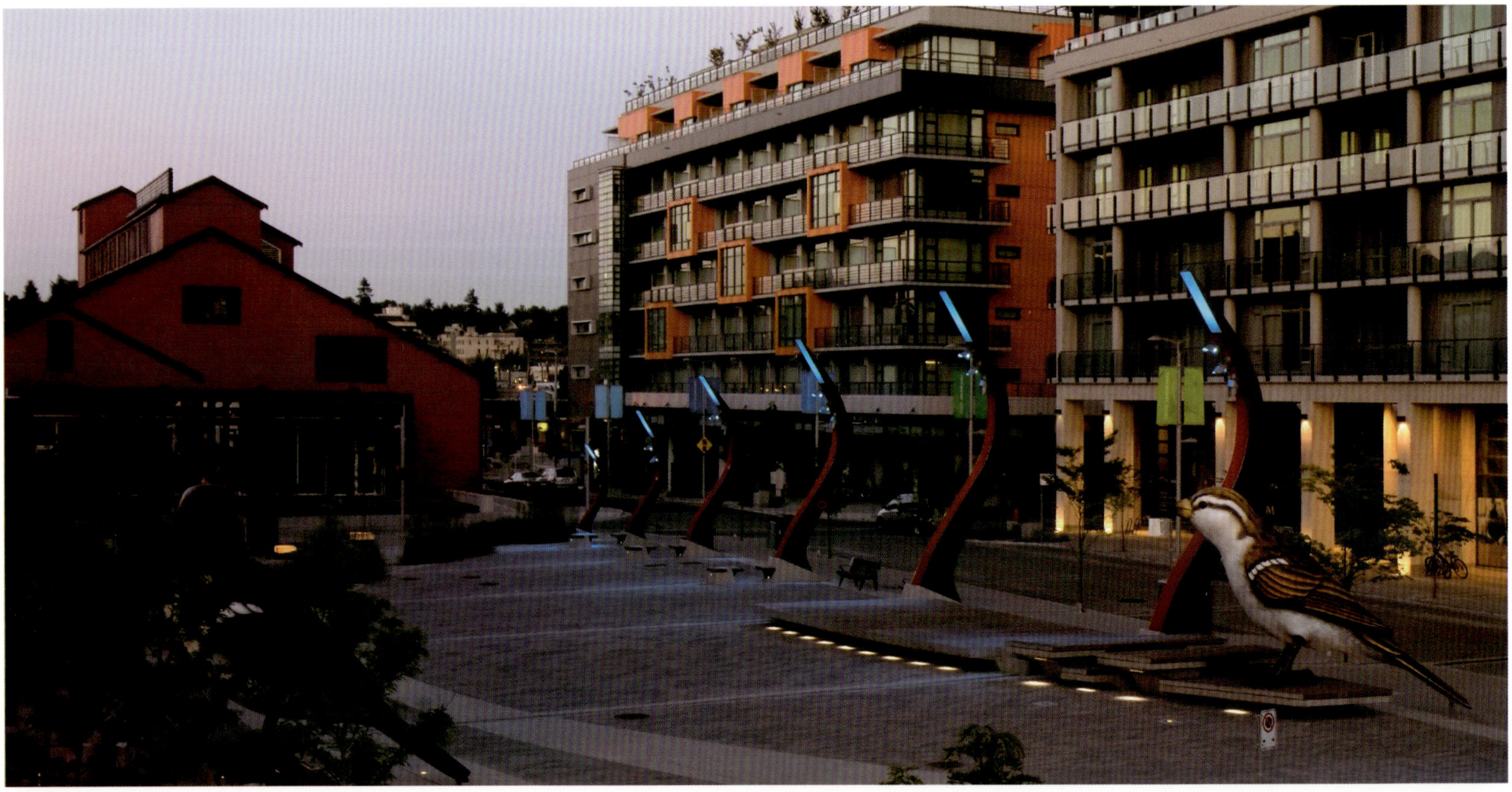

Upper right: Site funiture

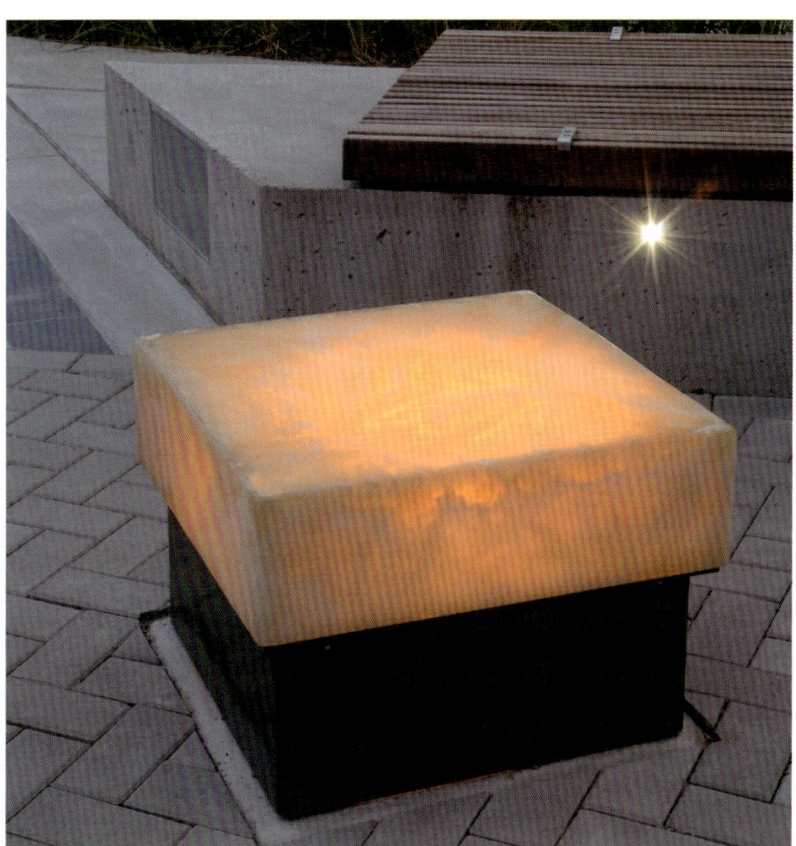

Fahrzeugwerke Falkenried

Location: Hamburg, Germany **Designer:** FSWLA Landschaftsarchitektur GmbH
Completion date: 2005 **Site area:** 30,000 sqm

Industrial monuments combine with a variety of modern architectures lend this new district of town a lively ambience. The homogeneous design of the outdoor space provides formal cohesion. The designers have deliberately confined their input to three elements: material(ity), trees and light.

Public and private spaces acquire form and distinctive identity simply from surfaces, density of vegetation and strength of light. All squares, streets and paths have the same paving. Asphalt on driving surfaces is light in color and matches the paving. The roads are not been designed in the classical manner; instead there are smooth, gradeless transitions between the roadway, kerb and pavement.

Everything is similar yet different. The same goes for the planting. The designers have used only one type of tree for the whole site: maple from all over the globe, free-standing in shrub or tree form, but different arrangements and varying sub-species. Depending whether its setting is a square, street, courtyard or garden, the maple appears in a group, row, block, loose cluster or solitary.

All the surfaces are equipped with the same simple, industrial-style lighting. Lone trees on squares are illuminated individually and in color. The leafy canopy over the central piazza has been staged as a forest of light.

1. Entry Feature
2. Traffic and Logistics
3. Urban Space
4. Recreation and Leisure Area
5. Private Area

Right: Large maple tree

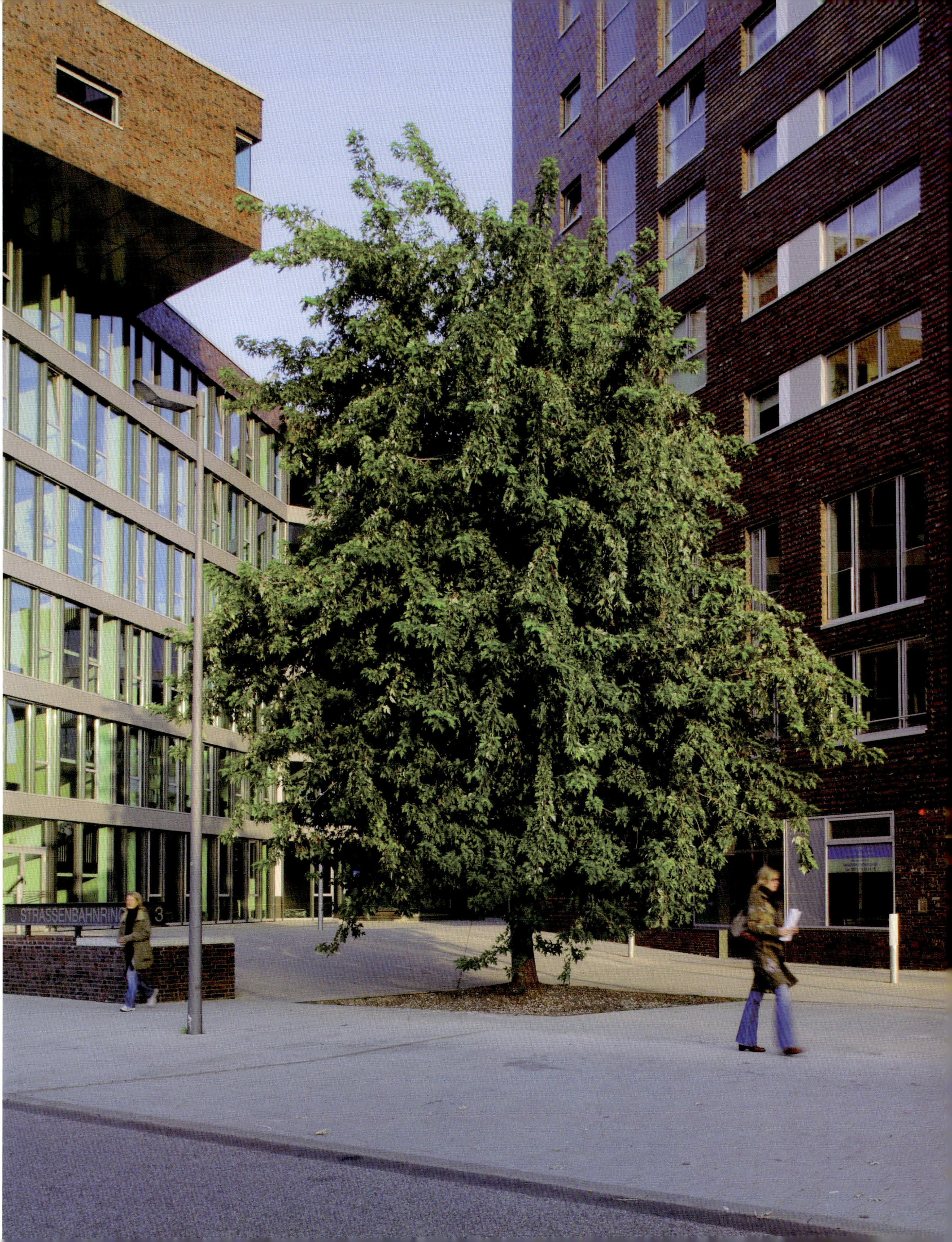
STRASSENBAHNRIN 3

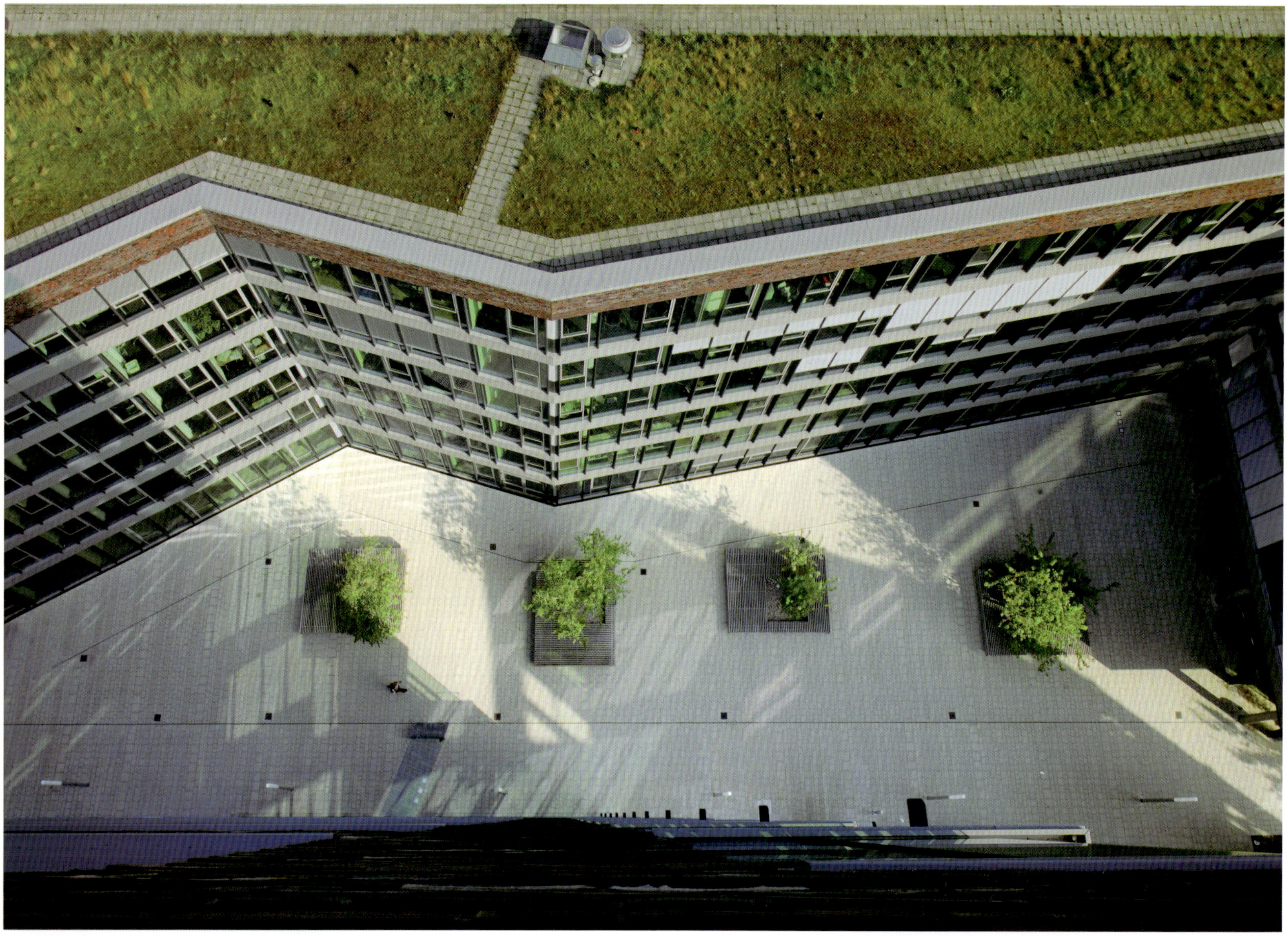

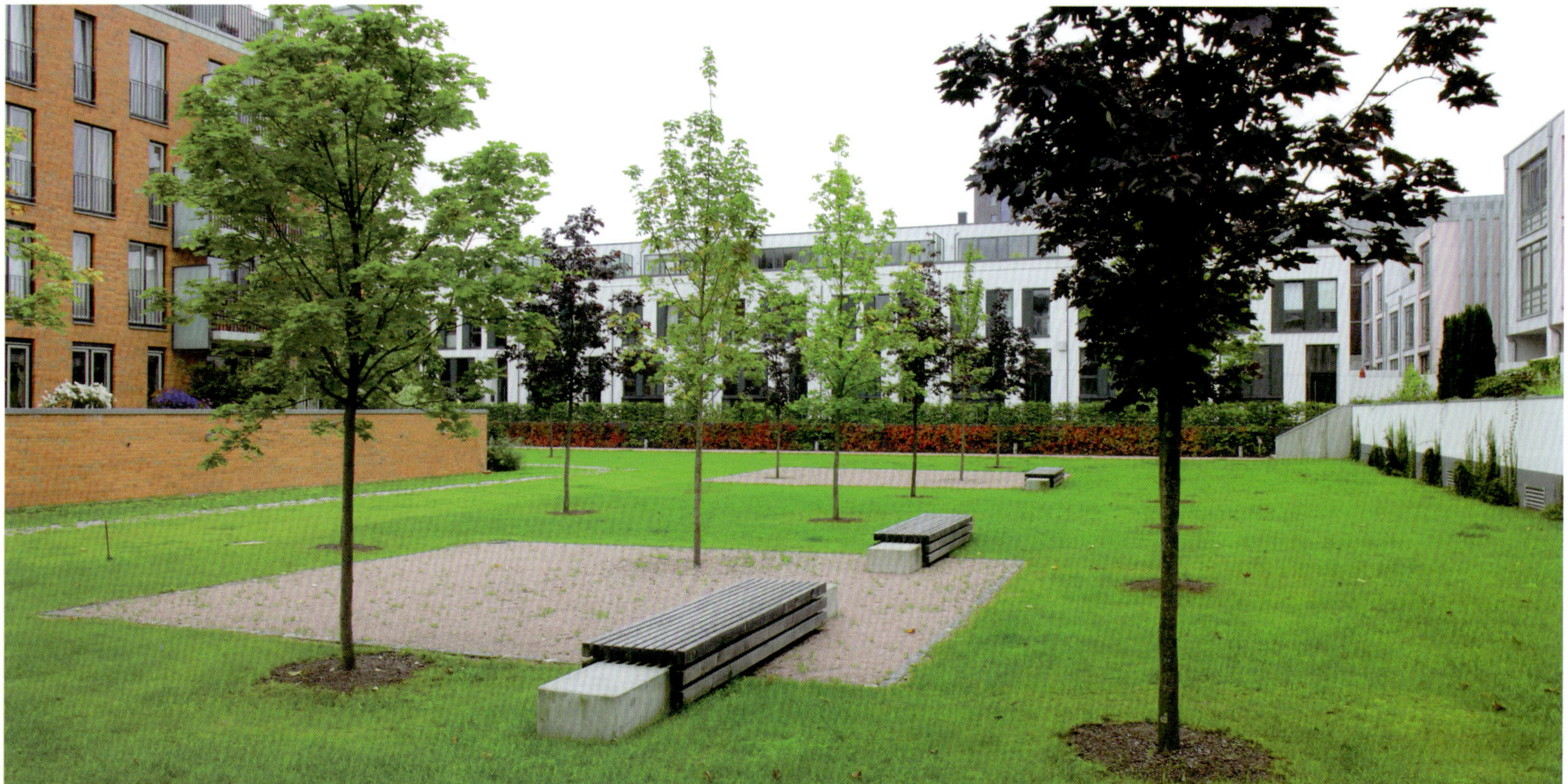

Upper left: Courtyard between two buildings
Lower left: Playground
Upper right: Main axis
Lower right: Steps

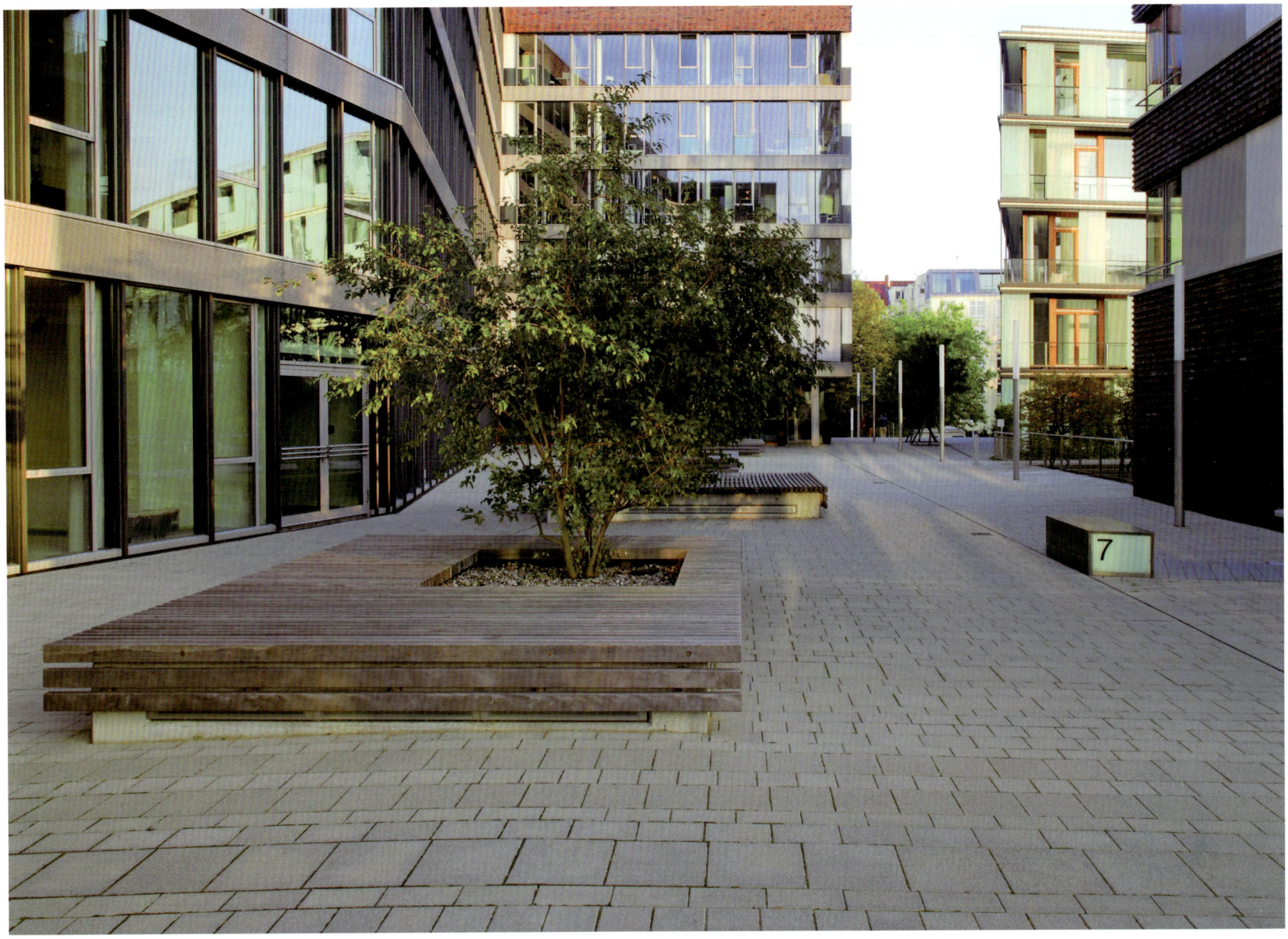
7

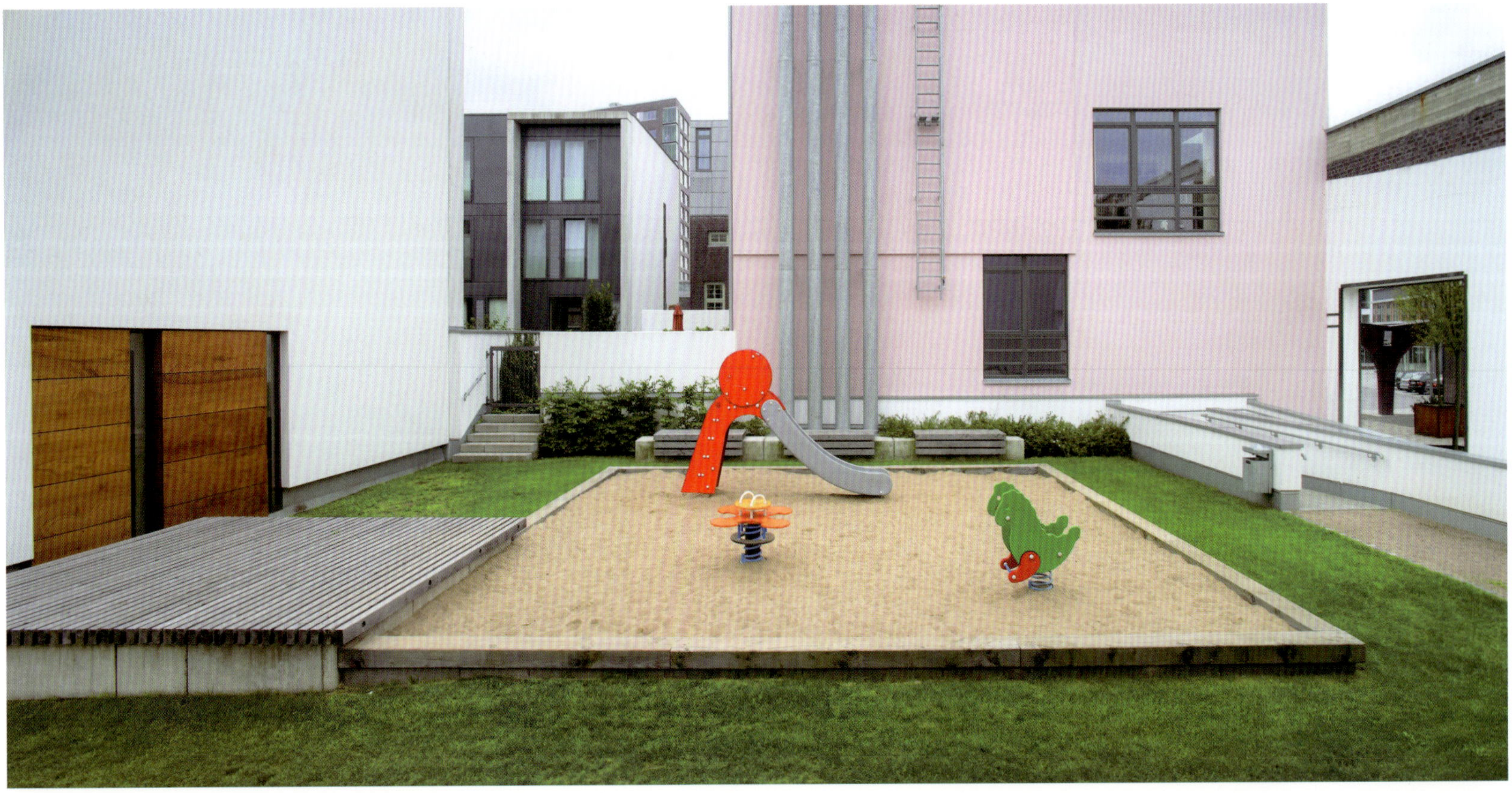

Upper left: Courtyard
Lower left: Playground
Lower right: Steps

Fontana Square in Quinto de Stampi

Location: Milano, Italy **Designer:** Labics **Photographer:** Luigi Filietici **Completion date:** 2009 **Site area:** 6,200 sqm

The project for Piazza Fontana is the project of a soil, the making of a landscape, capable of welcoming, answering and amplifying, with its articulation, the changing and complex needs of those who will use it. In fact, the project stems from the will to create a space triggering different and non-scheduled usages, from the will to create a complicated place, whose identity is unified and whose usage is manifold.

The geometrical pattern of the square is made of a thick grid of golden rectangles, sized according to the main size of the context determining every element of the square, from the main geometry to the drawing of the flooring.

The topic of soil bending was introduced inside this deeply characterizing texture. The 3D modeling of soil has a two-fold role to play; on the one hand it identifies milieus with different spatial qualities, to the other it strengthens spatial tensions that already exist in these places and simultaneously brings in new tensions.

The system of triangular fields inside the geometrical pattern represents a strong element of unity and identity for the project and, at the same time, thanks to its declination whose matter, size and combination always vary, is the tool to build manifold and varied situations inside this landscape where the balance between natural and artificial is unstable.

1. Rest Area
2. Playground
3. Fountain
4. Porta Europa
5. Lawn

Right: The playground

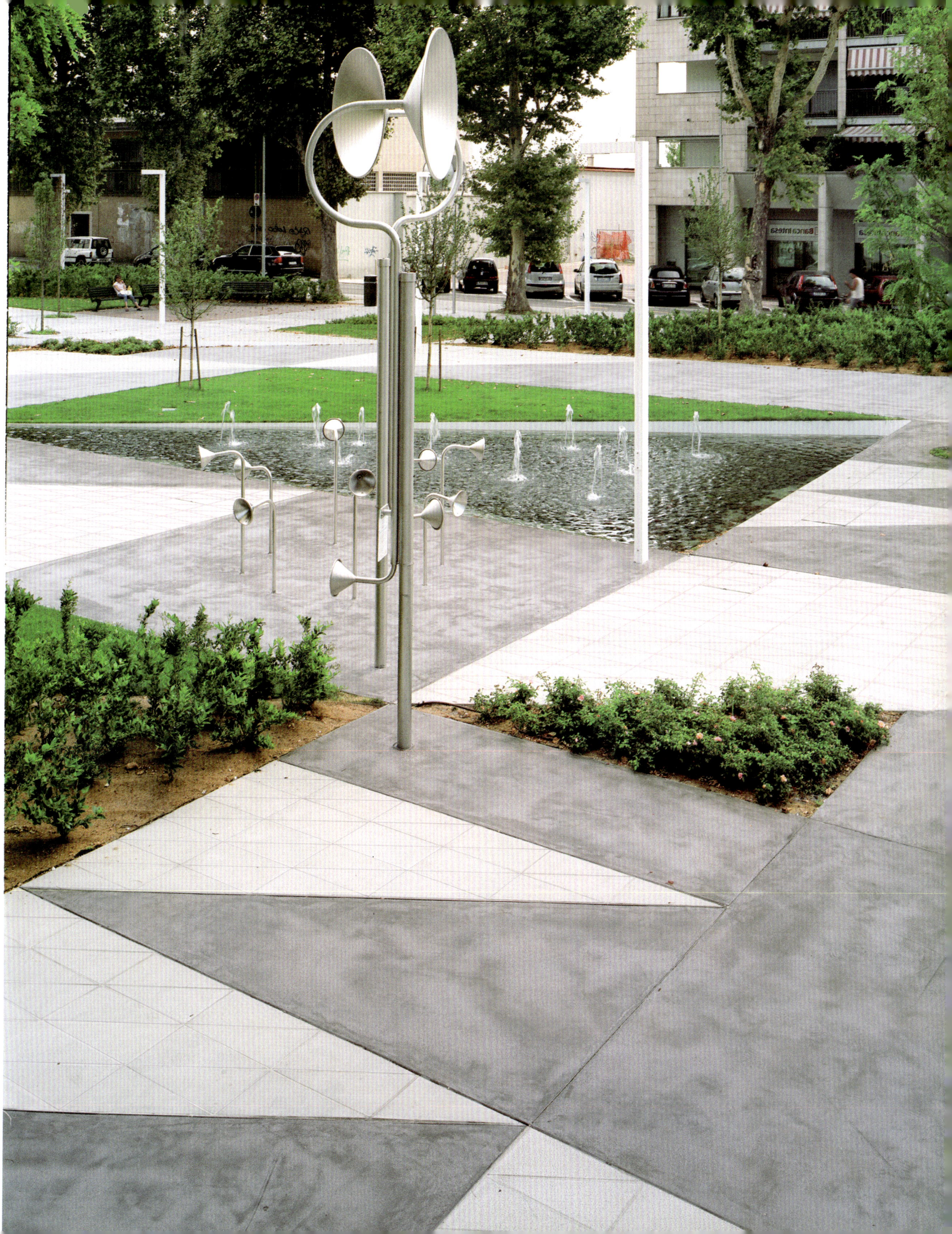

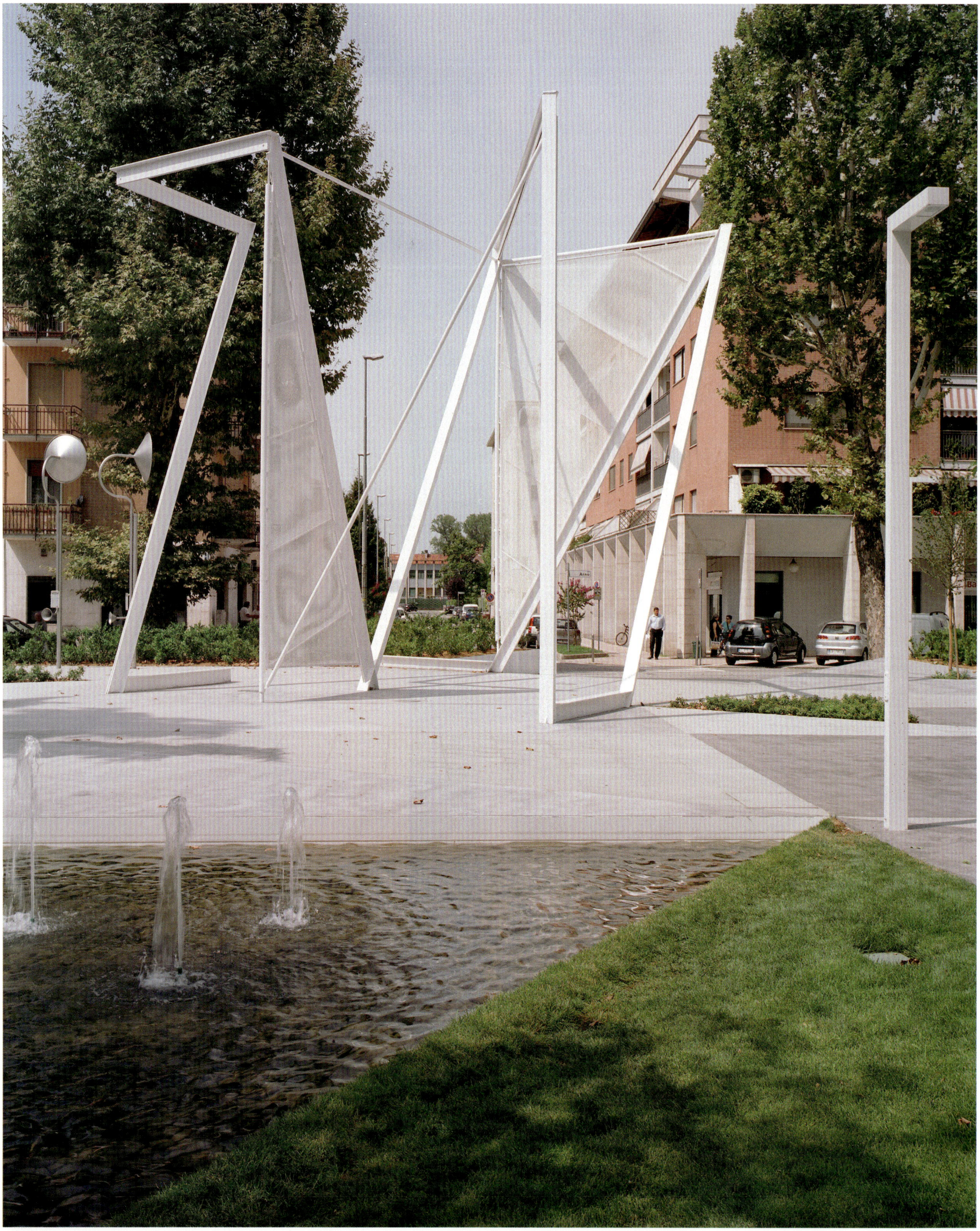

Left: Porta Europa
Upper right: General view
Lower right: The ground texture and the fountain

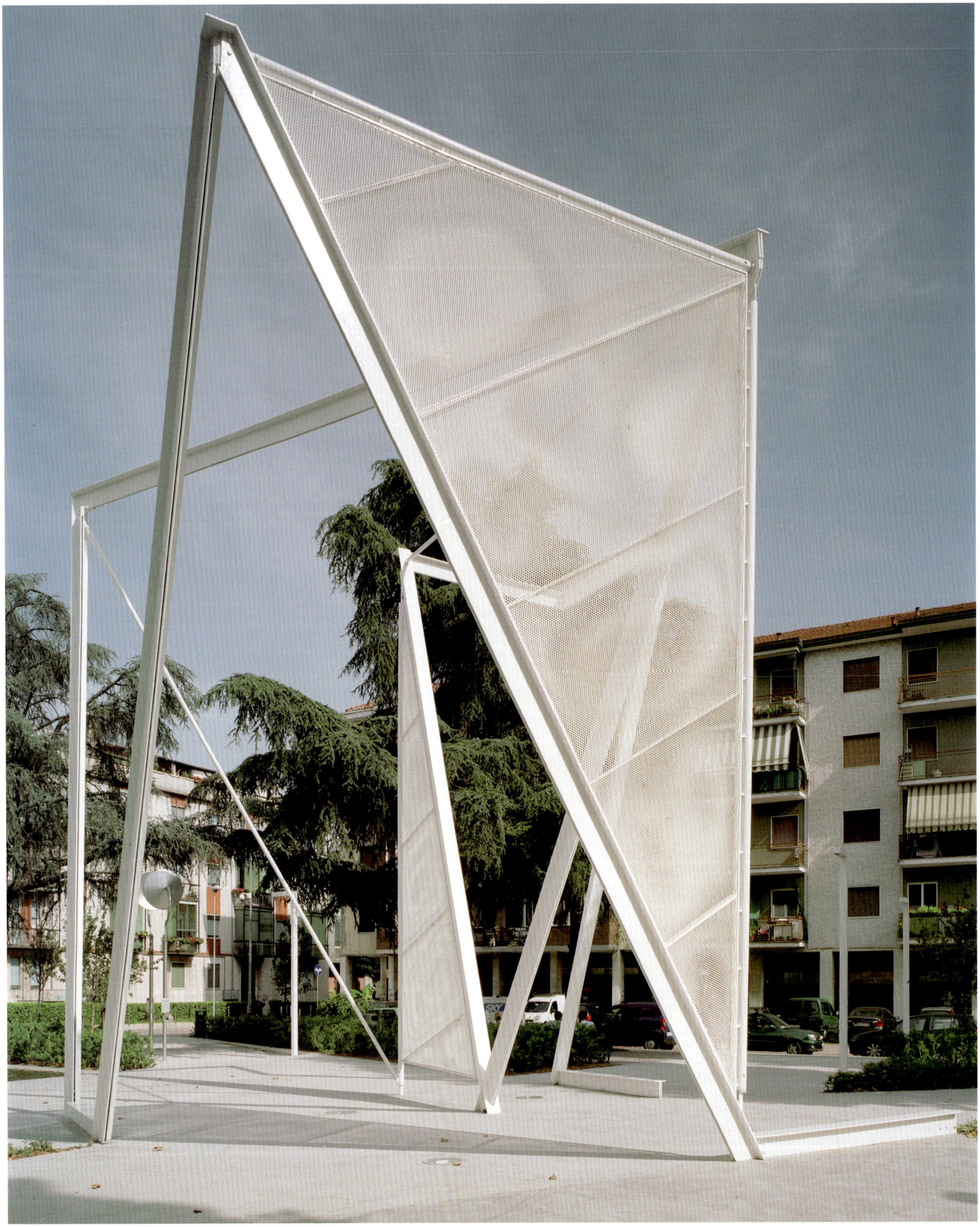

Left: Close view of Porta Europa
Upper right: Bird's eye view
Lower right: Detail of Porta Europa

Coquitlam Spirit Square

Location: British Columbia, Canada **Designer:** Phillips Farevaag Smallenberg
Photographer: Scott Massey **Completion date:** 2010 **Site area:** 7,300 sqm

The integration of art into the design of the Coquitlam Spirit Square is one of the key objectives of the project. Coquitlam is known today for its natural assets – creeks, forests and mountains. Though the City of Coquitlam's history is rooted in the early settlement of the First Nation people it is now a multi-cultural city with a rapidly changing demography. The City is growing quickly and the city's goal is to manage this growth in a sustainable way.

The City of Coquitlam received the Spirit Square funding for a new public plaza in the heart of their rapidly developing City Center. The site completes and revitalizes the public space already implemented across the street south of City Hall. The design process engaged the community through community workshops. The symbolism of the salmon, or red fish, that gives Coquitlam its name, was used to inspire the detailing and public art on the plaza. A key component of the first phase will be a flexible open area that is readily adapted to performances and special events with permanent supports and services for temporary installations.

1. Buchanan Square
2. Water Feature 'Source'
3. Water Feature 'Waterfall'
4. Civic Celebration Space
5. Water Feature 'River'
6. Games Area
7. 'River'
8. Neighborhood Yard
9. Kwikwetlem Feature
10. Stage

Right: Bird's view of the plaza

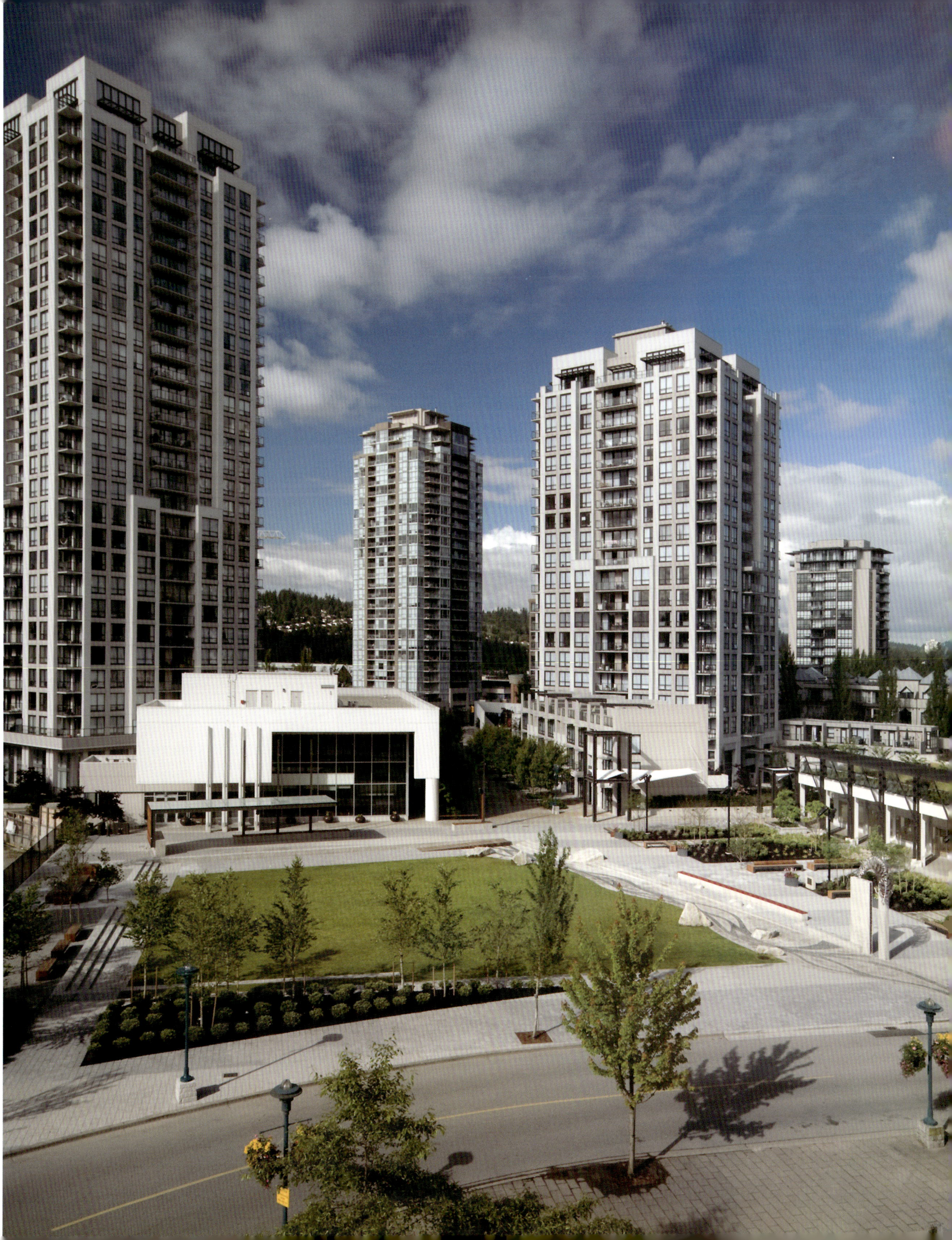

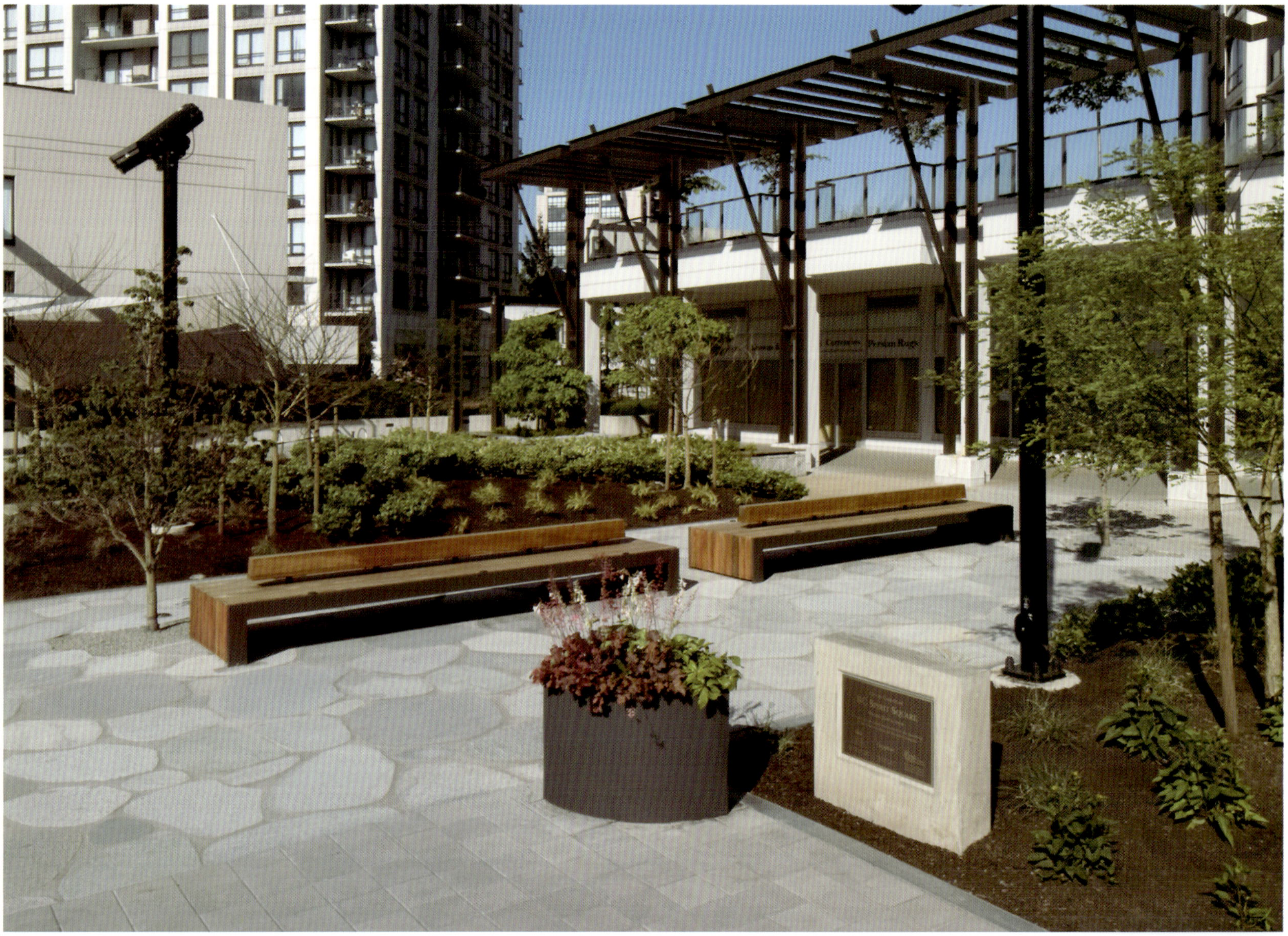
Persian Rugs

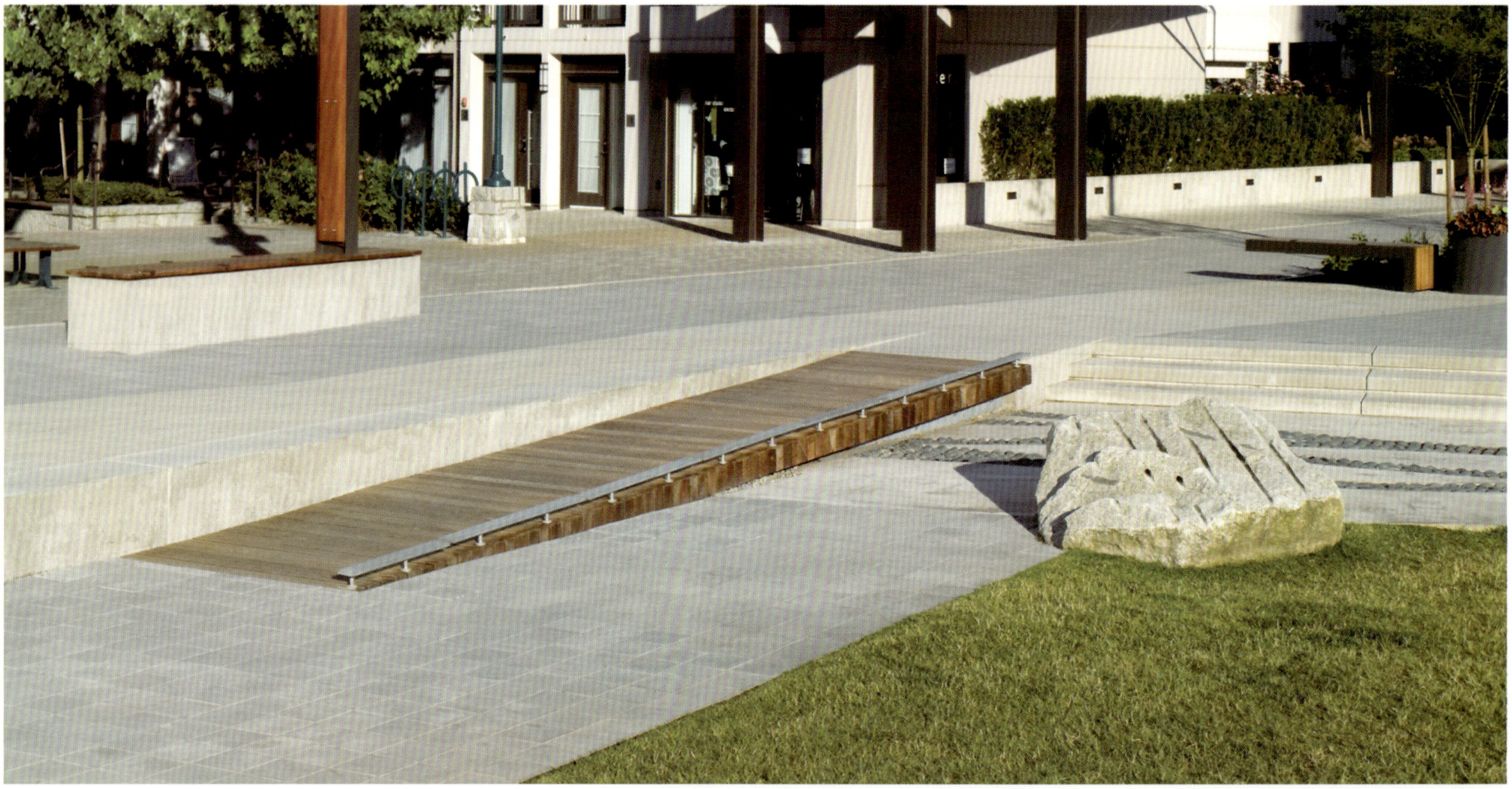

Upper left: Planting area with benches
Lower left: Accessible ramp
Upper right: Edge planting
Lower right: Featured dry stream

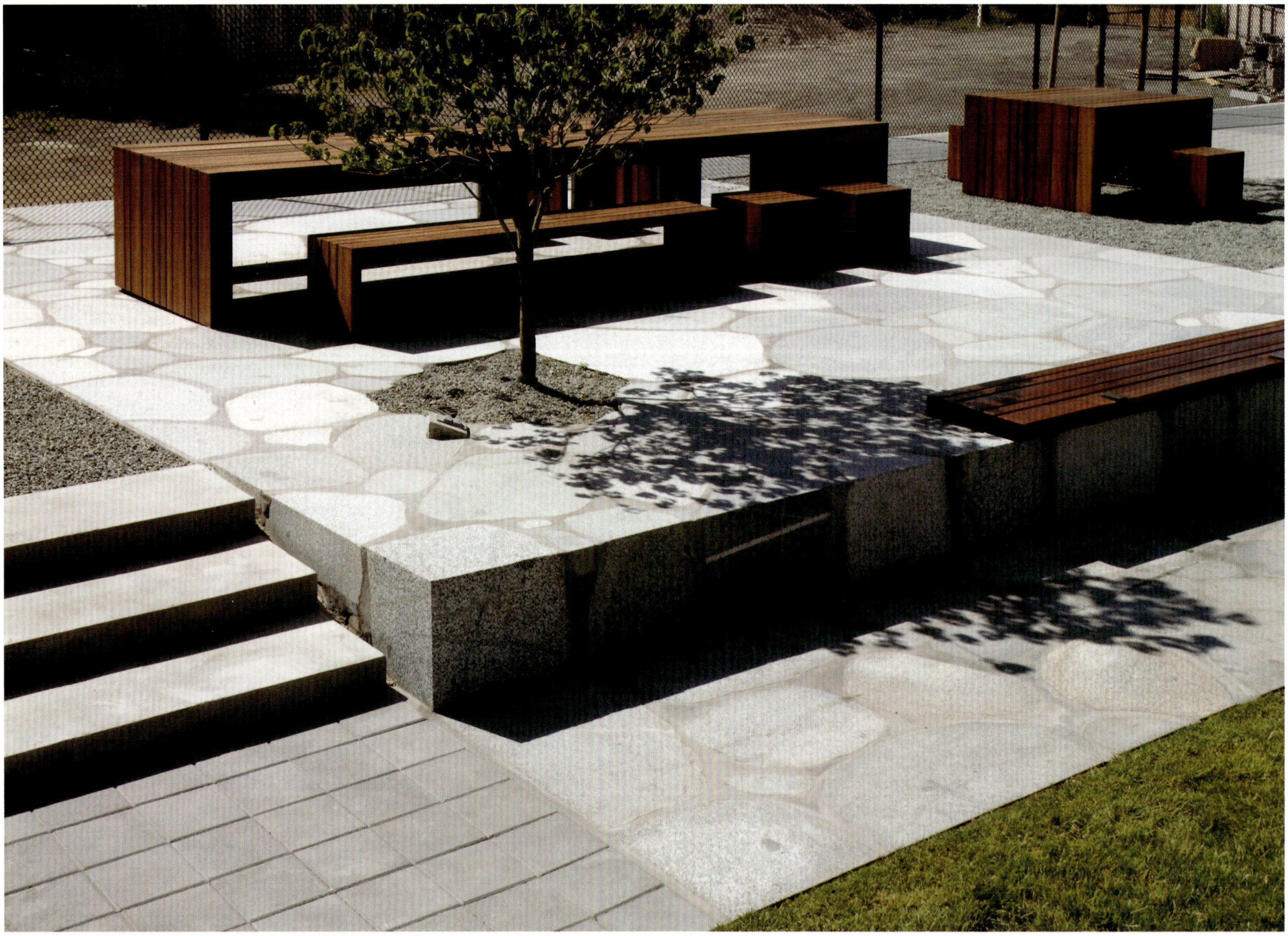

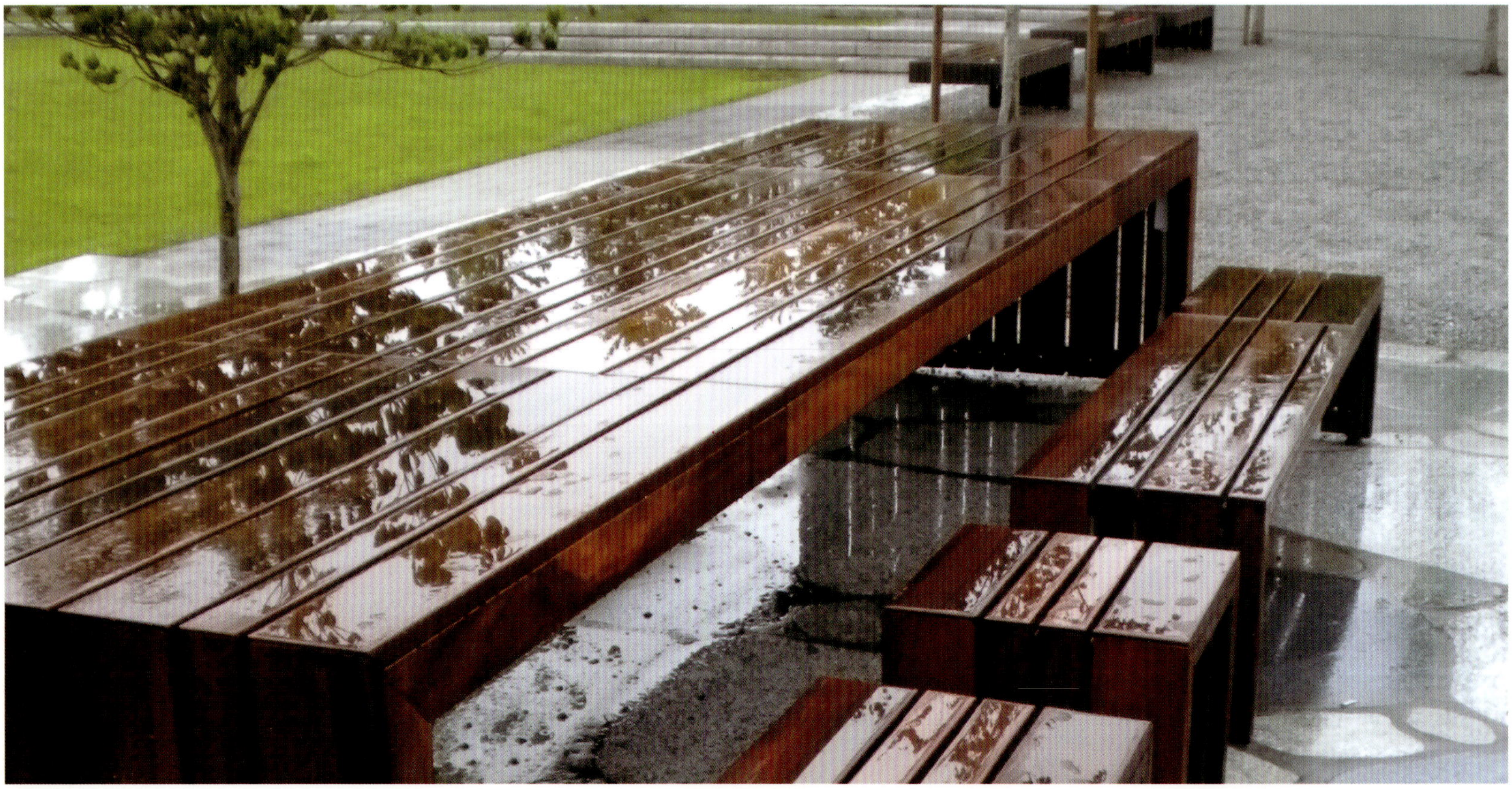

Upper left: Fixed tables and chairs for board games
Lower left: Details of the table and chairs
Upper right: Seating wall
Lower right: Detail of the bench

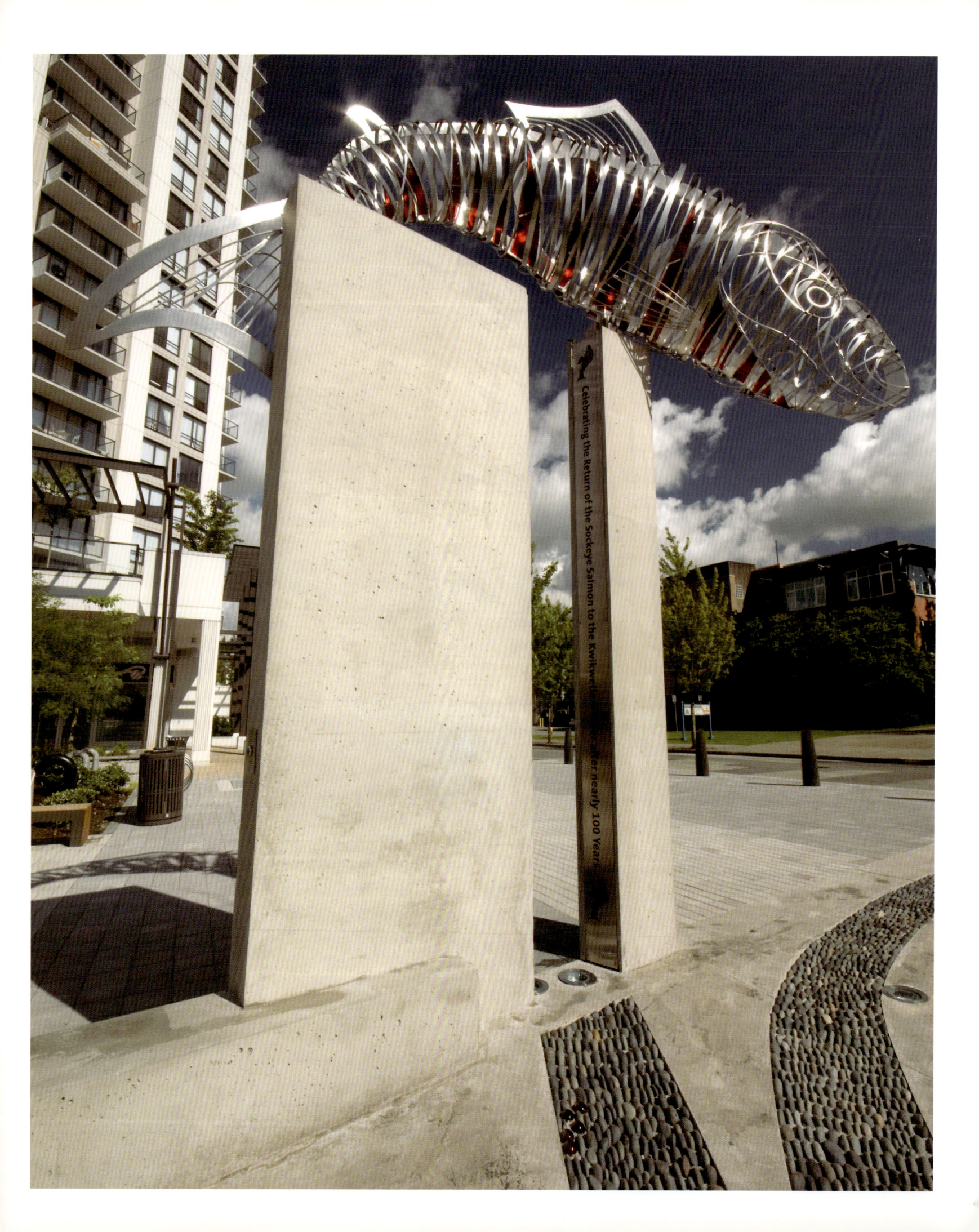

Celebrating the Return of the Sockeye Salmon to the Kwikwetlem after nearly 100 Years

Left: Public art
Upper right: Evening lighting
Lower right: Details of paving

INDEX

1. Ross Barney Architects
Phone: 312 832 0600
Fax: 312 832 0601

2. Natkevicius
Phone: +37 61 454169
Fax: +37 37 320814

3. Affleck + de la Riva Architectes
Phone: 514 861 0133
Fax: 514 861 5776

4. Claude Cormier Architects Paysagistes Inc.
Phone: 514 849 8262
Fax: 514 279 8076

5/43. DAOUST LESTAGE Inc. Architecture Design Urbain
Phone: +514 982 0877

6/22. ASPECT Studios Pty Ltd
Phone: +86 21 5302 8555
Fax: +86 21 5302 0815

7/32. The Office of James Burnett
Phone: 858 793 6970
Fax: 858 793 6905

8. Planet Earth Ltd
Phone: +01 342 825 825

9. BCA Landscape UK
Phone: +01 51 242 6161
Fax: +01 51 236 4467

10. 360°Landscape Architects
Phone: +61 2 9212 2204
Fax: +61 2 9212 2256

11. Chyutin Architects Ltd
Phone: +972 3 7320064
Fax: +972 3 7312760

12. Henningsen Landschaftsarchitekten BDLA Berlin
Phone: +49 30 69533005-0
Fax: +49 30 69533005-9

13/19. Rios Clementi Hale Studios
Phone: +323 785 1800
Fax: +323 785 1801

14. Thomas Biro Associates
Phone: +1 908 359 0091

15/31. Gnuechtel Triebswetter Landscape Architects
Phone: +49 561 78946-0
Fax: +49 561 78946-11

16. McGregor Coxall
Phone: +61 02 9977 3853
Fax: +61 02 9976 5501

17. Karres en Brands Landschaps Architecten bv
Phone: +31 35 642 29 62

18. ONG&ONG Pte Ltd
Phone: +65 6258 8666
Fax: +65 6259 8648

20. Alsop Architects
Phone: +44 20 7978 7878

21. SWA Group
Phone: +86 21 3217 0603
Fax: +86 21 6272 7355

23. Rush\Wright Associates
Phone: +61 3 9600 4255
Fax: +61 3 9600 4266

24. Raymond Jungles, Inc.
Phone: +305 858 6777
Fax: +305 856 0742

25. MANGADO & ASOC. SL.
Phone: +34 948 276202
Fax: +34 948 176505

26. Metropolis Peru
Phone: +511 4375635
Fax: +511 4376538

27/29. PLACE Design Group
Phone: +61 7 3852 3922
Fax: +61 7 3852 4766

28. The Jerde Partnership,Inc.
Phone: +31 0 399 1987
Fax: +31 0 392 1316

30. EARTHSCAPE, Inc.
Phone: +81 978 448 0300

33. Atlas Landscape Architecture
Phone: +503 224 5238

34. Scape Landschaftsarchitekten
Phone: +49 211 302037 13
Fax: +49 211 302037 20

35. Lodewijk Baljon Landschapsarchitecten
Phone: +31 (0)20 625 88 35

36. Rehwaldt Landschaftsarchitekten
Phone: 0351-8119690
Fax: 0351-8119699

37. L'Escaut Architectures
Phone: +32 (0)2 426 48 15
Fax: +32 (0)2 420 17 98

38/51. FSWLA Landschaftsarchitektur GmbH
Phone: +49 211 29106 47
Fax: +49 211 29106 20

39. Oslund.and.Assoc.
Phone: +612 359 9144
Fax: +612 359 9625

40. JAAM Sociedad de Arquitectura s.l.p.
Phone: +34 944 029654
Fax: +34 944 029654

41. PWL Partnership Landscape Architects Inc.
Phone: 604 688 6111
Fax: 604 688 6112

42. SLA
Phone: +45 3391 1316

44. Buro Lubbers Landschapsarchitectuur&Stedelijk ontwerp
Phone: +073 614 93 21
Fax: +073 614 09 20

45. Janet Rosenberg + Associates (JRA)
Phone: +416 656 6665
Fax: +416 656 5756

46. MICROSCAPE Architecture_Urban Design
Phone: +39 0583 469686
Fax: +39 0583 469686

47. SQLA Inc.
Phone: +213 383 1788
Fax: +213 613 0878

48. Grupo de Diseño Urbano S.C.
Phone: +52 55 5553 1248
Fax: +52 55 5286 1013

49. Auböck + Kárász
Phone: +43 1 523 72 20
Fax: +43 1 523 79 676

50/53. Phillips Farevaag Smallenberg
Phone: +604 736 5168
Fax: +604 736 5167

52. Labics
Phone: +39 06 572 880 49
Fax: +39 06 571 378 08

54. Roland Halbe Fotografie
Phone: +49 711 6074073
Fax: +49 711 6074178
www.rolandhalbe.de

©2010 by Design Media Publishing Limited
This edition published in August 2011

Design Media Publishing Limited
20/F Manulife Tower
169 Electric Rd, North Point
Hong Kong
Tel: 00852-28672587
Fax: 00852-25050411
E-mail: Kevinchoy@designmediahk.com
www.designmediahk.com

Editing: Arthur Gao
Proofreading: Qian Yin
Design/Layout: Ning Li

All rights reserved. No part of this publication may be reproduced or transmitted in any form or by any means, electronic or mechanical, including photocopy, recording or any information storage and retrieval system, without prior permission in writing from the publisher.

ISBN 978-988-15069-7-9

Printed in China